EAST ASIAN SOCIAL SCIENCE MONOGRAPHS

INEQUALITY AND ECONOMIC DEVELOPMENT IN MALAYSIA

INEQUALITY AND ECONOMIC DEVELOPMENT IN MALAYSIA

DONALD R. SNODGRASS

A study sponsored by the Harvard Institute for International Development

KUALA LUMPUR
OXFORD UNIVERSITY PRESS
OXFORD NEW YORK MELBOURNE
1980

Oxford University Press
OXFORD LONDON GLASGOW
NEW YORK TORONTO MELBOURNE WELLINGTON
KUALA LUMPUR SINGAPORE HONG KONG TOKYO
DELHI BOMBAY CALCUTTA MADRAS KARACHI
NAIROBI DAR ES SALAAM CAPE TOWN

ISBN 0 19 580431 7 (*boards*)
ISBN 0 19 580442 2 (*limp*)

Printed in Singapore by Dainippon Tien Wah Printing (Pte.) Ltd.
Published by Oxford University Press, 3, Jalan 13/3,
Petaling Jaya, Selangor, Malaysia

For Anne, Jacquelyn and Ted

Preface

I was moved to write this book by my two tours as an economic adviser to the Economic Planning Unit (EPU) of the Prime Minister's Department, Government of Malaysia. The first of these tours, which was sponsored by the Ford Foundation and stretched from September 1964 to August 1966, took place during the late stages of decolonization (at the time I arrived the EPU was still headed by a United Nations expert supplied under an Operating Executives, or 'OPEX', arrangement) and coincided with the end both of Malaysia as originally constituted to include Singapore and of Indonesian Confrontation. During these years the government was preoccupied with defence, internal security and (before August 1965) Lee Kuan Yew's attempt to gain a share of power in Malaysia, as well as (after August 1965) the need to adjust to the fact of Singapore's expulsion from the Federation.

In this bygone era, the ethnic (or 'racial', as they are commonly termed in Malaysia) motivations for, or results of, economic development programmes and policies were seldom made explicit. Economic growth was, without much examination, accepted as the probable solution to the country's ethnic problems. It was to be achieved by a liberal economic policy which assigned the development of mining, industry and much of commercial agriculture to the private sector—overwhelmingly foreign and ethnic Chinese in its ownership and management—and cast the government as a rather passive facilitator of such development, as well as a more active promoter of rural development, which was intended to improve the lot of the predominantly rural ethnic Malays. Few people questioned this approach at the time. The only real controversy over development strategy during my first tour with the EPU dealt only with the scale of the effort: how much money should be budgeted as 'development expenditure' in the First Malaysia Plan (1966–70), to be spent mainly on rural development, infrastructure and social services and to be financed primarily from taxes on foreign and Chinese incomes? The strategy itself was unquestioned, at least within the circles in which I moved.

My second tour with the EPU (again financed by the Ford Foundation but this time as a member of a team supplied by Harvard University's Development Advisory Service) began in December 1968 and ended in April 1972. By all odds the most dramatic event of this period was the unexpected and severe ethnic rioting of May 1969, which began less than a mile away from our house in Kuala Lumpur. The initial impact of this traumatic event on politicians and economic planners alike was to produce something akin to a state of shock. The politicians recovered first, each group of them hastening to interpret events according to its own lights. All assumed some connexion between the riots and economic development, but while some Chinese politicians concluded that the problem was insufficient private investment and economic growth (there had been a recession in 1967–8, which the government had done little to counter), the emerging view of many Malays was that the riots resulted from 'economic imbalances', not only in income but in employment patterns and in the ownership and control of wealth. Since the Malaysian political system is deliberately structured to give heaviest weighting to the needs of the Malay community, as interpreted and enunciated by the relatively small but growing Malay élite, it was the Malay view that eventually became official policy. A 'New Economic Policy' was enunciated, the aims and general principles of which were embodied in the Second Malaysia Plan (1971–5), a document which could not be released until the plan period was nearly six months old because of the need to formulate and express the new approach. As finally announced, the policy pledged the government to work for the virtual elimination of all the 'economic imbalances' over a twenty-year period—specifically, to see that by 1990 the income disparity between Malays and non-Malays was substantially reduced, the Malay share in all levels and types of employment was made to reflect the community's share in total population and the Malay stake in the ownership and control of all scales and types of economic enterprise was brought from its current negligible level up to 30 per cent of the total.

These were bold proposals indeed, little precedented in other developing countries and all the more startling for having emerged from what had previously been regarded by many as a 'conservative' and 'pro-free enterprise' government. They were also highly emotive proposals, which generated strong emotional responses from both Malaysian participants and foreign observers. The reactions of the Malaysians were generally, although not always, predictable on the basis of ethnic group membership. The reactions of the foreigners, often no weaker or less emotional, seemed to derive from the observer's background and political predilections. Thus, a moderately conservative American might invoke the merit principle and support the right of the ethnic Chinese to enjoy the major share of the wealth which, after all, they were primarily responsible for creating. Conversely, a European democratic socialist would tend to see the Malays as poor and exploited, and the Chinese (and still more foreign business interests) as exploiters. Marxist observers, of whom there have been few in Malaysia itself, have tended to see the whole ethnic conflict as something arranged, first by the colonial régime and later by the foreign neo-colonialists and their Malaysian collaborators, to divert the attention of the masses of all ethnic groups from their common interest in overthrowing an exploitative system.

None of these viewpoints (admittedly somewhat caricatured in the interest of brevity) struck me as an adequate basis for planning and policy-making. Each seemed to derive at least as much from preconception and self-interest as from analysis of the facts of the case. Indeed, many of the participants in the debate lacked significant pieces of information about what was actually happening in Malaysia, let alone *why*. There is a tendency in Malaysia for everyone, even the foreigners who work there temporarily (from the British colonial servants and 'advisers' to the Malay Rulers to the present-day technical assistance 'expert'), to gravitate toward strong partisanship. Few are willing or able genuinely to cast themselves in the classic role of the policy adviser, in which one accepts the goals of policy as defined by the political leadership, weighs the alternative means by which those goals might be attained and finally recommends those particular means which are thought to offer the highest possible level of goal satisfaction. While this classic definition of the policy adviser's role has been subjected to justifiable criticism (politicians seldom specify the ends precisely enough; no adviser is ever completely objective), I still believe that such an attempt to carry out dispassionate analysis within a circumscribed sphere has much to recommend it. This conviction is responsible for my decision to write this book once my second tour as an economic adviser was completed.

I have just referred to the 'attempt' to carry out dispassionate analysis. Although I wish to assert here that the attempt has been a sincere one, the judgement as to how successful it has been will have to be left to the reader. Foreign economic advisers, such as I was in Malaysia, are sometimes accused by radical critics of being 'unwitting tools of international capitalism'. Such a charge, even when one believes it to be totally false, can never be refuted to the satisfaction of those who regard one as unaware of one's own biases. No doubt some readers will see this book as pro-Malay and some as pro-Chinese, some as pro-capitalist and some as pro-socialist. To this I can only reply that aside from being pro-Malaysian, in the sense of having a great sympathy and affection for the country and all its people, whom I certainly wish well, I have tried to purge myself of any possible political bias. Perhaps some bias—resulting from my nationality (United States), my personal politics (liberal Democrat), my academic discipline (economics) or the position from which I viewed the Malaysian scene (from an institution which was at least nominally the government's chief development planning agency, but which was also sometimes the object of Malay distrust)—has nevertheless crept in. If so, it will be despite a very real attempt to be objective and dispassionate.

The purpose of this book, as spelled out at greater length in Chapter 1, is to examine the origins, nature, extent and possible rectification of economic inequality (particularly ethnic-group related inequality) in the Peninsular (western) portion of Malaysia. I have devoted to this effort whatever I have learned through personal experience in the country, all the pertinent statistics that I could lay my hands on and as full a survey of the relevant social science literature (especially that specific to Malaysia, but also a fair amount of relevant general literature) as I could manage. This process of reflective study has necessarily taken a fair period of time, the length of which has been further extended by competition from other claims on my time since leaving Kuala Lumpur to join the staff of the Development Advisory Service (subsequently the Harvard Institute for International Development) in Cambridge, Massachusetts. Even so, the returns on Malaysia's New Economic Policy, which is no longer so new, are by no means all in. The programmes and policies undertaken since 1969 have still not been in operation long enough for a definitive evaluation to be made; few of the statistics on which such an evaluation would have to be based are publicly available. This study thus represents more of an interim report than one would ideally want, although to some extent that failing is inevitable when one is dealing with on-going social phenomena.

The preceding paragraph's list of resources on which I have drawn is incomplete, in that it fails to mention the many perceptive people from whom I have learned more than from any books or statistical compendia. The most important groups of such colleagues are the numerous Malaysian officials from various government agencies and the succeeding Ford Foundation and Harvard DAS advisers with whom I worked on a day-to-day basis for over five years. I will desist from mentioning any of these individuals, so as to avoid both the risk that some will be inadvertently omitted and the risk that those mentioned will be incorrectly associated in the reader's mind with views for which I wish to assume sole responsibility. I have also benefited from discussions with academics and students. For comments on earlier drafts of the book, I would like to thank John Dixon, Charles Hirschman, Lim Lin Lean, R. S. Milne, Dwight Perkins, Michael Roemer, Jomo Sundaram and Tan Tat-wai, as well as members of the informal Malaysia Seminar held at Harvard University in 1975–6. For support and encouragement to complete this study in competition with other work which may have been more significant in institutional terms, I thank Lester Gordon, Director of the Harvard Institute for International Development. Finally, for expert typing of successive drafts of the manuscript, I owe thanks to Mary-Anita Browne, Mary Lavallee, Daphnie Crooks and Carol Murphy.

In concluding this Preface, I want to point out something which will be evident to many readers. This study is broad rather than deep. It takes on a wide range of issues and includes many quick analyses and back-of-the-envelope calculations, both my own and those of other scholars, policy-makers and advisers. I fully realize that I have not said the last word on the subject of economic inequality, growth and ethnicity in Malaysia. What I have tried to do is produce a broad, reasoned, readable survey of the subject which will inform the general reader and leave the specialist lots of room to conduct deeper, more detailed analyses in various areas of it.

This study was sponsored by the Harvard Institute for International Development, under whose auspices (and those of its predecessor organization, the Development Advisory Service) the work was carried out in

Kuala Lumpur and Cambridge. All interpretations, as well as any error which may have crept in, are however my own individual responsibility and should not be attributed to HIID as an institution.

Cambridge, Massachusetts DONALD R. SNODGRASS
May 1979

Note

Throughout this study terms are used—especially for groups of people and for entities in physical or political geography—which may be unknown to, or misunderstood by, readers who are not intimately familiar with Malaysia and its history. Such terms are starred when they first appear in the text. This will serve to refer the reader to the Glossary which appears at the end of the book.

All references to dollars ($) are to Malaysian (formerly Straits) dollars, now officially termed *ringgit*. From 1947 to 1974 M$3.00 ≏ US$1.00. The *ringgit* has since appreciated, and the current rate is about M$2.30 = US$1.00.

Contents

PART II POLICIES AND PROGRAMMES

Tables

Abbreviations

CGC	Credit Guarantee Corporation
CIC	Capital Investment Committee
DAP	Democratic Action Party
DID	Drainage and Irrigation Department
EPF	Employees Provident Fund
EPU	Economic Planning Unit
FAMA	Federal Agricultural Marketing Authority
FAO	Food and Agricultural Organization of the United Nations
FELDA	Federal Land Development Authority
FIDA	Federal Industrial Development Authority
FIMA	Food Industries of Malaysia
FLDA	(See FELDA)
FMP	First Malaysia Plan
FMS	Federated Malay States
FSS	Federation Savings Survey 1959
GMP	Guaranteed Minimum Price
GNP	Gross National Product
GRM	*Gerakan Rakyat Malaysia*
HBS	Household Budget Survey 1957/58
IBRD	International Bank for Reconstruction and Development (World Bank)
ICA	Industrial Co-ordination Act
KLDA	Kelantan Land Development Authority
LCE	Lower Certificate of Education
LPN	*Lembaga Padi dan Beras Negara* (National Padi and Rice Authority)
MADS	Malaysian Administrative and Diplomatic Service
MARA	*Majlis Amanah Rakyat* (Council of Trust for the Indigenous People)
MARDI	Malaysian Agricultural Research Institute
MCA	Malaysian Chinese Association
MCE	Malaysian Certificate of Education
MIC	Malaysia Indian Congress
MIDF	Malaysian Industrial Development Finance Sdn. Bhd.
MIDFIC	MIDF Industrial Consultants Sdn. Bhd.
MIEL	Malaysian Industrial Estates Ltd.

MSSEE	Malaysian Secondary School Entrance Examination
MTR-SMP	Mid-Term Review of the Second Malaysia Plan
NEB	National Electricity Board
NEP	New Economic Policy
NFPB	National Family Planning Board
NOC	National Operations Council
NPC	National Productivity Centre
OPEC	Organization of Petroleum Exporting Countries
PAP	People's Action Party
PERNAS	*Perbadanan Nasional* (National Corporation)
PES	Post Enumeration Survey 1970
PETRONAS	*Petroleum Nasional*
PMIP	Pan-Malayan Islamic Party
PPP	People's Progressive Party
PWD	Public Works Department
RIDA	Rural and Industrial Development Authority
RISDA	Rubber Industry Smallholders Development Authority
RRIM	Rubber Research Institute of Malaya
RSS	Ribbed Smoked Sheet
SEDC	State Economic Development Corporation
SES	Malaysian Socio-Economic Sample Survey of Households 1967–8
SMP	Second Malaysia Plan
SMR	Standard Malaysian Rubber
SRM	Survey Research Malaysia
SS	Straits Settlements
TMP	Third Malaysia Plan
UDA	Urban Development Authority
UMNO	United Malays National Organization
UMS	Unfederated Malay States
WHO	World Health Organization

PART I
Origins and Scope of Inequality

1 An Introduction to the Problem

> The most useful way to approach the problem of income distribution and economic growth appears to be through study of size distribution to persons, not in terms of abstract classifications of income receivers, but in relation to identifiable socioeconomic or regional groups whose normal propensities and regular behavior can be examined in the light of their contribution to economic growth (or whose needs can be assessed from a humanitarian point of view).
>
> United Nations Research Institute for Social Development, 1969, p. 23

THIS is a study of the interrelationships among inequality, economic development and ethnicity in a single country—Malaysia.* These subjects became matters of urgent concern for all Malaysians* after the jarring events of May 1969. Coincidentally, however, there was a worldwide surge of interest in the inequality-growth relationship—although not yet enough attention, in my opinion, to ethnicity. Thus, this book is not only a study of Malaysia for its own sake but also a Malaysia-based case study of problems which Malaysia shares, in varying degrees, with many other countries. Chapter 1 will serve to set the scene, from both the global and the national points of view.

THE GLOBAL CONTEXT

The 1970s have seen some striking shifts of focus within the broad and loosely structured field known as development economics. During the 1960s rates of economic growth in the poor countries were generally somewhat higher than had been expected, yet the results of that growth were looked on by many observers with a sense of disappointment.[1] For a number of reasons—especially, although not entirely rationally, widespread disenchantment with economic growth in the intellectually influential rich countries—attention was increasingly focused on a number of socio-economic problems which remained unsolved in the wake of even some of the most successful growth programmes. Existing doctrine, it was said, did not deal with these problems adequately. High on the list of the newly spotlighted problems was economic inequality. Badly skewed income distributions and other forms of inequality seemed not only to persist but often to worsen with the passage of time and rise of GNP. Constant or growing inequality occasioned frequently articulated dismay among international scholars and activists of political inclinations ranging from humanist to revolutionary. It also caused concern, less openly expressed, in the poor countries themselves, even—or perhaps especially—among those élites who stood to lose most if the dispossessed turned to extreme forms of protest.[2]

With the burgeoning interest in inequality, income distribution research has moved beyond its traditional preoccupation with measurement problems.[3] Inquiry was pushed back, so to speak, into the complex question of what causes inequality, as well as forward into issues of policy: how inequality can be reduced and how efforts to reduce it affect economic growth.

It has frequently been noted that in many countries where GNP is growing the average income of the bottom three or four deciles in the size distribution has risen little if at all. Since the income flow is usually measured over intervals of a year or less rather than some longer period, one might ask how stable the membership of this low-income group is. As Simon Kuznets (1963, pp. 8–10) has pointed out, high year-to-year variability in income or high rates of 'income mobility' from one decile to another can vitiate the hardships of income inequality as usually measured. However, it seems unlikely that these forms of relief are important enough in poor countries to modify significantly the conclusion that large parts of the population are being left behind in the process of development.

A situation in which this conclusion obviously holds is the one in which the poor are not just a statistical abstraction ('the lowest three deciles') but a large, distinct, independently identifiable social group which has its own history and plays a particular role in the political and economic life of the nation. If such a group consistently lags behind other elements of the population, it is evident that the problem is not merely one of short-run variability in income. And it is at least doubtful whether socio-economic mobility or other forces related to development will lead automatically to a breakdown of the pattern over time. The problem is undoubtedly a deep-rooted one and it may require radical changes and strong measures for its solution. Certainly the members of the deprived group, as they become increasingly conscious of their relative deprivation and increasingly politicized, will call for such measures in more and more definite terms.[4]

This states the problem from the viewpoint of the poorer, more backward group. Alternatively, since *relative* income levels are involved, one could ask why some social groups are so *successful* in economic endeavours and enjoy relatively *high* incomes as a result. That some social groups have a particular affinity for economic activity has been observed in many contexts, although—like poverty—it is a problem with which traditional economics does not deal comfortably.

Why do some social groups receive high and rising incomes while others have to accept low and stagnant ones? What forces maintain such a pattern of inequality over time? Will future economic growth strengthen or undermine them? Does the pattern of inequality hamper or promote growth? If a government wants to break the pattern, or is pressured to do so by its constituents, what is the best way to go about it? What policies will be effective in reducing inequality? Which ones will have some effect yet not seriously retard economic growth or unnecessarily disrupt the social order? How do ethnic and class interests interact? Is evolutionary change possible, or does the power of the wealthy preclude effective social action to reduce inequality? Is revolution a necessity?

These are the important questions with which this study deals. Final answers to them are hardly to be expected, but even marginal expansion of our understanding in such an important area should be socially beneficial.

MALAYSIA AS A CASE

There are many ways in which one could go about a study of inequality and development. The method used here is a single-country case study. Malaysia, is, I think, a good case to study because it has much in common with a significant group of poor countries yet it is in some important respects a polar case, in which widespread problems and possibilities appear with particular vividness and urgency.

Low-income countries are notoriously diverse, and the Malaysian case has only limited relevance to some of them. Those with which it does share many features form a considerable group of poor countries in Asia, Africa and, to a lesser extent, the Americas. The unifying characteristic of these countries is that they became independent in the post-World War II period after a history of colonial rule, one of whose legacies was a population consisting of two or more distinct communities. In any individual case, these communities may be identifiable by their separate races, religions, tribes, languages or customs. Whatever the objective basis for the distinction, however, the important point is that each group encompasses individuals who feel a strong sense of similarity to each other and differentness from members of other groups. This makes the communities major facts of political and economic life in all those countries where the 'plural society' (Furnivall, 1939 and 1948) exists. The relationship of cultural pluralism to economic inequality in a post-colonial society has not been closely examined.[5] This is a strange omission from the literature of development, since the economic progress, political stability and maybe even survival of many low-income countries depends largely on how well they solve, or at least learn to live with, the problems of cultural pluralism.

The polarity of the Malaysian case derives from three circumstances: (1) the division of the Malaysian population into three major communities, which coalesce into two almost equally numerous groups for many political purposes; (2) a pattern of political strength which diverges from that of economic strength and thus assures that the government is motivated to do something about economic inequality; and (3) a resource situation which is favourable enough to offer a significant chance of success in such an endeavour. While these characteristics—singly, let alone as a group—are polar in relation to the position of most low-income countries, this should only heighten the interest of the Malaysian case from the viewpoints of other poor countries and of students of development. For Malaysia *must* try to do now things that other countries can afford to put off for a while—even though they will probably have to face them eventually. And Malaysia *can* attempt to reduce inequality under sufficiently favourable circumstances that at least some of the lessons which it will provide to the world will probably be examples of success rather than failure.

When the plural society of Peninsular Malaysia*[6] emerged from British tutelage to become the independent Federation of Malaya* in 1957, both its socio-economic problems and its development potentials could be judged enormous. Perhaps the major items on the national balance sheet at the time were as follows:

Liabilities

1. A pattern of ethnic cleavage, in which the two largest groups (the Malays,* with 50 per cent of the population, and the Chinese,* with 37 per cent) differed sharply in culture, occupational pattern and income level; these groups, which had formerly co-existed peacefully, but separately and very differently, under the umbrella of Pax Britannica, would now be interacting more and would be forced to work out the terms of this interaction for themselves.

2. An over-specialized economy, subject to strong export-induced fluctuations and too dependent on a single crop whose continued viability was being threatened by competition from a synthetic substitute.

3. An explosive demographic potential, which had already raised the rate of natural increase above 3 per cent per annum and threatened to keep it there indefinitely.

Assets

1. The beginnings of a political system in which Malay, Chinese and Indian* representatives participated in the Alliance Party, a permanent coalition aimed at resolving conflicts of group interests through élite bargaining, based on 'the bargain of 1957', which specified that the Chinese would be given free range for their entrepreneurial talents (subject to provision of special programmes to aid the economic advance of the Malays) while the Malays would be allowed to dominate the government (subject to citizenship rights and junior-partner participation for the Chinese, the Indians and the several much smaller minorities).

2. A strong heritage of physical and administrative infrastructure.

3. A favourable ratio of land and other natural resources to population, which offered generally promising chances to raise income per head despite the high rate of population increase.

In 1957 it was hard to say just where the balance between the significant assets and liabilities should be struck, whether the net worth of the new nation was positive or negative. However, experience up to 1969, when the third post-Independence general elections were held, appeared to most observers to tip the balance solidly in the positive direction. During this twelve-year period West Malaysia's* Gross National Product increased by 86 per cent.[7] This substantial growth was achieved in the face of a declining price trend for natural rubber, which had provided nearly one-third of the country's export receipts in 1957. Although some observers thought that with appropriate economic policies West Malaysia could have attained a still higher rate of growth—perhaps 8–10 per cent a year instead of the 5.3 per cent implied by the actual 1957–69 performance—its achievement was clearly one of the better ones in South-East Asia and among poor countries generally. This comparatively strong economic performance was usually attributed to the assets listed in the balance sheet above, plus a liberal and outward-looking economic policy framework which stressed foreign trade and private enterprise.[8]

It was hardly a secret before 1969 that different segments of Peninsular Malaysia's communities were neither contributing equally to economic growth nor benefiting equally from it. The Malay half of the population dominated politics but was relatively poor, counting among its numbers large blocs of low-productivity agriculturalists—rice cultivators, small-scale rubber growers and fishermen. The largest minority, the Chinese, was systematically the most prosperous group, although only a small number of Chinese were actually rich. The Chinese had been leaders in economic advance since early British days, had always been the first to seize any new economic opportunity and had as a result become not only the wealthiest but also the most urbanized and best educated segment of the community. The smaller Indian minority, 11 per cent of the population, were less well off than the Chinese but somewhat better off than the Malays; large numbers of Indians were still attached to the plantation jobs which they had originally come to Malaya* to perform. The remaining 1–2 per cent of the population consisted of a mosaic of other groups, including a small number of Europeans* and Japanese, who played a disproportionately large role in the economy, owning and managing most of the large-scale commercial and industrial concerns while the Chinese dominated small-scale business.

Known inequalities in the economy were highly correlated with membership in these ethnic groups. An estimate for 1957 made by T. H. Silcock (1963) suggested that the mean income of the Chinese was 2.4 times as great as that of the Malays. Although there was no firm evidence, many thought that this 'racial economic disparity' had become even greater since Independence. In any case, one thing which did continue to rise—at a rate of natural increase of 3 per cent or more in each year from 1952 to 1964—was the population. This demographic burst in time created a rapidly growing labour force, which could not be absorbed smoothly into productive employment. Unemployment increased by perhaps two points, from 6 per cent to 8 per cent, during the 1960s, becoming much higher among the young; underemployment probably also increased. The former was greater among the more urbanized Chinese and Indians, the latter among the rural Malays.

The Malaysian Government was by no means heedless of these inequalities. As a constitutional government dependent on the support of a broad spectrum of the population, but especially of the Malay community, it could hardly afford to be. Even before the Alliance Party took the reins of government it was active in the promotion of programmes intended to provide economic benefits for the Malays, especially rural development programmes. Under these programmes progress had been made in irrigating rice land for double-cropping, opening up new areas for export agriculture and spreading education and other social services into the rural areas. An imaginative system had been devised to relate rural development planning to grassroots desires and to assure that approved projects were actually implemented. For this the government was praised by foreign observers and contrasted favourably with other developing countries (e.g. by Wilcox, 1965; and Ness, 1967).

The indirect approach to the problem of ethnic economic inequality through rural development was characteristic of the Alliance method of dealing with delicate matters. There was little direct reference to the problem, since it was believed that open discussion of it could be inflammatory. Some government policies to reduce inequality were undertaken quietly or even covertly. In some areas goal conflicts and indecision were evident. Thus new private investment in manufacturing was a frequently enunciated goal yet the necessary approvals were frequently held back (often by the states rather than the national government), presumably from fear that the old patterns of ownership, management and employment which had largely excluded the Malays would be replicated in the new establishments. This kind of indecision was partly responsible for the fact that economic growth, although respectable, fell short of potential.

There were signs that all was not well even before 1969. As in the past, the growth rate varied sharply from year to year, although limited export diversification and a small decline in the ratio of exports to GNP had moderated the problem a bit. In addition, the independent government was less prone to meet an export slump with austerity in the public finances, thus worsening the situation, than the colonial government had been. By the mid-1960s, although the basic private-enterprise policy remained in effect, public revenue and expenditure had risen substantially.

In the spirit of the 'bargain of 1957', government revenues were raised largely from taxes on Chinese and foreign businesses and spent largely to benefit rural Malays. How far this process should go was naturally a difficult question to resolve. As it turned out, the government shrank from further expansion of the public sector during the early years of the First Malaysia Plan (1966–68). Since this period of stagnant public expenditure fortuitously coincided with yet another export downturn, the result was three years of very indifferent economic growth.

In this setting the general elections of May 1969 were held. They produced stunning setbacks for the Alliance Party, setbacks which fell short of a clear-cut national defeat but which drastically weakened the national Alliance and created two very ambiguous outcomes in important State

Assembly elections. Three days after the vote the tensions produced by the campaign and its outcome erupted in the worst outbreak of ethnic violence in Peninsular Malaysia's history. After order was restored, the very next item on the national agenda was to determine what had gone wrong and how Malaysia's development could be resumed in a manner consistent with ethnic harmony, or at least avoidance of any recurrence of violence.

It was apparently the Malays who had initiated the violence, under greater or lesser provocation from the non-Malays according to the version of the story that one heard. In the election, both Malays and non-Malays had deserted the Alliance in large numbers. It was hard to say what part economic grievances had played on either side, although it was known that many Malays envied the higher standard of living enjoyed by the Chinese, while the Chinese (and Indians) in turn resented the special advantages which the government had provided for the Malays. In its own interpretation of the facts, the government chose to stress the economic disabilities of the Malays as the problem which now had to be solved. This choice was undoubtedly influenced heavily by the need which the leaders of UMNO (the United Malays National Organization), the senior partner in the Alliance coalition, now felt to regain the support of their Malay constituents. A more dispassionate observer can, however, agree with the immediate objective, to attain a healthier economic balance among the communities, as desirable on its own merit, while remaining open-minded (or even sceptical) about whether Malaysia will necessarily be a more tranquil country when the Malays are better off relative to the Chinese—and especially about the ease with which the transition to that situation from the present one can be effected without exacerbating tensions. The next question, then, is how to do it.

In the early post-May 1969 discussions, two schools of thought on this matter quickly emerged.

The *pro-growth, or 'trickle-down', school* argued that it would be unfair to ascribe past problems to adherence to a strategy of rapid growth, that in fact this adherence had not been strong enough or implemented with sufficient consistency and determination. Had not private investment approvals been held up in the past by a combination of inefficiency and Malay foot-dragging, and could not this situation be remedied by 'cutting through red tape'? Should not land development be speeded up to take advantage of Malaysia's great unused land resources, even if this meant large-scale new land development by non-Malays? While this might seem only to worsen the problem of ethnic inequality, a sophisticated version of the argument contended that the Malays would benefit in the longer run—by attainment of full employment by sometime in the 1980s, which would raise the wages of unskilled labour and draw Malays into the non-agricultural sector—and in fact that this was the best way, perhaps even the only feasible way, to improve the economic position of the Malays.

The *pro-redistribution, or interventionist, school* hotly disputed this kind of 'trickle-down' prescription, arguing that the time to do something about ethnic inequality had indisputably arrived and that the necessary means were much more direct intervention in the economy, if need be at the cost of economic growth. This school proposed a range of interventions in those parts of the economy traditionally dominated by Chinese and foreign interests, ranging from ethnic employment quotas to training programmes, the reservation of stock issues for the Malays, the 'creation' of Malay entrepreneurs, Malay-foreign joint ventures and even public sector ownership.

These two views were often voiced by Chinese and Malay spokesmen respectively, although not all Chinese took a consistently pro-growth position while Malay politicians and intellectuals varied widely in their enthusiasm for intervention. As noted in the Preface, foreign advisers and observers also tended to line up on one side or the other according to their sympathies and ideological preconceptions. The setting for a debate which would generate much heat and little light could hardly have been better, since in retrospect it is evident that:

1. the facts of ethnic inequality were only dimly perceived: how great it was, what patterns it assumed and whether it was increasing or decreasing through time and as the economy grew and fluctuated.

2. the causes of whatever inequality did exist were even more uncertain; partial, contending theories involving cultural differences, discrimination, monopoly and government policies past and present were advanced (or, more often, used implicitly as backing for particular policy positions without being spelled out explicitly at all); no tests of these theories were offered.

3. past policies to reduce ethnic economic inequality had seldom been evaluated and new policies were often put forth without considering what the success or failure of past policies boded for their own prospects.

4. all this debate was conducted in an inward-looking, self-conscious atmosphere, with little reference to the burgeoning interest in similar problems in many other countries, both 'developing' and 'developed'.

This is a formidable list of defects to be remedied. Since May 1969 agencies of the Malaysian Government, as well as a number of private researchers, both Malaysian and foreign, have done useful work on aspects of the problem. New analyses are becoming available to go along with the additional statistics which are being generated by the heightened interest in problems of economic inequality and increased willingness to face these problems head-on rather than deal with them by euphemism and indirection. These analyses and statistics provide much usable input for the broad and objective survey attempted in this book.

PLAN OF THE STUDY

The study tries to deal with the various aspects of inequality and development in Malaysia in a systematic fashion. Its major parts concern (1) the historical background; (2) the extent and nature of inequality in the post-Independence period; (3) statements and tests of theories of its causes; (4) evaluation of possible policies to reconcile inequality and growth and their consequences; and (5) conclusions regarding the effects of inequality on growth and vice versa.

Before examining the current situation it will be useful to learn something about its historical origins. Chapter 2 surveys Peninsular Malaysia's political and economic history up to Independence in 1957, emphasizing those aspects which appear to be most pertinent to the modern problems with which this book deals. The development of a plural society, which offered Malays, Chinese and Indians differing opportunities for economic and social advancement, is stressed. Chapter 3 discusses the creation of an independent state and major events up to about 1970.

In Chapter 4 an attempt is made to measure inequality in contemporary Peninsular Malaysia. There is a fairly large, if uneven and sometimes conflicting, body of data which bears on the questions of the extent and nature of inequality, and trends therein from 1957 into the 1970s. As best possible, this information is reconciled into a consistent and accurate picture of what has really happened.

Neither history nor measurement automatically provides the level of understanding of causal mechanisms which is a prerequisite for developing effective policy measures. This requires explicit theorizing about the way historical or other forces have worked to produce and perpetuate inequality. Such theorizing, as applied to the Malaysian case, is reviewed in Chapter 6, which goes on to consider how available evidence substantiates or casts doubt upon the theories.

These efforts to gain some insight into the causes of inequality serve as a basis for considering possible means of dealing with it. Chapters 6–9 evaluate four types of policy for reducing inequality: fiscal redistribution (Chapter 6); rural development (Chapter 7); Malay participation in urban economic activity (Chapter 8); and education and other 'general' policies (Chapter 9). The study ends with Chapter 10, which comments on very recent experience, peers into the uncertain future and attempts to generalize about the interrelations among inequality, growth and ethnicity in Malaysia and elsewhere.

ETHNICITY AND INEQUALITY

Before proceeding to Chapter 2, it is necessary to say a word about the use of ethnic categories as a fundamental element in the structure of this study. The validity of these categories has often been questioned,[9] but their use, at least in *hypotheses* relating to inequality and development, seems to me to be justified by the obvious importance that 'race', as they call it, is accorded by Malaysians themselves.

As will be seen, members of each of the ethnic groups[10] which make up Malaysian society have in their own minds a definite idea of what it means to be a Malay, Chinese or Indian. This kind of self-identification appears to transcend social class distinctions. Self-identification in ethnic terms is not visibly weakening, nor is it common for an individual to cross the line from one group to another—although this does occasionally happen in certain limited kinds of cases.[11]

To the criterion of self-identification can be added the fact of official recognition of 'race'—in many statistics, in law and often in policy. This practice follows the precedent of the British administration, but it is wrong to regard it as mere perseveration. The governments of independent Malaya and Malaysia have not found it useful to do away with these distinctions—on the contrary, they have been forced by the nature of Malaysian society to retain them and in some instances to widen their use.

It thus seems self-evident that ethnicity is important in Malaysia. The observed facts that most Malays are poor and that most well-off Malaysians are Chinese are almost certainly not explained by coincidence. *Some* hypothesized role for ethnicity in explaining the observed pattern of inequality is irresistible. What is not clear is just *what* role ethnicity has played, is playing and will play in the future; *what other forces* enter into the determination of inequality; or *how* ethnicity and the other forces interact. It is these things that the study will try to determine.

1. 'The state of development in most of the developing world today is unacceptable—and growing more so' (Robert W. McNamara, President, World Bank Group, Address to the United Nations Conference on Trade and Development, Santiago, Chile, 14 April 1972). Among many similar statements, see Huq (1972), pp. 60–8. For an attempt to define the policy lessons of the disappointment with past performance, see Healey (1972).

2. 'We obviously do not like to have a large and growing pool of educated unemployed *because that would adversely affect our political, and eventually our financial and economic stability as well*' [my italics]. Tun Tan Siew Sin (Malaysian Minister of Finance) (1969), p. 50.

3. 'With some small degree of exaggeration, most writings on income distribution in less developed countries which deal in numbers are nine-tenths description of statistical estimations, pitfalls and approximations, and one-tenth analysis of the end product.' Turnham (1972), p. 38.

4. Albert Hirschman (1973) has postulated the existence of a 'tunnel effect', whereby A's tolerance of his own inferiority in relative income increases (at least for a while) when B's income rises because A takes this as a prediction of future increases in his own income. This is put forward as an alternative to the usual assumption that A's tolerance of inequality is negatively related to his 'relative deprivation'. The operation of the 'tunnel effect' would appear to be dependent on the existence of a relatively homogeneous society, in which A regarded his prospects as essentially similar to B's. If, on the contrary, A and B were members of ethnic groups which regarded each other as fundamentally different, then B's advance would bring no comfort to A. At best, A would be indifferent, regarding B's rising income as irrelevant to himself. At worst, A would harbour a strong sense of injustice and even resentment and malice toward B.

5. The classic treatments for the *colonial* society are the works of Furnivall, who coined the term 'plural society'.

6. Peninsular Malaysia is chosen as the area to be studied in preference to all of Malaysia because its ethnic problems are different from and more important than those of the East Malaysian states of Sabah and Sarawak, and because many data are available for Peninsular Malaysia only. Another possibility would have been to include Singapore in the study along with Peninsular Malaysia, but this too was rejected because Singapore has been independent since 1965 and its political context and ethnic proportions (76 per cent Chinese in 1970) are very different from Peninsular Malaysia's.

7. This growth is measured in current prices; it thus fails to take account of domestic inflation during the period, but this was negligible in any case. Real output—i.e. GNP deflated for domestic inflation but adjusted upward to compensate for terms of trade deterioration—grew by considerably more than 86 per cent.

8. Among the admirers (with varying degrees of discernment) of Malaysia's economic policies have been Roger A. Freeman (1968), Wolfgang E. Kasper (1974), and Hla Myint (1967).

9. Maurice Freedman (1960, p. 158n) lists several critics of the 'plural society' concept. For a more recent, if somewhat obscure, criticism, see Robert W. Tellander (1970). Judith A. Nagata (1975) provides an excellent assessment of the present pattern of social relations, defining it as 'more stratified than plural' but noting the strong element of 'subjective pluralism' which colours the perceptions of most contemporary Malaysians.

10. I will generally refer to the Malays, Chinese and Indians as 'ethnic groups', even though the usual Malaysian term is 'race'. This change of terminology avoids unintended biological connotations.

11. Intermarriage (still rare), adoption (especially of Chinese girl babies by Malays), religious conversion (to Islam, a process which often involves *masuk Melayu*, 'becoming a Malay') and self-redefinition (see the entry 'Ceylonese' in the Glossary).

2 History: Before Merdeka

> The development of Malaya is one of the most remarkable of the achievements of British traders, planters, and administrators in the period after 1870 both in the rapidity of the transformation and the success of the undertaking.
>
> Knowles, 1924, p. 485

INTRODUCTION

MANY find the roots of ethnicity and inequality in Malaysia's history. This chapter and the following one unearth some of those roots to examine their connexion with contemporary concerns. In Chapter 2, a brief review of the general historical background is followed by a study of the origins of the plural society in Malaysia. Since this book is intended for both Malaysian and non-Malaysian readers—groups whose knowledge of the relevant history may vary widely—a balance between saying too much and saying too little is sought. Appropriate references to possible supplementary readings will be made.[1] Those who prefer to skip the history and proceed directly to a discussion of contemporary inequality are invited to turn immediately to Chapter 4.

GENERAL BACKGROUND

The pre-colonial history of the Malaysian area consists of a series of migrations. Around 2500 B.C. a New Stone Age people called the Proto-Malays apparently displaced the previously resident Negrito tribes, only to be pushed out itself by a more advanced group known as the Deutero-Malays *c*. 300 B.C. Both immigrant groups are believed to have originated in southern China. In each case the displaced group retreated to the hills, where it survived by following a nomadic way of life.

The Deutero-Malays are the ancestors of the Malays of today (although as will be seen, the Malays also received large admixtures of later migrants). They established small, widely scattered settlements along the rivers. Gradually over the centuries there was increasing contact with both the immediately surrounding region and the two more distant great civilizations between which the Malay world lay: India and China. Seasonal wind patterns made the Peninsula equally accessible, at different times of the year, from India, China and the Malay Archipelago

(Courtenay, 1972, p. 55). This promoted the development of Indianized trading settlements, the first of which was founded in the fifth or sixth century A.D. (Lamb, 1964, p. 105).

The Indian traders brought both Buddhism and Hinduism to the area along with other aspects of their culture. Political power was in the hands of Indianized Malay rulers.

In 1414 the ruler of Malacca embraced Islam, which had been introduced to South-East Asia by Arab traders in the thirteenth century. Thereafter, Malacca became the dominant power in the region and the most important centre for diffusion of the new religion.

Prior to the Portuguese conquest of Malacca in 1511, the population of the area now known as Peninsular Malaysia was small and scattered (McGee, 1964). Malacca itself is reported to have had 6,000 inhabitants in 1414—mainly Malays, with a good number of foreign traders.[2] Most of the population inhabited the small river settlements and relied on sedentary agriculture (especially wet and dry rice cultivation), fishing and trade in jungle produce and small quantities of tin and gold for their livelihood. An aboriginal minority, dependent on hunting and shifting cultivation, was thinly distributed over the mountainous interior.

As in other South and South-East Asian countries, European colonialism in Malaysia had its succeeding Portuguese, Dutch and British periods. The influence of the Portuguese (1511–1641) was slight, as was that of the Dutch, who supplanted them. The British period began in 1786, when Francis Light took possession of Penang on behalf of the British East India Company. Five years later a treaty was signed in which the Sultan of the adjoining state of Kedah formally ceded the island to the company. In 1795, while Holland was occupied during the wars of the French Revolution, the British seized Malacca. Five years later Penang's defences were strengthened by the purchase of a strip of the mainland (which was named Province Wellesley) from the Sultan of Kedah.

The Company's attitude toward the Indies was ambivalent; the new settlement of Penang, although it grew in population and trade, was never treated generously. Imperial greatness had to be thrust upon the Company by its famous servant, Thomas Stamford Raffles. By founding Singapore in 1819, an act in which he considerably exceeded his instructions, Raffles guaranteed Britain a major place in the colonization of South-East Asia. Its perfect location in the centre of the trading nexus (in contrast to Penang, which was somewhat out of the way), plus the free-trade policy which Raffles established (in sharp contrast to Dutch efforts to achieve a trading monopoly), made Singapore an immediate economic success. Its political future was assured by the Treaty of London (1824), which recognized British sovereignty over Singapore, Penang, Malacca and the Peninsula generally in return for unquestioned Dutch rule over the Islands (Tregonning, 1965; Mills, 1966).

For some time, the three Straits Settlements* (as they were titled formally in 1829) continued as outposts of the East India Company. In varying degrees—Singapore most, Malacca least—they prospered. Traders of many nationalities were attracted by the free-trade policy and the orderly conditions which the British established. From early times the trade was dominated by the Chinese. The Chinese also initiated modernization of tin mining, the earliest of Malaysia's great industries, in the process instigating the spread of British influence throughout the present area of Peninsular Malaysia.

During the early nineteenth century, as the population and prosperity of the Straits Settlements grew, the Malay areas on the mainland also began to change. There was considerable migration of Malay peoples from Sumatra and other parts of present-day Indonesia. Although the immigrants were of various subgroups, distinctions among them disappeared fairly rapidly, usually in one generation, in the unifying presence of common language, religion and customs.[3] Malay villages (*kampung*) were grouped in districts (*daerah*) headed by chiefs, which in turn were combined to form states (*negeri*) (Gullick, 1965). The head of a state was the Ruler (Sultan or Raja), although actual power was often largely dispersed among the chiefs. The early Malay state generally followed the contours of a river valley and had its capital at the mouth of the principal river, from which point the ruler could attempt to control his state and levy duties on trade. Since district chiefs also taxed trade there was a highly restrictive pattern of trade barriers similar to that which existed in medieval Europe.

Minerals, especially tin and gold, had been mined in small quantities in the Malay Peninsula for centuries.[4] The Sultans and chiefs had maintained a tight control over this profitable activity, either through taxes or by keeping ownership of the mines in their own hands. With the establishment of the Straits Settlements, the coming of large numbers of Chinese, growth in world demand for tin and the discovery of ever greater ore deposits, this control now slipped from their grasp. Chinese miners first moved into the more accessible coastal areas and then, in the 1840s and 1850s, to the much richer fields discovered further inland in Perak and Selangor. Meanwhile, world demand for tin for use in tinplating was rising sharply. In 1853 Britain removed the import duty which had been used to protect its Cornwall mines (Courtenay, 1972, pp. 78–92).

Chinese tin miners introduced new forms of organization and technology. The Malays and other early miners had panned or sluiced tin sporadically and on a small scale. Now large and diligent 'coolie' work forces were brought in. The chain pump—a hydraulic device originally used to irrigate rice fields in South China and then adapted to tin mining in Bangka—was introduced. Also as a result of their mining experience elsewhere, the Chinese were able to employ a variety of clay and brick kilns which were much more efficient than the simple ovens used by the Malays. So efficient were the Chinese that not only were the Malays driven from the industry but the Europeans themselves, despite their many political and economic advantages, were unable to penetrate it successfully until after the introduction of the high-pressure gravel pump and the coal-fired smelter in the mid-1890s (Sadka, 1968, pp. 348–51; Wong,

1965, pp. 32–43, 119–54, 211–27; Allen and Donnithorne, 1962, pp. 149–55).

The growth of tin mining led directly to British 'intervention' in the Malay States.*[5] The prosperity of the Straits Settlements (which came under Colonial Office jurisdiction in 1867) had become increasingly dependent on conditions in the Malay States. The Chinese who were moving rapidly into the Malay States by the 1860s were organized into secret societies. Civil war broke out in Selangor and Perak as rival factions, each with its Malay allies, fought for control of the tin fields. The British Government, under the growing influence of the Straits traders, eventually decided to intervene and stabilize the situation.

Under the Pangkor Engagement (the official instrument of intervention, signed in 1874), the Sultan of Perak accepted a British Resident, whose advice 'must be asked and acted upon on all questions other than those touching Malay religion and custom'. This set the pattern for British domination of the Peninsula, an alternative to outright annexation which came to be known as indirect rule. Similar agreements were signed with other states, and in 1895 the Federated Malay States* (Perak, Selangor, Negri Sembilan, and Pahang) were formally constituted to coordinate and simplify the governing of the four important central states which had accepted British Residents. Johore, to the south, remained outside the FMS but signed a treaty of protection with Britain which had much the same effect. The remaining four states of present-day Peninsular Malaysia (Perlis, Kedah, Kelantan, and Trengganu) did not come under British influence until they were ceded by Thailand in 1909 and accepted British Advisers. From 1909 on, therefore, despite the Balkanization and differences in terms, procedures, and legal fictions, all of Malaya was in effect under British rule.[6]

By the late nineteenth century tin was the premier industry. British participation in tin mining increased after the Kinta Valley in Perak, the world's richest tin field, was opened up in the 1890s. By the first decade of the twentieth century Malayan tin production was nearly 50,000 tons a year, constituting more than half the world's output (Yip, 1969, p. 392). In 1911 there were 196,000 tin miners in the FMS, of whom 189,000 were Chinese (Yip, 1969, p. 384).

The growth of tin mining, and of the British stake in it, created pressures for the establishment of a transportation system. The earliest railroads (begun in 1885) linked the minefields in Perak and Selangor to nearby ports; later these were joined to a north–south mainline which eventually (1923) stretched from Singapore to the Thai border. The FMS also built its own port: Port Swettenham (now called Port Klang), in Selangor. Development of Malaya's fine road network had to await the emergence of the rubber industry, which required good access to many parts of the country which had not been involved in tin mining.

Commercial agriculture in Malaya, Chinese and European, dates back to the late eighteenth century (James C. Jackson, 1968). The Chinese planted pepper, gambier (a dyestuff) and tapioca in Singapore, Johore, and Malacca. The Europeans started with spices but quickly moved to their first major plantation crop, sugar, which was grown in Province Wellesley. Ex-coffee planters displaced from Ceylon after the coffee industry there was destroyed by a fungus in 1870s were the first cultivators to become interested in the possibilities of Para rubber. After 1900 the rapid growth of the American automobile industry created a boom market for rubber. Malayan plantings reached 85,000 acres in 1906 and, buoyed by World War I, 2,475,000 acres by 1920. Net exports in 1920 were 174,300 tons, 51 per cent of total world supply (Lim Chong Yah, 1967, pp. 94, 328).

Unlike tin mining, rubber planting was a European venture from the start, an application to a new product of the plantation system with which the planters had been familiar in other parts of the world. Once rubber became profitable, Chinese and Indian capitalists, as well as peasant smallholders from all three of the major ethnic groups, followed the Europeans into the industry.

The plantation system requires large quantities of land and labour. Malaya's dominance of world natural rubber production is attributable to the ample supply of suitable land which could be made available to European planters through British influence to the Sultans. Early rubber planting was concentrated in the Straits Settlements (to the extent that land availability permitted) and in the western Federated States: Perak, Selangor and Negri Sembilan. Pahang, the fourth component of the FMS, was much less touched by estate development because of its location on the East Coast, away from the transportation grid originally designed to serve the tin mines. Johore was also an early participant in estate agriculture, while the remaining Unfederated States came into the picture only in 1909. Thereafter, Perlis and Kedah on the West Coast became the scene of many European estates, while the East Coast states of Kelantan and Trengganu remained isolated (the road network did not even reach them until after World War II).[7]

The concomitant of land availability is labour scarcity. As in other countries where the plantation system was introduced, the indigenous population did not offer itself in significant numbers for work on the estates; nor were Malays considered very suitable for such work by the European planters. The planters wanted a labour force which would be more disciplined, industrious and numerous than the Malays and more docile than the Chinese. For a solution to their problems, they turned to the Tamils of South India, with whom some of the planters were already familiar from their previous planting experience in Ceylon. Tamil immigration was tightly managed, first under an indenture system and subsequently through officially-subsidized migration of free labourers (J. Norman Parmer, 1960; R.N. Jackson, 1961).

By the late 1920s, Malaya was the most successful exemplar of what has been called the colonial export economy. (For varying perspectives, see Levin, 1960; Snodgrass, 1966; Beckford, 1972.) Its population (including Singapore) was over four million, of which more than half were of the immigrant groups. The vast quantities of rubber and tin which it supplied to world markets supported a prosperous group of

European businessmen, a government whose standards of public services were probably the highest in the colonial world and a relatively good living standard for its Asian population. This system was to be sorely tested in the decades to come.

First, the Depression devastated the trade-dependent Malayan economy. In the dark days of 1932, both rubber and tin became virtually worthless in world trade. Thereafter, prices showed a slow rising trend, broken by a brief downturn in 1938 and then capped by the feverish efforts to supply growing war needs in 1939–41. The colonial administration reacted in several ways to the massive economic setback of the 1930s. The classic adjustment mechanism of the colonial export economy, repatriation of immigrant labour, was brought into play on a large scale in 1930–2 (Parmer, 1960, pp. 222–48). More far-reaching changes in immigration regulations, stimulated by the discovery in the 1931 Census that the immigrant population had far out-distanced the Malay population, saw the era of open immigration ended forever in 1933.[8]

The government also sought means of strengthening the economy. Rubber and tin came under international supply restriction schemes (Knorr, 1945, 1945a). Expansion of rubber acreage was halted and production quotas were assigned to the estates and smallholders, to the considerable disadvantage of the latter (Bauer, 1948). Another effect of the Depression was to open a long-running debate on economic diversification. In the atmosphere of the Depression it was easy to believe that the Malayan economy was over-specialized. Dependence on imported rice—to the extent of 74 per cent of consumption in 1926–30 (Lim, 1967, p. 45)—was a particular cause for concern, but public policy was paralysed by an unwillingness either to let Chinese into the Malay preserve of rice cultivation, to protect domestic rice growing (and thus raise the price of principal wage good) or to subsidize the industry from the public treasury (Report of the Rice Cultivation Committee, 1932; Thompson, 1943, pp. 32–42). Hence the only significant action taken in the 1930s was to begin large-scale public investment in drainage and irrigation (Lim, 1967, pp. 162–6).

The outbreak of World War II at first affected Malaya only by stimulating demand for its products. But on 7 December 1941 the Japanese landed in Kelantan, opening a campaign which ended with the fall of Singapore on 15 February 1942. The Japanese occupation, which lasted until September 1945, was a period of deprivation in which inter-group relations worsened under the strain of sharply differing treatment by the Japanese and reactions to them. For the Chinese and Indians, the situation was conditioned by events in their countries of origin. China and Japan had been at war since 1937; the Chinese received much the harshest treatment during the occupation of Malaya and provided practically all the underground oppositions. By contrast, the Malays and Indians accepted the occupation with more equanimity and in many cases actively co-operated with the Japanese. Many Indians proved susceptible to Japanese promises of aid in the struggle for Indian independence.

The most fundamental effect of World War II, however, was to destroy the myth of natural European supremacy and perpetual colonial rule. In sharp contrast to the pre-war period, the era ushered in by re-establishment of British administration in 1945 was to feature continuous discussion of the nature of the new self-governing state now generally assumed to be in the making.

Nationalistic forces had been slow to emerge in the apolitical atmosphere of British Malaya.* The administration, against the cumulating evidence of a growing immigrant population, continued to regard the Chinese and Indians as temporary sojourners rather than permanent residents and potential future citizens of the country. Indeed, members of these groups themselves looked to their countries of origin and did not assert for themselves a role in local politics. The origins of 'Malay nationalism' have been traced to around the turn of the century (Roff, 1967), but nationalistic forces developed slowly in a predominantly rural and conservative community which moreover tended to look to the British as its protector *vis-a-vis* the more aggresive immigrant groups. Thus a unified Malayan nationalism was non-existent before World War II and even 'Malay nationalism' (i.e., pan-Malay communalism) remained weak.

Japan's surrender was followed in Malaya by a brief period of chaos. This period, which ended with the establishment of a British Military Administration, saw the exacerbation of ethnic tensions as wartime scores were settled and Chinese guerrilla groups temporarily seized control of several towns.

Post-war planners in London had prepared a blueprint for a Malayan Union,* which would establish unified and centralized control over an area consisting of the pre-war FMS, the five Unfederated Malay States and the Straits Settlements of Penang and Malacca. Singapore was to remain a colony because of its strategic importance and because inclusion of its overwhelmingly Chinese population in the Malayan Union would have created a Chinese majority in the new state. The Malayan Union government was to be highly centralized; the status of the Sultans and powers of the state governments were to be sharply curtailed. A common citizenship was to be made available to all persons born in the country or resident there during ten of the previous fifteen years.

The Malayan Union scheme, hastily instituted in 1946, generated an unprecedented stir of political activity. The long-feeble force of Malay nationalism was aroused to a fever pitch of opposition under the leadership of Dato Onn bin Jaafar, founder of the United Malays National Organization (UMNO). The non-Malays, still preoccupied with events in China and India, were slow to organize in defence of a constitution that gave them citizenship rights which they would covet later on. Eventually the British Government backed down and initiated discussions with the Rulers and UMNO—the non-Malays were not represented—which culminated in the Federation of Malaya Agreement of 1948 (Allen, 1967; Simandjuntak, 1969; Mohamed Noordin Sopiee, 1974).

This new Agreement, which formed the foundation for the later constitutions of independent Malaya (1957) and Malaysia (1963), abandoned or compromised most of the disputed points in the Malayan Union scheme. The idea of a unified colony was dropped in favour of continued indirect rule throughout a wider federation covering the same area as the Malayan Union. The Sultans regained their honorific positions but the power of the central government was greatly strengthened. A common multi-racial citizenship was retained from the Malayan Union plan but the residence requirement was lengthened (to fifteen of the past twenty-five years) and applicants were required to declare their intention to settle permanently in the Federation and to demonstrate their ability to speak either Malay or English, the two official languages. In sum, the Federation of Malaya which came into existence in 1948 was a strong federation in which the trappings of indirect rule were preserved in conjunction with strengthened central government control. It offered a place to all long-term residents but accorded special recognition to the status of the Malays.

The Federation of Malaya Agreement provided for a Legistative Council made up of appointed official and unofficial members. Elections were introduced at the local level in 1951 and at the national level in 1955. It was the Kuala Lumpur Municipal Council elections of 1952 which produced the Malay–Chinese 'Alliance', at first merely a no-contest pact but subsequently (beginning in 1953) a formally constituted Alliance Party.[9]

Promulgation of the new Federation in 1948 had coincided with the outbreak of a Communist-led insurrection, euphemistically termed the 'Emergency'. This uprising, which was almost exclusively Chinese in membership, achieved considerable success in its early years, disrupting the economy and terrorizing the countryside although it never succeeded in establishing liberated areas. It received much support from working-class Chinese but failed utterly among the Malays and Indians, who saw it as an exclusively Chinese affair. Although the outcome was initially in doubt, the British Government succeeded in gradually choking off the rebellion. By 1953 the tide had turned, although officially the Emergency was not terminated until 1960.

The insurrection had had as one of its early objectives the disruption of the Malayan economy. This effort was frustrated by the forbearance of the working population, and by the world commodity boom created by the Korean War, which generated large balance of payments surpluses in 1950 and 1951. The GNP of Malaya (including Singapore) *doubled* between 1949 and 1951 (International Bank for Reconstruction and Development, 1955, pp. 677–92). Thereafter, exports and GNP both declined again, but not before some of the pre-war prosperity of the Malayan governments and peoples had been restored. This hardly increased their sympathy for the revolutionary cause.

Without the Emergency, the Federation of Malaya might have achieved its Independence in the late 1940s or early 1950s, like many other Asian colonies. Paradoxically, however, it was the Communist insurrection which ultimately prompted Britain to promise Independence, as part of a 'hearts and minds' campaign to undermine popular support for the rebellion. The general election of 1955, in which the Alliance Party swept to victory in 51 out of 52 elected Legislative Council seats, was an important step toward Independence. It was followed by internal self-government, with Tengku Abdul Rahman, a prince of the Kedah royal family who had become president of UMNO upon the resignation of Dato Onn in 1951, as Chief Minister. Then in 1956 negotiations were held preparatory to the granting of full independence. These will be discussed in Chapter 3.

THE EMERGENCE OF A PLURAL SOCIETY

Although the small numbers of exotic traders and miners residing in the area from the fifth or sixth century on probably did not qualify Malaya to be regarded as a plural society, the mass migration which occurred during the period of British influence unquestionably did. Malays, Chinese and Indians have differed in many ways: language, religion, customs (to the extent of one group revelling in what another group abhorred), even physical features. These differences continue virtually unabated today. Only in very special circumstances have individuals moved from one group to another.[10] And while there are senses in which the groups have been drawn closer together by political, economic and social change, there are also senses in which they have been driven further apart.[11] The vast majority of Malaysians today have uppermost in their consciousness their identity as Malays, Chinese or Indians.

The internal homogeneity of the Malay, Chinese and Indian cultural groups is more debatable than their distinctiveness. Each group has its class divisions and each is to some extent composed of identifiable cultural sub-groups. The Malays are surely the most integrated group, since their sub-group divisions, which were important in earlier times, have been largely obliterated by uniformity in language, religion and custom, as well as by the need for political unity in the face of external challenges. Their hierarchical social structure has survived relatively intact to the present day, but the bonds among Malays at differing levels of society appear much stronger than any affinity which exists at particular class levels across communal groups.

The Chinese and Indian communities in Malaya are admittedly more heterogeneous. The Chinese virtually all came from Southern China but were drawn from several provinces and arrived in Malaya speaking a number of different, often mutually unintelligible, dialects. This led them to form dialect group clusters in particular regions of the country and lines of economic activity. In the late nineteenth century, therefore, one could seriously debate whether the Chinese in Malaya could be said to form a single community. Twentieth-century developments have weakened the distinctions among Chinese sub-groups: the common focus on Chinese nationalism, quickened by the revolution of 1911; the spreading use of the Chinese National Language (*Kuo-yu*); extensive intermarriage and social mobility; and, after World War II, the need to promote interests common to all Chinese. By the present day, differences among

Chinese sub-groups, although still visible, have become blurred and are of minor importance compared to the distinction between the Chinese as a whole and the other major groups.

The Indian group is the most heterogeneous. The great majority of Indians (84 per cent in 1970) are from the South Indian Tamil linguistic group, while an additional 8 per cent are Malayalis or Telegus, also from South India.[12] These people virtually all came to Malaya as estate or government labourers and most of them remain in such a working-class status, frequently in identical jobs, today. This majority is fairly sharply distinguished from a minority who came to Malaya, from all parts of India, with higher socio-economic status as traders, clerical workers and even technicians and professionals. The minority was much more diverse in language and religion (it included Muslims and Sikhs as well as Hindus) than the majority. In Malaya its interests were middle-class and urban; its language increasingly came to be English. There has been relatively little interchange between these two groups of Indians (and the minority is so diverse as to hardly constitute a group on its own), although a common background and shared interest in the independence movement and other events in the Indian homeland have created some bonds of sympathy. 'The Indians' is the least defensible of the three major Malaysian cultural groups (Tellander, 1970), but it will be used here because of its convenience (many data are collected on that basis) and limited validity.

Since Independence the Chinese, Indians and Others* have, for limited political purposes, tended to merge into a single group commonly referred to as the non-Malays. This has come about through the focus of political debate on questions of the 'special rights of the Malays' versus the 'legitimate interests of the other communities', which has given the Chinese and Indians a set of common political interests. Specifically Indian interests exist, of course—for example, the employment and livelihood of displaced estate workers—but political parties, including the Malayan Indian Congress, have been weak instruments for pressing these concerns because of the smallness of the Indian community and its geographic dispersion (no Parliamentary district has an Indian majority).

Table 2.1 shows the evolution of the population in terms of ethnic group and sex from 1833 to 1970.

The plural society emerged during the British colonial period. In the early decades of the nineteenth century, when the emphasis was still on trading, the number of immigrants remained small. By 1833–4 there were only 24,000 Chinese, 15,000 Indians and 8,000 other non-Malays in the Straits Settlements. It was the expansion of tin mining in the middle and latter part of the century which drew large numbers of Chinese into the Straits Settlements and Malay States, through both its direct labour requirements and its indirect effect on the volume of trade and other economic activity.

After British intervention in the Malay states, separate demographic patterns can be defined for the three political jurisdictions which emerged. The Straits Settlements, with their essentially urban commer-

TABLE 2.1
POPULATION BY ETHNIC GROUP AND SEX, 1833–1970
(Thousands)

Area and date	Malays		Other Malaysians[1]		Chinese		Indians[2]		Others		All		
	Male	Female	Male	Female	Male	Female	Male	Female	Male	Female	Male	Female	Total
Straits Settlements													
1833–4	—89[3]—		..	..	—24—		—15—		—8—		..	..	137
1850–2	72[3]	63[3]	..	..	53	10	13	4	4	4	143	80	223
1871	74	74	8	5	87	17	26	8	6	4	200	108	308
1891	92	93	16	10	183	44	41	13	10	7	342	167	509
1901	93	97	14	10	219	63	42	13	10	8	378	192	569
1911	98	103	19	12	273	97	62	19	13	10	466	242	708
1921	108	111	19	11	340	161	77	25	17	11	560	319	879
1931	117	122	21	14	410	249	97	32	21	15	666	433	1,098
Federated Malay States													
1891	—219—		—16—		—165—		—20—		—2—		..	..	422
1901	151	138	16	10	275	27	45	13	3	2	490	191	683
1911	178	168	48	33	367	69	133	41	6	5	731	315	1,046
1921	213	202	58	43	369	129	214	95	8	6	862	476	1,337
1931	226	225	84	66	482	237	249	136	17	11	1,058	675	1,733
Unfederated Malay States													
1911	346	353	34	25	97	15	10	3	9	8	497	403	900
1921	391	395	45	31	145	36	46	16	11	10	638	487	1,125
1931	458	466	76	56	239	92	76	35	15	14	865	662	1,527
Peninsular Malaysia													
1911	610	611	90	62	572	123	182	58	18	17	1,471	871	2,342
1921	694	692	107	76	633	224	309	131	23	20	1,767	1,143	2,910
1931	781	794	164	124	865	420	378	195	38	29	2,226	1,563	3,789
1947	1,064	1,098	143	122	1,039	846	319	216	45	31	2,610	2,313	4,923
1957	1,384	1,419	169	154	1,212	1,122	399	297	75	49	3,238	3,041	6,279
1970	2,182	2,210	148	145	1,578	1,545	495	437	37	33	4,449[4]	4,371[4]	8,820[4]

Sources: M. V. del Tufo (1949); H. Fell (1960); R. Chander (1971).

[1]A category used in censuses from 1871 to 1947 to designate immigrants of Malay stock, as well as aborigines.

[2]Generally includes those originating in present-day Pakistan and Bangladesh.

[3]Includes 'Other Malaysians'.

[4]Components fail to add to totals because of the presence of a few thousand unallocated transients.

TABLE 2.2

POPULATION BY ETHNIC GROUP AND BIRTH-PLACE, 1911–1957

(Per cent of total)

	Straits Settlements				*Federated Malay States*				*Unfederated States*				*Peninsular Malaysia*			
	Malay	*Chin.*	*Ind.*	*Other*	*Malay*	*Chin.*	*Ind.*	*Other*	*Malay*	*Chin.*	*Ind.*	*Other*	*Malay*	*Chin.*	*Ind.*	*Other*
1911																
State of residence	..	..	..	..	72	6	5	14	..	..	..	..	..	..	..	..
Other Malaya	..	..	..	..	12	2	2	18	..	..	..	..	..	..	..	..
Elsewhere	..	..	..	..	17	92	93	68	..	..	..	..	..	..	..	..
1921																
State of residence	49	21	16	53	71	14	10	37	88	14	5	79	83	18	10	62
Other Malaya	44	10	2		10	3	1		5	3	4		6	3	2	
Elsewhere	7	69	82	47	19	83	89	63	7	83	91	21	10	79	88	38
1931																
State of residence	84	36	20	48	78	26	20	26	88	20	11	76	86	27	18	53
Other Malaya	7	2	3		9	3	2		5	4	5		6	3	3	
Elsewhere	9	62	77	52	12	71	78	74	7	76	84	24	8	70	79	47
1947																
State of residence	84	60	40	59	86	58	46	56	93	53	34	86	91	58	44	70
Other Malaya	9	3	6		8	5	6		4	7	10		6	5	7	
Elsewhere	7	37	53	41	6	37	47	44	3	40	55	14	3	37	49	30
1957																
State of residence	90	70	54	39	84	66	57	33	92	64	49	53	89	67	55	41
Other Malaya	9	9	11	13	13	9	9	14	6	10	13	7	8	9	10	11
Elsewhere	1	21	35	47	4	25	34	53	2	26	38	41	3	24	35	48

Sources: A. M. Pountney (1911); J. E. Nathan (1922); C. A. Vlieland (1932); M. V. del Tufo (1949); H. Fell (1960).

cial and administrative populations (although Penang and Malacca, unlike Singapore, included significant agricultural hinterlands), continued to grow at around 2 per cent a year, mainly through immigration but also partly through natural increase. In the process, the Settlements became increasingly populated by the immigrant groups. Malays (including 'Other Malaysians'*) had made up 52 per cent of their population in 1871, but this percentage fell to 41 per cent by 1891 and to only 25 per cent by 1931 as immigrants, especially Chinese, consistently accounted for the largest share of population growth.

The first population censuses in what were to become the Federated Malay States were conducted in 1891. By that time Chinese immigrants, mainly adult male tin miners, already numbered 165,000 and made up 40 per cent of the population. Chinese immigration continued on a large scale up to the 1930s. Periodically there were checks to male migration, as when the tin mines were mechanized just before World War I and when the Depression hit, but accelerating migration of females to right the highly unbalanced sex ratio (10 : 1 in 1901) made up much of the slack. Chinese immigration was at first related directly to tin mining but later continued for other reasons after mining employment declined. Large-scale Indian migration to the FMS was always related to the growth of the rubber industry. Its peak period was 1900–20, but significant migration continued until the Depression. As in the Straits Settlements, the Malay community could not keep up with the high rates of non-Malay immigration into the FMS. Its share in total population (again counting 'Other Malaysians' as Malays) fell from 56 per cent in 1891 to 37 per cent in 1931.

In the UMS the first censuses were taken only in 1911, two years after Perlis, Kedah, Kelantan and Trengganu came under British protection. As might be expected, their populations were found to be heavily Malay (84 per cent). During the next two decades some parts of the UMS experienced heavy immigration, particularly Johore and sections of Kedah. However, the process was cut short by the Depression and the population of the five unfederated states remained 69 per cent Malay in 1931.

Throughout this period, despite the large-scale net immigration, many labourers came to Malaya to work there temporarily. Departures of Chinese averaged 45 per cent of arrivals between 1916 and 1929. Departures of South Indian deck passengers from Penang averaged 65 per cent of arrivals in 1916–29 (Parmer, 1960, pp. 270–1).

As nearly as one can tell, immigration more than accounted for the growth of the non-Malay population up to 1931. That is, deaths among these groups exceeded births. This phenomenon was caused partly by the harsh conditions in which many of the immigrants worked but primarily by the dearth of women among them and their high average age,[13] factors which raised the death rate and lowered the birth rate.

The incessant two-way flow of migrants led colonial administrators to regard the Chinese and Indians as 'birds of passage'. It would seem that the rising percentage of locally-born non-Malays (Table 2.2) and sharp increases in the female population should have been taken as indications of increases in the numbers of permanently settled Chinese and Indians. But as late as 1932 the Census Superintendent argued that the Chinese and Indians were no more permanent in Malaya than the Europeans:

> When we bear in mind the great increase in the ratio of females to males, and the constantly increasing number of births in Malaya from immigrant parents in recent years, we find nothing in this small increase in the Malayan-born component of the population to suggest a growing tendency toward permanent settlement. What the figures do suggest is the rapid 'turn-over' in the migrant population of Malaya, and the shortness of the average stay in Malaya of the individual immigrant. Europeans, Chinese, and Indians alike come to Malaya, not to make their home, but in the hope of making a living and amassing wealth, or at least a competence, with which to return to their native lands. To a much increased extent, they bring their womenfolk with them, and their children are largely born in Malaya. The more are so born the more 'Malayan-borns' will be caught in each successive draught of the census net, but few are caught twice, and fewer still are caught three times or more. Adult or child, it is the same story; like Gerillau's ants, they come and go (Vlieland, 1932, p. 67).

There was perhaps some justification for this view before the Depression brought immigration restrictions and forced immigrants already in Malaya to decide whether to stay or return 'home'. During the 1930s net immigration was much reduced (although it apparently remained positive for the decade as a whole; Courtenay, 1972, pp. 131–2), the death rate fell and the crude birth rate rose sharply. Natural increase thus began to take over from immigration as the main source of population growth. When the first post-war census was taken in 1947 it was found that the population had grown by over a million since 1931 (Table 2.1). Both the Malay and Chinese communities were much larger than they had been in 1931, while the Indian community was somewhat smaller. The Chinese and Indians both showed much better balance in terms of sexes and age groups. With immigration now largely closed off, it was evident (Smith, 1962, pp. 1–3) that a new demographic era was dawning, in which the three communities would be made up almost entirely of permanent residents and their relative sizes determined almost wholly by natural increase.

The Malays (and their sympathizers) had long feared that they would someday be outnumbered by the immigrant groups. While mass immigration continued these fears had ample basis. In 1911 the Malays, including immigrant Malays, had constituted 59 per cent of the population of what is now Peninsular Malaysia, or 53 per cent if Singapore is included (Table 2.1). Immigration during the 1911–21 intercensal period cut the former share to 53 per cent and the latter to 49 per cent. By 1931 the Malays had lost their majority, even with Singapore disregarded. In that year, the population of the latter-day Peninsular Malaysia was found to be only 49 per cent Malay, while the share for Malaya as a whole had dipped to 44 per cent. Despite the anxieties occasioned by this sharp and persistent decline in the Malay share of the population, it is likely that mass immigration would have continued, leading to a decisive decline of the Malay community into minority status, had prosperity continued into the 1930s. However, the onset of the Depression, followed by World War II, changed all that by sealing off immigration and redirecting the attention of those concerned with the numerical balance of Malaya's ethnic groups to comparative rates of natural increase.

Strangely, the balance of Malays and non-Malays in the population of Peninsular Malaysia was unaffected by the cataclysmic events of the 1931–47 intercensal period. The Malay share, including a slightly reduced number of people who identified themselves as 'Other Malaysians', remained at 49 per cent.

Fears that the Malays would be reduced to minority status outlived the era of mass migration. In the early post-war period these fears had some slender basis in the vital statistics. The Chinese rate of natural increase was higher than that of the Malays until around 1956, when the Malay rate moved decisively ahead as Chinese fertility declined. Fertility declined later among the Indians but by 1966 they too had a more slowly growing population than the Malays. The natural increase of the entire population has been rapid through most of the post-war period, running at 3 per cent or more in each year from 1952 through 1964.

The demographic pattern has involved a continuous decline in mortality and an initial rise, followed by a gradual decline after the mid-1950s, in natality (Saw, 1967; Cho, Palmore and Saunders, 1968). All groups shared these trends but the Malays were the last to experience the reduction in natality and also benefited most from the fall in the death rate. The result was that whereas they had only held their ground—at just under 50 per cent of the Peninsular Malaysian population—during the 1947–57 intercensal period, by 1970 they had moved ahead of the non-Malays to a 53 per cent share. There appears to be no way that the Malays, who control immigration and work-permit policies, can ever again be outnumbered. The projection is that the Malay share will experience some further increase and then stabilize as Malay birth and death rates become similar to those of the non-Malays. The fear—or, in other quarters, hope—that an immigrant majority will emerge, although once very real, can thus be laid to rest.

COMPONENTS OF THE PLURAL SOCIETY

Although Malaysia's ethnic groups have shared many historical experiences, their respective histories are in many ways separate and different. Present-day economic inequalities are often attributed to these differences. The validity of such arguments will be examined in due course; at this point the aim is merely to establish what the major historical differences among the groups are. Each of the three major groups will be discussed in turn, in terms of its colonial experience, its initial contact with the colonial system and its subsequent experience in colonial economic development.

The Malays

The main features of pre-colonial Malay society have already been sketched.[14] The small, scattered population was organized along feudal lines. The nominal apex of its hierarchy was the Sultan, ruler of the state. But the low population density, weak power instruments and lack of effective communication left much of the actual power in the hands of district and village chiefs. This system was viable until the appearance in numbers of Chinese and Europeans unleashed forces beyond its power to control. Although early British writers often characterized the Malay political system as unstable and exploitative, it is likely that it functioned well enough up to the mid-nineteenth century.

Culturally, the peninsular Malays were part of the broader, sea-linked Malay world. Living on the western edge of that world, they were most readily subject to cultural influences emanating from the West, which touched them first and affected them most. But the ties with Malay peoples elsewhere, especially those in nearby Sumatra, remained strong.

Pre-colonial Malay society consisted of a small aristocracy and a mass of peasants. Trading and mining were a monopoly of the aristocracy; peasants grew rice, fished and gathered jungle produce. The masses were subject to feudal labour obligations and were cut off from most forms of social or economic advancement. One opportunity which was open to them was migration to another area where there was unused land. This softened the impact of feudalism on the average Malay.

The terms on which the colonizing British and the Malays contacted each other exercised a major influence on later developments. In choosing to work through the Malay élite, the British changed its role in Malay society. The formal hierarchy of political power, with the Ruler at its apex, was strengthened. Even though the Rulers had increasingly to bow to the dictates of the British Residents and Advisers who appeared in their courts, and also lost many of their opportunities to take part in business, their prestige as symbols of the Malay community and its political legitimacy was gradually enhanced. (When seriously challenged for the first and only time under the Malayan Union proposal of the 1940s, the position of the Rulers proved to be impregnable.) This powerfully buttressed conservative forces in the Malay community.

Having come to terms with the Malay aristocracy, the British were free to go about their business in virtual disregard of the pre-existing Malay society and economy. Because of the sparseness of the population, mines, plantations and towns could all be established with minimal disturbance of the rural, rice-based Malay society. Nevertheless, some opportunities were created for mass Malay participation in new forms of economic activity, especially (1) employment in the mines, estates and other modern-sector organizations; (2) the supply of rice and other needed foodstuffs to the enclave populations; and (3) participation as smallholders in the production of export crops. These opportunities were seized to widely varying degrees.

It has already been seen that the Malay response to the growing demand for labour to work in the mines and estates was negligible.[15] Malays never came to represent a significant fraction of employment in any of the sectors which boomed after intervention. The mining labour force was always over 90 per cent Chinese. Chinese-owned estates also preferred Chinese labour. European estates relied mainly on South Indian labourers.

The unwillingness of rural Malays to work steadily on the estates led to the stereotype of the 'lazy' Malay, with his supposed backward-bending supply curve of labour. Yet in retrospect it is clear that this was not a particularly attractive opportunity for the Malays, either economically or in terms of their cultural values. The plantations required disciplined, low-wage labour while the *kampung* economy, with its favourable land–man ratio, probably offered a comparable living standard within a more familiar and comfortable social framework. Malays clearly preferred *kampung* life to the regimented existence in the estate 'lines'. Their devotion to rice cultivation carried with it heavy seasonal labour requirements, with '. . . every able-bodied man and woman . . . required to help with the planting of rice . . .' (Chai, 1964, p. 99). Malays were not, as will be seen, unresponsive to economic opportunities presented by colonial development when those opportunities were consistent with the continuation of *kampung* life and no radical change in life-style was required.

By contrast, the Malay response to opportunities which could be seized while still remaining a peasant farmer was significant. The rapid growth of the estate, mine and urban populations generated enormous increases in the demand for rice. Rice was the wage-good in the labour-intensive mining and plantation industries, and this fact resulted in strong pressure to assure an adequate supply at a low price. Up to the Depression, official policy favoured specialization on export crops and importation of rice from nearby and low-cost sources, Burma and Siam (Lim, 1967, pp. 174–8; Doering, 1973, pp. 15–21). Although the area planted with rice in Malaya, average yield and actual production all seem to have risen strongly during the 1920s[16]—and market-oriented rice-surplus areas began to emerge in Kedah, Perlis, Province Wellesley, northern Perak and Kelantan—local supply simply could not keep up with the soaring demand. Imports rose to nearly three-fourths of consumption in the late 1920s (Doering, 1973, p. 18). Any tendency for non-Malays to gain a position in rice cultivation was throttled by protective land reservation which began to be enacted early in the century and became far more widespread with the onset of the Depression.

The changed official attitude toward rice cultivation which resulted from the Depression brought about the first serious government efforts to enhance the economy of the rural Malays. The very limited government measures to promote rice output during the 1930s have been mentioned above. To the small amounts of additional infrastructural investment and research and extension services provided was added a legal requirement that land 'gazetted' for padi production be used *only* to grow padi. This legislation remains in effect today, although it is believed to be widely ignored.

Partly because of their own preferences and partly as a result of the effort to keep them in rice production, the Malays supplied little of the rapidly growing demand for subsidiary foodstuffs. Market gardening, poultry-raising and, of course, pig-rearing came to be dominated by the Chinese.

However, no policy could prevent the Malays from joining other groups in pursuit of the higher incomes which could be earned by planting rubber. The attractiveness of this opportunity has been demonstrated by Bauer (1948, p. 61), who showed that even at the depth of the Depression an average acre of land yielded more income in rubber than in rice. Malays responded by converting small plots of land from other uses, or from jungle, into rubber smallholdings. By 1953 there were nearly 200,000 Malay-owned rubber smallholdings (Lim, 1967, p. 332). But they were nearly all very small, averaging 3.3 acres; only 300 or so holdings were as large as 25 acres.

It is worth emphasizing that the surge of rural Malays into rubber cultivation occurred despite considerable official opposition. Not only were efforts made to keep the Malays in padi production, but Malay (and other) smallholders were discriminated against under the output restriction scheme of the 1930s. This discrimination, which has been documented by Bauer (1948), continued in somewhat abated form after World War II and even into the era of Independence.

Malay access to many important forms of employment—professional, administrative, clerical—was largely a function of education. Colonial policy quite explicitly held the Malays back from the types of education which would provide such access. There was much talk about making education 'practical' and 'suitable to the student's environment', while fears of the political effects of widespread English-language, urban-oriented education for Malays were often explicit in official pronouncements of the times (Loh, 1969, pp. 156–76; Chai, 1964, pp. 226–81). Government-sponsored secondary and higher education were offered almost entirely in English and expanded very slowly. Education in Malay was rural in its orientation, aiming 'to make the son of the fisherman or peasant a more intelligent fisherman or peasant than his father had been, and a man whose education will enable him to understand how his own lot fits in with the scheme of life around him'.[17] The small amount of Malay-medium secondary education which was provided beginning in 1905 was at first limited to sons of the nobility and later extended to teacher trainees for Malay-medium schools. A few urban and well connected Malays were able to benefit from English-medium schooling. Rural Malays were believed to be less interested in educating their children than other elements of the population, but there is evidence that their lower educational achievement is attributable in large part to the greatly inferior access to schooling which they were offered, particularly in the Unfederated States (Hirschman, 1972).

As Table 2.3 shows, economically active Malays remained concentrated in a small number of *kampung*-related occupations throughout the colonial period. There were changes within this pattern—people shifted some of their attention from rice to rubber, village handicrafts died out—but occupations which required one to leave the *kampung* were

TABLE 2.3

TEN LEADING MALAY OCCUPATIONS, 1911–1957

Occupation	*1911 (FMS only)* Rank	*1911 (FMS only)* Employment ('000)	1921 Rank	1921 Employment ('000)	*1931* Rank	*1931* Employment ('000)	*1947* Rank	*1947* Employment ('000)	*1957* Rank	*1957* Employment ('000)
Padi planters	1	108.2	1	452.0	1	366.2	1	417.1		
Agricultural labourers	2	29.2	2	94.8						
Agricultural owners and managers	3	18.3	4	29.8					1	424.1
Atap makers and sellers	4	5.5								
Coconut cultivators	5	4.6			5	19.3	5	21.8		
Tailors and seamstresses	6	3.9								
Labourers (unspecified)	7	2.9	8	8.2	6	17.4	7	18.8	5	33.1
Fishermen	8	3.2	3	35.0	4	35.4	3	41.4	3	41.3
Planters (unspecified)	9	2.4	5	26.3						
Weavers	10	2.1	6	11.2						
Proprietors and managers of businesses			7	10.8					7	14.3
Domestic servants			9	7.7	9	7.9				
Hawkers			10	7.2			9	14.8	10	7.7
Rubber cultivators (excluding managers)					2	123.5	2	147.4	2	247.3
Miscellaneous agriculturalists					3	50.9				
Poultry and livestock rearers					7	16.0				
Drivers, conductors, etc.					8	11.6	10	9.9		

TABLE 2.3
(continued)

Occupation	*1911 (FMS only)* Rank	*1911 (FMS only)* Employment ('000)	*1921* Rank	*1921* Employment ('000)	*1931* Rank	*1931* Employment ('000)	*1947* Rank	*1947* Employment ('000)	*1957* Rank	*1957* Employment ('000)
Salesmen					10	7.8				
Rubber estate owners and managers							4	22.7		
Fruit and vegetable growers							6	19.7		
Basketry and rattan workers							8	18.2		
Police									4	40.5
Teachers									6	19.5
Armed forces									8	12.1
Miscellaneous production workers									9	9.7
All other occupations		31.9		94.0		98.7		129.3		154.6
Total employment		212.3		777.1		754.7		861.1		1,004.3

Source: Population censuses.

Note: Occupational titles have been standardized as much as possible but some non-comparabilities remain, especially with respect to agricultural occupations. The geographic scope of the table is present-day Peninsular Malaysia.

slow to emerge. Only at the very end of the colonial period do the occupations through which the largest numbers of Malays have entered life outside the *kampung*—policeman, teacher, soldier—enter the list of the ten most common occupations for Malays.

Interpretation of the Malay experience under colonialism is a matter of keen interest and some controversy. The key issues are the true nature of government policy toward the Malays and the Malay response to the economic opportunities posed by these policies and by other circumstances of the world around them.

Most British colonial officials *liked* the Malays better than the Chinese or Indians, frequently expressing a romantic admiration for the Malay way of life. Moreover, the Malays posed no competitive threat to European economic interests. For these reasons, any allegation that colonial policy deliberately held back Malay economic advancement would have to rest on alleged fear of the *political* consequences. For this belief there is some basis. Since the British ruled through a legal relationship with the topmost layer of Malay society they had a vested interest in maintaining the existing social order within the Malay community. For this reason they were not kindly disposed toward, and in some ways actively impeded, social mobility among Malays. This can be seen in educational policy and in the rules regarding the use of Malay land for rice and other crops. The Malays were no economic threat to the existing order, but because of their political legitimacy in Malaya, which was never directly challenged, they were by far the greatest potential political threat. This fact does seem to provide at least partial explanation for official policies which limited Malay economic opportunities.

As for the Malay response to opportunity, the true picture seems more complex than the stereotype. What happened with smallholder rubber, and to a lesser extent with rice, contradicts the view that Malay society was totally static and unresponsive. On the other hand, both the will and the ability to make more sophisticated and far-reaching adjustments to changes in opportunity—adjustments which would have required changes in place of residence and style of living—do seem to have been weak, especially by comparison to the impressive abilities of the Chinese along these lines.

The Chinese

Where the Chinese (and Indians) are concerned, only part of the relevant pre-colonial experience—and very possibly the less important part, at that—occurred in Malaya. The other, more significant, segment of early experience took place in the homelands from which they originated.[18]

The small Chinese and Indian communities which existed in Malaya before the European contact acted as vehicles for the transmission of outside cultural influences to the Malays, but they also tended to take on local coloration. The outstanding example is the Straits-born, or 'Baba', Chinese community of Penang, Malacca and Singapore (Purcell, 1965, pp. 61–2). While remaining non-Islamic and continuing to eat pork, the

Straits Chinese adapted in other fashions, for example in their use of the Malay language. They posed no threat to the balance of political power and are often cited by contemporary Malay speakers and writers as models of cultural assimilation—in pointed contrast to later immigrants.[19]

Chinese immigrants brought with them elements of the great and ancient civilization from which they came. Just what this invisible cultural baggage consisted of is a matter for conjecture. However, two basic points seem unassailable:

1. In terms of economic anthropology, Chinese immigrants were products of a vastly more sophisticated economic system than their Malay contemporaries. Freedman (1959) has taken familiarity with money as a touchstone of this sophistication and suggested that the importation of credit institutions indigenous to South China was a critical element in the successful economic performance of Chinese immigrants in South-East Asia, as elsewhere.[20]

2. The social structure of the Chinese immigrants had economic advantages, both because it was Chinese and because it was immigrant. From the start, the immigrant preserved traditional social ties—within the nuclear family, clan and linguistic group—as valuable means of assuring survival and eventual prosperity in a strange and sometimes hostile land. During the pre-colonial period these ties provided a form of self-government in what otherwise would have been an anarchic situation. (They did not, however, suffice to prevent social disruption in circumstances of keen competition for high stakes, such as the Perak 'tin wars' of the 1860s and 1870s.) Later, they enabled the colonial authorities to follow a 'hands-off' policy once basic order had been established.

The Chinese were beginning to take an active interest in what were to become the peninsula's leading industries—mining and commercial agriculture—before the British appeared on the scene. When the British for the first time established settled conditions throughout Malaya these efforts were greatly facilitated. One might think that Chinese enterprise would have been hampered by the use of governmental power to further European (and perhaps also Malay) interests.

Europeans did in fact receive privileged access to land and mineral rights which the State could bestow. But British power was not monolithic. Many early colonial administrators set great stock in the 'development' of the country—by which they meant the growth of trade, population and government revenues—and were less concerned with the narrowed aim of enriching European entrepreneurs. In the broader objective the Chinese were confederates, not competitors. 'Development'-minded administrators, of whom Raffles was the prototype, thus welcomed them with open arms. Unlike the Dutch in the Indies, the British never let commercial rivalry lead them into suppression of Chinese enterprise. Not that a great deal was done actively to promote it either—it was not needed.. Law, order and *laissez-faire* were sufficient.

The Chinese community was prepared to respond vigorously to such minimal facilitating conditions. Chinese in numbers began to appear in

Penang, Malacca and Singapore virtually on the heels of the founders of British colonial rule. Throughout the colonial era the Straits Settlements remained a kind of home base for Chinese enterprise on the Peninsula. At first, forays into the Malay States were an adventure which could be justified only by the prospect of exceptionally high returns. After intervention the Chinese moved into the western Federated States and Johore in larger numbers to engage in mining, the production of commercial crops and trade. By the late nineteenth century mining camps and trading posts were developing into prosperous towns such as Taiping, Ipoh and Kuala Lumpur.

The forms of social organization adopted by the Chinese in Malaya drew heavily on forms existing in China but also began to grow in new directions as soon as they were transplanted to Malayan soil (Purcell, 1965 and 1967; Newell, 1962). In the absence of any systematic application of law and administration to the Chinese community by either the British colonialists or the Malay rulers, these customs and institutions became the legal framework of the Chinese immigrant.

Chinese newcomers to Malaya (*sinkehs*) were frequently recruited in China by an agent, who collected his commission when he delivered them to a labour depot in Singapore. The *sinkeh* was then typically indentured as a labourer in a tin mine or on a plantation. Life there was harsh and exploitative, with low pay, rugged working conditions and low life expectancy—especially in areas recently cleared of jungle, which tended to be malarial. Diversions were few, centring on gambling, prostitution and opium smoking—all of which were probably used consciously by the *towkays* (businessmen) to keep the coolies permanently dependent and in debt. Moreover, the *towkays* dominated the secret societies, using them to further their control of the labour force.

Late nineteenth- and early twentieth-century Malaya abounded with stories of penniless and illiterate coolies who, through years of hard work and saving, lifted themselves to prosperity, eventually dying rich and respected. Such success stories, widely circulated in the provinces of South China, undoubtedly helped to keep the immigrants coming. Although there are a number of verified case histories of remarkable Chinese achievement in Malaya—for example, that of Yap Ah Loy, founder of Kuala Lumpur (Middlebrook, 1951; Gullick, 1956)—sober assessment of the conditions under which the coolies lived and worked suggests that exceedingly few of them would have been able to save enough to escape the labourer's life and set themselves up in business. Probably the great majority of those who did achieve wealth started with at least some advantages in life—perhaps primary schooling and a relative or two already in business. The coolie who rose to riches is surely in large part a romantic myth.

Chinese immigrants in Malaya clustered in groups based on dialect, place of origin and clan. Members of any particular group showed a strong tendency to live close together and follow the same occupations. This behaviour built on institutions brought from their homeland, strengthened by the need for mutual protection in an alien environment.

Various types of societies grew out of this general behaviour pattern: trade guilds, welfare organizations, friendly associations and the infamous secret societies (Blythe, 1960).

Chinese labourers gravitated to industries and firms which were Chinese-owned and managed. In the less common case in which the employer was European, Chinese were often hired indirectly through labour contractors. Communal living in *kongsi* houses, dormitories of co-operating labourers belonging to a single dialect group and secret society, was common, especially on outlying mines and estates.[21] Similarly, various forms of commerce and industry were dominated by particular dialect and clan groups, which usually respected each other's jurisdictional boundary lines. Individual enterprises were typically partnerships, but they could actually draw on a much broader pre-existing social group for trade connexions, working capital and emergency relief if reverses were encountered.[22]

In the broader range of social affairs, early Chinese communities organized themselves under the leadership of a '*Kapitan China*', who was responsible to the royal or colonial authorities for the good behaviour of the Chinese as a whole. In a rowdy frontier atmosphere almost totally lacking in settled family life, this was a major undertaking. But toleration was great as long as fundamental public order was not threatened. Only toward the end of the nineteenth century did the government begin to involve itself with the welfare of the Chinese population. In 1877 a Chinese Protectorate was established, charged with ameliorating exploitation and dealing with 'social problems' such as opium and prostitution. This action represents a grudging acceptance by the colonial authorities of the task of beginning to incorporate the Chinese community into a general rule of law. Less charitably, it can also be interpreted as an attempt to lessen the competitive advantage which the *towkays* gained from their ability to exploit their Chinese labourers.

The authorities were slow to accept any obligation to provide the Chinese with social services. Health conditions in the mining camps and early Peninsular towns were appalling and the provision of education was exclusively a private-sector undertaking. Chinese-medium primary schools, of widely varying quality, were provided by community subscription. Secondary education was principally missionary-sponsored and in English. These schools were confined to the heavily Chinese Straits Settlements and a few large towns. They served as important aids to the exceptionally high rate of social mobility exhibited by ethnic Chinese in urban Malaya during the twentieth century.

The Chinese were systematically excluded from some important parts of the economy. They were not allowed into senior administrative posts in the Malay States, although they became increasingly numerous in the technical and clerical services, where they gradually replaced the Indians. Very few Chinese were permitted into the army or police—nor, thanks to long China-derived tradition, did many seek such employment. Chinese holdings of agricultural land were gradually stabilized during the first decades of the twentieth century through the progressive exclusion of the

TABLE 2.4

TEN LEADING CHINESE OCCUPATIONS, 1911–1957

Occupation	*1911 (FMS only)* Rank	*1911 (FMS only)* Employment ('000)	1921 Rank	1921 Employment ('000)	*1931* Rank	*1931* Employment ('000)	*1947* Rank	*1947* Employment ('000)	*1957* Rank	*1957* Employment ('000)
Mining labourers	1	149.1	2	71.4	2	78.9	7	30.2		
Agricultural labourers	2	39.8	1	144.4						
Fruit and vegetable growers	3	16.9	5	25.7	5	50.9	2	90.8		
Labourers (unspecified)	4	12.5	3	43.2	3	56.1	10	18.0	3	51.0
Domestic servants	5	11.8	6	24.6	4	55.2	8	25.6		
Tailors and seamstresses	6	8.0								
Rickshaw owners and pullers	7	7.8								
Gardeners	8	7.2								
Carpenters	9	6.5	9	15.6	10	18.3			9	19.1
Woodcutters	10	6.1								
Proprietors and managers of businesses			4	37.0	6	37.5	5	35.7	5	35.0
Hawkers			7	18.5	9	28.6	4	40.1	6	30.1
Salesmen			8	18.0	8	31.2	6	26.2	4	48.2
Planters (unspecified)			10	14.8						
Rubber cultivators (excluding managers)					1	174.6	1	153.0	1	176.9
Miscellaneous agriculturalists					7	34.1			2	68.1
Padi planters							3	44.6		
Typists, stenographers, clerks							9	20.8	8	20.7
Miscellaneous production workers									7	25.5
Fishermen									10	18.7
All other occupations		94.3		166.8		171.6		231.8		265.7
Total employment		360.1		579.8		736.9		716.8		759.0

Chinese from the development of jungle land and increasing legal protection of cultivated land owned by Malays. Although some further expansion occurred as a result of purchases of land owned by Europeans, these measures had the effect of diverting most Chinese entrepreneurial attention to non-agricultural activities. This effect was reinforced during the early 1950s, when over 400,000 Chinese 'squatters', who had fled towns during the Depression and Japanese occupation, were gathered together into semi-urban 'NewVillages' as a means of reducing support for the Communist insurrectionists.

Exclusion from some areas of activity seemed merely to accentuate the vigour of Chinese mobility into promising new areas of profit and wage opportunity. As Table 2.4 shows, the number of ordinary labourers—'coolies', in colonial parlance—declined during the early twentieth century, while the numbers of Chinese in commercial and clerical occupations rose.

These changes reflected the gradual establishment of a permanent Chinese community in Malaya. Although the Director of Census denied it as late as 1932, one had only to look at the rapidly rising female share of the Chinese population, the growing number of fixed investments owned by Chinese and the progressive establishment of normal family life by the immigrants to appreciate that increasing numbers of Chinese had abandoned any intention of returning to China and, perhaps without realizing it, begun to accept Malaya as their new home. Thus there were 538,000 non-working Chinese dependants in latter-day Peninsular Malaysia in 1931, compared to only 275,000 a decade before.

The rise of the Chinese worker from coolie status was temporarily checked by World War II. Ill-treated by the Japanese occupying forces and deprived of some previous forms of employment, thousands of Chinese retreated to a near-subsistence existence on the jungle's fringe. This disruption is reflected in the appearance of padi planting and fishing on the list of ten leading Chinese occupations in 1947 for the first and only time. By 1957, with peace and order restored, many rapidly expanding and remunerative occupations in the professions, commerce and clerical work had become Chinese-dominated. In addition, 62 per cent of craftsmen and production process workers were Chinese. This movement of Chinese into the middle and upper echelons of a modernizing economy continued through the early years of Independence.

The Indians[23]

Two different streams of Indian immigration have been noted. The earlier but smaller stream consisted of traders, clerks, policemen and labourers who moved to Malaya to exploit opportunities created by British rule. Those who came to trade were following the example set by their countrymen in many other parts of the Empire. In Malaya, however, they failed to gain the grip on wholesale and retail trade which they achieved in places such as Burma and East Africa—surely because of the presence of the competent and competitive Chinese. In the colonial public service, the Indians (and Ceylonese) had a more formidable advantage derived from their longer familiarity with British rule and greater competence in the English language. Thus substantial parts of the public service—the Public Works Department, the railway, the clerical service and some technical services—came to be Indian-dominated.

The second, and much larger, stream of Indian migrants arrived later—mostly during the first three decades of the twentieth century—and under much less favourable conditions. This group consisted of poverty-stricken South Indian peasants, who were brought to Malaya either under indenture, through recruitment by estate *kanganies* or under a government-sponsored scheme of subsidized immigration with guaranteed repatriation. They lived under closely managed conditions on the European estates—isolated, leaderless and dependent.

The vast majority of Indian immigrants came to Malaya as common labourers and departed, retired or died years later in the same status. Such labourers—whether employed by an estate, the P.W.D. or the Malayan Railway—lived in employer-provided barracks-like 'lines' and fitted their entire lives to the demands of the enterprise which they served. The atmosphere of their combined work-place and home was stultifyingly paternalistic. All benefits flowed from the employer through his appointed intermediary, the Indian *kangany* or *mandore*, to whom abject subservience was due. Basic needs for the continuation of life within this rigid framework were generally adequately provided: food through wage payment in kind or through the estate shop, shelter in the 'lines', rudimentary education and health services through the primary schools and clinics which the government provided or required the employer to provide (in the case of the larger estates).

Daily life in the 'lines' was dominated by the unending work routine, which frequently included the women and older children as well as the men. Not surprisingly, morale and ambition were generally low. 'Social problems', such as production of illicit and occasionally lethal spirits, were rife. Opportunities for escape, other than return to India, were slim. Education was in Tamil or another Indian language and ended with four to six years of primary school. Their customs and language cut the estate population off from other Malayan communities, among whom they were held in low regard. Employment opportunities outside the estate were essentially limited to the Railway, the P.W.D. and municipal sanitation departments. It is therefore not surprising (see Table 2.5) that Indians in Malaya exhibited a low rate of socio-economic mobility—perhaps even lower than that of the Malays. The paucity of opportunities to advance in the Malayan context is reflected in the fact that the population of working-age Indians reached its peak at the threshold of the Depression and declined thereafter. The 1931 Census, which was taken at a time when repatriation had already begun, showed 380,000 Indians employed in what is now Peninsular Malaysia. The figure for 1957, the year of Merdeka, was only 307,000.

The experience of the Indians in Malaya thus stands in contrast to that of both the Chinese and the Malays. Like the Chinese they were immigrants, but like the Malays they—at least the main mass of them—

TABLE 2.5

TEN LEADING INDIAN OCCUPATIONS, 1911–1957

Occupation	1911 (FMS only) Rank	1911 (FMS only) Employment ('000)	1921 Rank	1921 Employment ('000)	1931 Rank	1931 Employment ('000)	1947 Rank	1947 Employment ('000)	1957 Rank	1957 Employment ('000)
Agricultural labourers	1	80.4	1	213.5						
Labourers (unspecified)	2	11.1	2	16.1	2	51.1	2	26.0	2	32.5
Cart owners and drivers	3	7.0	6	6.6						
Government labourers	4	4.9	3	11.6						
Domestic servants	5	4.6	4	11.2	3	14.5	4	7.7		
Railway labourers	6	4.3	7	6.2	9	5.2				
Mining labourers	7	3.1								
Watchmen	8	2.3								
Overseers	9	2.3	8	4.7					9	6.7
Salesmen	10	1.6			7	7.0	8	6.7	3	13.7
Proprietors and managers of businesses			5	7.9	6	8.7	6	7.3	6	8.3
Typists, stenographers, clerks			9	3.6	10	5.1	10	5.7	7-8	7.1
Hawkers			10	3.2	8	6.0	7	7.2	7-8	7.1
Rubber cultivators (excluding managers)					1	189.0	1	141.5	1	128.6
Miscellaneous agriculturalists					4	12.9			5	8.9
Coconut cultivators (excluding managers)					5	9.5	3	8.2		
Estate rubber factory workers							5	7.5		
Oil palm cultivators (excluding managers)							9	5.9		
Miscellaneous production workers									4	10.9
Gardeners									10	6.1
All other occupations		23.0		55.0		71.5		76.4		77.2
Total employment		143.5		339.6		380.6		300.3		307.2

showed a low rate of socio-economic mobility and little tendency to be entrepreneurial. Without really being able to explain why, the writers agree that the South Indian was the ideal estate labourer in part because his propensity to move on to other things was so low.[24]

COMMENT: THE INFLUENCE OF HISTORY

Although the importance of historical influences relative to other causes of the trends observed in post-Independence Malaya and Malaysia remains to be explored, it is obvious that Merdeka found the Malays, Chinese and Indians in widely differing positions. Economically the Chinese were in by far the strongest position, not only because they had amassed relatively large amounts of wealth, education, and experience but also because of their demonstrated capacity to adapt to changing circumstances and seize newly-offered opportunities. In the political arena however, the Malays had already seized the initiative, based on their historical advantage of legitimacy and their earlier development of nationalism focused on Malaya. Through their preoccupation with the fast-moving affairs in their homelands, the Chinese and Indians had bungled whatever chance they had for a major political say in post-war Malaya. When they finally decided to opt for Malaya it was too late to obtain anything more than a junior-partner role. Thus the stage was set for the drama of independent Malaya and Malaysia.

1. There are several good, brief, general histories of Malaysia, including N. J. Ryan (1967), K. G. Tregonning (1963), J. M. Gullick (1969) and Joseph Kennedy (1970). For Malaysian history in its South-East Asian context, see John F. Cady (1964), D. G. E. Hall (1968) or, for a briefer treatment, Brian Harrison (1963). There is no comprehensive scholarly history of the country; specialized works dealing with particular periods and problems will be cited at appropriate places in the text. Finally, John Bastin and Robin W. Winks (1966) is a compilation of documents from all periods which breathe life into episodes in Malaysian history.

2. The traders were mostly Indians and Arabs. The date at which a permanent Chinese community was established is uncertain but surely prior to 1511. See Kernial Singh Sandhu (1961, p. 6).

3. '...only a small proportion of immigrants from Sumatra regard themselves, or are regarded by the native Malay, as in any way alien...in the vast majority of cases the children of immigrant peoples [from Sumatra] become merged at once in the Malay population, and regard British Malaya as their own country. In the case of the Javanese, on the other hand, the process of absorption or subjective "naturalization" is much slower, and commonly takes several generations, the determining factor frequently being intermarriage.' (C. A. Vlieland, 1932, p. 71.)

4. The very early history of the mining industry and the identity of the early miners are obscure. The Malays and Thais played a role but it is clear that the Chinese were early participants, both in the Peninsula and on the Island of Bangka, where tin had been discovered in 1711 (Wong Lin Ken, 1965, pp. 17 ff.; see also Yip Yat Hoong, 1969).

5. British intervention has been studied intensively by C. D. Cowan (1961) and C. Northcote Parkinson (1964). For the period immediately following intervention, see E. Sadka (1968) and Philip Loh Fook Seng (1969).

6. Important works dealing with the late nineteenth and early twentieth centuries which have not been mentioned previously are Chai Hon-Chan (1964) and Eunice Thio (1969).

7. The history of the Malayan rubber industry has been an oddly neglected area of scholarship. John Drabble (1973) deals with the early period, as do Jackson (1968) and, in a regional context, Voon (1976); Barlow (1978) is a recent comprehensive treatment.

8. Immigration quotas were established for the first time. At first these applied only to males, as Chinese female immigration was actively encouraged so as to improve the balance between the sexes in the Chinese community. Large numbers of Chinese females did in fact come in before the quota system was extended to them during the recession of 1938. Indians, as British subjects, were not affected by the restrictions, although they were repatriated in large numbers (Lim, 1967, pp. 187–9).

9. Originally, the Alliance brought together UMNO and the Malayan Chinese Association (MCA), which had been formed in 1949 as an anti-Communist focus of Chinese loyalties and a welfare body to assist squatters resettled in the Emergency. An Indian component, the Malayan Indian Congress (MIC), was added in 1954. Like national political parties in the United States, the Alliance is active at election time and quiescent during other periods. Continuing political activity is undertaken by its constituent parties, which are ethnically exclusive. There is no authoritative history of the Alliance Party, but for a brief treatment see R. S. Milne (1967, pp. 87–113).

10. Miscegenation has been rare, with the small European community perhaps the leading practitioners. The Eurasian community numbered 14,000 in 1970 (Chander, 1972, p. 85). As noted earlier, Malay status can be acquired and fairly commonly is: most frequently when Chinese girl babies are adopted by Malay families, when non-Malays marry Malays (which generally involves conversion to Islam and adoption of Malay customs) and when Chinese, aborigines or others convert and adopt Malay customs, as they have done in small numbers. There are also cases of redefinition of one's own status (see the entry 'Ceylonese' in the Glossary). However, all these forms of inter-group movement together can hardly affect more than 1 per cent of the population.

11. While there is a tendency for the groups to live and work in closer proximity to each other, independence has meant a sharpened definition of, and mobilization behind, divisive group interests. It has also meant some enlarging of ethnic groups, as 'Arabs' and 'Other Malaysians', for example, have increasingly identified themselves as Malays.

12. The statement refers only to those who categorize themselves as 'Indians', as opposed to 'Pakistanis' and 'Ceylonese', whom the 1970 Census categorizes broadly as 'Indians' (formerly, they were usually included in 'Others') (Chander, 1972, p. 84).

13. Vlieland (1932, pp. 105–6) somewhat defensively attributes the phenomenon entirely to the latter two factors.

14. Among the best sources, and those upon which this summary is based, are Richard Winstedt (1961) and Gullick (1965). In addition, Maurice Freedman (1960) provides an incisive summary of much of the material presented in this section and Karl Von Vorys (1975, pp. 21–52) goes over much the same ground.

15. 'Early records show that indigenous Malays could be obtained for wage labour and occasionally did offer themselves for employment when the wage was high enough. But Chinese employers preferred to deal with their own kind, and neither Chinese nor European employers found the Malays sufficient in number, as steady in their habits or cheap enough for their needs. The Malay, being native to the country, invariably had some tie with land where he could obtain a living usually in a more congenial manner than by working on the mines and estates. Employers necessarily turned to immigrant labor.' (Parmer, 1960, p. 16.)

16. Cheng Siok Hwa (1969). Although the data are suspect (cf. Lim, 1967, p. 149) the broad upward trends in acreage, yield and output during the 1920s and 1930s are unmistakable.

17. This often-quoted statement was made by George Maxwell, a colonial administrator, in 1927. See Chapter 9, below.

18. The standard, unrivalled studies of the Chinese in Malaya are those of Victor Purcell (1965, pp. 223–356; 1967).

19. Purcell, the student and frequent advocate of the Chinese, agreed: 'If the Chinese immigrants to Malaya had continued to be almost exclusively male, if return to China had continued to be as infrequent as it was in Portuguese and Dutch times (as we infer it to have been) and had the flood gates of Chinese immigration not been opened in the nineteenth century, there would be no Sino-Malay problem in Malaya today. The Babas adapted themselves prefectly to their surroundings, but they retained their Chinese dress, religion and customs with singular pertinacity. But they had in some essential respects and

will continue to have the "Malayan outlook" '(Purcell, 1947, p. 125).

20. This same argument is made with respect to Chinese and Japanese immigrants (as contrasted to Blacks) in the United States by Ivan H. Light (1972).

21. The history of Chinese labour in Malaya is surveyed by Purcell (1967, pp. 194–208) and W. L. Blythe (1947).

22. A detailed history of Chinese enterprise in Malaya has yet to be written. The best short treatment is Taku Suyama (1962).

23. Several good accounts, of varying length, of the Indian experience in Malaya are available. The most comprehensive is Kernial Singh Sandhu (1969). A briefer volume is Sinnappah Arasaratnam (1970). Finally, Sandhu (1962) provides a compact treatment.

24. 'Altogether, the South Indian was perhaps the most satisfactory type of laborer, for in addition to being a British subject, accustomed to British rule, he was a good worker, not too ambitious and easily manageable. He had none of the self-reliance nor the capacity of the Chinese, but he was the most amenable to the comparatively lowly paid and rather regimented life of estates and government projects. He was well-behaved, docile and had neither the education nor the enterprise to rise, as the Chinese often did, above the level of manual labor...' Sandhu (1962, p. 47). One interpretation is that the Indian estate labourer can be seen as the European businessman's answer to the coolie labour force dominated by this Chinese competitor.

3 History: Since Merdeka

> The present multi-racial character of the country is the direct result of British economic policy before the war which encouraged mass non-Malay immigration . . . Malaya's vast economic potential and the liberal, tolerant attitude of the Malays, exploited by the colonial government, caused an influx of Chinese and Indian immigrants, and mass migration continued until the thirties.
>
> A striking feature of the Malayan society at the time (which continues today, slightly abated) was the voluntary cultural segregation—while the Malays lived in a cultural milieu that institutionally continued in a local context, there was no effort made by the colonial authorities to orientate the increasing number of immigrant races toward local institutions. For the most part, the immigrant races were administered independently and led an independent existence. This partly explains some current attitudes among certain sections of the non-Malay communities, and some difficulties experienced today in nation-building.
>
> National Operations Council, 1969, p.1

THE 'BARGAIN OF 1957'

THE narrative of Malaysian political and economic history in 'General Background' of the preceding chapter ended with the 1956 Federation of Malaya independence negotiations. Since these negotiations had great influence on subsequent developments, they are worth examining in some detail.

There were actually two sets of negotiations in 1956. Formal talks took place in London between Her Majesty's Government and a Malayan delegation consisting of Alliance Party officials and representatives of the Sultans. These discussions, assisted by the report of a learned Constitutional Commission, formally determined the structure of the new state. Most of what was agreed to in the formal negotiations, however, had previously been worked out in internal discussions within the Malayan delegation.

The latter informal but critical discussions involved the élites of each ethnic group, with the UMNO Malays—who were surely more sensitized to the concerns of the broader majority of their ethnic group than the MCA and MIC representatives—dominating.

The final agreement established a Constitutional Monarchy, with a Head of State (*Yang Dipertuan Agung*) chosen for a five-year term from among the reigning Sultans of the nine Malay States. A bicameral Parliament replaced the Legislative Council. Many other features of the new Constitution were taken directly from the 1948 Federation of Malaya Agreement.[1] The most controversial constitutional issues, however, concerned citizenship, the national language and the rights of the various communities. These were negotiated within the Malayan delegation—in particular, between UMNO and the MCA.

By 1956 there was no longer any question that the majority of Chinese and Indians would remain in Malaya. On the other hand, the special position of the Malays, traditionally recognized by the British, had been reaffirmed by the Federation of Malaya Agreement and subsequent British policy. Potentials for ethnic conflict were thus increased, and the major constitution-writing problem was to reach a mutually acceptable balance between the interests of the two groups.[2] The balance struck, which came to be known as the 'Bargain of 1957', constitutes the most important part of the constitutional negotiations from the point of view of this study.

By 1956 the non-Malays—particularly the middle-class, English-speaking group whose interests were best represented by the MCA and MIC—wanted citizenship, a secular state, continued official use of English in addition to the Malay language, a meritocracy and a *laissez-faire* economy. The demands of the Malays—also voiced by upper-class representatives—concentrated on recognition of their special position as the indigenous people of the country and measures to accelerate their socio-economic progress in competition with the more aggressive immigrants. The Malays feared being swamped by new non-Malay citizens and losing their political hegemony, which they saw as a counter-balance to the economic strength of the Chinese.

The essence of the compromise was that the Malays made substantial concessions with respect to citizenship, while the non-Malays recognized the special position of the Malays without limit of time.

The 1957 Constitution accorded citizenship by *jus soli* to every person born in the Federation after Merdeka Day (31 August 1957). Those born in the Federation before Merdeka Day could become citizens by registration if they satisfied the government that they (a) had resided in the Federation during five of the preceding seven years; (b) intended to do so permanently; (c) were of good character; and (d) had elementary knowledge of the Malay (or in 1957–67, English) language. More than a million non-Malays became citizens by registration in the two years following Merdeka Day. A much smaller number of persons born abroad acquired citizenship by naturalization, the third method provided under the Constitution.[3]

In return for their liberality on the citizenship issue the Malays received certain tangible and intangible benefits. The symbols and institutions of the new state were Malay (where they were not British). Islam was made the state religion, although tolerance of all religions was guaranteed. Malay was designated as the national language, but the use of English as a second official language was guaranteed for a period of ten years. (The private use of other languages was specifically guaranteed, but they were accorded no official status.) Finally, Article 153 of the new Constitution stated that 'it shall be the responsibility of the Yang diPertuan Agung to safeguard the special position of the Malays and the legitimate interests of the other communities. . . .' Under this rubric, certain measures which had been enacted in the past to benefit the Malay community were formally entrenched in the constitution. These included employment quotas in the public services, scholarships, business permits and licences and (in Article 89) the reservation of certain land for exclusive use by the Malays. The 'legitimate interests of the other communities' were recognized in Clause 8 of Article 153, which states that the reservation of licences and permits for Malays cannot be used to deprive 'any person of any right, privilege, permit or licence accrued to or enjoyed or held by him' or to exclude anyone from a trade or business for which no licence was previously required.

FROM MERDEKA TO MAY 1969

The period since 1957 has seen accelerating change: the transition to independence and political maturity, economic growth at a pace unknown since the 1920s (and including for the first time industrialization on a significant scale), continued high-speed population growth. Related to all these developments, and to the dramatic expansion of the educational system, have been important (if unmeasurable) changes in the values, attitudes, ambitions and expectations of Malaysians of all ethnic groups.

After Merdeka, the first need of the new government was to establish its *bona fides* with the electorate. It soon became clear that the Alliance government's appeal to the voters would be based largely on its dedication to development. The fashion for economic planning had reached Malaya in the early post-war period. There was a rudimentary 'plan' (actually a simple list of investment projects) for 1950–5 (High Commissioner's Office, 1950) but the major impetus to development planning was given by a large World Bank mission which visited the country in 1954. This mission published a thick report (IBRD, 1955), made a number of important institutional recommendations which were subsequently acted upon and prepared an investment programme which became the Federation's first real development plan.[4] A Planning Secretariat (which became the Economic Planning Unit in 1961) was established in the Prime Minister's Department and a separate development budget was instituted. These new institutions paved the way for an expanded development effort, in which the government was to play a more active role than it had before.

Development was an attractive political platform for the new Alliance government. On the one hand, it made it possible to continue, with very little change at first, the colonial policies of liberal capitalism and monetary and fiscal conservatism.[5] This was what powerful foreign and Chinese business interests wanted and what the World Bank recommended.

On the other hand, the Alliance was impelled by political self-interest to launch a broad programme of rural development, through which it hoped to cement its support among the rural Malays who provided the main numerical backing for UMNO and thus for the Alliance. Rural development had the enormous advantage that it could benefit the Malay mass without directly challenging urban Chinese interests. The only costs to be borne by the Chinese (and by foreign interests) were the higher taxes and protection-inflated rice prices used to support the expanded programme of public expenditure.

The new government's rural development campaign built upon programmes which had been created by the old. RIDA—the Rural and Industrial Development Authority—had been established in 1950 (Dato Onn was its first Chairman), with the purpose of stimulating the economy of the rural Malays. It made loans for productive projects and carried out a variety of self-help schemes.[6] The Federal Land Development Authority (the FLDA, later called FELDA) was founded in 1956, originally as a co-ordinator and financier of land development schemes carried out by state governments and subsequently as the principal direct implementing agency for federal land development. To these was added, in 1959, a Ministry of Rural Development headed by the then Deputy Prime Minister, Tun Abdul Razak.

The new government's programmes received an early test in the general elections of 1959. The Alliance had won easily in the pre-Independence election of 1955, but by 1959 the franchise had been broadened considerably; Malays were now only 57 per cent of the electorate, versus 84 per cent in 1955. Nevertheless, the Alliance won 74 seats out of 104, despite a fall in its share of the popular vote from 79.6 per cent to 51.8 per cent.[7] It was repudiated in the poor, heavily Malay states of Kelantan and Trengganu, where it lost the State Assemblies and won only 2 of 16 Parliamentary seats. On the other hand, it did relatively well in the mainly non-Malay urban areas, where the MCA and MIC placed more members in Parliament than their non-Malay oriented opponents. Overall, the 1959 election was a qualified success for Alliance politics.

The election won, the next task was to consolidate the gains by building a stronger economy and more unified population under Alliance rule. This was the main thrust of the period up to the start of Indonesian Confrontation in 1963. The notable features of this period in the area of social and economic policy were the continued stress on rural development, the rapid expansion of the educational system and the heavy emphasis on public infrastructural investments. These added up to a development effort which attracted considerable international attention and favourable comment.[8]

In rural development there were the achievements of RIDA and of the FLDA, which had opened 22 land development schemes in nine states by 1960. Malay rice cultivators benefited from an expansion of irrigated rice land from 270,000 acres to 390,000 in 1955–60. Other rural programmes—agricultural extension, co-operatives, rural road construction, new water supplies and the extension of social services to rural areas—also expanded rapidly during the late 1950s and early 1960s.

School enrolments multiplied and access to education was liberalized. In 1956 there had been 767,000 students in primary schools and 89,000 in secondary schools; the corresponding figures for 1965 were 1,252,000 and 345,000 respectively. Primary enrolments as a percentage of primary-school age population rose, exceeding 90 per cent by the mid-1960s. Even more spectacular developments took place in secondary education, which had been small and mainly in English. The rapid growth of Chinese-language secondary schools during the 1950s was halted by the withdrawal of official assistance in 1961; this led to even faster growth of English-medium education. During the early 1960s Malay-medium secondary education began to be built up and in 1964 the secondary school entrance examination was abolished, leading to still more rapid enrolment growth in the later years of the decade.

In 1961 a new plan, the Second Five-year Plan, was published. The mood in which it was prepared was one of growing development ambitions buttressed by an improved financial position (rubber and tin prices had turned up again in 1959). The new plan called for public sector development expenditure of $2,150 million, twice what had been achieved in 1956–60. This no doubt seemed like an ambitious target at the time, but in actuality the achievement was well above the target, as Table 3.1 shows.

Development in Malaya during this period emphasized popular participation in decision-making and strong implementation. Project proposals were solicited at the grassroots level and then brought together by the Ministry of Rural Development in a set of 'Red Books'. After decisions had been made on which projects to carry out, the implications for local areas were spelled out in the same Red Books, which then served as a standard against which implementation could be judged. There was a progress reporting system and the Deputy Prime Minister conducted a series of inspection trips, progress reviews and meetings to resolve inter-agency co-ordination problems. The result was that a large increase in activity was coaxed out of a limited bureaucracy. Biases were introduced in the process—in favour of physical construction over more complex feats of social engineering and the policies and staffing needed to operate the newly-built institutions effectively—but the government did achieve action and make a name for itself in the process.[9]

It was largely on the basis of the successes enjoyed by the Federation of Malaya Government in its first five years of Independence that the Malaysia scheme was launched.[10] This plan sought to unite the disparate remaining areas of British responsibility—Singapore, Sarawak, North Borneo and Brunei—into a broader Malaysian federation. After an extended negotiating process, toward the end of which Brunei withdrew from the plan, Malaysia was finally inaugurated on 16 September 1963. The ceremony was delayed by two weeks in a last-minute attempt to placate President Sukarno of Indonesia, whose opposition to the new federation had been growing stronger as the reality of it neared. The Republic of the Philippines joined Indonesia in non-recognition of

TABLE 3.1
PUBLIC SECTOR DEVELOPMENT EXPENDITURE
IN PENINSULAR MALAYSIA
UNDER FOUR DEVELOPMENT PLANS

Expenditure category	*1956–60* $m.	*1956–60* % of total	*1961–5* $m.	*1961–5* % of total	*1966–70* $m.	*1966–70* % of total	*1971–5* $m.	*1971–5* % of total
Agriculture	227	23	468	18	911	25	1,747	22
Rubber replanting	153	15	131	5	116	3	116	1
Drainage and irrigation	38	4	109	4	329	9	240	3
Land development	17	2	130	5	310	9	992	12
Other	19	2	99	4	157	4	398	5
Transportation	230	23	589	22	357	10	1,219	15
Road	119	12	417	16	186	5	689	9
Rail	71	7	51	2	47	1	95	1
Port	37	4	61	2	83	2	291	4
Aviation	3	*	60	2	41	1	144	2
Communication	52	5	113	4	158	4	464	6
Telecommunication	47	5	85	3	119	3	393	5
Broadcasting	3	*	23	1	35	1	56	1
Post	2	*	5	*	4	*	15	*
Utilities	239	24	535	20	654	18	790	10
Electricity	142	14	353	13	518	14	516	6
Water supply	81	8	175	7	129	4	254	3
Sewerage	16	2	8	*	7	*	20	*
Commerce & industry	12	1	59	2	137	4	1,543	19
Social services	139	14	414	16	638	18	1,113	14
Education and training	61	6	237	9	287	8	576	7
Health and family planning	13	1	102	4	114	3	144	2
Housing	65	6	69	3	181	5	186	2
Social welfare and other[1]	—	—	6	*	56	2	207	3
General administration[1]	65	6	167	6	109	3	256	3
Sub-total: Non-security	964	96	2,344	88	2,965	82	7,132	88
Defence	35	3	245	9	532	15	765	9
Internal security	8	1	63	2	113	3	179	2
Total	1,007	100	2,652	100	3,610	100	8,076	100

Sources: *First Malaysia Plan 1966–1970* (1965, pp. 28–9); *Second Malaysia Plan 1971–1975* (1971, pp. 68–71); *Third Malaysia Plan 1976–1980* (1976, pp. 240–1).

*Indicates less than 0.5 per cent.

[1]There is some non-comparability among plans in these lines, certain items having been shifted from general administration as time went by.

Malaysia, although not in the armed hostilities which Sukarno launched as part of his 'Crush Malaysia' campaign.

The most significant consequences of the 'Confrontation' between Indonesia and Malaysia were political rather than military or economic. Except for unsuccessful parachute drops and amphibious landings in Johore in 1964 (which failed to stimulate the hoped-for uprisings of Chinese and Malays of Indonesian origin), Indonesian military action was limited to Sarawak and Sabah (as North Borneo was renamed upon joining Malaysia). Economic warfare took the form of a trade embargo, which hurt Singapore and Penang in its early stages but weakened through time as a result of Indonesia's inability to enforce the embargo on its own and third-country traders. In the States of Malaya,* as the eleven states of the former Federation were now called, the only economic effects were some discouragement of private investment and the diversion of public-sector funds and energies from development to security.[11]

According to one theory, Sukarno chose to confront Malaysia largely to divert the suffering Indonesian population from its domestic miseries. In Malaysia, too, the troubles with Indonesia turned attention away from domestic differences and lent urgency to appeals for national unity. Required by the old Federation of Malaya Constitution to hold elections in the States of Malaya in 1964, the Alliance Party not unnaturally chose loyalty to Malaysia in her hour of peril as its rallying cry (Vasil, 1965; Ratnam and Milne, 1967). The Alliance also stressed its development achievements and plans, especially in the rural areas, while the opposition parties sought to embarrass it by raising difficult matters such as language and education policy. But 'the main feature of the election was perhaps the preeminence of a single issue . . . Indonesian "confrontation" of Malaysia and the threat which it posed to the country's security' (Ratnam and Milne, 1967, p. 110).

The result of the 1964 election was a smashing Alliance victory, not up to the 1955 standard but far exceeding the comparatively slender win of 1959. The Alliance captured 89 Parliamentary seats out of 104, a gain of 15 over its 1959 total. Its share of the popular vote was 58.5 per cent, well above the 51.8 per cent achieved in 1959 despite the fact that there were 20 more opposition candidates in the field than there had been in the previous election. It did much better in urban and quasi-urban constituencies and polled nearly as many non-Malay votes as all the opposition parties combined while holding more than two-thirds of the Malay vote (ibid., pp. 365, 375). The only significant disappointment suffered by the Alliance in the 1964 election was its failure to take control of the Kelantan state government away from the PMIP.[12]

One significant feature of the 1964 election was an attempt by Lee Kuan Yew's People's Action Party (PAP) to establish a foothold in Peninsular politics, in effect challenging the MCA for Chinese loyalty. The theme of the PAP's campaign, 'A Malaysian Malaysia', was an implicit attack on Malay special rights. Although only one out of nine PAP candidates was elected, immense resentment of Lee and the PAP was created. This led directly to Singapore's sudden and unceremonious ejection from Malaysia on 9 August 1965.

A few weeks later came the unsuccessful *coup d'état* in Indonesia. With Sukarno and the Communists weakened there, the threat of a strong and possibly Chinese-dominated Malaysia removed by Singapore's expulsion and the Indonesian population war-weary and poorer than ever, Confrontation rapidly came to an end. Malaysia and Indonesia were both permitted to look inward once more.

The Malaysian economy was growing rapidly at this point, with high rubber prices and private and public investment both at record levels. In 1965, a new five-year plan, called the *First Malaysia Plan* (*FMP*), was published. The new plan was a mixture of forward movement and caution. Building on the unprecedented increases in public investment which had occurred during the previous plan period, the FMP called for further increases but at a declining rate. Planned development expenditure in Malaya was put at $3,713 million, compared to the $2,651 million realized in 1961–5.[13] An attempt was made to change the pattern of investment, replacing the Malayan Second Five-Year Plan's heavy emphasis on infrastructure, especially road construction, with larger allocations for directly productive facilities. Since the government continued to leave mining, industry and commerce almost entirely to the private sector—putting in practically no public money and exerting only loose regulatory functions—this meant larger outlays for agriculture: an allocation of $900 million (versus actual expenditure in 1961–5 of $468 million), of which the largest shares were for land development ($335 million) and drainage and irrigation ($319 million). Other areas of major expansion were education (which was growing rapidly at the secondary and higher levels) and defence.

The caution in the FMP arose from fears of renewed balance of payments difficulties (the relatively high export prices of 1965 were not expected to last) and from the politically sensitive issue of how large the public sector should be. Federal revenue had grown from 14 per cent of GNP in 1958 to 19 per cent in 1965 (Edwards, 1970, pp. 48–9), and the major political forces represented in the Alliance could not agree on what an appropriate levelling-off point would be. Although there was tacit acceptance of the basic principle that Chinese (and foreign) private enterprise should be taxed to finance public expenditure largely for the benefit of the rural Malays,[14] determining the amount to be thus transferred was difficult.[15] The compromise embodied in the FMP was a relatively large development expenditure target, but with actual expenditure of the money largely conditional on much greater use of foreign loan and grant financing than had been made in the past.[16] Since as it happened the FMP was promulgated at a time when international development assistance had lost most of its earlier dynamism,[17] the condition was strongly operative over most of the plan period and was the main reason why development expenditure virtually stagnated until 1969.[18]

Aside from its qualified endorsement of the principle of continued growth of a public sector with important though limited powers to promote Malay economic progress, the FMP took little notice of what E. K. Fisk (1962) has delicately termed 'the special development problems of a plural society'. The broad outlines of the policy framework remained *laissez-faire*, although 'special programmes' to benefit the Malays continued to expand under the increasing political pressure brought to bear through the structure of UMNO.[19] MARA (Majlis

Amanah Raayat; Council of Trust for the Indigenous People), as RIDA had been renamed in 1965, expanded its programmes, notably by establishing an Institute of Technology in 1967. A Malay bank (Bank Bumiputra) was launched in an attempt to break the Chinese–foreign monopoly of the banking industry. A Federal Agricultural Marketing Authority (FAMA) was set up as a means of attacking the exploitation by middlemen which allegedly reduced the incomes and incentives of Malay farmers. The growth of these programmes, though significant (see Chapters 6–9 below), did not at this stage challenge the pattern of ownership and control which gave foreigners and ethnic Chinese practically total domination of large-scale commercial agriculture and of all forms of non-agricultural enterprise (Tan, 1977). Nor, in general, did it dispute the reality that the vast majority of Malays were still agriculturalists while urban employment, except for public administration and a few low-skill jobs, was overwhelmingly non-Malay.[20]

A new economic problem which was brought to the public's attention around this time was unemployment. The first reliable information on the subject had been collected through a sample survey conducted in 1962 (Department of Statistics, 1963) which found about 6 per cent of the labour force to be unemployed and also measured substantial underemployment, especially in agriculture. Follow-up surveys conducted in 1965 and 1967–8 showed unemployment to be increasing. By 1967–8, 194,000 workers—6.8 per cent of the Peninsular Malaysian labour force—appear to have been unemployed in the standard sense and another 61,000 'passively unemployed', i.e. without a job and willing to take one but not, for some reason, actively seeking work.[21] Although definitional differences obscured comparison of rural underemployment between the 1962 and 1967–8 surveys, it seemed likely that it had also risen. As might be expected from the rapid growth of the labour force (which reached 3 per cent per annum sometime in the late 1960s) and the spread of post-primary education, open unemployment was heavy among (in fact was mainly a phenomenon of) young, relatively well educated workers. Because of their higher levels of urbanization, Chinese and Indians tended to be somewhat harder hit by unemployment than Malays.[22] Involuntary underemployment was undoubtedly greater among the Malays.

Yet another downturn in rubber prices, together with the cautious fiscal policy of the first three years of the FMP, led to low GNP growth rates, and probably further increases in unemployment, in 1966–8. This in turn may have contributed to the upheaval of May 1969, but the proximate cause was the antagonisms stirred up during the 1969 election campaign.

Since no opinion polls were taken there is no way to gauge the state of ethnic attitudes at the start of the campaign. It seems probable, however, that the spread of education and improvement of communication during four distraction-free post-Confrontation years had been gradually eroding Malay acceptance of their economic inferiority. Many Malays believed that their relative income was worsening, that development was benefiting only the non-Malays. Their communal self-confidence seems to have been growing and their willingness to accept the *status quo* declining *pari passu*.[23] The non-Malays, meanwhile, continued to be wary of efforts to use the powers of government to advance Malay primacy and welfare. Particularly sensitive were language issues, which seemed to have been settled in the compromise National Language Act of 1967 but refused to die, especially the question of language policy in education (Ratnam, 1965, pp. 126–41; Roff, 1967; Snider, 1970). The stage was thus amply set for a campaign which would fan these fears and discontents.

By 1969 the maximum five-year interval between elections once again had passed. Parliamentary and state elections were scheduled to take place (for the first time, throughout Malaysia) in May. Without much basis for thinking so, most observers expected that the Alliance would suffer some net losses but, in general, have little difficulty carrying the day against the divided opposition which it had to face.[24] The Alliance itself set its target as a two-thirds majority in the federal Parliament plus recapture of the Kelantan state government from the PMIP. It appealed for support to voters of all races on its record of economic progress, seeking to convince the Malays that they were best off under the Alliance (the people of Kelantan were lured with promises of federal projects if they voted the Alliance into power) and simultaneously keep at least a substantial minority of the non-Malays in the Alliance fold. The opposition parties—except for the recently formed and legitimately non-communal Gerakan Raayat Malaysia (GRM)—were under no compulsion to make such a broad appeal and hammered away lustily at the grievances which their respective constituencies had accumulated during thirteen years of Alliance rule.

As it turned out, the cumulative effect of these grievances had been under-estimated by everyone, including opposition party leaders. When the vote was counted in Peninsular Malaysia it was found that the Alliance had suffered a crippling setback. It lost 22 seats in the Federal Parliament,[25] experienced sharply reduced margins everywhere and fell to the status of a minority party with only 49.1 per cent of the popular vote.[26] By far the heaviest blows were absorbed by the MCA, which lost 14 of its 27 seats, including all the constituencies which it held in major urban areas. UMNO had a net loss of 7 seats while the MIC retained two of its three seats by tiny margins. Three Ministers were defeated and the Prime Minister himself held his Kedah constituency by a sharply reduced majority.

The outcome of the Parliamentary and state elections (see below) gave the impression that the non-Malays had deserted the Alliance. This impression was severely distorted, however, by the way in which the Parliamentary districts are designed to over-represent the Malays and by the effectiveness with which the opposition parties combined to defeat MCA candidates. In fact, if one looks at changes in the popular vote since 1959, Malays had deserted the Alliance to an even greater extent than non-Malays. The Alliance received approximately 54 per cent of the Malay vote and 43 per cent of the non-Malay vote in 1969.[27] Comparable estimates for 1964 are 67 per cent of the Malay vote and 48 per cent of the non-Malay vote (Ratnam and Milne, 1967, pp. 374–6). Going back to 1959, it seems that the share of the Malay vote was even higher than in 1964 while the share of the non-Malay vote was about the same (ibid., pp. 376–7). This decline in previously very strong Malay support for UMNO is attributable partly to the unprecedented number of candidates whom the PMIP put in the field in 1969 and partly to increasing support for the PMIP in head-on races with UMNO.

If the Parliamentary results were a shock, Alliance setbacks in the Peninsular Malaysian state assembly elections were even more stunning. The Alliance again failed to take Kelantan from the PMIP, although it did succeed in preventing the PMIP from returning to power in Trengganu. That it lost Penang, the only state with a majority of non-Malays, to a coalition headed by the Gerakan was not too surprising. The worst damage was done in Perak, where the Alliance won only 19 out of 40 seats (although the opposition parties subsequently proved incapable of forming a coalition), and in Selangor, where the result was a 14–14 deadlock. These were the two most populous and prosperous states in Peninsular Malaysia and the heart of the old FMS. Selangor included Kuala Lumpur, the seat of the federal government and a city with which many Malays felt a strong sense of identification despite the fact that its population was over 50 per cent Chinese (Provencher, 1971, p. 14). If non-Malay opposition parties succeeded in controlling the governments of these two states, would this not constitute the long-feared frontal attack on Malay political power?

As far as one can tell, it was the ambiguous outcome of these two state elections which led to the severe racial violence which broke out in Kuala Lumpur on the evening of 13 May, three days after the election.[28] The riots began, by the government's own admission (National Operations Council, 1969, pp. 42–57), when a Malay rally gathered at the residence of Selangor's *Mentri Besar* (Chief Minister) turned violent and began to attack Chinese passers-by. Several days of chaos followed, as continuing disorder in the heart of the federal capital hampered the government's usually effective machinery for dealing with civil disturbances. Unwise statements and actions by government figures fanned rumour and fears on the part of the non-Malays that UMNO was moving to establish a Malay dictatorship.[29] There was little violence in other parts of the country. In all, 196 people died, according to the official report—rumours put the number of deaths much higher—and many shops and homes were destroyed. The country's previously good record of avoiding racial violence[30] was badly scarred. Worst of all, its carefully constructed and hitherto efficient political machinery for coping with communal differences had all but been destroyed by the election and its aftermath.

At the crux of the matter was the apparent withdrawal of Chinese support for the MCA and the consequent conclusion by many Malays that the Chinese were in effect repudiating the 'Bargain of 1957' and directly challenging the Malays for political control.[31] Since Malay economic backwardness had not been overcome while awareness of the disparities and determination to do something about them had increased, such a challenge was frightening to the Malays. A 13 May announcement by a depressed Tan Siew Sin that the MCA would withdraw from the Cabinet, although it would continue to support the Alliance in Parliament, had seemed to confirm the impression that the Alliance formula of inter-ethnic politics was bankrupt.

FROM MAY 13 TO THE NEW ECONOMIC POLICY

To assist in restoring order, a State of Emergency had been declared by the Yang Dipertuan Agung on 14 May 1969. The power to make such a declaration, which suspended the operation of the Constitution, had been granted to the Yang Dipertuan Agung (when the Parliament was not sitting) by the Constitution itself. After physical security had been restored, it was decided to use the Emergency powers to try to deal with some of the fundamental problems which had led to the riots. An appointed body, called the National Operations Council (NOC), was established to manage the Emergency. Although Tengku Abdul Rahman remained as Prime Minister, most of the responsibility for running the government devolved to Deputy Prime Minister Tun Abdul Razak, who headed the NOC as Director of Operations (a title borrowed from the 1948–60 Emergency and connoting combined civil and military authority).

The NOC period lasted until February 1971. Fears of a Malay dictatorship gradually abated as it became clear that the intention was to return to Parliamentary government, but under a changed set of rules. The new rules were intended to reduce the chance of future violence by more deeply entrenching the 'Bargain of 1957' and removing the main elements of that bargain from the arena of political debate. When Parliament was reconvened it was instructed to pass a series of amendments to the Constitution and to the Sedition Act. Among other things, these forbade anyone to question the position of the Malay rulers, the use of Malay as the national language, the 'special position' of the Malays or the rights of non-Malay citizens to their citizenship (Malaysia, 1971; Mohamed Suffian, 1972, pp. 192–201). Henceforth, no one could propose the abolition of any of these provisions although it was explicitly permitted to raise questions about the manner of their implementation. Within these limits, it was felt, democracy could be practised. The Alliance position in Parliament had been bolstered by a sweep in the Sabah elections, postponed from May 1969 to June 1970, and by the formation of a coalition government in Sarawak. With the two-thirds majority needed to amend the Constitution thus assured, and the ultimate weapon of power to declare an Emergency in the government's hands anyway, the opposition members in Parliament bowed to the inevitable.[32] Shortly before, in September 1970, Tengku Abdul Rahman had retired and Tun Abdul Razak had succeeded him as Prime Minister.

There is no way to prove or disprove any particular theory about the causes of the Alliance's electoral setback and the riots of May 1969.[33]

Many people, both Malays and Chinese, argued that economic factors constituted an important part of the problem. The slow growth of the economy since 1965 had contributed to the worsening of unemployment. Even though the unemployed were mostly Chinese and Indians, the slack labour market made it harder for Malay migrants to the towns to find jobs. Malay youths were now completing secondary education in significant numbers for the first time and were often frustrated not to receive either of the major benefits bestowed on secondary school leavers in the past: urban white-collar employment or admission to higher education. Growth in the number of good jobs had not kept pace with enrolment expansion, while access to higher education was often blocked by inferior educational preparation and lack of facility in English.

Certainly these and other socio-economic problems did exist, and offered grounds for concern regardless of their contribution to causing the riots. Those who agreed that they had been a major cause divided when it came to prescribing a remedy. Two broad groups emerged, one endorsing the past lines of economic policy but arguing that implementation had been too sluggish in the past, and the other calling for major increases in intervention in the economy to benefit the Malays, if necessary at the cost of economic growth.

There is little doubt that faster economic growth could have been achieved before 1969. Visiting economists had frequently wondered why Malaysia was not enjoying the 8 to 10 per cent growth rates achieved by some other small East Asian countries. In 1967 a group of foreign economic advisers had drawn up a detailed perspective plan (Gates, Goering and Keare, 1967) which had shown how a high investment rate and a big push to open up more land for export agriculture could achieve full employment of the labour force by the mid-1980s, despite labour force growth at 3 per cent per annum. This, they argued, would be the best thing the government could do for the Malays, since the tight labour market which would result from successful execution of the plan would draw Malay labour out of agriculture into urban pursuits, forcing rises in the productivity and incomes of those who remained behind in the agricultural sector. The plan was a logical extension of the main policy line being followed by the government before 1969. That it did not become a reality is attributable partly to the problem of limited implementation capacity which had plagued the public sector since the early 1960s,[34] but even more to unwillingness to accept the plan's implications for ownership and management of economic enterprise. For there to be more rapid growth in manufacturing and other urban activities, and even for land to be developed at the pace envisaged in the advisers' plan, would have required the government to give a much freer hand to the Chinese and foreign investors who already dominated the economy than it was willing to give.

The actions which the government took in the economic field after May 1969 were, as usual, conditioned by the need to make political compromises and were not wholly consistent with each other. A Capital Investments Committee established with Tan Siew Sin as Chairman cleared away a large backlog of private investment approvals, leading directly to a boom in private investment in 1970 (another cause was a rubber price upsurge which had occurred in late 1968 and early 1969). But at about the same time new statistics were released showing the total domination of the modern sectors of the economy by foreign and Chinese interests, with only a tiny Malay share (*SMP*, 1971, p. 40). Many Malays resolved that the pattern must be broken. Predictably, a new round of Malay 'special interest' economic programmes appeared in the months following the riots. An Urban Development Authority (UDA) was set up to speed Malay entry into urban commerce, as well as to perform other urban planning functions. Pernas (the *Perbadanan Nasional* or National Corporation), established in 1970, was empowered to purchase existing businesses, found new ones and enter into joint ventures. State Economic Development Corporations (SEDCs) were set up by all the state governments, largely as a response to grassroots pressure for action to assist the Malays. Unlike their predecessors, these programmes focused mainly on urban, non-agricultural activities. This reflected the gradual change in Malay interests and ambitions during the 1960s. The changes came to be known collectively as the 'New Economic Policy' (NEP).

Soon after the riots, in July 1969, an important change in social policy was announced. The then Minister of Education, known as a Malay radical, succeeded in committing the government to implementation of the long-delayed policy change of eliminating English-medium education and replacing it with education in the Malay medium.[35] This was to be done a year at a time, beginning with the class which entered primary school in 1970. The transition would thus not be completed until this class graduated from Form VI in 1982, but the significant fact (which gratified most Malays and caused great consternation among middle-class non-Malays) was that a definite timetable had been established after years of compromise and delay.

The first summing-up of the economic policy discussions which followed the May 1969 riots came in the Second Malaysia Plan (SMP), published in June 1971. In its rhetoric, the new Plan took much more explicit and extensive account of the problems of economic inequality than had its predecessors. Over the long run, it pledged the government to improve 'racial economic balance', measured in terms of employment patterns, relative incomes and shares in ownership and control of assets. The period over which balance was to be achieved was twenty years, one generation. In the Plan's most specific commitment, it promised that 'within a period of 20 years, Malays and other indigenous people will manage and own at least 30% of the total commercial and industrial activities in all categories and scales of operation' (*SMP*, 1971, pp. 41–2). At the same time, in the spirit of the 1957 Constitution, the SMP asserted that the Plan would work 'in an ever expanding economy in which the growing volume of goods and services is enjoyed by all groups in the Malaysian society' and that 'the Government will ensure that no particular group will experience any loss or feel any sense of deprivation'.

The Plan also made an inter-communal appeal with its promise to 'eradicate poverty irrespective of race' (ibid., pp. 1, 43).

While the general tone of the SMP and its long-run targets differentiated it sharply from previous plans, there was much less departure from the past in its specific five-year targets. The planned average annual growth rate of 6.5 per cent (Malaysia-wide) was only slightly more than had been achieved in the preceding five years. As with the FMP, the size of the development expenditure target proved to be a difficult issue to resolve and was the subject of a rather odd compromise. The expenditure estimates published in the Plan totalled $7,250 million (Malaysia-wide) while the public finance framework provided for expenditure of only $6,000 million. The rationale given for this discrepancy was that the basic problem was one of implementation capacity and if expenditure of more than $6,000 million proved to be possible additional financing would be provided (ibid., pp. 66–81).[36] The pattern of development expenditure was similar to that of 1966–70, although there were significant increases in land development, commerce and industry, transportation and communications, and offsetting cuts in the relative importance of drainage and irrigation, utilities and social services other than education (ibid., pp. 68–71). Recognition was accorded to the growing unemployment problem but the Plan could offer nothing more promising than containment of percentage unemployment in Peninsular Malaysia at its estimated 1970 rate of 8 per cent (ibid., pp. 95–111).

In summary, the SMP was a blend of radical rhetoric and bold promises for the long-range future, on the one hand, and only moderately increasing expenditure levels and general continuity with past policies, on the other. It was perhaps inevitable that this dichotomy should emerge, in view of the relatively short period of time intervening between May 1969 and publication of the Plan, the lack of much of the information which would be needed to formulate rational programmes for the reduction of economic inequality and the pragmatic nature of Malaysian politics, which often favours postponement of the definition and resolution of those issues which can be postponed. Greater specificity on the New Economic Policy was provided by the Mid-Term Review of the Second Malaysia Plan published in late 1973 (*MTR-SMP*, 1973, pp. 1–21). This document stated the 'two-pronged strategy' of the NEP, aimed at the overriding objective of promoting national unity, in the following terms:

(a) eradicating poverty by raising income levels and increasing employment opportunities for all Malaysians, regardless of race. This is to be achieved by programmes aimed at raising the productivity and income of those in low productivity occupations, the expansion of opportunities for intersectoral movements from low productivity to higher productivity activities and the provision of a wide range of social services especially designed to raise the living standards of the low income groups;

(b) accelerating the process of restructuring Malay society to correct economic imbalance, so as to reduce and eventually eliminate the identification of race with economic function. Programmes for this purpose include the modernisa-

> tion of rural life, the rapid and balanced development of urban activities, the establishment of new growth centres and the creation of a Malay commercial and industrial community in all categories and at all levels of operation. The objective is to ensure that Malays and other indigenous people will become full partners in all aspects of the economic life of the nation (*MTR-SMP*, 1973, p. 1).

This statement elaborated the NEP's objectives in terms of a hierarchy of goals and sub-goals. At the apex of the hierarchy was the overriding goal—national unity. This objective, it was postulated, could be attained through the achievement of two sub-goals: poverty eradication and the restructuring of Malaysian society. Some of the possible means of achieving the two sub-goals were specified in general terms. Other new departures in the Mid-Term Review were the publication of new information on the extent of existing inequalities and the specification, in an 'outline perspective plan' for 1970–90, of quantitative interim and end-year targets for employment structure and share capital ownership.

CONCLUSION

The New Economic Policy represented a genuine new departure for Malaysian development policy, in that it boldly recognized and confronted the problem of Malay economic inferiority and prescribed remedies which stressed intersectoral movement and urbanization in addition to the rural development measures undertaken in the past. In launching the NEP the government went far to cover its flank against charges of 'not doing enough to help the Malays'. At the same time, non-Malays were placated by the poverty eradication goal of the NEP, which in effect promised to assist Chinese and Indians living in circumstances comparable to those of the majority of low-income Malays. As later chapters will show, the NEP also offered many opportunities to the Malay elite while in some respects threatening the status and well-being of the English-speaking Chinese and Indian élites.

Official statements of the NEP have, not surprisingly, played down certain ambiguities and likely conflicts in its logical structure. How seriously will the poverty eradication goal be taken? No quantitative targets have yet been set for the absolute or relative income levels of the poor. And what will be the relationship between the restructuring objective and economic growth? Although a growing pool of resources is obviously needed for the NEP's objectives to be met, some of its provisions—notably the squeeze on the foreign and ethnic Chinese shares of capital ownership and management—could depress economic growth rates. In typically Malaysian fashion, such difficult issues have been put aside for later resolution on a pragmatic case-by-case basis.

With the launching of the NEP this survey of the major historical influences on ethnicity and economic inequality in Malaysia is completed. After a closer examination (in Chapter 4) of patterns and trends in equality, some theories which try to explain these facts in terms of historical and other factors will be considered (in Chapter 5). Thereafter, the remaining chapters of the book will discuss the experience of the NEP during its first few years, among other things.

1. For description and analysis of the Malayan Constitution, see H. E. Groves (1964), Milne (1967, pp. 36–42) and Tan Sri Mohamed Suffian bin Harun (1972).

2. Ratnam (1965) analyses in detail the exchanges over these issues during the 1950s; see also Von Vorys (1975).

3. Mohamed Suffian (1972, p. 243) states that from Merdeka Day through 1970, 1,743,051 non-Malays acquired citizenship by registration and 15,773 got it by naturalization.

4. The Bank Mission's recommendations included an Economic Committee of the Executive Council (later Cabinet), an Economic Secretariat, a Technical Advisory Committee of high-level civil servants (later established as the National Development Planning Committee), a Central Bank and an industrial credit institution (later Malayan Industrial Development Finance). For the plan, prepared by the Economic Secretariat based on World Bank recommendations, see Malaya (1956).

5. There was no significant increase in public ownership (beyond the public utilities which had been government-owned under the British) until the late 1960s. Currency regulation remained under the completely automatic currency board system until 1967. Fiscal policy continued to be cautiously conservative through the 1960s.

6. RIDA's early activities were evaluated in D. E. M. Fiennes (1957). For an analysis of the whole rural development programme and the institutions created to carry it out, see Gayl D. Ness (1967).

7. The percentage of the popular vote won can be a misleading measure, as it is sensitive to the number of parties contesting and the number of districts in which they choose to field candidates. In this case, it exaggerates the decline in support for the Alliance. Popular vote shares in the 1959 and 1964 Parliamentary elections are given in K. J. Ratman and R. S. Milne (1967, p. 361).

8. For example, by Ness (1967), whose sympathetic book has already been cited, and by Wilcox (1965, p. 23), who concluded that in the South-East Asian context,

> 'Development planning in Malaysia is unique in three respects. The content of development plans has been determined, to an unusual degree, by the choices of the people, in cities, towns, and villages. The annual phases of the plans have been incorporated, with extraordinary success, in governmental budgets. Execution of the plans has been supervised and expedited through procedures that are both ingenious and effective.'

9. Malayan planning and implementation procedures in this period are described by Wilcox (1965, pp. 23–33). The system lost much of its dynamism after the attention of the Deputy Prime Minister was distracted by Confrontation in late 1963.

10. See Milton E. Osborne (1964), Willard A. Hanna (1964), T. E. Smith (1963), Emily Sadka (1961), and Robert O. Tilman (1963).

11. Confrontation initiated a process of military and police build-up which continued into the early 1970s. Malaysia's dependence on Britain and Australia for its defence had been one of the features of the new federation to which Sukarno objected most violently. After Confrontation ended, efforts were made to reduce this dependence. These were still going on when the 1969 troubles provided a fresh motive for strengthening the security forces. The impact of military and police expenditures on successive development plans is suggested in Table 3.1.

12. Trengganu, the other state won by the PMIP in 1959, had been captured by the Alliance in 1961 when several PMIP assemblymen defected.

13. FMP, 1965, pp. 69–70. The comparison is on a States of Malaya basis: for all of Malaysia, including Sabah and Sarawak, the FMP target was $4,550 million, compared to actual expenditure in 1961–5 of $3,108 million.

14. This is not to say that all public expenditure benefited rural Malays. On the contrary, the colonial and immediately post-colonial pattern of public expenditure benefited the higher income groups and more developed regions to a considerable extent. As will be

seen in Chapter 6, below, this pattern had changed to one of greater progressivity, especially where poor Malays were involved, by the late 1960s.

15. There were also increasing transfers from Peninsular Malaysia to Sabah and Sarawak to reckon with. Direct transfers from the federal government to the Sabah and Sarawak state governments totalled about $250 million in both 1964 and 1965. In addition, federal current and development expenditure in Sabah and Sarawak exceeded federal revenue by a sum which rose from $130 million in 1964 to $268 million by 1967 (Donald R. Snodgrass, 1971, p. 42).

16. The foreign financing target of the FMP was in fact absurdly ambitious. This is shown in the following Table, which also indicates how far short of targets net foreign borrowing and foreign grants fell in 1966–70 and suggests how this caused development expenditure to miss its target as well. The Table (in $ millions) is on an all-Malaysia basis and for the consolidated public sector (*FMP*, 1965, pp. 33, 75; *SMP*, 1971, p. 81).

	Actual 1961–5	*Plan 1966–70*	*Actual 1966–70*	*Plan 1971–75*
1. Development expenditure	3,109	4,550	4,242	6,000
2. Net foreign borrowing	305	1,000	458	720
3. Foreign grants	255	900	243	190
4. Total foreign finance (2 + 3)	560	1,900	701	910
5. Foreign-financed share (4 ÷ 1)	18.0%	41.8%	16.5%	15.2%

17. Net official aid disbursements by members of the OECD Development Assistance Committee were stagnant from 1961 to 1965, after which they did manage to grow by 23 per cent in 1965–9 (Edwin M. Martin, 1970, p. 172). Malaysia enjoyed some upsurge in British and Commonwealth aid to assist its formation and later in compensation for the military withdrawal, but this subsided and overall Malaysia did no better than the average aid-receiving country. As shown in footnote 24, net foreign financing for the Malaysian public sector was just 25 per cent higher in 1966–70 than it had been in 1961–5 ($701 million compared to $560 million).

18. Consolidated public sector development expenditure (Malaysia-wide) had risen from $641 million in 1964, Malaysia's first full year, to $841 million in 1966. The three years of near-stagnation produced figures of $821 million in 1967, $854 million in 1968, and $867 million in 1969. Thereafter, vigorous growth resumed and by 1972 development expenditure was up to $1,650 million (Treasury, 1974, pp. xl–xli).

19. A first 'Bumiputra Economic Congress' was held in June 1965 and a second in September 1968. These were opportunities for a wide cross-section of Malays ('Sons of the Soil') to air their grievances and propose remedies, although under circumstances which were carefully orchestrated by the UMNO leadership.

20. One of the earliest departures from this tendency to accept the *status quo* apparently occurred in the implementation of the Pioneer Industries programme, in which the government insisted that employment patterns in firms receiving special tax inducements 'should reflect the multiracial character of the population'. The circumspection with which these quotas were enforced is suggested by the fact that I can find no printed reference to them which pre-dates 1969.

21. See Department of Statistics (1966) and N. S. Choudhry (1970). The figures given in the text differ somewhat from those in the surveys, since they have been adjusted for biases and definitional differences; see Donald R. Snodgrass (1972).

22. Choudhry (1970) found rates of active unemployment of 10.5 per cent for Indians, 7.0 per cent for Chinese and 6.0 per cent for Malays. Indians were especially hard-hit because of their pattern of dependence on estate employment, which declined from 311,000 in 1959 to 263,000 in 1969 (*Monthly Statistical Bulletin of West Malaysia*, July 1971, p. 202).

23. These statements are clearly somewhat conjectural. See, however, two accounts of politicization in the *kampung*, Peter J. Wilson (1967) and Marvin L. Rogers (1969).

24. The major opposition for Malay votes again came from the PMIP. Opposition appeals for non-Malay votes centred on three parties which succeeded in putting together a no-contest pact: the Democratic Action Party (previously the PAP), the Gerakan Raayat Malaysia (GRM) and the People's Progressive Party (PPP) of Perak. The DAP and PPP

made exclusively ethnic appeals, while the GRM, a new group, presented itself as a multi-racial party. The far left boycotted the election. On the 1969 elections, see Martin Rudner (1970), Stuart Drummond and David Hawkins (1970), R. K. Vasil (1972), and von Vorys (1975, pp. 251–307).

25. The Alliance had held 89 Peninsular Malaysian Parliamentary seats. It won 67 in the May election and probably would have won one other, which was not contested because of the death of the Alliance candidate.

26. As noted earlier, popular vote shares are hard to interpret. The fact that the Alliance had 56 fewer opposition candidates to face than in 1964—119 instead of 175—should have helped to raise its popular vote share in 1969. On the other hand, the opposition conceded it the surprisingly high total of 9 seats on nomination day; this should have had the opposite effect. In any case, the measured drop (from 58.5 per cent to 49.1 per cent) is so large that the genuineness of a significant decline in support is indisputable.

27. Drummond and Hawkins (1970, p. 333); the estimate assumes that Malays cast 55 per cent of the valid ballots.

28. Accounts of the 13 May violence published in its wake tended to be sketchy, emotional and biased. The fullest and most balanced is Anthony Reid (1969). Tengku Abdul Rahman (1969) is a highly subjective account, while John Slimming (1969) is scarred by the kind of strong ethnics bias (in his case pro-Chinese, anti-Malay) which is all too common among foreigners who have lived and worked in Malaysia. The National Operations Council report (1969) gives the official version of the facts and interprets them, generally from a Malay point of view. Even today, several key questions of fact and interpretation remain open, at least in so far as the public record is concerned; see von Vorys (1975, pp. 308–69).

29. These included the attribution of the trouble to the Communists, arrests of some newly-elected opposition politicians, alleged favouritism in security-force operations, inept handling of information policy and the widely-reported statement by an UMNO Minister that 'democracy is dead in this country. It died at the hands of the opposition parties.' See Reid (1969, pp. 269–74).

30. There had in fact been periodic outbreaks of communal violence in the past: in Penang in 1957, on Pangkor Island in 1959, in Province Wellesley and in Singapore (then part of Malaysia) in 1964 and in Penang again in 1967. However, these were all small and limited incidents which were prevented from growing by prompt police action. Given the depth of the ethnic divisions and emotions, this was generally considered to be a good record.

31. As Reid (1969, pp. 260–3) points out, there was a tendency to look only at the outcome in terms of seats and ignore the fact that the decline in popular support for the Alliance was at least as great among Malays as among non-Malays. That UMNO quickly came to appreciate this point is shown by its subsequent strong measures to reconsolidate its political base.

32. The government had made it clear that passage of the legislation was a condition for terminating the Emergency. Under the circumstances, only the DAP and the PPP remained intransigent in opposing the Bill, which was passed by 125 votes to 17.

33. Reid (1969, pp. 275–6) suggests that the NOC's own analysis attributed the major blame to three factors:

(i) Malay dissatisfaction over the non-implementation of long-standing policies to make Malay the effective National Language;

(ii) non-Malay provocation of Malay sensitivities by challenging their privileged position under Article 153 of the Constitution;

(iii) urban and small-town unemployment on the part of school-leavers, both Malay and non-Malay.

The remedies prescribed were the elimination of English-medium education, the Constitutional and Sedition Act amendments and the New Economic Policy.

34. This too was partly an ethnic problem. Although most high-level administrative generalists in the government were Malays, the technical specialists needed to carry out many development projects were predominantly Chinese or Indian. The government wanted a larger share of technical jobs to be held by Malays but faced a shortage of qualified individuals. This led to high vacancy rates in technical positions and consequent loss of implementation capacity. A related problem was discrimination in salary structure against technical posts, a holdover from colonial times which made it hard for the government to attract and retain technicians in competition with the private sector.

35. Only English-medium schools, which had constituted the road to employment

opportunity since the withdrawal of support from Chinese-medium secondary education in the early 1960s, were affected. Chinese and Tamil-medium schools were permitted to continue but are essentially dead-ends in employment terms, except that Chinese schools do lead to jobs in small Chinese firms and Chinese-controlled trades.

36. As it happened, development expenditure rose sharply in 1971 (from $979 million to $1,427 million, Malaysia-wide) and continued to increase sharply throughout the plan period, except for a lull in 1973 intended as an anti-inflationary measure (Ministry of Finance, 1976, p. xxvii). Total expenditure in 1971–5 eventually totalled $9,820 million (*TMP*, 1976, p. 233), although some of the increase was attributable to inflation, which became significant in Malaysia for the first time in late 1972.

4 Patterns and Trends in Economic Inequality

> The direct link between per capita income and the numbers living in poverty is income distribution.... A 'plan' which conveys no targets for reducing poverty, unemployment and inequality can hardly be called a 'development plan'.... Suppose, for example, that a perspective plan specified that the per capita income of Brazil doubled in the next thirty years, but assumed no change in distribution or the number unemployed. Then at the turn of the century, a big landowner in the Mato Grasso would run two cars, instead of one, and a peasant in the North-East would have two pieces of meat a month, instead of one. His son might well be out of work. Can we really call that 'development'?
>
> Seers, 1969

INTRODUCTION

AT the time the New Economic Policy was formulated knowledge of the actual dimensions of economic inequality in Peninsular Malaysia was sparse and impressionistic. Not surprisingly, more work on the subject has been done since 1969, so that now there is considerable information on, and understanding of, both the pattern of inequality *c.* 1970 and trends in inequality during the 1957–70 period. In addition, considerable amounts of information on post-NEP trends have been collected by the government; however, few of the findings have been released to the public, so conclusions about what has happened since 1970 retain a large element of conjecture.

This chapter summarizes what is known about economic inequality in Malaysia. The first step is to consider some significant definitional issues.

1. *Inequality of outcomes, or results, versus inequality of inputs, or causes.* Other discussions of inequality and policies for reducing it have shown this to be an important distinction because in a state of imperfect knowledge equalization of known causes does not assume equalization of results. Results are usually measured by income or wealth. Causes can be measured in various ways, depending on the causal forces postulated (education, degree of monopoly power, ability, preferences as between income and leisure or present consumption and future consumption, etc.). If the relationship between causes and results could be specified fully and unambiguously, and all causes could be affected by policy

measures, equality in causes would ensure equality in results. But full specification is usually impossible; at best, the analyst succeeds in establishing only a few causal factors and roughly suggesting their pattern of interaction. Equality in these partial causes does *not* insure equality of results.

This chapter looks only at results, leaving the effort to explain observed inequality to later chapters.

2. *How to measure results*. The most frequently used measure, monthly or annual income—usually taken before the payment of taxes and fees to the government and the receipt of public consumption benefits and transfer payments from it—is dictated mainly by statistical availability. Wealth has some appeal as either an alternative or a supplementary measure of welfare, but it has been much less studied because it poses greater statistical difficulties and data on it are therefore sparse. This study is driven by these same forces to put primary emphasis on income before taxes. But the content of the discussion in Malaysia and the nature of official targets strongly recommend against exclusive use of the income measure.

The Second Malaysia Plan (*SMP*, 1971, pp. 36–41) cites three kinds of 'economic imbalance' as significant in Malaysia: imbalances in income, in employment and in ownership and control of wealth. This might be regarded as mere rhetorical redundancy; jobs and ownership and control of wealth could be considered significant only for the income which they provide. However, the heavy emphasis placed on bringing Malays into the kinds of modern-sector employment in which they have been lightly represented in the past and on carving out a significant Malay share in the ownership and control of modern-sector wealth suggests that this is not the case. Instead, there appear to be strong motivations which make employment, ownership and control significant criteria of economic inequality in their own right. One such motivation is political and rather obvious: many Malays doubt that they can long hold on to political power if their community continues to be economically weak in terms of power and skills. Another is psychological and more subtle: Malay self-confidence and feelings of self-worth, although still rooted largely in traditional cultural and religious values, are surely becoming increasingly dependent on improvements in status and ability to participate effectively in the modern economy. Such motivations carry significant weight in influencing policy; there is thus little doubt that economic inequality in Malaysia must be defined in terms of multiple criteria.

3. *How to measure inequality*. One could measure *relative income inequality* in terms of the overall size distribution or in sub-distributions such as those internal to the various ethnic groups. It is also possible to examine the *absolute poverty or wealth* of particular groups. Since it is by no means clear which of these measures is superior, either in broad ethical terms or in its relationship to social discontent and possible upheaval, the study takes an eclectic approach, employing both relative and absolute measures.

4. *How to evaluate the inequality measured*. It is usually possible to say

whether inequality is large or small and whether it has increased or decreased over time—although different statistical measures do not invariably give identical answers even to these seemingly straightforward questions—but it is much harder to say how much inequality is 'bad' or 'dangerous'. Efforts to develop universally acceptable ethical standards invariably run into difficulty (Sen, 1973) and the prediction of discontent and rebellion in relation to patterns of inequality is in its infancy. The present study finesses such questions of ultimate objectives and standards by simply assuming that the present degree of inequality—at least in inter-communal terms and perhaps also in overall size distribution terms—is both ethically objectionable and potentially dangerous to the society. It follows that any observed increases in inequality are also bad and potentially dangerous, while at least some reduction in inequality is desirable both for its own sake and as a contributor to social tranquility.[1]

INCOME INEQUALITY SINCE 1957[2]

Introduction

The primary income measure to be used here is monthly income per household. The main reason for this choice is that it alone permits us to compare the results of five sample surveys of household income conducted between 1957 and 1970. Kuznets (1963, pp. 3–8) stresses that one should start from household rather than individual income because the allocation to individuals of incomes earned in family enterprises or from property is often arbitrary. The disadvantage of the household is that it is not a standard unit, varying in size and composition in terms of age groups, sexes and socio-economic roles. Kuznets therefore recommends that household income be recalculated on a per capita or adult equivalent basis wherever possible. The data do not permit one to follow this advice in the present case but there is reason to believe that variations in household size and composition explain only a small part of inter-household income variation in Malaysia.[3]

A more significant reason for returning to the analysis of individual incomes later on arises in connexion with 'causal' (or associative) analysis aimed at uncovering some of the more interesting determinants of income. Most of the potential correlates of income are attributes of individuals rather than entire households. Thus one can by no means ignore the distribution of income among individuals. But it seems best to begin with household income, using it to evaluate our statistical sources and establish the broad distributional patterns and trends before adding refinements.

The plan of this section is as follows. First, the overall size distribution is examined to see whether inequality has changed over time and how great it is in Malaysia compared to other countries. Then attention turns to particular groups which command special interest: the poor, the major ethnic groups and the rural and urban strata.

Overall Size Distribution

1. *Total household income.* Before examining the size distribution of income among households, it will be useful to establish a benchmark by estimating the growth of *total* household income. This can be done using

TABLE 4.1

NATIONAL ACCOUNTS-BASED ESTIMATES OF AGGREGATE PERSONAL AND PRIVATE INCOME, 1957–1970[1]

($ million)

	Period[2]				
	April 1957– March 1958	*1959*	*June 1967– May 1968*	*October 1967– September 1968*	*1970*
Personal consumption expenditure	3,230	3,390	5,330	5,380	5,980
Direct taxes on households	110	110	280	290	350
Transfers to general government	20	20	80	80	100
Transfers to rest of world	200	210	200	200	220
Total household expenditure	3,560	3,370	5,890	5,950	6,650
Personal savings[3]	160	240	280	280	790
Personal income	3,720	3,970	6,170	6,230	7,440
Retained company earnings	160	180	100	90	300
Direct taxes on companies	100	100	260	260	330
Net private income	3,980	4,250	6,530	6,580	8,070
Depreciation	230	250	470	470	530
Gross private income	4,210	4,500	7,000	7,050	8,600

[1]In this Table, aggregate personal income is reconstructed from the national accounts, based on measures of the *uses* of personal income, which are probably more reliable than the measures of sources of such income. Most data for 1967–8 are taken from Department of Statistics (1972). Data for 1957–9 are taken in part from Department of Statistics (n.d.), although many components for these years are guestimates based on related data and figures for later years. Data for 1970 are primarily estimates based on unpublished data; final data published subsequently are based on a revised system of national accounts and are therefore non-comparable to earlier figures. For all years, the estimation of personal saving is a problem: see footnote 3, below. All figures in the Table are rounded to the nearest $10 million.

[2]The periods selected correspond with those of the household income surveys cited below. Estimates for split years are interpolations of published figures for calendar years.

[3]Total *private* savings can be estimated by the residual method as gross domestic capital formation minus the sum of depreciation, government savings, surpluses of public corporations and the nation's deficit on current account. A split of this total between households and companies is not regularly published. However, direct estimates of company retained earnings are obtainable for 1966 and later years from the Financial Surveys of Limited Companies (Department of Statistics, 1969 and subsequent years). For earlier years the breakdown of private savings into personal savings and retained savings is a guess, but since personal savings is only a small fraction of personal income, its roughness does not have much effect on the far larger total.

the national accounts statistics. The data (Table 4.1) suggest that aggregate personal income doubled between 1957–8 and 1970. The sum of retained company earnings, direct taxes on companies and depreciation allowances—private income items which are normally excluded from analyses of income size distribution but which are too sizeable to be ignored in the Malaysian case—more than doubled during the same period.

TABLE 4.2

NATIONAL ACCOUNTS-BASED ESTIMATES OF INCOME PER HOUSEHOLD, 1957–1970[1]

	April 1957– March 1958	*1959*	*June 1967– May 1968*	*Oct. 1967– Sept. 1968*	*1970*
Personal income[2] ($ million)	3,720	3,970	6,170	6,230	7,440
Population ('000)[3]	6,420	6,700	8,610	8,670	9,150
In institutions[4]	180	180	260	260	300
In private households	6,240	6,520	8,350	8,410	8,850
Mean household size[5]	5.5[6]	5.5	5.5	5.5	5.5
Number of households ('000)	1,130[6]	1,190	1,520	1,530	1,610
Income of private households[7] ($/million)	3,620	3,860	5,980	6,040	7,200
Mean income of private households ($/month)	270[6]	270	330	330	370

[1]All totals in this Table have been rounded to the nearest ten units.

[2]From Table 4.1.

[3]*Source*: Charles Hirschman (1974a).

[4]Institutional population includes those living in military and police barracks, hotels, maternity homes, welfare homes, temples and prisons. It was measured at 182,000 in the 1957 census. An independent estimate of the components for 1967 yielded a figure of 260,000. Other figures are guesses.

[5]Mean household size is a matter of some uncertainty. Fell (1960, p. 16) implies a figure of 4.8, the *HBS* a mean of 5.5, the 1966–7 Family Planning Survey (p. 23) 5.6, the *SES* 5.5, the *SRM/Ford* survey 5.4, the 1970 population census field count summary 5.5 on an actual occupancy basis, and the 1970 housing census 5.6 on a usual occupancy basis. Given the weight of evidence favouring a figure of about 5.5, it seems likely that the lower 1957 census figures result from a definitional variation rather than a trend toward larger households (although this cannot be confirmed). Accordingly, a constant value of 5.5 is assumed here.

[6]Mean household size has been assumed to have been 5.5 in 1957, as explained in the preceding note. The census enumerated 1,257,000 households, implying a mean of 4.8. If the latter figures were used, estimated mean household income in 1957 would be $240 per month.

[7]Presumably what is being measured by household surveys is not total personal income but only that portion of it which accrues to persons residing in private households. In the absence of information on the respective mean incomes of the institutional and private household population, it is assumed that they are equal; private households have thus been allocated a share of personal income equal to their share of the population.

A more difficult task is determining what this growth of aggregate income meant for the average household. Although there are several estimates of both population and mean household size, it appears (Table 4.2) that the mean income of private households was around $270 per month in 1957–8 and rose to approximately $370 by 1970. These are rough estimates, since a degree of uncertainty attaches to the measures of national accounts aggregates, population growth and mean household size; however, Table 4.2 does provide a general indication of what happened to the income of the average household during the first sixteen years of independence. The next question is how these income gains were distributed.

2. *Five household surveys.* In search of an answer to this question, the findings of five household surveys conducted between 1957 and 1970 will be examined. Each of these surveys yields estimates of mean income per household, median income and the shape of the distribution as measured by decile income shares and by the Gini concentration ratio, which is one of several possible summary measures of the degree of inequality in the distribution as a whole.[4]

The surveys in question are:

1. *The Household Budget Survey of the Federation of Malaya 1957–58*, which will be referred to as the *HBS*.
2. *The Federation Saving Survey* (1959) (*FSS*).
3. *The Socio-Economic Sample Survey of Households 1967–68* (*SES*).
4. *The SRM/Ford Social and Economic Survey 1967/68*.
5. The Post Enumeration Survey of the 1970 population census (PES).[5]

None of these sources can be accepted as accurate without evaluation. They have been tested in Snodgrass (1975b), using three main tools of evaluation: (1) circumstantial evidence about the survey which suggests the likelihood of sampling and non-sampling errors; (2) consistency checks with non-survey data, including the national accounts estimates shown in Tables 4.1 and 4.2; (3) consistency checks against each other. These checks are not necessarily conclusive, since it is impossible to transcend the limited quantity and quality of data available. But they do permit use of the surveys, despite their varying definitional bases and biases, to gain a reasonably clear idea of what happened to the size distribution of income among households in 1957–70.

a. *The Household Budget Survey, 1957–58.* The *HBS* was a pioneer household survey whose main purpose was to measure consumption patterns for use as weights in consumer price indices. After extended enumerator contact with a sample household, an income question was posed. Little is known of the precise definition of income used (if indeed there was one). The data collected were arranged in a size distribution; some freehand smoothing was done 'to remove irregularities and give a smooth curve. This is believed to give a better distribution of income than from the uncorrected data . . . [but nevertheless] the tables on income distribution of households are not as accurate as those for consumption . . .' (Department of Statistics, n.d., p. 3).

The *HBS* sample was 2,760 households, only a 0.2 per cent sample of private households. Separate urban and rural samples were drawn. Only Malays, Chinese and Indians were covered in the survey and all households with incomes above $1,000 per month were excluded.

In the *HBS* report, household frequencies are given for twenty-eight income-size groups—for the whole sample and for each of the six ethnic group-by-stratum cells.[6] These data (Department of Statistics, n.d., p. 39) show a mean value of $196 per household per month and a Gini ratio of .368, indicating a relatively equal income distribution.[7] Mean household income as shown in the survey ($196) is only 73 per cent of the mean derived in Table 4.2 ($270).

There are two identifiable sources of understatement in the *HBS*: (1) the omission of 'Others', who made up only 2 per cent of the 1957 census population but undoubtedly had incomes well above the mean; and (2) the omission of all households with incomes over $1,000 a month. Income tax assessment data offer a way of adding the latter group in. Despite definitional differences between the two data sets and undoubted under-reporting of income for tax purposes, this seems a worthwhile adjustment.[8] The distribution of household income in 1957–8, as estimated from the *HBS* corrected for exclusion of higher-income households, is shown in Table 4.3.[9]

TABLE 4.3

DISTRIBUTION OF HOUSEHOLD INCOME IN 1957–1958
ACCORDING TO THE HOUSEHOLD BUDGET SURVEY
(Adjusted)

	Per cent of total income			
Per cent of households	*Total sample*	*Malays*	*Chinese*	*Indians*
Top 5%	22.1	18.1	19.6	19.5
Top 10%	33.2	27.6	30.5	29.5
Top 20%	48.6	42.5	45.8	43.7
Top 30%	60.1	54.4	57.3	54.9
Top 40%	69.6	64.3	66.9	64.4
Top 50%	77.4	72.9	75.0	72.9
Top 60%	84.1	80.5	82.0	80.3
Top 70%	89.7	87.2	88.0	86.8
Top 80%	94.3	92.9	93.2	92.4
Top 90%	97.9	97.3	97.4	97.0
Mean ($/month)	215	139	300	237
Median ($/month)	156	112	223	188
Gini ratio	0.412	0.342	0.374	0.347

The corrected estimate suggests that income inequality at the time of Merdeka, although marked, was less than in most other developing countries. The Gini ratio of 0.412 can be compared with estimates of 0.51 for the Philippines in 1965, 0.50 for Thailand in 1966 and 0.45 for

Ceylon in 1963; on the other hand, it is above the 0.36 value measured for Taiwan in 1964 (Oshima, 1970). The top 5 per cent of households received 22 per cent of the income, compared to 30 per cent or more in many developing countries.[10] The poorest 40 per cent of households had to make do with only 16 per cent of the income, but even this was more than they received in most other countries at Malaya's stage of development.[11]

These findings are generally consistent with what is known about the relationship between size inequality of income distribution and economic growth. On the one hand, Malaya's distributional pattern was unequal relative to the developed countries of Europe and North America; inequality is thought to rise during the early stages of development and incline during the later stages.[12] On the other hand, inequality was less than in other countries at a similar level of development.

Table 4.3 (like Tables 4.5 to 4.7, below) also shows data for the three major ethnic groups. These will be discussed later on.

b. *The Federation Saving Survey*. Like the *HBS*, the *FSS* collected income data as a matter of secondary interest. Its main purpose was to measure savings by various segments of the population. A sample of 5,691 households (drawn in a manner which is not clear from surviving descriptions) was surveyed in February to May 1960, using the calendar year 1959 as the reference period. The survey was conducted by students from the University of Malaya, Singapore, under the direction of K.R. Chou. Lee Hock Lock (1971) states that defects in training and publicity, along with language problems and deliberate lying or suppression of information, limited the accuracy of the survey results. In his tabulations, Lee discarded 544 questionnaires, mainly because of missing or inconsistent data on income. Also among the discarded, however, were all households headed by unemployed persons or pensioners, since Lee was not interested in their savings behaviour.

The only reasonably comprehensive source of *FSS* income findings is Lee Hock Lock (1971, pp. 9–36, especially p. 36). The results given

TABLE 4.4

DISTRIBUTION OF HOUSEHOLD INCOME IN 1959
ACCORDING TO THE FEDERATION SAVING SURVEY

Per cent of households	*Per cent of income*	*Per cent of households*	*Per cent of income*
Top 5	30.6	Top 60	90.5
Top 10	44.3	Top 70	94.2
Top 20	61.5	Top 80	97.1
Top 30	72.0	Top 90	99.0
Top 40	79.7	Mean ($/month)	246
Top 50	85.8	Median ($/month)	129
		Gini ratio	.549

there, regrouped into deciles, appear in Table 4.4. Lee's tabulation is strikingly at variance with the adjusted *HBS*. It indicates an exceedingly unequal distribution, in which the top decile of income recipients gets 44 per cent of the total and the Gini ratio is of a magnitude found only in cases of extreme inequality. The reasons for the sharp discrepancy between the *HBS* and *FSS* are not clear. Although one is tempted to seek grounds for rejecting the *FSS*, since it is inconsistent with an otherwise reasonably coherent pattern, statistical consistency checks provide no definite basis for doing so. The strongest case for rejection can be derived from the circumstantial evidence. The unclear criteria for selection of the sample, weak supervision of enumerators[13] and selective tabulation of the returns are all major grounds for scepticism.

c. *The Socio-Economic Sample Survey of Households 1967/68*. The next household income survey was not taken until the late 1960s, when the Department of Statistics returned to the field and private market research organizations appeared in the country.[14] The Statistics Department's *SES* was the first large-sample, multiple-purpose household survey undertaken in Malaysia. Originally intended to run continuously on the model of the Indian National Sample Survey of Households, its published results are confined to the period from June 1967 through May 1968. During this period data were collected on employment and unemployment, housing, demography and cash income. The income data were gathered last. Separate questions were asked for individual earners and the household as a whole but there was no probing and not even necessarily any checking for consistency of the replies for individuals and the household. The replies were grouped into eight intervals, the lowest being zero cash income and the highest $750 or more per month.

A new sample frame was created for the *SES*. Sampling fractions varied by stratum, ranging from 1/30 in the largest towns to 1/50 in the rural areas. The aim was to cover about 30,000 households or some 2.5 per cent of the presumed total. Population estimates were then obtained by multiplying sample results by the inverse of the sampling fraction.

The basic results of the *SES* with respect to cash household income are displayed in Table 4.5. They show a low mean household income (only 60 per cent of the hypothetical total) and high overall inequality. A probable reason for these findings is that the *SES*, unlike the other surveys discussed here, limited itself strictly to cash income. Non-cash income[15] would be expected to be somewhat more evenly distributed than cash income, so its exclusion should heighten measured inequality. A second possible reason for the greater inequality found in the *SES* may be its lesser tendency to smooth out monthly variations in income. There is a higher incidence of zero-income households in the *SES* than in other sources.

The *SES* measured income distribution within a much larger sample than had been used in previous surveys. Its principal defects were that it limited itself to cash income, failed to probe the answers given, and used an insufficient number of income intervals with too large an open interval at the high end of the range. Despite all this, it can be said that the

TABLE 4.5
DISTRIBUTION OF HOUSEHOLD CASH INCOME IN 1967–1968 ACCORDING TO THE SOCIO-ECONOMIC SAMPLE SURVEY OF HOUSEHOLDS

	Per cent of total income			
Per cent of households	*Total sample*	*Malays*	*Chinese*	*Indians*
Top 5	26.6	26.1	..	24.2
Top 10	39.7	38.3	34.3	36.2
Top 20	56.8	55.1	51.1	51.6
Top 30	68.7	67.9	63.4	62.6
Top 40	77.9	77.4	72.9	71.4
Top 50	85.3	84.8	80.9	79.0
Top 60	90.9	90.7	87.4	85.5
Top 70	95.2	95.2	92.7	91.0
Top 80	98.2	98.3	96.9	95.6
Top 90	99.8	99.8	99.6	98.8
Mean ($/month)	199	125	290	234
Median ($/month)	130	83	208	165
Gini ratio	0.525	0.515	0.458	0.445

findings of the *SES* fit fairly smoothly into the broad picture created by the other surveys. Its tendency toward under-reporting is shared with the *SRM/Ford* survey (see below), and discrepancies *vis-à-vis* that survey appear to be explained mainly by the use of the cash income concept in the *SES*.

d. *The SRM/Ford Social and Economic Survey 1967/68*. The 'SRM/Ford survey' is a tabulation of economic and social data collected by Survey Research Malaysia Sendirian Berhad for its 'Media Index', instituted in 1967–8 and replicated in subsequent years. The survey is based on a stratified random sample of individuals aged 15 and over (originally 6,696 in number), drawn from the *SES* sampling frame. For comparability to other surveys, it has been converted into a random sample of households by multiplying each observation by the inverse of its household size in terms of number of adults. This compensates for the fact that a member of a six-adult household, say, is six times as likely to be selected in the original sample as a member of a one-adult household. The survey deliberately oversamples urban areas, correcting for this (and for suspected variations in response rates) by applying sample findings for each ethnic group and stratum to frequencies estimated to hold in the universe rather than the frequencies found in the sample itself.

The survey tabulations array household income data in six intervals only, for the total sample and by ethnic group and stratum. The highest interval is an open one beginning at $1,000 a month.

Mean household income in the *SRM/Ford* survey is $240 per month (Table 4.6), an increase of 12 per cent over the adjusted *HBS* of more than a decade before. The *SRM/Ford* median is actually below the

TABLE 4.6
DISTRIBUTION OF HOUSEHOLD INCOME IN 1967–1968 ACCORDING TO THE SRM/FORD SOCIAL AND ECONOMIC SURVEY

	Per cent of total income			
Per cent of households	*Total sample*	*Malays*	*Chinese*	*Indians*
Top 5%	23.6	22.2	19.9	22.3
Top 10%	35.5	32.7	31.7	32.7
Top 20%	51.3	48.2	46.7	48.1
Top 30%	62.9	59.6	58.5	59.4
Top 40%	72.3	68.4	68.0	69.0
Top 50%	79.8	76.2	76.1	77.1
Top 60%	85.7	83.0	83.0	83.7
Top 70%	90.7	89.0	89.0	89.1
Top 80%	94.9	94.0	93.9	93.7
Top 90%	98.1	98.2	97.8	97.4
Mean ($/month)	240	163	349	260
Median ($/month)	154	120	261	191
Gini ratio	0.444	0.400	0.391	0.403

adjusted *HBS* median. Mean income in the *SRM/Ford* survey is 73 per cent of the hypothetical total.

Aside from this understatement, the *SRM/Ford* results seem broadly plausible. The circumstantial evidence surrounding *SRM*'s survey techniques suggests competent professionalism, but there are hints of corner-cutting to reduce costs.[16] The data suffer from the fact that income information is collected only as background to the media and product data which are the firm's principal concern. This means, among other things, that responses to the income questions are not probed for fear of heightening respondent resistance and that there is an inadequate number of size classes.

e. *The Post Enumeration Survey 1970*. The *PES*, taken in conjunction with the 1970 population and housing census, had three purposes: (1) to check the accuracy of the censuses; (2) to collect information on family planning knowledge, attitudes and practices as a follow-up to the Family Planning Survey of 1966–7; and (3) to provide yet another measure of household income distribution. Using the house lists from the census as a frame, a random sample of about 28,000 households was selected for the survey.

The *PES* employed a comprehensive definition of income, including all forms of income in the national accounts sense, plus transfer receipts. Household income was the sum of incomes of individual earners, which in turn were collected in two different ways: by simply asking and by probing through separate questions on eleven different income components. The latter, computed, income measure appears to provide more carefully collected income data than have been available hitherto. The responses have been coded into sixteen income classes, the last of which begins at the high level of $5,000 per month. In data collection and presentation, the *PES* thus has substantial advantages over previous surveys.

The *PES* (Table 4.7) yields a mean household income of $267 a month, about 11 per cent above the *SRM/Ford* mean for 1967–8 and 72 per cent of the hypothetical total shown in Table 4.2. Overall size inequality in the *PES* data is high: less than that of the *FSS*, which undoubtedly overstated inequality, or the *SES*, with its cash income concept, but much more than that of the adjusted *HBS* or the *SRM/Ford* survey.

TABLE 4.7
DISTRIBUTION OF HOUSEHOLD INCOME IN 1970
ACCORDING TO THE POST ENUMERATION SURVEY

	Per cent of total income			
Per cent of households	*Total sample*	*Malays*	*Chinese*	*Indians*
Top 5%	28.5	24.6	25.3	28.2
Top 10%	40.4	36.2	37.1	39.6
Top 20%	56.1	52.5	52.6	54.2
Top 30%	67.3	64.3	63.7	64.4
Top 40%	76.2	73.5	72.6	72.8
Top 50%	83.1	81.1	79.9	79.7
Top 60%	88.8	87.3	86.1	85.7
Top 70%	93.3	92.3	92.3	90.8
Top 80%	96.7	96.3	95.4	95.1
Top 90%	99.1	99.2	98.5	98.5
Mean ($/month)	267	177	399	310
Median ($/month)	167	122	269	195
Gini ratio	0.502	0.466	0.455	0.463

Trends in Overall Size Inequality

What do the five household surveys have to say about the trend in overall inequality of size distribution between 1957 and 1970? On the face of it, the rise of the Gini ratio from 0.412 in the adjusted *HBS* (1957/58) to 0.444 in the *SRM/Ford* survey (1967/68) and then to 0.502 in the *PES* (1970) suggests a substantial increase in inequality between Merdeka and the start of the New Economic Policy.[17] Could this increase be overstated? Is it, perhaps, impossible to say anything at all about trends in inequality in this period because of the considerable limitations of the data?

I believe that an increase in inequality of about the extent measured probably occurred, although this cannot be demonstrated conclusively.[18]

The trend measurement essentially rests on the *HBS*, the *SRM/Ford* survey and the *PES*. Apparent shortcomings, reviewed above and in more detail in Snodgrass (1975b), do not suggest a rising upward bias in measured inequality through time. Of course, there could easily be other differences (e.g. in enumeration procedures) which are not so apparent but could have the same result. But there is no basis to assume that such undetected biases would work in this particular direction; in the absence of indications to the contrary, it seems logical to suppose that unobservable differences among the surveys could as easily have led to *understatement* of the growth in inequality as to overstatement, or to have had no marked effect on it in either direction. And because the *HBS*, *SRM/Ford* survey and *PES* all appear to have been generally competent, professionally designed and directed surveys, I doubt that the magnitude of such biases, in whatever direction they work, would negate the rather striking trend apparent in their results.

In particular, tests reported in Snodgrass (1975b) demonstrate that neither the mingling of income tax data with survey data nor the varying treatment of zero-income households in the surveys could have biased the trend upward enough to upset this basic conclusion.

A different point, which has merit, is that some of the contrast between measured inequality in 1957–8 and 1967–8, on the one hand, and 1970, on the other, is probably attributable to short-term fluctuations rather than a long-term trend. Throughout the period aggregate income fluctuated from year to year, mainly as a result of variations in export prices. As it happens, 1957–8 and 1967–8 were low points in terms of these fluctuations while 1970 was a near-peak. Although the income benefits of an upswing in export prices are fairly widespread, it seems likely that high-income groups benefit more, in relative terms, and that inequality is thus positively related to the export price index.[19] Since there are neither year-by-year estimates of income distribution nor comprehensive data on the split between property income and labour income, this proposition cannot be proven and its magnitude estimated.[20] However, it clearly has some effect on the results.[21] Given that it was necessary to use 1957–8 and 1970 as end years in the trend calculation, some of the measured increase is probably cyclical rather than secular.

There is, however, a countervailing factor which surely leads to *understatement* of the trend toward greater income inequality. In Malaysia significant portions of private income never find their way into the household at all, being either retained in firms or taxed away as company direct taxes. Table 4.1 suggests that this sum rose from $490 million in 1957–8 to $1,160 million in 1970, or by a faster rate than personal income. If these property incomes could be attributed to the households which own the companies involved, one would undoubtedly find that they accrue overwhelmingly to high-income households. It therefore seems safe to conclude that the distribution of total private income is significantly more unequal than the distribution of personal income alone and that its trend toward increased inequality is also more pronounced.

All the above discussion refers to the situation before taxes.[22] The effects of the tax system, and of government services and transfer payments, on the income distribution are discussed in Chapter 6. As can be seen there, some increase in the progressivity of the fiscal system, on both its revenue and expenditure sides, has probably moderated the trend toward greater inequality in pre-tax income.

A final point is that, whatever happened to income inequality between 1957 and 1970, the trail of verifiable evidence regrettably ends in 1970. Four different surveys conducted since that year[23] reportedly contain information of the distribution of household income, but their results—except for certain summary measures published in the Mid-Term Review of the Third Malaysia Plan (*MTR-TMP*) and cited below—have not yet been published or otherwise made available to researchers. One possible reason for withholding these results is that the newer surveys are said to contradict each other on the question of whether inequality has increased further, remained constant or lessened since 1970. This is a matter of some importance, since the year to which the last publicly available data refer also marks the beginning of the NEP.

Position of Particular Groups

The overall size distribution of income is an abstraction with which most individuals and governments find it hard to identify. Greater interest is attached to the question of how particular groups of social and political importance fare in the process of development—what productive contributions they make and what income benefits they receive in return. This is at least as true of Malaysia as of other countries. The early emphasis on rural development was distribution-motivated; the First Malaysia Plan aimed to 'increase the well-being of Malaysia's rural inhabitants and other low-income groups, primarily by raising their productivity and thus their income-earning capacity' (*FMP*, 1975, p. 2). Later, income-redistribution objectives were broadened and made more explicit. Two distribution-related objectives of the Second Malaysia Plan have already been noted: 'to reduce and eventually eliminate poverty . . . irrespective of race' and 'to correct economic imbalance, so as to reduce and eventually eliminate the identification of race with economic function' (*SMP*, 1971, p. 1). These official specifications suggest three ways of categorizing Malaysian society which are important for income distribution purposes: by rural and urban strata, by poor and non-poor, and by ethnic groups. These will now be examined in turn.

1. *Rural and urban strata*. The five sample surveys suggest that inequality increased both between rural and urban areas and within each of them between 1957 and 1970. Comparing the mean income of urban households to that of rural households, the ratios shown in Table 4.8 are obtained. Both the *SRM/Ford* survey and the *PES* show wider disparities than the *HBS*. It thus seems likely that rural development from 1957 to 1970, impressive though it was in many ways, did not prevent a worsening of the relative incomes of rural residents. It would also appear that the considerable rural–urban migration which took place during the period (Hirschman and Singh, 1975; Hirschman, 1976) was still insufficient to keep population pressure from holding down rural earn-

ings.[24] This trend toward increasing rural–urban disparity continued into the 1970s, according to data recently published by the government (Table 4.8).

All the available surveys agree that inequality is greater in urban areas. Urban inequality is generally greater than inequality in the economy as a whole, while rural inequality is less than overall inequality.[25] Comparison of the *PES* with the *HBS* suggests a considerable rise of inequality within each sector during the pre-NEP years, while the *SRM/Ford* survey indicates a more moderate increase.

TABLE 4.8

SUMMARY OF URBAN AND RURAL INCOME DISTRIBUTIONS, 1957–1976

Year and Survey	*(1) Urban mean* (*$/month*)	*(2) Rural mean* (*$/month*)	*(3) Ratio of means* *(1) ÷ (2)*	*(4) Gini concentration ratios* *Urban*	*(5)* *Rural*
1957–8 (Adjusted *HBS*)	319	173	1.84	0.429	0.374
1967–8 (*SRM/Ford* survey)	360	185	1.95	0.447	0.399
1970 (*PES*)	432	202	2.14	0.494	0.463
1973–4	579	269	2.15	NA	NA
1976	936	417	2.24	NA	NA

Sources: For 1957–8 and 1967–8, as cited above. Data for 1970 are from *MTR-SMP* (1973, p. 4); the Table published in this source excludes zero-income households, which have been added back in here. Data for 1973–4 and 1976 are from *MTR-TMP* (1979, p. 44); they are based, respectively, on a weighted average of data from the Household Income Survey (1973) and Labour Force Survey (1974) and on preliminary results of the Agriculture Census (1976). (See note 23.)

Note: NA = not available.

2. *Poverty*. There is no generally accepted definition of poverty. One view is that poverty constitutes an income level below some minimum standard which society establishes. Such a standard is not absolute (the 'subsistence level of income' is notoriously difficult to quantify) but differs among countries and rises through time with the average level of income. Moreover, for a given time and place it should be geared to the circumstances of the household concerned: the number and ages of its consuming members, as well as the number of earners and their hours of work (a household in which three members must work to earn a given total income is really poorer than one in which a single earner receives the same amount). Finally, the 'poverty line' should be defined in real terms, to allow for inter-temporal and spatial variations in consumer prices.

No such sophisticated concept of the poverty line can be implemented using the data available to me. However, a much cruder concept can be applied. The *HBS* gives average consumption in 1957–8 of the income group earning less than $510 per month as approximately $100 a month, of which nearly $70 went for food. A slightly higher figure, say $120, can be taken as the poverty line. Available consumer price indices show only negligible price increases between 1957–8 and 1970, so the $120 standard can be used in all years. Since information on household size and composition and on spatial price variations (for example, between urban and rural areas) is lacking, these factors regrettably must be ignored.[26]

TABLE 4.9

PERCENTAGE OF HOUSEHOLDS IN VARIOUS CATEGORIES WITH INCOMES OF LESS THAN $120 PER MONTH

	Category					
	Malays	*Chinese*	*Indians*	*All rural households*	*All urban households*	*All households*
1957–8 (Adjusted *HBS*)	55.7	13.1	19.8	44.2	16.8	34.9
1967–8 (*SRM*/*Ford* survey)	50.2	12.3	25.6	42.4	17.6	34.7
1970 (*PES*)	49.3	13.9	20.2	41.7	15.2	34.9

Sources: All as cited above, except the *PES* data, which are taken from *MTR-SMP* (1973, pp. 3–4). The estimates for 1967–8 and 1970 may be less reliable than those for 1957–8, since the smaller number of income size groups tabulated in the *Ford/SRM* survey and shown in the *Mid-Term Review* necessitated more interpolation to estimate the number of households below the poverty line.

From these somewhat rough estimates (Table 4.9) it appears that there was no real change in the overall share of households living in poverty from Independence up to 1970. Since the number of households increased significantly, this means that the absolute amount of poverty in the country clearly rose.[27] The above analysis is based conservatively on a poverty line which is held constant (in real terms) over a period of thirteen years. If the poverty line were raised to reflect the considerable achievements and rising ambitions which occurred after 1957, the results of the calculation would be even less favourable.

For the period since 1970 official estimates of the prevalence of poverty are available. These show a rise in the number of Peninsular Malaysian households living in poverty from 791,800 in 1970 to 835,100 in 1975 (*TMP*, 1976, p. 163), followed by a decline to 776,300 in 1978 (*MTR-TMP*, 1979, p. 28). As a percentage of all households, these figures imply a steady drop: from 49.3 per cent in 1970 to 43.9 per cent in 1975 and 36.6 per cent in 1978. However, the poverty line used is not clearly defined, except to say that it 'takes account of minimum nutritional and other non-food requirements of each household to sustain a decent standard of living' (*TMP*, 1976, p. 160), so it is not clear to what extent inflation may have eroded the poverty line standard used in the computation.

The poverty line analysis is relatively reliable because it does not depend on precise measurement of household incomes at various points along the income scale. Another commonly-used approach to the measurement of poverty makes greater demands of questionable data. It looks at the mean incomes and shares in income growth of various ranges within the size distribution of income. Such an analysis, covering the 1957–70 period, is presented in Table 4.10.

TABLE 4.10

MEAN INCOME AND SHARES IN INCOME GROWTH, BY INCOME SIZE GROUP, 1957/8–1970

Income size group	*Mean income per household ($/month)*		*Income growth, 1957/8–70*		*Total personal income ($ million per annum)*			*Per cent share of increase*
	1957/8	*1970*	*In $/month*	*In per cent*	*In 1957/58*	*In 1970*	*Increase*	
Top 5%	953	1,520	+567	+59	638	1,477	839	36
Top 10%	716	1,078	+363	+51	957	2,096	1,139	49
Top 20%	524	749	+225	+43	1,403	2,911	1,508	65
Next 40%	191	218	+27	+14	1,023	1,693	670	29
Bottom 40%	86	75	–11	–13	459	584	125	5
Total	215	267	+52	+24	2,885	5,188	2,303	100

Again, the results of the analysis are discouraging. The data suggest that the top 10 per cent of income recipients were able to increase their incomes by 51 per cent on average, while the lowest 40 per cent of households actually suffered a decline in mean income. Some 49 per cent of the additional income created accrued to the top 10 per cent. It thus seems possible that the growth of population and labour force pressure during the period prevented the poorest groups in Malaysian society—rural labourers, padi planters, fishermen, the urban unskilled—from sharing in the substantial growth in total income experienced during the period. This finding has parallels in other developing countries.

It is well known that social services in rural areas improved significantly during the 1960s. Social indicators such as school enrolment ratios; doctors, clinics and hospital beds per thousand of population; and life expectancy at birth all rose noticeably. It thus appears that the social consumption of the poor increased while their private income and consumption did not.

It should not be inferred from this that all the fruits of Malaysian economic growth up to 1970 were plucked by the rich. On the contrary, the statistics show that the size of the 'middle class'—which is actually a highly privileged class in relation to the population in general—increased tremendously. Clearly there is no completely satisfactory objective definition of the middle class but it can be defined roughly, as was the poverty line. Say that a household was 'middle class' if it earned between $750 and $3,000 per month. Comparison of the *PES* with the adjusted *HBS* suggests that the number of such households grew from 22,000 in

1957 to 85,000 in 1970 (from 2 per cent of all households to over 5 per cent).

3. *Ethnic groups*. By contrast to nebulous socio-economic constructs such as 'the poor' and the 'middle class', the separate identities of the major ethnic groups are all too explicit a part of Malaysian society.

The simplest measure of income differences among the ethnic groups has been termed the 'disparity ratio': the ratio of the mean income of the non-Malays (or sometimes of the Chinese alone) to that of the Malays. The disparity ratios implied by the household surveys are given in Table 4.11, along with more recent estimates based on data published by the government. There is general agreement that the income of the average non-Malay household or of the average Chinese household alone has consistently been a bit more than twice that of the average Malay household. Although it is commonly believed that the disparity ratio has risen since Merdeka, Table 4.11 suggests that the value of the ratio changed little over the years.

TABLE 4.11
'DISPARITY RATIOS', 1957/8–1970

Year and source	*Non-Malay ÷ Malay*	*Chinese ÷ Malay*
A. Per household		
1957/8 adjusted *HBS*	2.21	2.16
1967/8 *SES* (cash income only)	2.26	2.32
1967/8 *SRM/Ford* survey	2.01	2.14
1970 *PES*	2.18	2.25
1973/4	2.14	2.21
1976	2.30	2.49
B. Per head		
1957/8 adjusted *HBS*	1.89	1.74
1967/8 *SES* (cash income only)	2.04	2.00
1967/8 *SRM/Ford* survey	1.94	1.84
1970 *PES*	2.12	2.03

Sources: Cited surveys, except for 1973/4 and 1976. The latter estimates are based on *MTR-TMP* (1979, pp. 44–5).

The household is a less satisfactory unit of observation for the study of ethnic income differences than it was for previous parts of this study because Malay, Chinese, Indian and Other households differ systematically in size and composition. The average Chinese household is largest in both earners and total members. Accordingly, the second part of Table 4.11 shows disparity ratios recalculated on a per capita basis, using estimates of mean household size generated by the various surveys. It can be seen that this redefinition reduces the values of all the ratios given, but only slightly. There is still no clear trend in the value of the ratio. Recalculation on a per earner basis would give similar results. It thus can be seen that differences in individual income account for most of the inter-group differences in mean household income, and that variations in the number of earners per household are a significant but much smaller influence.

One who looked only at the disparity ratio would miss much that is important with respect to income distribution among and within ethnic groups. For one thing, this measure is based entirely on relative incomes and tells nothing about changes in the absolute incomes of the various groups. Table 4.12 recalculates the measures given earlier in Table 4.10, with the population now divided up by ethnic groups rather than income size groups. This calculation shows that all three major ethnic groups shared significantly in aggregate income growth. Their shares in aggregate personal income were quite similar in 1970 to what they had been in 1957–8.[28]

TABLE 4.12
MEAN INCOME AND SHARES IN INCOME GROWTH, BY ETHNIC GROUP, 1957/8–1970
(MALAYS, CHINESE, AND INDIANS ONLY)

Ethnic group	*Mean income per household ($/month)*		*Income growth, 1957/8–70*		*Total personal income ($ million/year)*			*Per cent share of increase*
	1957/8	*1970*	*In $/month*	*In per cent*	*In 1957/8*	*In 1970*	*Increase*	
Malays	139	177	39	28	1,008	1,954	946	41
Chinese	300	399	100	33	1,299	2,426	1,127	49
Indians	237	310	74	31	358	673	315	14
Total	203	262	59	29	2,665	5,053	2,388	100

Finally, there remains the seldom-discussed topic of income distribution *within* ethnic groups. As before, the adjusted *HBS*, *SRM/Ford* survey and *PES* can be taken to define the best available estimate of actual trends. The relevant findings appear in Table 4.13, which is based on Tables 4.3, 4.6 and 4.7. They indicate that in each year inequality within each of the three major ethnic groups was less than within the population as a whole.[29] Over the 1957–70 period intra-group inequality rose for each group, but most for the Malays and least for the Chinese. Whereas in 1957–8 intra-group inequality was highest for the Chinese and lowest for the Malays, by 1970 this ranking was reversed. This finding accords well with the observation that the Chinese movement into modern, well-paid activities was more rapid and broadly-based than that of the Malays (or Indians). Few Chinese males remained employed in low-productivity agricultural or service-sector jobs by the late 1960s (Chinese females so employed were generally supplementary earners). The others had gone on to better-paid jobs in the urban economy or, increasingly toward the end of the period, in Singapore—to whose tight-

TABLE 4.13
DISTRIBUTION OF INCOME WITHIN MAJOR ETHNIC GROUPS, 1957/8–1970

Year and survey	*Per cent of total income*							
	Top 5 per cent	*Top 10 per cent*	*Top 20 per cent*	*Next 40 per cent*	*Bottom 40 per cent*	*Mean income ($/month)*	*Median income ($/month)*	*Gini ratio*
				Malays				
1957/8 Adjusted *HBS*	18.1	27.6	42.5	38.0	19.5	139	112	0.342
1967/8 *SRM/Ford* survey	22.2	32.7	48.2	34.8	17.0	163	120	0.400
1970 *PES*	24.6	36.2	52.5	34.8	12.7	177	122	0.466
				Chinese				
1957/8	19.6	30.5	45.8	36.2	18.1	300	223	0.374
1967/8	19.9	31.7	46.7	36.3	17.0	349	261	0.391
1970	25.3	37.1	52.6	33.5	13.9	399	269	0.455
				Indians				
1957/8	19.5	29.5	43.7	36.6	19.7	237	188	0.347
1967/8	22.3	32.7	48.1	35.6	16.3	260	191	0.403
1970	28.2	39.6	54.2	31.5	14.3	310	195	0.463

ening labour market they had easy access. By contrast, Malay movement into high-income jobs, largely in the public sector, was far more selective; masses of Malays—the great majority of them, in fact—remained in poorly-paid occupations such as rice cultivation, rubber smallholding and fishing.

On a more positive note, the 1957–70 period did see the beginnings of the creation of a Malay middle class. While fewer than 2,000 Malay households earned from $750 to $3,000 a month in 1957–8, some 18,000 did so in 1970. Malays thus joined, in significant numbers for the first time, those Chinese and Indians (52,000 and 11,000 households respectively) who were earning at this prosperous level.

Conclusions

This section has tried to formulate conclusions about trends and patterns of income inequality in Peninsular Malaysia since 1957. Caution is indicated because of the shaky data base and because of the importance of the subject—while accurate factual statements can contribute to constructive policy discussion, inaccurate ones can hardly do so. But however cautiously put, only tentative conclusions are possible. A number of researchers are at work on the subject, and survey data yet to be released may affect some of the conclusions about patterns and trends in inequality given here. In the meantime, the main conclusions indicated by this research can be briefly reiterated.

For 1957–70, the general trend is one of increasing inequality. This is evident in the overall distribution of personal income (and still more of total private income), in distributions within ethnic groups and in both urban and rural areas. The *share* of households living in poverty did not change substantially; the *absolute number* of such households therefore rose. The incomes of the higher income groups rose much faster, in percentage terms, than those in the bottom 80 per cent of the size distribution; many poor households probably experienced absolute income declines. Although all major ethnic groups shared significantly in the growth of aggregate personal income, non-Malay households continued to earn more than twice the income of Malay households on average.

Trends since 1970 are less fully documented. No full sets of income size distribution data for post-NEP years have yet been released. Summary measures published in the Mid-Term Review of the Third Malaysia Plan suggest that there may have been some further increase in overall inequality since 1970. As noted above, 'disparity ratios' and urban–rural differentials appear to have increased slightly. Mean incomes in the lowest four deciles of the income distribution rose less in 1970–6 than the mean for the distribution as a whole (based on *MTR-TMP*, 1979, pp. 29, 44; this observation applies to each of the major ethnic groups as well as the population as a whole). Yet the number of households living in poverty seems to have declined. So perhaps the pattern of growth since 1970 has been marginally more equitable than that which prevailed before 1970.

All these statements refer to incomes before the payment of taxes and

TABLE 4.14

EMPLOYMENT BY INDUSTRY, SEX AND ETHNIC GROUP, 1957 AND 1967
(Thousands)

	1957								
		Per cent distribution							
		Male				*Female*			
Industry	*Total (thousands)*	*Total*	*Malay*	*Chinese*	*Indian*	*Total*	*Malay*	*Chinese*	*Indian*
Agriculture, forestry, and fishing	1,223	67	43	16	8	33	18	9	6
Rubber estates	264	54	10	16	28	47	9	14	24
Rubber smallholdings	332	68	45	20	2	32	17	15	—
Other agriculture	545	69	56	10	2	31	25	4	2
Forestry	19	94	37	57	1	6	3	2	—
Fishing	61	99	67	31	1	1	1	—	—
Industry	288	86	19	53	13	14	3	9	1
Mining and quarrying	60	83	18	53	10	17	—	15	2
Manufacturing	160	85	13	58	12	16	6	9	1
Construction	68	92	32	42	16	8	—	5	2
Commerce	195	91	13	60	16	10	4	6	—
Public administration and defence	167	96	56	10	13	4	1	1	1
Other activities	277	79	25	33	18	21	4	14	2
Utilities	12	97	33	24	35	3	—	2	1
Transport and communication	78	98	36	38	21	2	—	1	—
Community services	76	72	33	24	13	29	9	13	4
Other services	110	69	13	38	17	31	4	25	3
Total	2,149	76	36	27	11	24	12	9	4

TABLE 4.14 (continued)

1967									
		Per cent distribution							
		Male				Female			
Industry	Total (thousands)	Total	Malay	Chinese	Indian	Total	Malay	Chinese	Indian
Agriculture, forestry and fishing	1,394	61	39	15	7	39	23	10	5
Rubber estates	222	49	12	15	23	51	12	15	23
Rubber smallholdings	474	59	41	13	5	41	24	15	1
Other agriculture	598	60	45	10	3	40	31	7	2
Forestry	31	96	39	58	—	4	2	2	—
Fishing	68	99	56	43	—	1	1	—	—
Industry	396	80	18	52	8	21	7	13	1
Mining and quarrying	69	88	19	59	9	12	1	9	1
Manufacturing	232	71	15	49	7	29	11	17	—
Construction	95	93	26	57	9	7	—	6	1
Commerce	312	80	18	53	9	20	8	12	—
Public administration and defence	210	95	65	14	14	6	2	2	1
Other activities	415	70	26	28	14	30	9	18	3
Utilities	17	95	44	13	38	5	—	1	3
Transport and communication	108	97	37	39	20	3	1	2	—
Community services	128	59	33	16	9	41	16	18	5
Other services	162	57	12	30	14	43	9	31	2
Total	2,727	70	33	26	9	30	15	11	3

Sources: Author's estimates, based primarily on Fell (1960) and Choudhry (1970), plus many secondary sources. Rubber estates data are from the Ministry of Labour. For methodological information see Snodgrass (1972; 1976). Percentages may not add to 100 because of rounding and the omission of Others.

Note: —indicates less than 0.5 per cent.

receipt of social benefits. As Chapter 6 will show, an increasing volume and improving incidence of fiscal redistribution helped to offset the increasing inequality of the distribution of private incomes during the 1957–70 period.

OTHER MEASURES OF INEQUALITY

This section summarizes the information available on other measures of inequality in economic results which are important to Malaysians: employment patterns and ownership and control of wealth.

Employment Patterns and Trends

The changes in employment structure associated with the growth and modernization of the economy before 1957, and the participation of the various ethnic groups in these changes, were discussed in Chapter 2. This section considers the nature and extent of the 'employment imbalance' referred to in the SMP and asks whether it improved or worsened after Independence.

Table 4.14 shows the employment structure of Peninsular Malaysia by major industry, sex, and ethnic group in 1957 and 1967. It can be seen that in 1957:

1. The industrial structure of employment was still fairly heavily agrarian; agricultural employment was 57 per cent of the total, industry only 13 per cent.

2. Malay employment was far less modernized than that of the other ethnic groups: 69 per cent of employed Malay males, and 88 per cent of the females, worked in agriculture; non-agricultural employment for Malays was concentrated in government-provided services.

3. The Chinese had the most modernized employment structure, with 66 per cent of the males (but only 42 per cent of the females) employed outside agriculture.

4. Indian employment was heavily concentrated in export agriculture, which engaged nearly 40 per cent of working Indian males and nearly 90 per cent of the females.

5. A marked pattern of ethnic concentration existed in many industries: public administration and rice cultivation were Malay-dominated; mining and commerce were Chinese-dominated, etc. Other important industries—rubber cultivation, much of the service sector—generally reflected the ethnic composition of the population.

Other aspects of 'employment imbalance' at the time of Independence do not emerge from tabulations of employment by industry. There was, and is, considerable heterogeneity within several industries with respect to the scale, technology and capital intensity of producing units. Thus rubber can be cultivated on tiny, weed-infested smallholdings or on vast, factory-like modern estates. Manufacturing employment can consist of cottage industries and repair shops or of large, machine-filled plants. Such differences imply considerable intra-industry variation in skill levels, output per worker and possibly pay.[30] Frequently, where there are such intra-industry differences, Malay employment is concentrated in the less modernized part of the industry. The true contrast between the industry structure of Malay employment and that of Chinese employment in 1957 is therefore greater than is indicated by Table 4.14. Malays were in fact under-represented in the more modern forms of production in agriculture and the service sector as well as in industry.

One set of data which strongly suggests these differences is shown in Table 4.15. In general, employees work in the more modern, organized enterprises while self-employed persons and unpaid family workers are engaged in more traditional forms of production.[31] Thus it is notable that many industries show striking differences between Malays and non-Malays as regards the prevalence of employee status in 1957. For example, 86 per cent of non-Malay forestry workers were employees but only 39 per cent of Malays were. Similarly, more than half of all Malays engaged in manufacturing were self-employed while 72 per cent of non-Malays were employees. These differences pervaded agriculture, industry and commerce in 1957, although they were much less evident in the service sector. Overall, twice as high a proportion of non-Malays as of Malays were employees.

TABLE 4.15
EMPLOYMENT STATUS BY INDUSTRY AND ETHNIC GROUP, 1957

		Per cent distribution					
		Malays			*Non-Malays*		
Industry	*Total (thousands)*	*Employees*	*Self-employed*	*Unpaid*	*Employees*	*Self-employed*	*Unpaid*
Agriculture, forestry and fishing	1,223	24	58	18	76	19	5
Rubber cultivation	596	57	36	7	91	7	1
Other agriculture	545	5	69	26	35	48	16
Forestry	19	39	54	7	86	13	1
Fishing	61	15	81	4	34	60	6
Industry	288	67	30	3	81	18	1
Mining and quarrying	60	98	1	—	94	6	—
Manufacturing	160	41	53	5	72	26	2
Construction	68	84	15	—	89	10	—
Commerce	195	23	71	6	44	52	4
Public administration and defence	167	100	—	—	100	—	—
Other activities	277	80	18	1	80	18	1
Utilities	12	99	1	—	98	2	—
Transport and communication	78	71	28	—	81	18	—
Community services	76	94	6	—	89	10	—
Other services	110	67	29	3	73	25	2
Total	2,149	37	49	14	74	22	3

Sources: Fell (1960, pp. 111–22); percentages may fail to add to 100 because of rounding.
Note: —indicates less than 0.5 per cent.

Table 4.16 corroborates these impressions by showing how the ethnic composition of employment in 1969 was correlated with plant size—and, through plant size, very probably with ethnicity of ownership (small manufacturing plants tend to be owned by Malaysian Chinese, while large ones are mostly foreign-owned). Employment in the small plants, as Table 4.16 shows, was at least three-quarters Chinese in 1969. Only in the larger units did Malay employment become significant. Moreover, the same can be said for Indians, Others and non-Malaysians: only in the larger firms did they appear in significant numbers. Clearly, industry-wide averages for ethnic employment shares can mask large intra-industry variations.[32]

TABLE 4.16

ETHNIC COMPOSITION OF MANUFACTURING EMPLOYMENT BY SIZE OF PLANT, DECEMBER 1969[1]

Number of full-time employees	*Malay*	*Chinese*	*Indian*	*Other Malaysian*	*Non-Malaysian*
1–4	7	87	4	0	2
5–9	14	79	4	0	3
10–19	16	76	5	0	3
20–29	14	78	5	0	2
30–49	19	72	6	0	3
50–99	23	66	7	0	4
100–199	28	60	7	1	4
200–499	38	48	9	1	4
500–	34	50	9	1	8
All sizes[2]	27	62	7	0	4

Source: Department of Statistics.

[1]Includes only plants covered by the 1969 *Survey of Manufacturing Industries*.

[2]Includes firms with no full-time employees.

Another dimension of 'employment imbalance' relates to the roles which workers play in the industries in which they are employed. This characteristic is imperfectly captured by the occupational statistics displayed in Table 4.17. Of the nine major occupational groups listed there, the first two could be considered to make up the economy's stock of high-level manpower. In 1957 Malays comprised 40 per cent of one of these groups (professional and technical) but only 16 per cent of the other (administrative, executive and managerial). This difference certainly bears some relationship to the fact that professional and technical jobs are concentrated in the public sector while administrative and managerial positions are more widely distributed among industries; 60 per cent of these categorized as professionals or technicians in 1957 were in fact teachers.

The next two occupational groups—clerical and sales—represent the lower ranges of 'white-collar' work. In both categories Malays were severely under-represented in 1957, even though many clerical jobs were in the government.

The remaining five occupational categories listed in Table 4.17 overlap so much with industry of employment that they add little to the knowledge gleaned from Table 4.14. (It does not help to learn that nearly all of those employed in agriculture are categorized occupationally as agricultural workers.)

Despite their limitations, the occupational data do help verify the Malay community's skimpy participation in white-collar work (except at the top level, and then only in the government) and in industrial blue-collar work. Statistically, Table 4.17 shows the Malays to be under-

TABLE 4.17
EMPLOYMENT BY OCCUPATIONAL GROUP, SEX AND ETHNIC GROUP, 1957 AND 1967

	Per cent distribution								
	Total	Male				Female			
Occupational group	*(thousands)*	*Total*	*Malay*	*Chinese*	*Indian*	*Total*	*Malay*	*Chinese*	*Indian*
1957									
Professional, technical, etc.	66	71	31	25	9	28	10	14	2
Administrative, managerial, etc.	25	98	17	61	12	2	—	1	—
Clerical	62	93	26	41	19	7	1	5	—
Sales and related	182	90	12	61	17	10	4	5	—
Agricultural	1,200	67	44	15	7	33	18	9	6
Miners	6	34	6	24	3	66	2	62	2
Transport and communication	67	98	41	39	16	2	—	1	—
Craftsmen, labourers, etc.	329	88	21	48	18	12	3	8	2
Service	183	79	36	18	11	21	4	15	2
Total	2,118	75	35	27	11	25	12	9	4
1967									
Professional, technical, etc.	135	68	34	22	6	32	13	14	5
Administrative, managerial, etc.	46	95	21	61	9	5	1	3	—
Clerical	113	79	26	37	14	21	4	14	1
Sales and related	262	76	16	51	9	24	10	14	—
Agricultural	1,318	59	40	11	6	41	25	11	6
Miners	27	74	14	51	8	26	2	25	—
Transport and communication	99	99	44	37	15	1	1	1	—
Craftsmen, labourers, etc.	506	80	29	38	13	20	7	11	1
Service	224	57	27	19	10	43	11	28	4
Total	2,727	68	34	24	9	32	16	12	4

Sources: Fell (1960, pp. 128–37); Choudhry (1970, Table 28).

Note: —indicates less than 0.5 per cent.

Totals may not add to 100 because of rounding and omission of Others. For 1967, adjustments were made to take account of the omission of institutional population from the Socio-Economic Survey and to adjust for sampling biases in terms of ethnic group.

represented in *every* major occupational category, except of course that of agricultural worker. The Chinese, by contrast, clearly supplied most of the rather modest skilled and educated labour inputs used by the economy in 1957. And of course most of the positions of greatest power and responsibility were still held in 1957 by Europeans, whose numbers were too small to be conspicuous in Table 4.17, except for the military forces then in the country to fight the 'Emergency'.

So much for ethnic imbalances in the 1957 employment pattern. As with income distribution, the next question to be considered is whether this form of inequality increased or lessened in the years after Merdeka.

Table 4.18 shows the ethnic composition of employment change by industry in 1957–67, together with value added per worker and mean cash income per worker by industry in 1967. It indicates that employment expansion during the decade was characterized by mild structural shifts. Agriculture, representing 57 per cent of initial employment, accounted for only 30 per cent of the increment and thus fell to 51 per cent of the total by 1967. The percentage points lost by agriculture were evenly distributed among industry, commerce and 'other activities'. Public administration and defence remained a constant share of total employment as a brisk rise in civilian employment was offset by a reduction in military forces.

Table 4.19 provides the equivalent information in terms of occupational groups. Here again there is a decline in agriculture's share and rises in all other categories—except service occupations, which fall slightly. Aside from agricultural jobs, the largest shares in employment growth are taken by craftsmen and labourers (29 per cent of the total), sales workers (13 per cent) and professionals and technicians (11 per cent).

What part did Malays take in this inter-sectoral labour transfer? The data[33] reveal some lessening of imbalance in both sectoral and occupational terms, although the extent of change is small. The inter-sectoral shift led Malays mainly into government employment, although they also scored some gains in the other non-agricultural industries, in which they had been so under-represented in the past. Actually, if one looks only at the five major industry groups shown in Table 4.18 one sees a rise in the Malay share of employment in *all five*—a phenomenon which statistically requires a rise in the Malay share of total employment, which did in fact occur according to my estimates. The relative shift, therefore, consists of the fact that the Malay share of employment in agriculture rose very little, while somewhat larger gains were made in industry and other activities, and the largest of all in public administration and defence and—for some reason—commerce.

Similarly, trends in ethnic shares in employment by occupational group show increases in the Malay share within each group but only a small increase for agricultural workers and much larger ones for other groups.

The major conclusions, therefore, with respect to 'employment imbalance' are (1) that it was indeed pronounced but (2) that it declined

TABLE 4.18

NET EMPLOYMENT CHANGES BY INDUSTRY, SEX AND ETHNIC GROUP, 1957–1967

Industry	*Value added per worker, 1967* ($)	*Cash income per worker, 1967* ($)		*Net employment increase, 1957–67 (thousands)*								
					Malays		*Chinese*		*Indians*		*Others*	
		Male	*Female*	*Total*	*M*	*F*	*M*	*F*	*M*	*F*	*M*	*F*
Agriculture, forestry, and fishing	1,500	1,000	400	+171	+9	+109	+12	+36	−1	−4	+2	+7
Rubber estates	1,500	1,100	600	−42	−1	+4	−8	−2	−23	−12	−1	—
Rubber smallholdings	1,100	(bracketed above)	(bracketed above)	+142	+42	+59	−4	+21	+17	+4	+1	+2
Other agriculture	1,600	800	200	+54	−34	+46	+7	+16	+6	+4	+1	+6
Forestry	3,200	1,200	300	+12	+5	—	+7	—	—	—	—	—
Fishing	3,200	(bracketed above)	(bracketed above)	+7	−3	—	+10	—	—	—	+1	—
Industry	4,200	2,200	700	+108	+19	+18	+53	+24	−5	−1	−1	+1
Mining and quarrying	7,600	2,400	1,100	+9	+2	+1	+9	−3	—	—	−1	—
Manufacturing	3,700	2,200	700	+72	+14	+17	+19	+25	−3	—	—	+1
Construction	3,000	2,100	1,000	+27	+3	—	+25	+2	−2	−1	—	—
Commerce	3,800	2,600	700	+117	+30	+17	+49	+26	−4	+1	—	—
Public administration and defence	2,200	3,700[1]	2,800[1]	+43	+43	+2	+13	+2	+8	+1	−25	—
Other activities	3,100	2,300[1]	1,000[1]	+138	+39	+25	+24	+37	+9	+6	−1	—
Electricity, water and sanitary services	11,000	2,700	2,000	+6	+3	—	+1	—	+1	—	—	—
Transport and communication	2,800	2,300	2,400	+30	+12	+1	+13	+1	+4	—	—	—
Community services	4,500	[1]	[1]	+51	+18	+14	+3	+13	+1	+4	—	—
Other services	1,500	2,100	800	+52	+6	+11	+7	+24	+3	+2	−2	—
Total[2]	2,500	1,700	900	+578	+140	+172	+150	+125	+6	+3	−26	+7

Sources: Value added per worker: Value added from Department of Statistics (1972). Employment from author's estimates. Data rounded to the nearest $100 per annum.

Cash income per worker: From special tabulation of data from the Socio-Economic Sample Survey of Households 1967–68. Income in kind is excluded, biasing the estimates against industries where it is important. However, allowance has been made for unpaid family workers, so that the figures refer to cash earnings *per worker*, not per earner. Data rounded to the nearest $100 per annum.

Employment increase: Same sources as Table 4.15. Failure of some of the rows and columns to add up is attributable to rounding.

[1]Community services included in Public administration and defence, and thus excluded from other activities.

[2]The number of workers whose industry was unspecified in the source fell from 18,000 in 1957 to 3,500 in 1967; this leads to a small overstatement of employment growth by industry, 1957–67.

gradually in the first decade after Independence.[34] After 1970 the government acted to accelerate that decline. Targets for the ethnic composition of employment in each major industry in 1990 were published in the *Mid-Term Review of the Second Malaysia Plan 1971–1975* (1973, pp. 76–80); subsequently the *Third Malaysia Plan 1976–1980* (1976, pp. 32–3, 186–9) listed official estimates of progress made in restructuring employment between 1970 and 1975. These data are reproduced in Table 4.20. They show significant increases in the Malay share of employment in all the industries in which Malays were seriously under-represented in the past: mining, manufacturing, construction and commerce. Similar gains were reported for major occupational groups. According to the TMP, these gains were made possible by high growth rates of total and Malay employment (at 3.5 and 4.0 per cent per annum respectively), coupled with slower rates of growth in Chinese and Indian employment (3.1 per cent and 2.8 per cent). Unemployment rates were reported to have fallen for Malays (from 8.1 per cent to 6.9 per cent), while rising slightly (from 7.0 to 7.2 per cent) for Chinese and sharply from an already high level for Indians (from 11.0 to 12.2 per cent). Further restructuring of employment was reported in the *Mid-Term Review of the Third Malaysia Plan* (1979, pp. 44–8). It is thus clear that the NEP has had a major effect on employment structure—conferring benefits on Malay job-seekers and further aggravating the job problems of Indians in particular.

Ownership and Control of Wealth

Although statistics relating to the ownership and control of wealth are sparse, the broad facts are obvious and spectacular enough. Wealth is held very unequally, regardless of whether one chooses to measure in terms of a size distribution, in terms of the division between Malaysian citizens and foreigners or in terms of ethnic groups. We can review the known facts in sectoral terms.[35]

In agriculture, the major crops are rubber (4.3 million acres planted in 1970), rice (1.3 million), oil palm (700,000) and coconut (500,000). Of these, only rice is a straightforward peasant crop. Rubber, oil palm and coconut are raised on plantings of widely varying sizes, which are conventionally divided into 'estates' and 'smallholdings' using 100 acres as the cut-off point. On this basis, nearly all the oil palm land, 37 per cent of the rubber and 10.5 per cent of the coconut area consisted of estates in 1970. Including FELDA schemes, estates aggregated 2.5 million acres, which was owned as shown in Table 4.21. Over 70 per cent of this land belonged to corporations, the stock of which was 70 per cent foreign-controlled. Malaysian ownership of shares in plantation corporations was almost exclusively Chinese. The non-corporate share has been increased in recent years through the activities of FELDA, which by 1970 accounted for about 15 per cent of estate acreage. Over 90 per cent of FELDA land has been allocated to Malays: FELDA is thus almost wholly responsible for the 350,000-acre (14 per cent) Malay stake in estate ownership in 1970.

TABLE 4.19

NET EMPLOYMENT CHANGE BY OCCUPATION, SEX AND ETHNIC GROUP, 1957–1967

	Cash income per worker, 1967 ($)			*Net employment increase, 1957–67 (thousands)*							
				Malays		*Chinese*		*Indians*		*Others*	
Occupational group	*Male*	*Female*	*Total*	*M*	*F*	*M*	*F*	*M*	*F*	*M*	*F*
Professional, technical, etc.	4,900	3,300	+69	+24	+10	+17	+9	+7	+4	−2	—
Administrative, managerial, etc.	6,700	4,600	+21	+5	+1	+14	+1	+1	—	—	—
Clerical	3,500	3,000	+51	+12	+5	+20	+12	+4	+1	−1	—
Sales and related	2,200	500	+80	+18	+16	+31	+23	−8	+1	−1	—
Agricultural	900	500	+118	+5	+101	−15	+27	−1	−4	+1	+6
Miners	2,200	1,000	+21	+4	—	+14	+3	+2	—	—	—
Transport and communication	2,100	1,500	+32	+14	—	+14	+3	+2	—	—	—
Craftsmen, labourers, etc.	1,700	700	+177	+70	+26	+51	+24	+5	—	—	+1
Service	2,600	900	+41	+9	+13	+7	+25	+2	+4	−21	+1
Total	1,700	800	+609	+159	+172	+151	+125	+15	+4	−24	+8

Sources: Cash income per worker: See notes to Table 4.17.
Employment increase: Same source as Table 4.16.

TABLE 4.20

ETHNIC COMPOSITION OF EMPLOYMENT BY INDUSTRY, 1970–1975

Industry	*1970* Total employment (thousands)	*1970* Ethnic shares (%) Malays	Chinese	Indians	*1975* Total employment (thousands)	*1975* Ethnic shares (%) Malays	Chinese	Indians
Agriculture, forestry and fishing	1,406.0	68	21	10	1,534.3	67	21	11
Mining	85.3	25	66	8	83.7	33	56	10
Manufacturing	263.9	29	65	5	362.8	33	60	7
Construction	77.6	22	72	6	97.4	29	60	10
Utilities	16.6	48	18	33	21.4	61	14	24
Transport and communication	119.4	43	40	17	161.0	47	38	15
Commerce	350.9	24	65	11	459.8	32	61	7
Service	474.0	49	36	14	596.8	51	36	11
Total	2,793.7	51	37	11	3,317.2	53	36	10

Source: *Third Malaysia Plan 1976–1980* (1976, p. 187). Components may not add to total because of rounding errors and exclusion of Others.

The fact that the foregoing data are defined initially in terms of citizenship, while earlier statistics on estate ownership use ethnicity as their primary classificatory-criterion, makes it hard to say what trends there have been in ownership shares.[36] The European share of rubber estate ownership declined significantly in 1947–57 and continued to drop between 1957 and 1966, the last year for which the old ownership data were published.[37] Some of this decline merely represents a shift of European acreage from rubber to oil palm, but it seems likely that the Asian share of estate acreage under all crops has been rising slowly. Most of this Asian acreage is Chinese-owned; the extent to which it is owned by citizens and non-citizens cannot easily be determined.

Smallholdings of rubber and coconut are generally less productive, acre for acre, than estates, and hence are less valuable. Perhaps two-thirds of rubber smallholdings belong to Malays but most Malay holdings are very small (three acres or less) and low in productivity. Probably less than half the acreage, and a still lower proportion of the wealth in monetary terms, is Malay. Coconut smallholdings are mostly Malay.

The smallholder share has risen since Independence in both rubber and coconut. In rubber it now amounts to more than 60 per cent (including FELDA acreage), compared to 46 per cent in 1957. There has been a similar trend in coconut cultivation, although precise numbers are not available. Smallholding ownership is obviously much more widely dispersed than shares in estate companies, so the shift of acreage to smallholdings evidently broadens the holding of productive agriculture-sector wealth. On the other hand, it has been argued (Swift, 1967; Fisk, 1961) that the ownership of the smallholdings themselves, particularly Malay-owned holdings, is becoming more concentrated over time.[38] Malay-owned rubber (and rice) lands, it is alleged, are gradually passing from the hands of the poorer peasants into those of a few richer peasants and of non-peasant landlords. Documentation for this thesis is sparse, although such a trend would be consistent with the income distribution trends discussed earlier, particularly the persistence of rural poverty.

Neither ethnicity nor foreign ownership is a major issue with respect to the rice-growing sector, which is practically all Malay-owned and operated.[39] There the more important question is tenancy, which affects about 40 per cent of Peninsular Malaysia's padi farms (see Chapter 7, below). There have been several studies of tenancy conditions *on operating holdings* in various parts of the country but none at all of *owners of padi land*. Hence nothing can be said, in general terms, about the degree of concentration of plot ownership. One would guess, however, that there is less agglomerated holding of rice land than of rubber land.

In the industrial sector, a distinction similar to that between estates and smallholdings can be made between 'modern' and 'traditional' mining, manufacturing and construction enterprise. A statistically viable proxy for 'modern' and 'traditional' is corporate and non-corporate.

TABLE 4.21

OWNERSHIP OF ESTATE ACREAGE, 1970[1]

	Corporations		*Others*		*Total*	
	'000 acres	*Per cent of total*	*'000 acres*	*Per cent of total*	*'000 acres*	*Per cent of total*
Malaysians	515.0	29.2	697.6	94.1	1,212.6	48.4
Malay	5.0	0.3	349.3	47.1	354.3	14.1
Chinese	457.0	25.9	243.3	32.8	700.3	27.9
Indian	4.9	0.3	74.8	10.1	79.7	3.2
Others	48.1	2.7	13.2	1.8	61.3	2.4
Government	—	—	17.0	2.3	17.0	0.7
Non-Malaysians	1,249.6	70.8	44.0	5.9	1,293.6	51.6
Total	1,764.6	100.0	741.6	100.0	2,506.2	100.0

Source: *MTR-SMP* (1973, p. 12).

[1]Includes all holdings of 100 acres or more planted with rubber, oil palm, coconut, or tea. FELDA schemes are included among 'Others' and classified by ethnic group (these schemes are individually owned in small plots but collectively managed at present on a scheme-wide basis). 'Government' holdings refer to government-owned estates.

Corporations accounted for 66 per cent of value added in mining, 60 per cent in manufacturing and 11 per cent in construction in 1967.[40] There were large foreign ownership shares in the former two cases—a long-established one in mining and one more recently built up through officially encouraged investment in manufacturing. As Table 4.22 shows, foreigners controlled nearly three-quarters of corporate capital in mining and 60 per cent in manufacturing in 1970. The foreign share in mining had recently declined from still higher levels through sales of assets to

TABLE 4.22

OWNERSHIP OF SHARE CAPITAL OF LIMITED COMPANIES OPERATING IN PENINSULAR MALAYSIA, BY SECTOR, 1970[1]

Ownership	Rubber		Other agriculture		Tin mining		Other mining		Manufacturing		Construction		Transport		Banks		Insurance companies	
	$m.	*Per cent*	*$m.*	*Per cent*	*$m.*	*Per cent*	*$m.*	*Per cent*	*$m.*	*Per cent*	*$m.*	*Per cent*	*$m.*	*Per cent*	*$m.*	*Per cent*	*$m.*	*Per cent*
Malay individuals and interests	3	—	11	4	3	1	1	—	34	2	1	2	11	13	3	3	—	—
Chinese individuals	150	13	27	9	73	17	18	17	296	22	31	53	35	43	24	26	2	22
Indian individuals	15	1	1	—	2	1	—	—	9	1	—	1	2	2	—	—	—	—
Governments and statutory bodies	—	—	5	2	—	—	—	—	15	1	—	—	3	3	10	11	—	—
Other residents and locally controlled companies[2]	85	7	55	19	44	10	7	6	190	14	6	10	21	26	24	25	2	22
Sub-total: Residents	254	22	99	33	124	29	26	24	544	40	38	66	72	88	61	65	3	45
Non-residents and foreign controlled companies	881	78	199	67	311	71	83	76	804	60	20	34	10	12	33	35	4	55
Total 1	1,134	100	298	100	434	100	109	100	1,348	100	58	100	82	100	94	100	8	100

TABLE 4.22 (continued)

Ownership	*Other financial institutions*		*Wholesale trade*		*Retail trade*		*Other industries*		*All industries*	
	$m.	*Per cent*	*$m.*	*Per cent*	*$m.*	*Per cent*	*$m.*	*Per cent*	*$m.*	*Per cent*
Malay individuals and interests	18	3	4	1	1	1	13	2	103	2
Chinese individuals	130	24	110	24	75	48	220	38	1,192	23
Indian individuals	4	1	1	—	3	2	13	2	52	1
Governments and statutory bodies	3	1	—	—	—	—	11	2	48	1
Other residents and locally controlled companies[2]	85	16	20	4	6	4	142	24	686	13
Sub-total: Residents	240	45	135	30	86	56	400	69	2,081	39
Non-residents and foreign controlled companies	296	55	316	70	69	45	183	31	3,208	61
Total	536	100	451	100	155	100	583	100	5,289	100

Source: Department of Statistics; see also *MTR-SMP* (1973, p. 12).

[1]In agriculture, share capital totals were estimated from acreage data; for government-held enterprises, value of fixed assets was used.

[2]The ownership of these controlling companies was apparently unascertainable, although it can be assumed to reflect the ethnic pattern reflected in the preceding lines of the Table.

Malaysians, nearly all ethnic Chinese.[41] Similarly, Chinese took an overwhelmingly dominant position within the domestically-owned portion of modern manufacturing. Corporations engaged in construction were nearly all Chinese-owned.

Foreign enterprise has long had a strong position in banking, insurance, other financial institutions and wholesale trade (Puthucheary, 1960; Tan, 1977). This continued to be the case in 1970, as Table 4.21 indicates, despite considerable expansion by domestically-owned institutions—predictably heavily Chinese. These are industries in which most of the business is done by corporations. The remaining sectors of the economy—transportation, retail trade and private services—are dominated by unincorporated enterprises and individuals. Foreigners have little stake in this part of the economy, and the Malay share is also small—except in transportation, where there has long been a policy to increase Malay involvement. Small firms are owned and managed primarily by Malaysian Chinese.[42] Independent professionals are nearly all Malaysians, mainly Chinese.[43]

In summary, it will be evident from the foregoing survey—impressionistic as it is—that the Malaysian economy in 1970 was strongly marked by two kinds of concentration, or imbalance, in ownership and control.

1. Large parts of modern agriculture, industry and commerce—overall, as much as 61 per cent of the corporate sector, according to Table 4.22—were in foreign hands.

2. The large minority of the corporate sector and the majority of unincorporated business which are Malaysian-owned and controlled were overwhelmingly Chinese. Up to 1970 Malay individuals and interests owned only such traditional productive facilities as rubber and coconut smallholdings, padi fields, and small fishing craft and gear—plus a few small, newly-established enterprises in transportation and other industries. Similarly, Indians—although a much smaller community—also had little stake in the ownership and control of enterprise.

Broadly speaking, there was no visible tendency for the structure of ownership and control to change before 1970. Since that year, according to summary statistics published by the government, the share of corporate capital held by foreigners has fallen from 63.3 per cent (1970) to 46.0 per cent (1978) (*TMP*, 1976, pp. 33–4, 190; *MTR-TMP*, 1979, pp. 48–50). The Malay share (including holdings by Malay interests) rose from 2.4 per cent to 10.3 per cent over the same period. These trends permitted a rise in the share of non-Malay Malaysians, so trends in the early 1970s seem consistent with the redistribution-at-the-margin principle of the NEP.[44]

This industry-by-industry survey of ownership and control, plus the survey of income distribution undertaken earlier, strongly suggests a highly skewed size distribution of personal wealth, as well as marked inter-communal differences. The personal distribution of wealth cannot be measured directly, but there are data on ownership of specific assets which hint at the extent of inter-communal disparities. Table 4.23 shows

TABLE 4.23

INDICATORS OF PERSONAL WEALTH, 1967–1968

	Malays	*Chinese*	*Indians*	*All urban*	*All rural*
Per cent of adults who own:					
Stocks	2	1	3	2	1
Life insurance	1	4	9	6	2
A bank account	8	12	10	15	8
Who live in a household possessing:					
An electric fan	8	31	16	37	8
A camera	2	9	4	12	2
An air conditioner	0	1	0	1	0
A refrigerator	4	16	9	22	3
A sewing machine	52	80	44	74	56
A radio	63	66	70	71	62
A typewriter	4	10	5	12	3
A gas stove	1	10	11	14	1
A television set	8	11	12	22	3
A motor-cycle	9	20	7	16	11
A car	5	17	7	20	5
Its own home	82	64	16	52	75

Source: *SRM/Ford Social and Economic Survey 1967/68.*

that Chinese were half again likely to own a bank account as Malays in 1967–8, twice as likely to own a motor-cycle and more than three times as likely to own a car. Ownership of other consumer durables shows similar differentials, although for two items which have widely pervaded Malaysian society—the radio and the sewing machine—inter-group differentials were much narrower. Malays are more likely to own their own homes than Chinese—and much more likely to do so than Indians—but this is more indicative of differences among *kampung*, town and estate life-styles than of the ownership of wealth in the form of housing. Data on the quality of housing—space occupied and access to various amenities—show the average Malay to be living under conditions far inferior to those of the average Chinese.

CONCLUSIONS

This chapter has examined three kinds of inequality in economic results. In all three cases—income, participation in modern-sector employment, and ownership and control of wealth—large inequalities have been found among individuals and ethnic groups. There can be no doubt that such inequalities are a marked feature of Malaysian society.

If one is interested in the amelioration of economic inequality then it is important to determine whether the extent of inequality is increasing or decreasing through time. Trends in inequality up to 1970 appear to be inconsistent across the three types of inequality surveyed.

1. *Income inequality* was found to have increased significantly in size-distribution terms and within the major ethnic groups, but not (or much less) as among ethnic groups.

2. Malay *participation* in modern-sector and high-status employment increased slowly in 1957–67; the ethnic specificity of employment by industry and occupational group declined.

3. *Ownership and control of wealth* in the modern sector continued to be divided between foreigners and Malaysian Chinese; no trend is perceptible in the fragmentary data available.

Since 1970 inequalities in participation and wealth ownership have declined, while income inequality may have continued to increase. However, the period since 1970 is short and only limited data are available. To understand what might be expected to happen in the future, one must go beyond these fragmentary indications of trends and examine the *inequalities in causes* which produced the observed *inequalities in results*. This will be done in Chapter 5.

1. To say that *greater equality* would be socially stabilizing does not imply that a *movement from greater to lesser inequality*—let alone *political action to bring about such a movement*—would necessarily be stabilizing. On the contrary, any such transition period is likely to be stormy, since it can arouse fears in those who are losing their previous privileged position while generating heightened expectations in the unprivileged which may not be capable of realization in the immediate future.

2. This section is a condensed and revised version of D. R. Snodgrass (1975b). Several other analysts (Sudhir Anand, 1973; Lim Lin Lean, 1971, 1974; Charles Hirschman, 1974; Eddy Lee, 1975) have studied the 1957–70 data, reaching generally similar but occasionally divergent conclusions.

3. Information on household size by income level is needed to convert income per household to income per capita. Such information is available only for the *SRM/Ford* survey, the *PES* and the *HES*. Anand (1973, p. 28) found very similar Lorenz curves for the distributions of household and per capita income; their Gini coefficients were 0.5129 and 0.4980 respectively. Table 4.11 calculates inter-communal 'disparity ratios' on a per household and a per head basis. I am similarly unable to take account of the age-structure influences on cross-sectional income distributions which Kuznets has stressed recently (1975).

4. There are well-known objections to the Gini ratio or to any other single measure of overall inequality. It is, however, possible to avoid ambiguity while achieving comparability with other studies by using the Gini ratio and checking it against the decile shares.

5. Availability of these sources is as follows:
HBS: Department of Statistics (n.d., *c*. 1960–1); no further information available.
FSS: Conducted by Department of Economics, University of Malaya, Singapore, 1960. Full results of this survey were never published and are now said to be lost. Many of the findings can be reconstructed from Tables given in Lee Hock Lock (1971). Partial results are given in K. R. Chou (1960).
SES: Department of Statistics (1974), plus some detailed breakdowns which have not been published.
SRM/Ford: This 'Survey' is a special tabulation of data collected for commercial purposes

by the marketing research firm Survey Research Malaysia.
PES: Department of Statistics, Kuala Lumpur. Detailed income data are forthcoming; selected distributions appear in the *Mid-Term Review of the Second Malaysia Plan 1971–1975* (1973). Related information has been published in Department of Statistics (1971).

6. Oddly, no zero-income households are reported. This should lead to understatement of inequality.

7. The theoretical range of the Gini concentration ratio is from zero (complete equality) to one (complete inequality). Values actually observed in income distributions usually lie between 0.3 and 0.6. All ratios cited here are approximations based on decile shares in the size distribution. There values are slightly lower than those which would result if a larger number of income classes were used.

8. The definitions of both income and a household differ between the two sources. Downward reporting bias is probably greater in the tax data, which are from Department of Inland Revenue (1960, p. 15; 1961, p. 14). The adjustment raises estimated household income to $2,885 million, or 80 per cent of the national accounts-based total. This adjustment of the *HBS* data was first made by Silcock in T. H. Silcock and E. K. Fisk (1963, pp. 1–3, 276–81), and also used by Charles McLure (1972).

9. Tables 4.3 to 4.7 show the distribution of income among percentage shares of households ranked by income size. These distributions are transformations of the original data, which give numbers of households in specific income ranges (e.g. $100–150 per month).

10. The most comprehensive comparative analysis is Felix Paukert (1973). In the US$201–300 range of GDP per head, in which Malaya fell in 1957–8, the mean share of the top 5 per cent is 32 per cent. Paukert (pp. 111–14), following Oshima, understates inequality in Malaya by using uncorrected *HBS* data.

11. Paukert's mean for the share of the lowest four deciles in countries in the US$201–300 range is only 12.8 per cent.

12. This is the famous 'Kuznets hypothesis', which was put forth as a speculation in Simon Kuznets (1955). The hypothesis has been questioned by several scholars, but it is consistent with the findings of Paukert (1973), who found the Gini ratio to be highest, on average (about 0.50), around GDP per capita of US$300, and to decline thereafter to an average of 0.365 for levels above US$2,000. It should be stressed that these findings are based on cross-section data and do not necessarily forecast future events in presently less developed countries—still less, in a particular country such as Malaysia.

13. One economist who served as an *FSS* enumerator while a student in 1960 reports that many forms 'were filled in while sitting beneath a tree'. His view is that the *FSS* findings cannot be taken seriously.

14. Not discussed here is the Family Planning Survey of 1966/67 (National Family Planning Board, 1968), which collected household income data as part of its background information. Except for the mean income found—which at $170–180 per month was very badly understated—the results were not published in its report and have not become available to me.

15. Non-cash income has three components: production for own consumption; employee payments in kind; and implied rent on owner-occupied housing. Together these represented a significant share of total household income, although a smaller one than in most Asian countries. A very rough estimate of non-cash income in Peninsular Malaysia in 1967–8 is $400–500 million, or $20–30 a month for the average household.

16. The 1970–1 round of the SRM survey, which was examined but is not discussed here, shows severe problems of non-response and understatement of income. These may arise from deviations from randomness in sample selection.

17. As already discussed, the *FSS* (1959) finding, which runs counter to this trend, is heavily discounted.

18. Lim (1974) and Hirschman (1974) concur with this conclusion, while Anand (1973) concludes—with excessive caution, in my view—that it is impossible to say anything about change in inequality in 1957–70.

19. Property incomes in rubber, tin and other export industries can rise tremendously during an export boom. In the presence of labour surplus and absence of strong trade unions, labour incomes are likely to rise much less if at all. Since property income is undoubtedly heavily concentrated in the hands of the top few per cent of income recipients, the short-term worsening of inequality could be considerable.

20. The following is an illustrative calculation for the rubber estate industry which traces the property and labour shares of income through the 1967–70 price cycle:

	1967	*1968*	*1969*	*1970*
1. Production ('000 tons)	525.8	563.0	593.4	617.9
2. Average price ($/ton)	1.211	1,190	1,564	1,264
3. Total revenue ($ million) (1 x 2)	636.7	670.0	928.1	781.0
4. Wage bill ($ million)	311.8	283.2	300.0	294.2
5. Wage share (%) (4 ÷ 3)	49	42	32	38
6. Property income plus non-labour costs ($ million)	324.9	386.8	628.1	486.8

Source: *Monthly Statistical Bulletin of West Malaysia*, various issues. Average price is the price of RSS 1 on the Malaysia/Singapore Rubber Exchange.

Note: The foregoing calculation is a rough one, since the price and wage bill data are rough and no allowance has been made for fluctuations in the cost of non-labour inputs. However, it is clearly indicative of the wide swings in property income induced by product price fluctuations.

21. Another comparison which suggests changes in the share of higher income recipients is that between income assessed for income tax purposes and the national accounts-based estimate of personal income which is reflected in Table 4.1. The comparison is as follows:

	(1) *Assessed income* (*$ million*)	(2) *Estimated personal income* (*$ million*)	*(3)* *(1)* ÷ (2)
1957	457	3,743	0.12
1958	475	3,656	0.13
1959	473	3,971	0.12
1960	724	4,229	0.17
1961	763	4,435	0.17
1962	859	4,687	0.18
1963	864	5,016	0.17
1964	998	5,335	0.19
1965	1,103	5,579	0.20
1966	1,294	5,811	0.22
1967	n.a.	6,060	n.a.
1968	1,325	6,284	0.21
1969	1,368	6,925	0.20

Source: Column (1) from *Annual Reports* of the Department of Inland Revenue. 'Assessed income' is the total assessed up to 31 December of the succeeding year for the years 1957–66, up to 31 March only for 1968 and 1969; data for 1967 have not been published. Column (2) derived as explained in footnotes to Table 4.1 above. Two things are notable in column (3) of the foregoing table: the secular rise in the share of personal income assessed for tax purposes and the tendency of the ratio to rise in boom years such as 1960 and 1964–5 (although not in 1969). The rising trend is probably attributable to a combination of improved tax enforcement (there was little expansion in legal coverage) and a rising share of income accruing to the high-income group liable to the tax. The spurts in 1960 and 1964–5 reinforce the suspicion that booms disproportionately increase the incomes of the rich. The absence of a similar spurt in 1969, which is the year of most rapid growth in estimated personal income, is undoubtedly explained by the disruptions of that year, which held down the amount of income which had been assessed by 31 March 1970.

22. At least, one hopes that it does. Since the definitions of the income concepts used in the various surveys are less explicit than one would like, the possibility that some incomes were erroneously reported after tax cannot be ruled out.

23. The four surveys are the Household Expenditure Survey (1973), the Household Income Survey (1973), the 1974 Labour Force Survey and the Agriculture Census (actually a 10 per cent sample of all households) (1976).

24. The difference in findings between the *SRM/Ford* survey of 1967/68 and the 1970 *PES* may result in large part from short-term fluctuations. Although rubber, tin and other export commodities are produced mainly in rural areas, it is likely that much of the income generated—and especially the more variable components of the income flow—accrues to urban residents. If so, this would cause the urban–rural differential to widen and narrow in step with trade-induced fluctuations in GNP.

25. If inequality in rural areas is less than in the economy as a whole, it may seem like a necessary condition that urban inequality should be greater than overall inequality. This is not the case, however, as will be seen when the patterns within ethnic groups are discussed. Inequality within the total population can be (and in that case is) greater than inequality in any of its components.

26. Note, however, that this makes *inter-group* comparisons rather risky. In comparing Malays with Chinese in Table 4.9, for example, one should take account of the fact that Malays are more predominantly rural and may therefore face lower prices (they may also have more omitted or understated non-cash income). On the other hand, Chinese households are larger in terms of both total members and adults. Such ambiguities are less important for inter-temporal comparisons, which are stressed in the text.

27. As explained in the footnotes to Table 4.2, growth in the number of households is hard to measure. Multiplying the estimates of total households adopted in Table 4.2 by the shares appearing in Table 4.10 gives the absolute number of households living in poverty as 390,000 in 1957–8; 534,000 in 1967–8; and 565,000 in 1970. Although these specific numbers are obviously questionable, the implied increase is large enough to make it clear that there is *some* rise in the number of households earning less than $120 a month between 1957 and 1970. Moreover, as Eddy Lee (1975; 1977) has pointed out, the numbers imply that the absolute incomes of many poor rural households declined between these two years.

28. 'Others' have been excluded from this Table because they are omitted from the 1957–8 data, except for households with $10,000 or more of assessed annual income. Judging from income tax data, their share in personal income may have declined absolutely between 1957–8 and 1970. Conversely, the 'Other' share in ownership, and in private incomes which escape inclusion in personal income because they are retained by firms, taxed away or remitted abroad, may well have increased.

29. This pattern is made possible by the fact that each of the three ethnic-group distributions had a different mean. There has been a tendency for each group's distribution to cluster around its own mean in a tighter distribution than the one produced by the cluster of incomes in the entire society around *their* mean. This might be taken to suggest the importance of ethnicity in the determination of household income, a matter which will be explored in Chapter 5.

30. Pay is often higher in the more modern establishments, especially if a higher skill level is required. But this is not invariably the case. Estate labourers, for example, receive a steadier income than smallholders but not necessarily a higher one (it is higher in years of low rubber prices but lower in good years); the skills involved are practically identical.

31. There are of course exceptions to this generalization (employers in modern establishments, independent professionals) but the numbers involved are small.

32. A study of employment patterns in Penang by Basil Moore (n.d., *c.* 1974–5) helps to sort out the size and ethnicity variables discussed here. Moore found that larger firms hired more Malays than smaller firms. When allowance was made for the average size difference in firm size, foreign-owned firms did not appear to employ a significantly larger fraction of Malays than did locally-owned firms as a group. Among locally-owned firms, however, those owned by Chinese hired about 12 per cent fewer Malays at each occupational level than did those owned by non-Chinese.

33. Malay shares in 1957 employment, 1957–67 employment growth and 1967 employment, respectively, are estimated to have been as follows:

	1957	*1957–67 change*	*1967*
Agriculture, forestry and fishing	61	69	62
Industry	22	34	26
Commerce	16	40	26
Public administration and defence	57	105	67
Other agriculture	30	46	35
Professional, technical, etc.	41	49	45

	1957	*1957–67 change*	*1967*
Administrative, managerial, etc.	16	29	22
Clerical	26	33	29
Sales and related	16	43	24
Agricultural	62	90	64
Miners	0	19	15
Transport and communication	42	44	43
Craftsmen, labourers, etc.	24	54	34
Service	40	54	42
Total employment	47	54	49

34. Charles Hirschman, who studied ethnic group changes in occupational patterns in 1931–67, also noted the slight lessening of 'employment imbalance' in the post-Independence decade. This, he said, represented a reversal of the 1947–57 experience:

'There is a trend toward similarity in the occupational distributions of Malays and Chinese from 1931 to 1947, but the gap widens from 1947 [to] 1957. This might be due to a trend toward shared poverty during the Depression and war years, when many marginal Chinese urban workers and tin miners became small farmers. However, the postwar era created new opportunities, and the Chinese occupational structure seemed to shift more than the other two during the years 1947 to 1957. Perhaps because of greater access to education and the urban milieu, Chinese had an advantage in the urban job market over Malays' (Hirschman, 1975, p. 78).

35. For a knowledgeable discussion of the distribution of wealth and its influence on the distribution of income, see Tan Tat-wai (1977, pp. 210 ff).

36. The data in Table 4.19 cannot be compared with the earlier data because an unknown proportion of non-Malaysians are Chinese (especially) and Indian.

37. Department of Statistics (1967). A handy summary of the historical data appears in Lim Chong Yah (1967, p. 331). The European share of estate acreage was 74.6 per cent in 1947, 64.3 per cent in 1957 and 55.8 per cent in 1966.

38. Statistics on smallholding ownership are very sparse. This pattern is documented for rubber smallholdings in 1953, however, by Lim (1967, p. 332).

39. This situation results in part from strong measures taken in the past, and continuing up to the present, to prevent the acquisition of rice land by non-Malays. See Chapter 7, below.

40. Based on a comparison of the data given in Department of Statistics (1969) and in Department of Statistics (1971a).

41. See Yip Yat Hoong (1968); Yip found that while share ownership in this traditionally European segment of the industry moved heavily into Malayan hands between 1954 and 1960, *control* of the firms involved remained in the hands of European directors.

42. An imperfect measure of small-firm ownership, which refers to industry and services together, is the ethnicity of registrations of unincorporated businesses. These data, for 1957 and 1971, are as follows:

	1957		*1971*	
Ethnic group	*('000)*	*Per cent of total*	*('000)*	*Per cent of total*
Malays	13.8	15.5	24.5	15.4
Chinese	66.1	74.3	113.7	71.1
Indians	8.7	9.8	20.8	13.0
Others	0.3	0.4	0.8	0.5
All groups	94.0	100.0	159.9	100.0

Source: Department of Inland Revenue (1960, p. 21; 1974, p. 74).

These data suggest that 70–75 per cent of unincorporated businesses are Chinese-owned and that any decline in this proportion is small. The statistics are only suggestive because (1) they only show *numbers* of businesses registered, with no weighting by size, and (2) there may be substantial under-registration, especially of the smaller firms and in the more remote parts of the country.

43. A Department of Statistics survey conducted in 1971 and covering lawyers, doctors, dentists, architects, engineers, accountants and surveyors showed 94 per cent of those members of these professions who were not government-employed to be Malaysians. By ethnic group, 71 per cent of the Malaysians were Chinese, 19 per cent Indian and 8 per cent Malay. The data reflect both the paucity of qualified Malays in these professions and the tendency for those who do exist to be employed in the public sector—as were 60 per cent of the Malays, compared to only 35 per cent of the non-Malay Malaysians.

44. For a study of shareholdings in manufacturing companies in 1974–5 which looks at the size distribution of holdings as well as the distribution in terms of citizenship and ethnicity, see Sieh-Lee Mei Ling (1977). One of the findings of this study is that non-Malaysian holdings are much more concentrated than Malaysian holdings. This suggests the possibility that foreign *control* of the corporate sector could be even more extensive than is indicated by the large foreign *ownership* share.

5 Social Science Analyses

Of race, class, and I.Q. [title of a 'Report From Kuala Lumpur', Schmid, 1973]

LARGE variations among ethnic groups with respect to mean levels of income, wealth and employment patterns have now been documented. Are these variations statistically significant, and, if so, what is the causal mechanism at work? These are important questions for anyone interested in policy prescription, since, as in medicine, accurate diagnosis is likely to be necessary before a cure can be effected. Some elementary manipulation of available income statistics will help to launch the inquiry.

DECOMPOSITIONS AND CORRELATIONS

That ethnicity is a statistically significant correlate of household and individual income in Malaysia on a simple correlation basis can be established by F tests[1] conducted on available income distributions. In the 1957/8 *HBS* distribution of income among households, for example, the null hypothesis that Malay, Chinese and Indian households are drawn from a homogeneous population is decisively rejected ($F_{.05} = 89.34$; $F_{.01} = 4.62$). Similar results are obtained for the *SES* (1967/8) and *PES* (1970). Moreover, ethnicity continues to be highly significant in unpublished cash income data from the *SES* which show the size distributions of cash incomes of male workers by ethnic group within major industrial and occupational categories (Table 5.1). Here the Chinese receive the highest mean income among the three major ethnic groups in all cases except five in which the Indians push them into second place. The value of F is highly significant in all cases, regardless of whether the 'Others', who are generally much more highly paid, are included in the analysis.

These results might seem to conflict with the findings of other researchers who find ethnicity *not* to be a major statistical determinant of income once certain 'other factors' are taken into account. Thus Sudhir Anand (1973) expressed inequality in the distribution of individual incomes in the *PES* sample in terms of a Theil index,[2] which permits decomposition into two components: a between-occupation component and a between-race component within occupational groups. Eight occupation groups and four ethnic groups were used. On this basis, Anand found that inter-occupation group variation constituted a much larger proportion of total variation than did inter-ethnic group variation within

TABLE 5.1
MEAN INDIVIDUAL CASH INCOME BY
ETHNIC GRÓUP, INDUSTRY, AND OCCUPATION, 1967–1968
($ per month)

	Malays	*Chinese*	*Indians*	*Others*	*All groups*
			Industries		
Agriculture: non-export	66	137	176	62	80
Agriculture: export	69	144	120	611	97
Mining and quarrying	170	210	175	742	198
Manufacturing	120	210	172	566	185
Construction	116	187	177	559	169
Utilities	188	352	200	631	221
Commerce	135	255	178	555	219
Transport and communication	161	212	211	421	191
Services	217	286	238	786	256
			Occupations		
Professional, technical and managerial	298	434	462	830	388
Administrative, executive and managerial	415	494	576	876	504
Clerical	264	284	333	491	290
Sales	119	237	143	183	198
Agricultural	64	133	106	158	82
Miners	162	176	168	864	178
Transport and communication	150	176	181	730	176
Craftsmen and production process workers	128	172	165	757	166
Labourers	121	157	133	219	134
Services	186	224	172	655	204

Source: *SES*, unpublished data.

occupational categories. A similar analysis in which industries replaced occupations yielded comparable results. Anand also fit a 'human capital model', using education and work experience as independent variables, to the earnings of male urban employees (a group selected in the hope of minimizing the effect of property income, which is an unknown proportion of total income as reported in the data). Using just these variables, and ignoring ethnicity, he 'explained' from 13 to 46 per cent of income variation within eight occupational groups and 42 per cent of variation among all urban male employees.

Similarly, Charles Hirschman (1975) studied the influence of ethnicity and other factors on income, educational attainment and occupational mobility using data from the 1966–7 West Malaysian Family Survey, which include the rare datum of father's occupation. His broad conclusion was that:

> Statistically controlling for social background reduces the ethnic gap (Malay-Chinese) in income by almost two-thirds and the educational gap by eighty per cent. For both income and education the social background factors which account for most of the ethnic gap are Father's Occupation and Birthplace. Effects of Years of Schooling and Occupation, net of other social background factors, seem not to have much effect on the inequality of income among ethnic groups. I interpreted these patterns as indicating that ethnic inequality is basically due to an inheritance of poverty, or of rural agrarian origin, rather than any strong effect of ethnicity alone . . . (Hirschman, 1975, p. 79).

The trouble with these analyses is that they might lull the unsuspecting reader into assuming that such 'other factors' as occupation and educational attainment are variables which are independent of ethnicity. If this assumption were correct, then the statistical analyses would indeed have established that ethnicity is a relatively unimportant influence on income inequality. But the assumption is not correct. As discussed in other chapters, ethnicity has had, and continues to have, an important bearing on occupation, education and practically every 'other factor' one can think of. So the conclusion would not be warranted. In fact, by appealing to variables which have so obviously been influenced by ethnicity the statistical analyses serve to emphasize rather than downgrade the ultimate importance of ethnicity. The question, therefore, is not whether there is a relationship between ethnicity and economic inequality but what the precise nature of the relationship is. To get at this issue requires explicit theorizing.

THE PROBLEM OF HIGH OR LOW ECONOMIC ACHIEVEMENT

Conventional economic theory does not take one very far toward an explanation of inequalities of the sort observed in the Malaysian case. The neo-classical theory of income distribution explains the size distribution of income in terms of the ownership pattern of assets used in the production process (physical and human capital), household labour supply and the relative returns to each of these assets. Certain useful conclusions about likely patterns and trends in income distribution flow from this theory, especially if account is taken of departures from competition likely to be found in the factor and product markets of developing countries. Additional explanatory power can be derived from classical (Ricardian and Marxian) distribution theories, while the more recently formulated job competition model helps to explain the effect of modern sector employment expansion on the size distribution of income.[3] But none of these theories explains why *particular* households possess more productive assets, and perhaps also obtain higher rates of return on them, thus earning consistently higher incomes than other households—why, for example, one community may have achieved a mean income twice as high as another community living beside it in the same country.

This is an absolutely fundamental problem of development, analogous to the question of why one country develops rapidly while another does not. Both questions are so complex that they can be explored but will probably never be fully resolved. In a sense, however, there are only two possible solutions:

1. The *opportunities* open to the groups differ (or at least have differed in the past) as a result of discrimination by other members of society or by the government. These discriminatory practices could be conscious or unconscious. They could be malevolent in intent, misguidedly benevolent or merely a side effect of actions taken for some unconnected purpose.

2. The *responsiveness* of the groups to economic opportunities is (or has been) different as a result of differences in tastes or abilities.

a. *Tastes* could differ systematically among groups with respect to key values such as the relative preference for work versus 'leisure' (more properly, activities not usually defined as 'work'), present consumption versus future consumption and surer gains versus larger but riskier ones. Greater work-orientation, greater future-orientation and perhaps also greater risk-preference could thus cause a group to become relatively richer through time, purely as a result of its preferences.

b. *Abilities*. Given identical tastes and opportunities, the capacities of different groups to respond might vary systematically. Such differences in ability could be inherent or they could be acquired through education, training and experience.

In the case of two groups occupying the same geographic area and living under the same political authority the opportunity factor is equalized to some extent (although it may still differ because of inherited advantages and disadvantages, or because of official or private discrimination). In these circumstances, it has been suggested that 'the group whose culture is best suited for the exploitation of a given environment tends to become dominant' (Shibutani and Kwan, 1965, quoted in Hirschman, 1975, p. 3). This theory does not appear to explain why immigrant groups so often out-perform indigenous groups, which presumably have had a better opportunity to adapt to the environment. In any case, performance cannot just be a matter of comparative rates of adaptation since contiguous groups interact so as to influence (positively or negatively) each other's opportunity structures. A common form of interaction is foreclosure of opportunities for the weaker groups through the activities of the stronger groups. As noted earlier, this may explain why Indian immigrants have failed to achieve the economic domination in Malaysia which they have attained elsewhere: the presence of the still more entrepreneurial Chinese may have forestalled them.

Over the years, the problem of high or low economic achievement has attracted much attention. Economists, sociologists, psychologists, anthropologists, geneticists, geographers and historians have all thought about the problem, using their own distinctive methodological frameworks. Some analysts have focused on the high economic achievement of particular groups as the phenomenon to be explained, while others have concentrated on the low economic achievers. A satisfactory general theory would have to explain both ends of the spectrum, of course, but such a theory does not yet exist. What does exist at present is a loose tangle of inconclusively contending general and special theories, most of which are potentially applicable to the Malaysian case.

At the risk of over-simplification, theories of economic inequality can be grouped under two major headings, which can be termed the *cultural hypothesis* and the *structural hypothesis*. Fundamentally, the cultural hypothesis would say that *something* in Malay culture—or could it be a 'culture of poverty' generated by Malay poverty itself?—makes the Malays immobile, irresponsive to economic opportunity, impecunious and therefore poor, while *something* in Chinese culture—or in a 'culture of immigrants'—makes the Chinese mobile, adept at seizing economic activities, thrifty and therefore relatively prosperous. As noted above, these *somethings* must go back to differing tastes and/or abilities, although they may also lead to increasing divergence of opportunities as time goes by. By contrast, the structural hypothesis would assert that differences in tastes and abilities are more apparent than real and stress differences in opportunities as the major cause of inequality.

Each hypothesis has its adherents among Malaysians and foreign commentators on Malaysia. Supporters of each view can draw on broader intellectual antecedents for support. The two groups come out quite differently in terms of policy implications. The remainder of this chapter consists of a review of the cultural and structural hypotheses.

THE CULTURAL HYPOTHESIS

The Theory

'Everybody knows' that Malays and Chinese are very different kinds of people, not least the Malays and Chinese themselves. Each group has a stereotyped view both of itself and of the others. (Because of the relative fewness and weakness of the Indians, it is the Malay and Chinese stereotypes that are critical.)

Malays and Chinese are in broad agreement about what kind of people they are, although each tends to put a favourable connotation on its own supposed characteristics and an unfavourable one on those of the other group.

> Malays regard themselves as scrupulous in their dealings with outsiders as well as one another, faithful in all obligations to their families, friends, religion and rulers, and concerned more with the quality of human relations and with the unhurried enjoyment of simple, decent living than with material acquisition.... [They] have a less flattering image of the Chinese: hard-working, ambitious, insatiably acquisitive, clever but unscrupulous in transactions outside their family, coarse and insensitive in interpersonal relations, ritually and physically unclean, unreliable in their values except their enduring obligation to ancestors and thus to Chinese culture and to China, regardless of the regime temporarily in power (Esman, 1972, p. 20).

For the Chinese, features in their own make-up which appear to the Malays to be vices turn out to be virtues, while the very qualities which seem to the Malays to constitute their own principal virtues as a group are identified as shortcomings. 'The Chinese firmly believe that their wealth and Malay poverty are the natural consequence of Chinese industry, thrift and adaptability to modern ways, and of Malay indolence, thriftlessness and conservatism' (Silock, 1965, p. 183). They

> ... regard themselves as hard-working, progressive, concerned with improving their lot through their own efforts in a competitive and often hostile environment, and faithful to their family and social obligations. To the Chinese, a 'typical' Malay is lazy and superstitious, without motivation to improve himself through education or hard work, preferring to subsist on handouts or patronage from relatives or the government than to earn his way through diligent work (Esman, 1972, pp. 20–1).

Yet it would be misleading to give the impression that all Malaysians are satisfied with their self-images. For many Malays, as a result of increasing contact with a larger world in which materialistic values are stressed and of fears that the Chinese will totally eclipse them in time, are losing confidence in the superiority of their own values and behaviour patterns. This change in attitude has been traced by William Roff (1967) to the importation of Islamic reformist doctrine from Cairo, beginning around the turn of the century. Reformist thinking, which slowly gained ground at least up to the late 1960s, generally began by acknowledging the virtue of traditional ways but then went on to conclude that the Malays must reform themselves—becoming more dynamic, industrious and technologically skilled—if they are to survive in a competitive modern world. Reformism has long separated the younger, better-educated Malays (the *kaum muda*) from the older traditionalists (the *kaum tua*). This line of thought found strong expression in *Revolusi Mental* (Senu *et al.*, 1971), an UMNO-sponsored tract published in 1971. This call for mental revolution presented a long list of attitudinal changes which would supposedly lift the Malays from poverty: they were urged to become more self-critical, realistic, positive, self-confident, conscientious, punctual, self-disciplined and so on. Even as the appeal was being framed, however, increasing numbers of Malays seem to have been rejecting reformism's implication that Malay poverty results primarily from the values and behaviour of the Malays themselves and espousing the alternative view that Malay economic problems are not primarily of their own making, that it is society, not Malay attitudes, which is most in need of reform.

Stereotypes often tell more about the attitudes of those doing the describing than about the behaviour of those being described. Thus the diagnosis and prescription of both the Malay reformists and the more radical group of societal reformers which has eclipsed them reflect changing Malay self-perceptions which increasingly stress their economic inferiority and, implicitly, give less emphasis to their self-perceived superiority with respect to qualities such as tranquility and religious purity. Similarly, colonial officials and businessmen of a few decades back reflected their own attitudes in their stereotypical characterizations of the Malays and Chinese.

A serious attempt to put forward a cultural hypothesis of the origins of economic inequality must go beyond this. It must state how, and why, the Malays and Chinese differ in ways which affect their respective economic performances. And it must in some sense be testable.

Probably the most explicit and systematic attempt to present the cultural explanation for the backwardness of the Malays which has been made in recent years is that of Brien Parkinson (1967). Parkinson postulated 'their attitude toward economic development' as a major cause of the economic retardation of the rural Malays. The essence of this attitude, according to Parkinson, is a resistance to economic change which is part of a broader resistance to change in general.[4] The rural Malay is very security-minded, partly because of factors which apply to peasants everywhere—living close to the margin of subsistence, prone to the operation of powerful natural forces—and partly as a lingering reaction to historical conditions in the nineteenth-century Malay state, where, it is argued, the farmer who amassed a surplus could expect to have it confiscated by a ruler or chief. As examples of the rural Malay's resistance to economic change Parkinson cites widespread refusals by padi farmers to double-crop or to establish wet-land seedbeds as urged by the government, slowness to form co-operatives, preference for coastal fishing over more lucrative deep-sea fishing, a tendency to hold savings in sterile forms such as cattle, land and jewellery and reluctance to send their children to school. As a result of this resistance to economic change, Parkinson argues, rural Malays are receptive only to innovations which do not require any radical change in *kampung* life.

Parkinson is careful to emphasize that he is making a positive, not a normative, judgement:

> [The] desire to succeed is not more absent from rural Malay society than it is from any other, but to the Malay success means something different from what it does, for example, to the Malaysian Chinese. The Chinese seem to regard success as being the improvement of their economic position even if this requires some fundamental change or innovation. The Malays seem to regard success as doing what their forebears have approved and practised, but doing it as well as they can. Wealth and economic advancement are desired by the Malays, but not at the expense of renouncing utterly the traditions and traditional occupations of their forefathers to which they have grown accustomed, and which offer them a level of satisfaction greater than that offered by the mere pursuit of economic advancement and wealth.
>
> ...The Chinese and the Malays, because they possess different cultures, attitudes, values and motivations, maximize different things. Neither one is necessarily superior to the other, it is simply that the maximizing postulates of the Chinese are *more* likely to lead to economic development in the Western sense than are the maximizing postulates of the Malays (Parkinson, 1967, pp. 42–3).

Parkinson does not deny the importance of structural forces; he simply argues that they cannot be the whole story. After all, were not both the Malays and the Chinese originally faced with much the same unfavourable economic environment? Even though the Chinese were more auspiciously placed in the urban areas and the rural Malays neglected and exploited, there must be characteristics internal to each group which help to explain the large variance in economic performance.

In his article, Parkinson named E. K. Fisk and Ungku Abdul Aziz as among those holding contrary views but noted (Parkinson, 1967, p. 32) that 'some anthropologists and European students of Malay language and custom' had 'stressed the importance of Malay attitudes', an emphasis 'which is not accepted by many Malaysian academics . . .'. His paper drew a heated reply from one anthropologist, William Wilder (1968), who scornfully accused Parkinson, an economist, of falling back on unconvincing non-economic arguments when his economic analysis failed him. Subsequently, Parkinson replied with equal heat (Parkinson, 1968), but the only really telling point made in the exchange appears to have been Wilder's criticism that Parkinson's strictures were loose and not proven. For example, would it necessarily have been economically beneficial for the farmers mentioned by Parkinson to adopt double-cropping? To specify more clearly and convincingly the effects of differences in values and abilities on the relative economic performance of the Malays and Chinese, it would appear that one must get down to cases.

Few studies have attempted systematically to define and analyse value differences between the Malays and Chinese which may have contributed to their divergent economic performances. James Guyot (1968) did succeed in demonstrating, through tests administered at the University of Malaya, that Chinese students were greatly superior to Malays in 'convergent learning' (measured through an English vocabulary test) while Malays were nearly equal to Chinese in 'divergent learning' (measured through a multiple meanings test). The implication is that 'Chinese are high powered and routine while Malays are more flexible' (Guyot, 1968, p. 8). Whether this difference applies to the mass of rural Malays as well as to the élite from which the university students were drawn—much less what its significance for economic inequality is—remains uncertain.

Although the Guyot finding is consistent with prevailing ethnic stereotypes, tests have sometimes refuted the common view. For example, Yoshimitsu Takei *et al*. (1973) found that Malay secondary school students polled in 1968–9 did *not* have career aspirations which were significantly lower than those of their Chinese and Indian counterparts. Their career *expectations*, no doubt stimulated by official sponsorship of Malays in education and employment, were actually higher than those of the Chinese and Indian students.

On the elusive question of abilities, there is a well-known article by Maurice Freedman which ascribes the economic prowess of the Chinese immigrants to their superior ability to handle money, especially their sophisticated systems of credit. Freedman traces this ability back to values prevalent within the community:

> Shrewdness in handling money was an important part of the equipment which ordinary Chinese took with them when they went overseas in search of a livelihood. Their financial skill rested above all on three characteristics of the society in which they were raised: the respectability of the pursuit of riches, relative immunity of surplus wealth from confiscation by political superiors, and the

legitimacy of careful and interested dealings between neighbors and even close kinsmen. The Chinese were economically successful in South-East Asia not simply because they were energetic immigrants, but more fundamentally because in their quest for riches they knew how to handle money and organize men in relation to money (Freedman, 1959, p. 65).

One can lengthen the list of economically valuable learned abilities to include the relatively high degrees of literacy and education which prevailed among overseas Chinese, as well as their greater experience with urban life and a more complex system of agricultural organization which featured land tenure based on private ownership and rental by means of formal written contracts, as well as complex systems to manage agricultural technology and irrigation water. This heritage of experience has been used by Dwight Perkins (1975) to explain, in part, the development successes of China since 1949, such as its ability to withstand the sudden withdrawal of all Soviet technicians in 1960. It seems equally applicable to the case of the Overseas Chinese. Just as the Overseas Chinese were adept enough to achieve domination of retail trade in their adopted lands, so their stay-at-home counterparts were able to forestall the efforts of European trading companies to accomplish a similar feat in China itself. And both these phenomena occurred despite the low status traditionally accorded to the merchant in Chinese society. This line of reasoning thus provides an alternative to sociological and psychological theories which postulate emigration as a major cause of high economic performance.[5]

Although discussions of economic inequality in Malaysia seldom refer explicitly to general theories of high or low economic achievement which have been proposed in the literature, there are several such theories to which appeal might be made by those seeking support for the cultural hypothesis. These include *marginality*, *achievement motivation* and *modernization* as potential explanations of high achievement, and the *culture of poverty* as a potential explanation of low achievement.

Marginality. Max Weber (1930) attributed the rise of capitalism in Western Europe to Protestantism and its doctrine of salvation for God's elect, who could be identified by their frugal, industrious behaviour on earth. Subsequently, numerous cases of high economic achievement among religious groups which stressed a direct relationship of man to God were noted. Still later, the theory was broadened to cover any form of social 'marginality'. The argument is that normal roads to social recognition are to some extent closed to marginal groups, causing them to seek new means of self-expression. Often the marginal group regards itself as superior to the majority, possessed of traditions and a religion which are not shared by the unenlightened mass. A high degree of internal cohesion, born of a need for mutual protection and reassurance, is common. All these characteristics, it is argued, favour achievement. Particularly if the group has had some past exposure to market relationships, the achievement is likely to take an economic form.

Groups can be marginal for any of several reasons. Immigrants are inherently marginal, since by the very act of migration they have differentiated themselves from the larger society to which they once belonged and moved into proximity with another society, into which they will be assimilated slowly, if at all.

The potential application of the marginality thesis to the Malaysian case is obvious. Chinese immigrants to Malaysia may have developed values favourable to economic achievement as a result of being immigrants rather than (or in addition to) as a result of being ethnic Chinese. Most Malays, as members of a stationary majority, would not have received whatever benefits marginality may confer.[6]

Achievement motivation. This features in the psychological theory of David McClelland (1961), which is similar to that of Everett Hagen (1962). Economic achievement, either individual or collective, is believed to result from a personality trait called need for achievement. Social classes and ethnic groups differ systematically in terms of the prevalence of this trait, although there are also substantial differences among individuals within groups. A general rise in need for achievement precedes an upsurge in economic activity in any society. Normally, a need for achievement originates in child-rearing practices, but individuals can be trained to have a higher need for achievement, according to the theory (McClelland and Winter, 1969).

Modernization. One group of sociologists, the 'modernization theorists', join McClelland and Hagen in stressing attitudinal change as prerequisite to economic development. Alex Inkeles (in Brode, 1969, p. vi) has stated that:

> Sustained development seems to depend on the wide diffusion throughout the population of certain attitudes, values, dispositions to act, and habits of doing things, which, in combination, characterize the 'industrial man' and differentiate him from the man of tradition who makes up the bulk of the population in most underdeveloped countries.

Inkeles and David H. Smith (1974) have made an ambitious attempt to define 'modern' or 'industrial' man and measure his prevalence in six low-income countries. They find modern man to be politically more 'active, interested, informed'. Moreover,

> Beyond politics, the modern man showed himself to perform differently from traditional man in many realms of action having practical bearing on the process of societal modernization. The more modern man is quicker to adopt technical innovation, and more ready to implement birth-control measures; he urges his son to go as far as he can in school, and, if it pays better, encourages him to accept industrial work rather than follow the more traditional penchant for office jobs; he informs himself about the goods produced in the more modern sector of the economy, and makes an effort to acquire them; he permits his wife and daughter to leave the home for more active participation in economic life... (Inkeles and Smith, 1974, p. 313).

The most important sources of individual modernization according to Inkeles and Smith are education, mass communications and—to a greater extent than suspected previously—new forms of work experience, particularly in the factory. This suggests that new economic experiences themselves tend to breed future economic achievement.

Modernization theory has been criticized for being value-laden in its stress on qualities characteristic of contemporary Western societies when these qualities may not be the ones most needed for accelerated late development efforts in non-Western societies (Portes, 1973). Whether the Chinese can be said to be more 'modern' than the Malays, and, if so, whether this accounts for their higher level of economic achievement, is surely debatable. But regardless of whether there is a unified psychosocial pattern which can legitimately be termed modernity, it does seem reasonable to believe that values differ among ethnic groups, that such differences contribute to differential economic performance and that values change over time as a result of experience. This, at least, is the line of thinking behind Freedman and Perkins's observations about the Chinese, quoted above.

Theories mentioned so far have been concerned with *high* economic response. Yet there is no reason to assume that high response is any more in need of explanation than low response. One theory which focuses on low response to economic opportunity argues that the poor *per se* can become a distinct cultural group, with its own values and behaviour patterns, which differ from those of the broader society and are transmitted from generation to generation as a *culture of poverty*. This theory, which was derived by the anthropologist Oscar Lewis from his studies of Latin American slum dwellers, grows out of the observation that the poor of many countries share certain characteristics; on the individual level, these add up to strong feelings of marginality, helplessness, dependency and inferiority (Lewis, 1968).

Although some such congruence is usually conceded, the extent to which the shared characteristics constitute an integrated culture (or subculture) and the extent to which this culture, if it exists, is transmitted between generations are controversial (Rossi and Blum, 1968). The alternative view is that the observed characteristics of the poor are merely a 'situational adaptation' to their poverty, and that values and behaviour would both change rapidly if the situation could somehow be altered for the better.

The 'culture of poverty' theory seems to apply to a situation in which traditional culture has been broken down by rural–urban migration and other factors but the economic basis for successful modernization has not been provided. It seems only marginally pertinent to Malaysia, where it perhaps best fits the circumstances of the South Indian labouring class. As for the Malays, they have retained substantial cultural integrity and have so far engaged in only rather limited rural–urban migration, bringing most of their traditional cultural apparatus with them when they do come to town (Provencher, 1971).

Both the 'traditional society' and the 'culture of poverty' seem intuitively to help explain poverty and relative backwardness. Both theories, however, remain untested, and probably untestable by virtue of the broad terms in which they are couched.

Evidence

Adherents of the cultural hypothesis, indeed, tend to regard the whole course of Malaysian economic history, and the wide differentials in income and wealth which it has produced after all groups started out poor, as *ipso facto* substantiation of their theory. But history is the furthest thing from a controlled experiment; it can never be 'run again', so as to tell us whether the outcome would have been the same if 'other factors', such as official policies which affected economic opportunity, had been different. Although the cultural hypothesis cannot be subjected to genuine controlled experimentation, there are two documented studies of the responses of Malays and Chinese to situations in which their opportunities were as nearly identical as it is possible to make them in the real world. These studies provide some genuine empirical support for the cultural hypothesis.

The first study involves one of the earliest FELDA land development schemes (the Kemendore Project, in Malacca state), on which previously landless rural dwellers, both Malay and Chinese, were settled.[7] The settlers were given a subsistence allowance of gradually declining amount during the first three (later extended to four) years. In return, they were to work for given periods on the immature rubber which would later become their main source of income and develop their homesteads, with attendant garden plots. Given the six-to-seven-year gestation period for rubber, the conception of the scheme depended on the ability of the settlers to support themselves, to an increasing extent, from the garden plots and other supplementary income sources.

Visiting the Kemendore Project about two years after its founding, a University of Malaya team found that the Chinese houses had been extended and redecorated at the settlers' own initiative, while the Malay houses remained as originally built. The houses of both groups contained appliances such as radios, paraffin lamps and kerosene stoves, but the team got the impression that the Malay settlers were much more heavily indebted for the purchase of these items than the Chinese. The Chinese had excelled in producing root crops, vegetables and spices as income-earning and subsistence-providing secondary crops. The Malays produced much smaller quantities of root crops, spices, bananas, rice and corn. Over half the Chinese had some surplus produce for sale, while fewer than 10 per cent of the Malays did. Some of the Chinese had also had success with pig-raising. Most significant of all, the Chinese were taking much better care of the young rubber trees than were the Malays:

> . . . despite similar levels of guidance and encouragement by the authorities, the Chinese holdings are apparently superior; by March 1963, for example, the trees on their Phase I plots had a 2-inch girth advantage in general over those on most Malay units (Wikkramatileke, 1964, p. 48).

These striking differences in performance under similar circumstances are attributed by the author of the Kemendore study only partly to cultural factors:

These disparities in levels of husbandry should not be attributed simply to differences in ability or drive alone. The Malays entered the project at a disadvantage in that their initial personal financial resources were comparably less and the gap was subsequently widened by the ability of the Chinese to make more profitable use of the [non-rubber] land use units within the project. It is significant that in 1960 it was observed that 70 per cent of the Chinese on Phase I worked as full-time farmers within the scheme, whereas 80 per cent of the Malays were compelled to seek sundry employment outside the project and thereby had less time to devote to nursing the rubber . . . (Wikkramatileke, 1964, p. 48).

The second study (Huang, 1974) also concerns Malay and Chinese farmers settled on new land under similar circumstances, this time in the rice fields of Tanjong Karang, Selangor. Tanjong Karang, a long coastal strip of former swamp land, was drained and developed for padi in the 1930s and 1940s. It is one of the few areas in Malaya in which there are Chinese padi planters. The study concerns the response to the government's efforts, beginning in the early 1960s, to persuade the farmers to double-crop. A survey taken in 1966 measured, for each holding, output, hired labour used, variable inputs purchased (expenditure on seed, fertilizer and pesticides), family labour used, area cultivated and non-rice income. The results are summarized in Table 5.2. The Chinese farmers achieved much higher yields by making significantly greater use of all inputs except family labour.

The study went on to calculate a Cobb-Douglas function based on the data. When a dummy variable was inserted in the equation to represent race (with one standing for Chinese farmers and zero for Malays) the value of its coefficient was positive but not statistically significant. Separate production functions were then calculated for each group. These permitted the marginal product of each of the principal inputs (land, hired labour, family labour and variable inputs) to be measured and compared with its opportunity cost. The calculation suggested that the

TABLE 5.2

MEAN VALUES OF VARIABLES FOR PADI FARMS IN TANJONG KARANG, 1966

	Malay farms	*Chinese farms*
Area cultivated (acres)	8.72	7.08
Production (*gantangs*)[1]	3,960	4,103
Yield (*gantangs*/acre)	443*	567*
Other income ($/year)	442*	719*
Family labour use (man-hours/acre)	282	270
Variable inputs use ($/acre)	4.32*	14.58*
Hired labour use ($/acre)	34.92*	87.10*

Source: Huang (1974, p. 178).

*These mean values are significantly different at the .99 level.

[1]A *gantang* is a local measure of volume, equal to 5.6 lb. of padi.

Chinese were using a relatively efficient input mix, while the Malays were more erratic—using far too few variable inputs and too much labour.[8]

Huang (1974, pp. 812–15) interprets his findings as follows:

1. The Malay and Chinese farmers do not differ significantly with respect to market information, average age, level of education or availability of resources.

2. The major difference is attitudinal: the Chinese 'are almost certain to be responsive, ambitious, willing to take risks and hence innovative', perhaps because they are immigrants; the author asserts that immigrants of Malay stock also tend to be more successful in rural enterprises than indigenous Malays.

3. For the Malays, padi growing is a way of life and a means of obtaining the dietary staple; for the Chinese, it is just one more way to make money—hence their greater use of hired labour and fertilizer.

4. Chinese social structure is more conducive to collective action on matters such as uniform planting schedules and pest control; the Chinese live in small villages, while the Malays live on their individual plots and are less likely to co-operate with each other.

5. The observed differences *may* only be temporary; given the great economic superiority of double-cropping, the Malays may in time respond and, in the process, change their attitudes and perceptions.

These two case studies strongly suggest that, given similar opportunities for economic advancement, the Chinese are likely to respond more quickly and strongly than the Malays. Why, specifically, this is so is less easy to establish. Stereotypically, the Chinese are regarded as harder working, readier to take risks and thriftier than the Malays. Yet none of these characterizations is easy to establish using available statistics.

1. The stereotype of the 'lazy' Malay has been attacked as a slur on the peasant who works long hours, often in a state of under-nourishment and disease (Abdul Aziz, Ungku, 1965, p. 27). Indeed, the backward-bending labour supply curve appears to have limited applicability to Malaysia at best.[9] Age-specific labour force participation rates for Malays do not differ systematically from those of Chinese or Indians in any way that could be taken to suggest a stronger preference for leisure. The same can be said of available statistics on hours of work.

2. As for risk-taking, there seems to be no obvious way to measure it systematically. It may be worth noting, however, that while some writers (e.g. Yukon Huang) find the Malays to be excessively cautious, others (e.g. E. K. Fisk, 1964) attribute to them a recklessness in pursuit of get-rich-quick schemes in commerce and industry. Both may be correct; that is, Malays may prefer familiar areas of activity like padi growing and government employment, and be conservative in their behaviour within those spheres, yet behave recklessly when induced to enter unfamiliar areas such as commerce and industry. But this is merely speculation based on observers' reports; it has yet to be documented.

3. Household budget data for 1957–8 suggest that Malay households save *more*, not less, at comparable incomes than Chinese or Indian

TABLE 5.3
HOUSEHOLD INCOME, CONSUMPTION AND SAVINGS, 1957–1958
($ per month)

Income range		*1–150*	*151–300*	*301–500*	*500–1,000*	*All*[1]
Malays:	Income	91	202	378	615	135
	Consumption	94	174	346	NA	128
	Savings	–3	28	32	NA	7
Chinese:	Income	109	215	376	682	270
	Consumption	122	213	348	569	259
	Savings	–13	2	28	113	11
Indians:	Income	108	211	370	642	216
	Consumption	115	208	363	NA	240
	Savings	–7	3	7	NA	–24

Source: Department of Statistics (n.d.).
Note: NA = not available.
[1]Excludes households earning more than $1,000 per month.

households (Table 5.3). This finding, which regrettably is based on rather weak data,[10] is clearly at variance with the notion of the profligate Malay.[11] What seems most wrong with Malay savings is not its low overall amount but the form it takes. The Malays have failed to organize informal capital markets with anything like the virtuosity of the Chinese (Swift, 1957, 1963, 1964).

In conclusion, it seems well established that the Malays have generally been less responsive to given opportunities than the Chinese, even when these opportunities have taken forms which require relatively little adaptation of the traditional life-style.[12] The reasons for the lower responsiveness have been established less firmly. Systematic differences in taste have frequently been alleged but cannot be traced in the available (admittedly weak) data on household economic behaviour. Differences in ability, especially in financial sophistication—the factor stressed by Freedman and Perkins—are more evident.

Policy Implications

The belief that there are inherent, or at least hard-to-change, cultural characteristics which largely determine each group's economic performance is a powerful deterrent to direct efforts to ameliorate economic inequality. Many Malaysians apparently think in terms of a static world, in which one individual or group's gain is inevitably another's loss (Scott, 1968). According to the cultural hypothesis, the real world is more complex but no more auspicious. When the government sets out to create economic opportunities for the Malays, it is argued, it is inevitably faced with the problem of how to prevent the Chinese from taking even greater advantage of them. It will try to do so but if the Malays are unresponsive one of two outcomes will occur: either (1) the exclusionary devices will be evaded, in which case the Chinese will become the prime beneficiaries (although they may have to make payments to Malay confederates and front-men), or (2) the Chinese will be effectively excluded, in which case opportunities will go unexploited and the GNP will be smaller than it otherwise would be. The moral is clear. Such policies can only impose costs. They cannot confer benefits, unless one defines containment of the disparity ratio by the sheer holding back of Chinese income increases as beneficial.

Adherents of the cultural hypothesis are therefore very reluctant to manipulate opportunities, preferring either to try to change individual tastes and abilities or to work indirectly through increasing opportunities for all.

Exhortations for 'mental revolution' are one example of policy—if they can be called that—derived from the cultural hypothesis. The big hope of many culturalists, however, is education (see Chapter 9, below). The rapid spread of education will definitely result in an improved distribution of some abilities which are of economic importance—for example, basic literacy and numeracy. It will also, in line with the findings of Inkeles and others, have a significant effect on values. However, there are many economically useful skills which are not taught in schools.[13] These skills (and, according to Inkeles and Smith, many important value changes as well) are probably best acquired on the job. This reopens the familiar issue of how to open up opportunities for Malays to get new kinds of employment.

The culturalist approach to policy is well illustrated by an article written shortly after Malayan Independence by Goh Keng Swee (1958), later a long-time Minister in the Government of Singapore. Goh noted that the new federation was blessed with a valuable resource which most less developed countries lack: a large and energetic entrepreneurial class. Yet the entrepreneurs, who were overwhelmingly non-Malay, were nervous because of the concentration of political power in the hands of the Malays and the 'possibility, even a probability, that measures will be taken through political action to redress the disparity in wealth between the components of the plural society' (Goh, 1958, p. 4). Conceding that action would be taken to reduce inequality, Goh Keng Swee asked himself what form of action would be best. One way to do it would be to increase the supply of Malay entrepreneurs. Some might hope for a spontaneous growth of entrepreneurship among the Malays, but that would be futile.[14] The alternative would be deliberate efforts to foster Malay entrepreneurship, but this too faces serious difficulties: (1) Protection of Malay entrepreneurs would be 'self-defeating in a free enterprise system'; who would select those potential entrepreneurs who could survive outside the protective walls, and how could they be induced to play a real economic role and depend for their income and benefits on their own efforts rather than on special privileges? (2) If the policy failed, as Goh implied it would, the result would be 'a reduction of business efficiency, and the burden of this will have to be borne by the consuming public in the form of higher costs and prices and inferior output of goods and services' (Goh, 1958, p. 5). Goh saw some opportunities for training

Malays in *management*—to the extent that there were large-scale enterprises which could employ them—but his basic conclusion was that 'it was preferable to abandon unattainable objectives and to concentrate on those about which more can be done.... A more promising approach towards the problem of economic imbalance is surely to concentrate efforts on general rural development and standards of living for everybody in the rural areas...' (Goh, 1958, p. 6).

This line of reasoning has been an influential one. In the early post-Merdeka years the government heavily emphasized rural development while giving non-Malay and foreign enterprises relatively free rein in the commercial and industrial sectors. There was in fact a preference during those years for *defining* the problem as one of imbalance between the urban and rural areas rather than among ethnic groups *per se*.[15] By defining the targets of government programmes as rural residents (presumed to be poor and known to be heavily Malay, but including a minority of rural non-Malays and excluding the relatively well-off urban Malays) rather than Malays as such, the strategy was made to sound less threatening to non-Malays. It established a more widely acceptable criterion (basically poverty) for receipt of assistance and preserved the meritocratic, or Darwinian, principle in the most dynamic sector of the economy. This made it an appealing rationale for policy until it was so suddenly and overwhelmingly repudiated by the electorate in May 1969.

As noted in Chapter 3, the most sophisticated enunciation of the indirect approach to inequality—implicitly based on a culturalist interpretation of the situation and on a devotion to meritocratic principles—was a paper prepared by three foreign economic advisers in 1967 (Gates, Goering and Keare, 1967). This paper showed how unrestricted growth of the economy, together with rapid development of uncultivated land, could bring about a tight labour market in twenty years or less—an outcome which would benefit the Malays, as the largest suppliers of unskilled labour. The authors obviously believed that they were proposing the best possible reconciliation of Malaysia's growth versus equity dilemma. Whether one agrees depends on such things as the relative importance attached to the reduction of inequality and the abolition of absolute poverty as social objectives, on one's evaluation of different policy instruments and on the explanation of inequality which one accepts.

THE STRUCTURAL HYPOTHESIS

The Theory

While the *cultural hypothesis* ascribes inter-group differences in economic performance to underlying cultural differences in values and/or abilities, the *structural hypothesis* emphasizes differences in opportunity. Since the policies of independent Malayan and Malaysian governments have been designed to favour the Malays, to the extent that any favouritism was intended, discrimination to limit the opportunities of the Malays must either be historical or, if contemporary, either private or official but unintended. All these possibilities have featured in the arguments of those who have espoused the structural hypothesis.

As noted earlier, two writers who have formulated more or less straightforwardly structural explanations of economic inequality in Malaysia are Ungku Abdul Aziz (1957, 1962, 1964, 1965) and E. K. Fisk (1962). Ungku Aziz, an uncompromising structuralist, attributes the poverty of Malay peasants to their own low productivity, to exploitation by other social groups and to official neglect.[16] He lists four forms of exploitation which are crucial in his view:

1. 'merchants who charge excessive margins for their services';
2. 'high rates of interest charged by moneylenders and shopkeepers who supply the farmers with credit in kind or loans in cash';
3. 'high rents on land and insecurity of tenure';
4. 'wage exploitation . . . practised on farmers who are so poor that they have to offer their labour for hire' (Abdul Aziz, Ungku, 1957).

The popular view is that Ungku Aziz blames the poverty of the rural Malays on exploitation by non-indigenous middlemen, but the list just cited shows that what he calls 'the M-M (monopoly-monopsony) system' is only part of his thesis. Although the merchants and moneylenders whom he lists as exploiters *are* predominantly non-Malays, the landlords and employers of rural labour who get equal billing are frequently Malays. And even the middlemen, Ungku Aziz (1957) says, are exploiters because of their economic role, not because of ethnicity *per se*. Malay middlemen would be just as bad.

Ungku Aziz rejects the cultural hypothesis explicitly and often derisively. In one of his papers (1965, pp. 24–30) he marshalls arguments to refute two 'myths' which he says are used to rationalize inaction on rural development—'the people are already happy' and 'rural folks are conservative'—plus four others which rationalize a slow rate of progress or programme failures: 'the Malays are lazy'; 'the rural Malays are improvident'; 'results will take time'; and 'the Malays are superstitious (incapable of rational thinking)'.

Fisk, writing in 1962 and citing figures which indicated a totally stagnant rural economy between 1950 and 1958, ascribed the stagnation to 'vicious circles'. The low and stagnant income level in rural areas leads to low savings and an inability to pay the costs either of education or of migration, the two principal means of social mobility, thus assuring continued poverty. By contrast, urban populations are in closer touch with opportunity and well enough off to benefit from it, so their prosperity also tends to be self-perpetuating. Fisk's argument is thus more directed to the question of why inequality persists than to the issue of its origins. Nevertheless, he clearly implies that the major impediments to policies which would try to reduce inequality are structural. Fisk is, however, less uncompromisingly structuralist than Ungku Aziz. For example, in discussing 'the shortage of Malay capital invested in commerce and industry', he states that the reasons are

> . . . several, of which three are particularly important:
>
> 1. The lower general level of income, and in particular of cash income,

amongst the Malays as compared with the other races, provided a smaller margin for saving, and therefore a smaller total of investable funds.

2. The ownership of land was a matter of tradition amongst the Malays, and carried considerable prestige and emotional value. This had a twofold effect, in that Malays tended to prefer investment in land to other forms of investment, and in that it tended to disassociate the purchase-price of land from its value as an income-earning investment, and so to inflate the price of land above its economic value. There was therefore not only a preference amongst Malays for investment in land, but the cost of exercising that preference was inflated and the remaining surplus available for other forms of investment was thereby further reduced.

3. With the relatively small amounts available for investment, the idea of earning a reasonable return on the investment, *qua* investment, was not particularly attractive, and as a result Malay investment tended to be undertaken in wildcat schemes where the hope was for much larger and quicker returns. . . . The result has been that a substantial proportion of Malay investment in commerce and industry has been in unsound projects with a high casualty rate, and Malay experience of such investment has frequently been discouraging (Fisk, 1964, p. 98).

Thus Fisk agrees with Ungku Aziz that low income, and the factors that lie behind it, are part of the explanation for the slowness of Malays to enter commerce and industry, but he parts company with Ungku Aziz in attributing another part of the explanation to culturally determined values.

At the root of the structuralist arguments of Aziz and Fisk is the concept of *discrimination*. However, use of this term as a synonym for inequality of economic opportunity raises semantic difficulties. Literally discrimination means only unequal treatment, but in common parlance the word has acquired the negative connotation of purposive action to limit the opportunities of others. For present purposes it seems important to ask how the inequality of opportunity came about, whether the unequal treatment was in fact intended to limit the opportunities of certain groups and whether it is a phenomenon of the past, the present or both. One should also distinguish between official and private discrimination.

Mention has already been made of the thesis that the different policies which the colonial government pursued towards the Malay and Chinese communities favoured the economic advance of the latter, even though the intention was if anything the opposite. Since Independence, of course, a policy of 'reverse discrimination' has been implemented to offset the alleged discrimination of the past—although some would argue that the announced policy is largely a matter of political symbolism and that the policy has often been ineffectual or even perverse in its effects. The issue of historical official discrimination has been touched on in Chapter 2, while the effects of post-1957 policies will be examined in Chapters 6–9.

Private discrimination is a concomitant of communalism. Whether or not there is much overt hostility among communal groups, there is bound to be a sense of separateness and difference, as well as a lack of communication. Each group normally prefers to deal with its own members, although it may also be happy to exercise any monopoly power it possesses over other groups.[17] When practised by the economically dominant group, this exclusiveness can significantly limit the opportunities of other groups. Although the dominant group will be quite willing to sell to them, to buy from them and to lend them money (especially if there are monopoly rents to be obtained), and *perhaps* willing (or even anxious) to hire them to do low-paid work, it will probably not be anxious to enter into partnerships with them, hire them in positions of responsibility or impart its skills to them. This is discrimination, even though it may not be directed *against* any specific group so much as *for* members of one's own group, and hence against all other groups equally.

Evidence

To prove the structural hypothesis, one would logically have to demonstrate both the existence of unequal opportunity and some responsiveness to its removal. That is, to accept the hypothesis, at least in its present form, one must show not only that the Malays are exploited or discriminated against in some sense, but also that it is this which is holding back their economic advance. There is in fact little evidence which can meet this demanding test.

Economists have come to regard exploitation simply as the exercise of monopoly (or monopsony) power, i.e., the maintenance in the long run of a product price higher than marginal cost (or of a factor payment lower than marginal product). Ungku Aziz has postulated the existence of exploitation in this sense in the main economic relationships engaged in by rural Malays: the marketing of their products, borrowing of capital for consumption or production purposes, renting of land and use of their services as paid agricultural labourers. In doing so, he places himself squarely in an intellectual tradition which is strong in Malaysia as in many other low-income countries but which has received very mixed reviews from those who have attempted to test it empirically.[18]

The Aziz position received support from an article by Clifton Wharton (1962). Arguing on theoretical grounds, Wharton picked smallholder rubber as a product for which middleman monopsony was likely to be present. A number of factors contributed to this expectation: the price inelasticity of smallholder output, the fact that first-buyer level rubber dealers are licensed, the tendency of such dealers to perform money-lending as well as dealer functions and finally the possibility of collusion among dealers of the same clan or extended family. To verify his thesis, Wharton called for factual research. The first such research, published in 1968 by Lim Sow Ching, examined the trading margins of 150 first-level dealers in the state of Selangor. This study strongly contradicted the expectations of Aziz and Wharton. Lim found that where good-quality rubber (ribbed smoked sheet) is concerned, the dealer's margin 'does not appear excessive and is certainly much lower than is commonly asserted'.[19] The study *did* uncover a problem with respect to poor-quality rubber (unsmoked sheet), for which marketing margins were much higher. This, however, probably has more to do with the high cost of marketing low-grade rubber than with any lack of competition. An earlier RRIM study (Barlow and Lim, 1965) had already shown the establishment of group processing centres, at which latex from Malay-owned smallholdings receives quality processing, to be a socially remunerative investment.

It seems probable, therefore, that rural Malays are *not* seriously exploited with respect to one service—marketing—rendered to producers of one major peasant crop—rubber. There is less conclusive evidence on other services and other crops. The marketing of padi, the other staple crop of Malay peasants, has often been described as fraught with exploitative practices (Thomson, 1954; Aziz Yassin, 1966; Selvadurai, 1972, pp. 37–43). The only careful study that I know of (Purcal, 1971, pp. 106–24), which refers to Province Wellesley in 1961–2, found that most farmers were anxious to sell their crop within six weeks of its harvest because they lacked storage space and drying facilities, had payments due to creditors and in some cases had to sell the harvest from one isolated plot so that they can move on to another. Nevertheless, the behaviour of the private rice dealers in the case studied seemed reasonably competitive and the looming threat of more active government intervention in the market tended to prevent them from exploiting fully their apparent market advantages. As a result, farmers in the area studied received between 75 and 80 per cent of the retail price for rice—surely an acceptable share, considering the milling, transportation, storage and vending services performed as the product passes from grower to ultimate consumer. What is not clear is how typical this case is, since similar studies have not been done for other areas and periods, and the author notes that at the time of his study padi farmers in Kedah and Selangor were less well paid than those in Province Wellesley (Purcal, 1971, p. 124).

No one suggests that marketing and other services are invariably rendered to Malay peasants through competitive markets and at least cost. But a recent thorough review of the evidence by Tan (1977, pp. 400–52) indicates that marketing margins are generally low as a result of the almost invariable existence of alternative buyers and suppliers, as well as easy entry conditions into retail trade and the lower levels of the wholesale trading network. Tan finds that *overall* marketing margins, as opposed to the margins of specific dealers, are high; this may be attributed to the heavily layered nature of the marketing system, as well as, possibly, monopsonistic price fixing by importers.

The type of crop for which Tan found most evidence of monopsonistic marketing conditions is fruit and vegetables. Ironically, this is the one area of agriculture which is dominated by Chinese farmers. However, Malays may also suffer, as did the Perak durian growers studied by T. B. Wilson (1954).[20]

Although further research could still change the picture, it does seem safe at this point to say that 'exploitation' of rural Malays is much less widespread than has been averred in some structuralist commentaries and that private markets have provided the peasant farmer with ancillary services far more competitively and efficiently than has been assumed by policy-makers eager to replace the private market with the government-sponsored institutional alternatives discussed in Chapter 7, below.

The foregoing results cast grave doubt upon the proposition that Malay peasants remain poor primarily because they are exploited by those with whom they have economic dealings. A different structuralist proposition is that Malays remain in farming and other occupations traditional to them because their efforts to move into new areas are continually frustrated by the collusion of the Chinese. Although support for this view is, as far as I know, entirely anecdotal, the position is a more plausible one on its face than the one just examined. Earlier the ways in which small Chinese firms grow out of Chinese social structure and relate to each other as part of that structure as well as merely through commercial dealings were discussed. Many a nascent Malay retailer has complained of favouritism to his Chinese rivals on the part of Chinese wholesalers. Although detailed, reasonably impartial examination of such charges is lacking, they are not without plausibility. The tendency for small Chinese-owned firms to be exclusively Chinese in staffing and for skills used in these businesses to be acquired in ways which are effectively closed to non-Chinese were noted earlier.

Even in the absence of conclusive evidence, therefore, there is reason to believe that there have in fact been powerful structural impediments to Malay movement into many sectors of the economy. (It is harder to say how great the response would have been if the impediments had not existed.) There are also grounds for thinking that another important route for social and economic mobility, education, has also been less accessible to Malays than to non-Malays. This was particularly true in colonial times, as has been revealed by a study by Charles Hirschman (1972). Working with data from the 1957 population census, Hirschman found that the lower overall educational attainment of the Malay community could be 'explained' statistically largely by reference to the differential provision of schooling among Malayan states. His work contradicts the stereotyped view that Malays have been less interested in education than other groups. In fact, retention rates proved to be higher for Malays than for others, suggesting a *greater* reliance on formal education as a means of advancement than that of the other groups, a finding which has been confirmed by more recent work (see Chapter 9, below).

In the field of education there can be no doubt about Malay responsiveness to widened opportunity. Enrolment of Malay students has grown tremendously in recent years. Greater concern is attached to the question of the quality and economic relevance of the education received, an issue which is pursued in Chapter 9.

Policy Implications

The structural hypothesis, because it postulates more accessible, less deep-rooted, causes of inequality, is much more activist in its policy implications than the cultural hypothesis.[21] Structuralists generally advocate policies which will widen Malay opportunities. This can take the form of attempts to eliminate present-day inequalities in opportunity, or it can go further and advocate preferential opportunities for Malays as compensation for alleged historical deprivation. It has been seen (in Chapter 3) how specific Malay 'special rights' were written into the 1957 Constitution and 'entrenched'—that is, made virtually undiscussable and unamendable—in 1971.[22] These 'rights' include the reservation of certain lands for Malay ownership and the establishment of ethnic quotas on scholarships and civil service jobs. Although 'special rights' are of great symbolic importance, they have clearly not been sufficient to make a major impact on the Malays' relative deprivation. Hence the search for other structuralist solutions.

Different structuralist writers have their own favourite recipes for policy intervention. Ungku Abdul Aziz, in a line of argument elaborated in several articles (1964, 1967, 1969), favours far-reaching structural reforms in the rural areas. These include the application of existing labour legislation to employees in the traditional rural sector, land reform to control rents and provide security of tenure, an extensive rural credit system run either by public bodies or co-operatives and a co-operative system of marketing for the main smallholder crops. Some elements of this ambitious programme of institutional reform—especially those dealing with credit and marketing—have been implemented over the years, as we shall see in Chapter 7, while other parts—those dealing with labour legislation and land tenure—have not.

E. K. Fisk—whose structuralism, as has been seen, is less strict than that of Ungku Aziz—has stressed two principles which he believes are essential to policies to reduce economic imbalance: increased access to opportunities and heightened ability to compete (Fisk, 1964, pp. 101–8). Increasing indigenous opportunities, Fisk recognizes, will require limiting the opportunities of others and thereby creating some inefficiencies. Measures which he stresses under the ability to compete rubric include the preferential provision of capital, entrepreneurial and skill development and policies to bring industrial employment opportunities and rural labour closer together—preferably by encouraging rural–urban migration, since Fisk regards policies to induce industries to locate in rural areas as generally ineffective. Finally, Fisk argues that problems of economic inequality should be attacked as soon as possible, since the inequalities tend to widen and the mechanisms which reinforce them tend to become stronger through time.

These and other policy proposals derived from a structuralist interpretation of economic inequality in Malaysia became prominent in the policy discussions which were stimulated by the events of May 1969. Among other suggestions made at the time were proposals to institute area development programmes (including urban as well as rural economic activities) on the East Coast, to place ethnic quotas on private-sector urban employment, to strengthen rural education so as to improve the 'feed' into higher levels of schooling, to grant tax concessions to Malay businesses and to establish public corporations to go directly into business on behalf of the Malays. All these policy possibilities will be encountered and evaluated in succeeding chapters.

THE POSSIBILITY OF SYNTHESIS

If there is one conclusion which emerges clearly from the foregoing survey of what have been called the cultural and structural hypotheses it is that although the two theories appear to be mutually exclusive, in fact they are not. Malays and Chinese logically *could*—and in reality almost certainly *do*—differ significantly with respect to values, abilities *and* opportunities. The illusion of diametrically opposed hypotheses is created mostly by the tendency of advocates of both theories to exaggerate the importance of the particular differences which feature in their own theory and downplay those which do not fit the theory. Overall, differences in values and abilities may be said to exist—contrary to the assumptions of thorough-going structuralists—but to be much smaller in magnitude and more readily subject to change than is assumed by thorough-going culturalists.

Charles Hirschman (1975, p. 3) has pointed out that one might investigate separately the question of how socio-economic differences among ethnic groups originated and the question of how they are maintained (or reduced or eliminated, as the case may be) over time. This suggests the possibility of a synthesis of the cultural and structural hypotheses. As regards the *origins* of inequality, the argument that something internal to their culture and experience enabled the Chinese to make more than the Malays out of roughly equal opportunities seems to be a strong one. However, as discussed above, the role of acquired abilities, as opposed to values and inherent abilities[23] may have been an important one, and this is not what most culturalists have in mind when they talk of inequality's cultural origins.

Since both values and abilities change over time, acceptance of a culturalist hypothesis about the origins of poverty does not necessarily imply a persisting or widening pattern of inequality through time. It is true that there are cumulative tendencies resulting from the faster acquisition by the dominant groups of wealth and economically valuable abilities. Indeed, Hirschman (1975, p. 79) argues that these cumulating advantages, rather than either cultural differences or the exercise of discrimination, are the main means by which income inequality is maintained from one generation to the next. But the distribution of wealth and the acquisition of abilities, as well as the structure of opportunities, are at least potentially manipulable by policy means. So despite inequality's probable cultural origins, it would not appear necessary to accept the culturalist's gloomy strictures about the futility of attempts to reduce inequality through public policy.

The discussion in succeeding chapters is based on the premise that it *is* possible to reduce ethnicity-related income inequality by altering the distribution of wealth, ability and opportunities. What cannot easily be determined is how fast and efficiently these mechanisms work—how much time will be required, how strong the incentive must be, how much output is likely to be lost in the process. These are the questions which must be kept in mind during the following examination of the more direct policy approach to dealing with inequality taken by the government since 1969.

1. The F test determines, at specified levels of confidence, whether differences among group means are great enough, given the variance among observations *within* each group, to reject the null hypothesis that all observations are in fact drawn from a homogeneous population.

2. The Theil index is a measure of inequality borrowed from information theory which has the advantage of being decomposable into between-class and within-class components. For a discussion see Amartya Sen (1973, pp. 34–6).

3. See William R. Cline (1975) for an excellent recent survey of the literature on distribution and development.

4. Parkinson (1967, pp. 38–9) ascribes this resistance to two factors: a love for retaining old ways and a fear or dislike of the unfamiliar. He cites the syncretization of Islam with earlier beliefs and practices as an indication of the former and the use of magic by rural Malays to 'familiarize themselves with the unfamiliar' as an indication of the latter.

5. Perkins notes that Chinese who emigrated can be distinguished from Chinese who stayed behind principally in terms of their greater poverty, their residence in south-eastern provinces which were closest to the countries of destination and their kinship to previous emigrants. Otherwise, 'there is no reason to believe that the Chinese who emigrated had substantially different traits from those who remained behind' (Perkins, 1975, pp. 10–11).

6. Oliver Popenoe (1970) found some evidence of marginality in the small groups of entrepreneurial Malays whom he identified and studied. His Malay entrepreneurs tended to be of higher socio-economic status, better educated and more orthodox religiously than Malays in general. Although a significant number were of aristocratic origin, many had experienced marginalizing experiences such as failure in school or family bankruptcy. A surprising number had virtually been forced to go into business by family or societal circumstances, especially the disruption of normal life during World War II.

7. See R. Wikkramatileke (1964). The scheme was started in 1958; later Felda projects settled Malay families almost exclusively.

8. The ratios of value of marginal product to opportunity cost were:

Input	*Malay farms*	*Chinese farms*
Land	2.66	2.32
Hired labour	1.61	1.24
Family labour	0.54	1.00
Variable inputs	7.33	1.73

Source: Huang (1974, p. 179).

9. Huang (1976) tested the responsiveness to economic opportunities (in terms of use of family labour and purchased inputs) of rice farmers in Kelantan, Selangor and Province Wellesley. His results were consistent with the backward-bending supply curve model for Kelantan but not in the other two cases. He concluded that:

'The limited aspirations of subsistence farmers in Kelantan are perhaps a consequence of both the law technology and the lack of social and cultural stimulation. The findings should be interpreted optimistically, since they indicate that, given an economic stimulus, peasant farmers may respond favorably, and if farmers have limited aspirations, it is perhaps as much due to the limited economic opportunities surrounding them as to social and cultural factors' (Huang, 1976, p. 208).

10. See the discussion of the Household Budget Survey in Chapter 4, above. Lee Hock Lock (1971, p. 47) also gives data on saving by income class and ethnic group for 1959.

These data show Malays saving more at given income levels than Chinese, although less than Indians. Given the contrasting means and distributions for each ethnic group (accentuated in the *FSS* data), Malays as a group save a smaller share of their income than Chinese or Indians. This may well be a more accurate picture than Table 5.3's depiction of a higher average savings ratio for the Malays as a group, despite their much lower mean income.

11. Two possible explanations of the phenomenon may be offered without proof: (1) Malays do not actually save more at given levels of *real* income, but their real incomes at given levels of nominal income are higher because they tend to live in rural areas, where prices are lower; hence they save more at given *nominal* income levels; (2) Malays actually do save more at given income levels because the generally lower incomes of their ethnic group give them a higher income *relative to their reference group* than Chinese and Indians with the same absolute income.

12. It may be desirable to state explicitly that while Malays appear to be *less responsive* to economic opportunity than the Chinese they are not *unresponsive*. Among many examples of Malay response to economic incentives, perhaps the most dramatic is the rush of rural Malays to establish rubber smallholdings in the 1920s and 1930s after their profitability had been demonstrated.

13. For an instructive analysis of methods of skill acquisition among the Chinese, see Chai Hon-Chan (1971).

14. 'I do not see this as in any way possible. The facts of the situation are against such a spontaneous growth. Quite apart from sociological facts such as their customs, religion and beliefs, and quite apart from their lack of experience in business affairs, the Malays have to contend with so many obstacles that I think it improbable that large numbers will succeed in rising to the top of the entrepreneurial ladder in a free competitive system. Where success in business depends not only on innate ability but also on the ease with which a person can form useful contacts in the business world, the barriers of the plural society act as a severe restraint to the formation of such contacts between the Malays and the others. And it is the others who are in strategic positions. The barriers are neither sinister nor are they planned by any group of persons; they merely form part of the natural facts of our plural society. And these barriers cannot be broken down merely by well-meaning exhortation directed toward the general population' (Goh, 1958, p. 4).

15. 'That the racial issue is exploited [by politicians] does not . . . invalidate the contention . . . that the true or basic problem is the rural versus urban conflict; the racial aspect may be seen simply as an accentuating factor' (Augustine H. H. Tan, 1964, p. 120).

16. 'Low productivity' does not appear to be on the same level of causation as 'exploitation' and 'neglect'; that is, it could well itself be a result of the other two, although it in turn could be said to 'cause' poverty. It is therefore ignored in the text discussion.

17. Breaking with an old tradition of representing discrimination as the exercise of monopoly power (exploitation), Gary Becker (1957) analysed discrimination in a competitive framework using the assumption that the behaviour of some of the participants is influenced by a 'taste for discrimination'. Although Becker has certainly established a new standard of elegance in discrimination theory, both Lester Thurow (1969, pp. 111–29) and Robinson Hollister (n.d.), who graciously lent me his unpublished book manuscript, have noted that observed real-world patterns of discrimination are seriously at variance with the predictions of his theory. One reason for this may be the weakness of competition in the real world. On the other hand, the main difficulty with monopoly theories is why competition does not work to undermine the discriminatory pattern—how, for example, U.S. employers could go on paying white workers more than their marginal product and black workers less, when there is a competitive advantage to be gained by hiring more blacks and thus lowering one's costs. Thurow (1969, pp. 126–9) suggests that the reason for this is a 'web of discrimination' which prevents employers from perceiving the true productivity of blacks, since they have less education, trade certification, etc. Different forms of discrimination tend to reinforce each other. Concluding his survey of discrimination theories, Hollister (n.d.) quotes Kenneth Arrow to the effect that whether discrimination has anything to do with profitability to the discriminating group should be regarded as an open question.

18. That interest rates or marketing margins are high does not prove the existence of monopoly/monopsony, since the *cost* of lending to, or the marketing the produce of, small farmers is also likely to be high. Some economists who have studied empirical evidence on the subject (e.g. Millard F. Long, 1968) have argued that observed margins are generally consistent with competition, while others (e.g. A. Bottomley, 1964) see a significant element of monopoly rent. The majority of economists would probably regard most such

markets as reasonably competitive, though few would dogmatically assert that this is the case in all times and places. For example, markets are more likely to be monopolized when production of a good is highly localized or when production is highly seasonal, creating a capital requirement to finance storage between time of harvest and time of consumption. Strong indirect evidence supporting the view that the private market handles these functions reasonably efficiently comes from the nearly universal difficulties which governments have had in trying to substitute public or co-operative credit or marketing services for private ones.

19. Lim Sow Ching (1968, p. 3). The dealer's 'surplus', which included his labour and management, interest on capital and taxes, averaged $4,900 a year, or 30 per cent of his investment.

20. Durians are a seasonal, highly perishable fruit which represent an important source of cash income in some *kampungs*. Wilson studied the operation of the market in the Parit district of Perak, finding that the need to get the fruit to market quickly resulted in high returns to the three to five dealers who intervened between *kampung* producer and urban consumer. On the basis of his data, the peasant producer appears to receive only one-third to one-half of the retail price. Wilson ascribed the wide price spread less to anti-competitive behaviour on the part of the dealers than to inefficiency in the systems of transport and marketing.

21. For this very reason, there is some tendency for those who support strong measures to reduce inequality to favour the structural explanation, while those more sympathetic to the *status quo* lean toward the cultural hypothesis.

22. For a discussion, see Gordon P. Means (1972.)

23. There has been little mention in recent years of the possibility of inherent biological differences. An exception is the thesis advanced by Mahathir bin Mohamad (1970, pp. 16–31), in his anguished post-1969 appraisal of 'the Malay dilemma', that the backwardness of the rural Malay is partly attributable to genetic weakness brought on by persistent inbreeding.

PART II
Policies and Programmes

Introduction to Part II

PART II is concerned with alternative policy approaches to ethnic-group related economic inequality. One might begin by asking what would be the future trend in economic inequality if the Malaysian Government took no direct measures to reduce inequality. Since Malaysia is approximately at that level of GNP per capita at which inequality in the size distribution is generally found to be greatest in cross-section studies, one could hope a lower degree of inequality will emerge in time as a by-product of economic growth. On the other hand, time-series studies of other countries' experience in recent years (Weisskoff, 1970; Turnham, 1972), to say nothing of the findings presented in Chapter 4, suggest that further increases in inequality are a distinct possibility for some years to come. An important hypothesis about why overall size inequality behaves as it does as growth proceeds is that the eventual downturn in inequality in many countries is largely dependent upon the successful absorption of surplus labour. 'Successful' labour absorption consists of boosting the demand for labour to the point at which unskilled labour becomes a scarce factor and its real wage rate begins to rise. Since unskilled labour is the most widely distributed factor of production, this brings about a lessening of overall size inequality. Expansion of education may have a similar effect, since it may lead to a narrowing of differentials in earned income. These may be the mechanisms which brought about reduced inequality in Korea and Taiwan's rapidly growing economies (Fei, Ranis and Kuo, 1975).

Rapid, labour-absorbing economic development *à la* Korea or Taiwan involves openness to new international trade opportunities and avoidance of the factor-price distortions which seem to have hampered labour absorption in many countries. If the aim of policy is to reduce overall size inequality of income distribution without a revolution, this may well be the fastest way to do it—supported, perhaps, by measures to redistribute assets such as land reform. Gates, Goering and Keare (1967) advocated such a strategy—with the characteristically Malaysian addition of rapid land development—as the solution for Malaysia's inequality problem. But there are two major difficulties posed by the Malaysian case of *ethnic* inequality which would not be present in the case of a more homogeneous population:

1. Response to incentives would differ among groups, as Donald Keesing (1972) has suggested and this study has shown. This could lead to continuing worsening of the distribution of wealth. The economic benefits of formal education would become more widely distributed, but

the same might not be true of skills acquired on the job (Chai, 1971). Prospects for reduced ethnic inequality may thus be less favourable than those for lower overall size inequality.

2. Questions of effects on the political system arise because of the slowness and possible weakness of the inequality-reducing effect. The apparent convergence of ethnic-group values and aspirations has been noted; this can lead to heightened inter-group competition and tension. As noted in Chapter 1, it is more likely to be a case of the sociologists' model of 'relative deprivation' than of Albert Hirschman's 'tunnel effect'. Tolerance of growing inequality is likely to be fragile. Pressure for a more interventionist policy will increase, quite independent of the wisdom or folly of such a move. Whether the potential for tension involved in *this* approach is greater or less than that produced by waiting for more indirect measures to take effect is politically moot in Malaysia's case.

Given that Malaysia is committed to direct action, the next question is what the range of possible policies looks like. The basic alternatives can be stated as follows:

1. The government can redistribute wealth and economic power from the wealthier group either to the public sector or directly into the hands of the poorer group.

2. It can alter the distribution of earned incomes by one of three means:

   a. Accelerating income growth in sectors in which the backward group is presently concentrated (e.g. through a general rural development bias).

   b. Emphasizing inter-sectoral mobility and penetration of the modern sectors by the backward group.

   c. Stressing productivity-raising policies which are independent of the pattern of employment (primary education, public health services, etc.).

3. It can further affect the distribution of welfare through redistribution policies, either:

   a. Explicitly, through the fiscal system (i.e., by the differential impact of taxation and public expenditures on various groups), or

   b. Implicitly, through tax- or subsidy-like policies which affect relative prices (e.g., protection from imports).

Type 1 policies—outright transfer of existing assets—have so far been rejected in Malaysia; all redistribution is to be accomplished out of economic growth. They thus scarcely enter into this discussion.

Type 2a policies are the least tension-provoking and the most acceptable to the richer group. They probably can have a significant effect on income distribution. In the context of long-run structural change they amount to temporizing, but this is not to say that they are unimportant. If the pattern of economic inequality is to be eliminated, most members of the poorer group must eventually move into the modern sectors. But this takes time, and reduction of inequality during the transition period would be a worthwhile achievement. In the post-1969 Malaysian political context, Type 2a policies could be described as necessary but no longer sufficient.

Type 2c policies—to skip Type 2b for the moment—are intended to ease the transition process. They create fewer direct conflicts than the types which follow, in that they merely strengthen the poorer group's ability to compete, without intervening in the labour market. (There are some hard choices to be made, however, with respect to who gets educated.) They do raise major questions about the effectiveness of education (especially in the absence of other policies) as a solution to the inequality problem, as well as about its budgetary costs and its possible destabilizing effect on expectations and aspirations.

Type 3 policies are probably the next hardest to carry out. Tax incidence in most low-income countries is thought to be approximately neutral, while benefit and expenditure incidence may well be regressive. This has led some economists to write off fiscal redistribution as a potential means of influencing inequality. However, Chapter 6 suggests the existence of at least modest and increasing progressivity, with the possibility of further increases if the government so desires. Thus redistribution seems to have a place in the overall strategy, at least as a cushion for inequality in earned incomes.

Finally, Type 2b policies are the most difficult in political terms and the most likely to create conflict. It is here that the biggest questions of effectiveness and cost arise. This category includes the means of achieving both the employment and the ownership and control targets of the current government. It is these policies which pose the dilemma discussed by Goh Keng Swee (1958), Oliver Popenoe (1970), Gordon Means (1970) and others: how a productive and self-reliant group of entrepreneurs and workers can be created under direct government sponsorship—whether, to put it more sharply, this procedure will not forever warp incentives, so that the beneficiaries seek ever-increasing amounts of government largess and resist submitting themselves to the rigours of the market. The dilemma is a familiar one to the economist; it has been debated for decades in connexion with the issue of tariff protection for new industry, among others. There, the following consensus may be said to have been reached: even though it is hard to say in advance where dynamic comparative advantage is likely to be found, and it is politically difficult to remove protection once it has been instituted (pre-arranged time limits are often proposed but seldom imposed), one cannot sustain a blanket rejection of the idea of protection if there are important national purposes to be served. So the search for more effective and efficient policies goes on.

Part II discusses past, present and possible future Malaysian policies using the categories just defined, although not in the order listed above. Chapter 6 deals with fiscal redistribution (Type 3 policies). Chapter 7 discusses rural development policies (Type 2a); Chapter 8, urban development policies (Type 2b). Chapter 9 analyses education and other general policies (Type 2c). The study concludes with Chapter 10, which comments among other things upon the political issues briefly raised above.

6 Fiscal Redistribution

> Shifts in the pattern of public expenditure represent one of the most effective techniques a government possesses to improve the conditions of the poor. Too often these expenditures—on health, on transport, on water supply, on education, and on many other sectors—end by benefiting the already privileged far more than the mass of the disadvantaged.... Governments can best begin to shift public expenditure towards those who need it the most by initiating surveys on the effects of their current patterns of disbursement: where do the funds really go, and who benefits the most?
>
> McNamara, 1972

INTRODUCTION

FUNDAMENTALLY, the Malaysian Government's ability to do anything at all about economic inequality depends on its capacity to re-allocate resources. This can be done by altering incentives so as to bring about the desired re-allocation within the private sector or through the use of public-sector programmes. In the latter case, two important questions arise. Can the government command the necessary share of society's resources? And can it use those resources effectively to achieve the desired objective—the reduction of economic inequality? The second of these questions will be dealt with in Chapters 7–9; the present chapter addresses the first of them.

Four related issues will be taken up:

1. To what extent does the government in fact redistribute income or welfare among ethnic groups, regions and income size groups?
2. Have the nature and extent of such redistribution changed since Merdeka?
3. Where there is redistribution, what form does it take? What taxes and what benefit programmes are significantly redistributive?
4. Is the pattern of public investment (i.e. provision for services to be rendered in the future) significantly different from the pattern of current services?

There is a long history of scepticism about the ability and willingness of low-income countries to use their fiscal systems for redistributive purposes. Their ability to do so, it is often asserted, is limited by the smallness and narrowness of the tax base, as well as by the tendency for government service networks to leave large sectors or social classes practically untouched in some instances. Willingness, meanwhile, is limited by the tendency to use the tax system for other purposes—raising revenue at least cost; assisting presumed leading sectors through tax concessions, subsidies and supportive public expenditures—which may preclude its use for redistributive purposes. Moreover, the greater political participation and power of the 'haves' is thought to pose a major barrier to progressive taxation and constitute a lobby for the promotion of expenditures beneficial to the privileged class.

Recently some evidence that these strictures are overdrawn has begun to accumulate.[1] Moreover, the pessimism is probably less applicable to Malaysia than to other developing countries. Malaysia's political system, far from suppressing the distribution issue, has brought it to the fore. Its fiscal system, which by the late 1960s was collecting 26–27 per cent of GDP as government revenue (including Employees Provident Fund contributions), is relatively well developed.[2] The Malaysian revenue system is fairly pervasive, reaching even small-scale independent producers through export, import and excise taxation. Similarly, the major government services are extended to practically the entire population. The exchange rate is near equilibrium and the system of protection does not, in general, severely distort internal prices.

These favourable circumstances have caused a significant share of the interest in the distributive impact of public sector financial operations to be focused on Malaysia. Studies of the incidence of taxes and/or expenditures have been carried out by Lai Ah Hoon (1968, 1975), Charles McLure (1972), Donald Snodgrass (1974, 1975), Fuat Andic (1977) and Jacob Meerman (1977, 1977a). Although these studies differ in coverage, distributive categories, dating and methodology (see Table 6.1), they are, in general, broadly consistent with each other, and can be pooled to gain approximate answers to the four issues raised earlier. This chapter will look first at the impact of taxes, then at expenditures and finally at the overall redistributive impact of both sides of the budget taken together.

TAX INCIDENCE

Methodology

McLure (1972) conducted the first tax incidence study for Peninsular Malaysia, covering the split year 1957–8, which was also the reference period for the *HBS*. Snodgrass (1974, 1975) marginally adjusted McLure's estimates, converting to a calendar year 1958 basis, and added a parallel estimate for 1968 to give an indication of trends in the post-Merdeka period. Subsequently, Andic (1977) conducted a similar study of tax incidence in 1970. McLure examined only the incidence of the tax system on income size groups, while Snodgrass looked also at ethnic groups and regions of the country. Andic focused on the poor and non-poor.

The methodology of the three studies is similar and traditional in empirical studies of tax incidence. It ignores the development of general equilibrium incidence theory which has occurred over the past fifteen years (Harberger, 1962; McLure, 1971, 1971a); although the general equilibrium approach is theoretically superior, it is hard to apply empirically. Detailed information is collected on (1) the composition of taxes and other forms of government revenue and (2) the incomes, assets, consumption patterns (i.e. tax bases) of the taxpaying groups being studied. The two sets of data are then linked to each other via a set of assumptions about who pays which taxes. Finally, the total taxes estimated to be paid by each taxpaying group are summed up and compared with the group's income base to determine the incidence of taxation on that group.

This methodology involves a lot of detailed work in assembling, consolidating and reclassifying masses of data. Moreover, it requires the researcher to bridge the frequent data gaps with numerous assumptions, not all of which are well supported. One of the most difficult areas is tax shifting; the burden of taxation is often not borne by the entities from which the government actually collects the money, and assumptions about where it does fall are often problematical. Because of these difficulties, even the most careful incidence studies must be regarded as indicative rather than definitive, as many critics have pointed out (e.g. Meerman, 1972; Bird and de Wulf, 1973).

The Snodgrass study covered the federal government and the Employees Provided Fund (EPF),[3] omitting the eleven state governments of Peninsular Malaysia, four municipalities and many smaller local governments. It thus includes about 80–85 per cent of the total fiscal system.[4] Receipts of the government, thus defined, were categorized as taxes,

TABLE 6.1

STUDIES OF FISCAL REDISTRIBUTION IN PENINSULAR MALAYSIA

Study	*Coverage*	*Distributive categories*	*Period of coverage*
Lai (1968, 1975)	Federal grants to state governments	By states	1948–63
McLure (1972)	Federal taxes + EPF contributions	By income size groups	1957–8
Snodgrass (1974, 1975)	Federal taxes + EPF contributions; federally financed expenditures	By income size groups, ethnic groups and regions	1958, 1968
Andic (1977)	Federal and state taxes	Poor and non-poor	1970
Meerman (1977, 1977a)	Selected federal expenditures (agriculture, education, health, pensions)	By income size groups, ethnic groups, regions and levels of urbanization	1974

payments for services, transfer payments received, loan account receipts and sales of assets. Greatest interest focuses on taxes, which are by far the largest and the most clearly coercive type of payment made to the government. Taxpayers were grouped into four income size groups, three ethnic groups (Malays, non-Malays, non-residents) and three regions.[5] Transactions with the rest of the world were omitted in the study, including (in 1968) those with East Malaysia.

Major Findings

The main findings of the Snodgrass study—including those relating to benefit incidence and the overall redistributive effect of the fiscal system, which will be discussed later—are summarized in Tables 6.2 and 6.3.

McLure (1972) found tax incidence by income size groups in 1957–8 to be U-shaped. That is, there was regressivity at the lower income levels and progressivity toward the top of the income range. This pattern resulted mainly from the importance of export duties on rubber and tin as revenue sources. Both contributed to the progressivity at the top and the rubber duty, through its effect on smallholders, also helped to make the structure regressive at the bottom. Had these two duties been ignored, McLure observed, the tax structure would have been approximately proportionate in 1957–8. McLure made no estimate for later years, but he speculated that the regressivity had probably been ironed out and the progressivity increased.

The Snodgrass study supported McLure's conclusion about 1958. It estimated tax incidence in that year as 22 per cent of adjusted income in the lowest group, 14–17 per cent in the middle group and 27 per cent in the highest (Table 6.2). But it confirmed only half of McLure's speculation about later trends. Although the 1968 rate of incidence was much higher than the 1958 rate in each income group,[6] the U-shaped pattern persisted in 1968. The under-$150 group seems to have been paying a lower share of total taxes than in 1958 but the levy on the average under-$150 household was significantly higher. On the other hand, the progressivity at the top of the structure does seem to have increased somewhat. The continuing regressivity at the low end of the income scale is attributable to large increases in revenues from import duties and excise taxes (including road transport fees), which probably fell heavily on the two lowest income groups (Snodgrass, 1975, p. 280). This influence far outweighs the effect of lighter payments for rubber export duties in its impact on under-$150 incomes.

Table 6.3 adds the ethnic dimension to the picture. It shows that the generally poorer Malay half of the population paid less than one-third of the tax bill in 1958. Tax incidence was also lighter for Malays in relation to adjusted income, although not dramatically so. As tax collections were raised to two-and-a-half times their 1958 level by 1968, a further share of the tax burden was shifted to the non-Malays. The Malay share dropped to about 28 per cent; while the average Malay paid $94 in taxes in 1968, the average non-Malay (whose adjusted income was twice as great) paid $251.

TABLE 6.2
MAJOR FINDINGS BY INCOME SIZE GROUPS

	1958				1968			
Income size ($)	*$ million*	*Per cent of total*	*Per cent of adjusted income*[1]	*$ per household*[2]	*$ million*	*Per cent of total*	*Per cent of adjusted income*[1]	*$ per household*[2]
				Taxes				
0–150	143.5	24.9	21.9	264	281.8	19.4	31.2	369
150–500	259.8	45.0	16.6	500	572.7	39.4	25.5	847
500–1,000	62.4	10.8	13.7	1,071	169.4	11.7	22.9	2,058
1,000+	111.7	19.3	26.7	7,071	429.8	29.6	50.8	14,326
Total	577.5	100.0	18.6	507	1,453.6	100.0	30.7	937
				Public Consumption I[3]				
0–150	63.4	34.7	9.7	116	160.2	43.2	17.8	210
150–500	85.0	46.4	5.4	164	163.2	44.0	7.3	241
500–1,000	10.3	5.6	2.3	176	26.9	7.2	3.6	327
1,000+	24.3	13.3	5.8	1,539	20.9	5.6	2.5	696
Total	182.9	100.0	5.9	161	371.1	100.0	7.8	239

TABLE 6.2 (continued)

Public Consumption II								
0–150	206.4	38.2	31.5	379	426.4	41.9	47.3	473
150–500	266.9	49.4	17.0	514	477.8	47.0	21.3	707
500–1,000	36.0	6.7	7.9	618	75.3	7.4	10.2	915
1,000+	31.1	5.8	7.4	1,969	37.7	3.7	4.5	1,255
Total	540.5	100.0	17.4	475	1,017.2	100.0	21.5	656
Transfer Payments								
0–150	134.0	51.7	20.4	246	240.4	41.3	26.6	315
150–500	107.8	41.6	6.9	208	273.0	46.9	12.1	404
500–1,000	14.1	5.4	3.1	242	40.6	7.0	5.5	493
1,000 +	3.3	1.3	0.8	210	28.3	4.9	3.4	945
Total	259.3	100.0	100.0	228	582.3	100.0	12.3	375
Net Current Balance[4]								
0–150	+176.8		+27.0	+328	+338.2		+37.5	+443
150–500	+71.9		+4.6	+138	+100.7		+4.5	+149
500–1,000	−21.2		−4.6	−364	−75.0		−10.1	−911
1,000 +	−84.1		−20.1	−5,324	−385.8		−45.6	−12,860
Total	+143.5		+4.6	+126	−21.9		−0.5	−14

TABLE 6.2 (continued)

Income size ($)	1958 $ million	1958 Per cent of total	1958 Per cent of adjusted income[1]	1958 $ per household[2]	1968 $ million	1968 Per cent of total	1968 Per cent of adjusted income[1]	1968 $ per household[2]
Public Investment I								
0–150	30.8	33.4	4.7	57	149.2	43.3	16.5	195
150–500	46.0	49.9	2.9	88	141.7	41.1	6.3	210
500–1,000	5.4	5.9	1.2	93	36.4	10.6	4.9	443
1,000+	10.0	10.8	2.4	632	17.1	5.0	2.0	570
Total	92.1	100.0	3.0	81	344.4	100.0	7.3	222
Public Investment II								
0–150	37.9	35.9	5.1	61	155.5	42.8	16.3	188
150–500	51.5	48.8	2.9	87	149.9	41.3	6.3	213
500–1,000	6.1	5.8	1.2	91	39.0	10.7	5.1	456
1,000+	10.0	9.5	2.6	796	18.6	5.1	2.1	628
Total	105.5	100.0	3.1	81	363.0	100.0	7.3	221

[1]Adjusted income includes export duties, company taxes and retained earnings; see Snodgrass (1975, pp. 285–8). The income estimate for 1968 is almost certainly biased downward, so all the figures in the 'Per cent of adjusted income' column for 1968 are overstated to an unknown degree.

[2]Household size and income are positively correlated. Thus $ per capita, which was not calculated, would at a minimum be less strongly correlated with income than is $ per household.

[3]'Public Consumption I' and 'Public Investment I' represent allocable items only. 'Public Consumption II' and 'Public Investment II' also include unallocable overheads, arbitrarily divided on an equal per capita basis.

[4]'Net Current Balance' consists of Public Consumption II plus Transfer Payments, less the sum of taxes, payments for services, and transfer receipts. The last two items, both small, are not shown separately here.

TABLE 6.3
MAJOR FINDINGS BY ETHNIC GROUPS

	1958				*1968*			
	$ million	*Per cent of total*	*Per cent of adjusted income*	*$ per capita*	*$ million*	*Per cent of total*	*Per cent of adjusted income*	*$ per capita*
				Taxes				
Malays	177.5	30.7	17.0	56	411.8	28.2	24.9	94
Non-Malays	400.0	69.3	19.5	128	1,048.5	71.8	34.0	251
Total	577.5	100.0	18.6	92	1,460.3	100.0	30.8	171
				Public Consumption I				
Malays	73.7	40.3	7.0	23	178.7	48.1	10.8	41
Non-Malays	109.1	59.7	5.3	35	192.5	51.9	6.2	46
Total	182.9	100.0	5.9	29	371.2	100.0	7.8	44
				Public Consumption II				
Malays	251.8	46.6	24.1	80	501.7	49.3	30.4	114
Non-Malays	288.6	53.4	14.1	92	515.6	50.7	16.7	123
Total	540.4	100.0	17.4	86	1,017.3	100.0	21.5	119

TABLE 6.3 (continued)

	1958				1968			
	$ million	*Per cent of total*	*Per cent of adjusted income*	*$ per capita*	*$ million*	*Per cent of total*	*Per cent of adjusted income*	*$ per capita*
Transfer Payments								
Malays	124.4	48.0	11.9	39	278.6	47.8	16.9	63
Non-Malays	135.0	52.0	6.6	43	303.8	52.2	9.8	73
Total	259.3	100.0	8.4	41	582.3	100.0	12.3	68
Net Current Balance								
Malays	+167.1		+16.0	+53	+300.3		+18.2	+68
Non-Malays	−23.7		−1.2	−8	−328.9		−10.7	−79
Total	+143.4		+4.6	+23	−28.6		−0.6	−3
Public Investment I								
Malays	36.2	39.2	3.5	11	211.2	61.3	12.8	48
Non-Malays	56.1	60.8	2.7	18	133.4	38.7	4.3	32
Total	92.3	100.0	3.0	15	344.6	100.0	7.3	40
Public Investment II								
Malays	42.6	40.5	4.1	14	220.4	60.7	13.3	50
Non-Malays	62.7	59.5	3.1	20	142.7	39.3	4.6	34
Total	105.3	100.0	3.4	17	363.0	100.0	7.7	43

The work of Andic (1977), which relates to 1970 and is based on the *PES* and preliminary consumption data from the 1973 Household Expenditure Survey, supports the McLure and Snodgrass results in some respects while differing sharply from them in others. Unlike the two earlier researchers, Andic included state taxes in his calculations but omitted EPF contributions. Focusing exclusively on poor households, defined as those receiving $150 or less per month, Andic found the tax system to be highly progressive. The poor, according to his estimates (Andic, 1977, p. 343), received 10 per cent of total income in 1970 while paying only 3–4 per cent of federal taxes. Snodgrass (1975, p. 277), by contrast, found them to pay 25 per cent of total taxes in 1958 and 19 per cent in 1968. McLure's estimate for 1957–8 was 21 per cent (McLure, 1972, p. 79). Comparing Andic's list of taxes paid by poor households in 1970 (Andic, 1977, p. 342) with those of Snodgrass for 1958 and 1968 (1975, p. 280) and McLure for 1957–8 (1972, pp. 78–9), it is evident that Andic allocated much smaller amounts of export duty, import duty and excise tax revenues to poor households while assuming that income taxes do not affect them at all. In addition, as already noted, he left EPF contributions, which in international practice would be treated as a tax, out of the calculation entirely. The overall effect would appear to be considerable overstatement of the degree of progressivity in the Malaysian tax system.[7]

The implication of the Andic study is that the Malaysian tax system is rather sharply progressive. By contrast, the McLure and Snodgrass studies suggest that it is regressive at low levels of income and progressive at high levels. The Snodgrass study, the only one which explicitly compares two different years (although McLure did project his 1957–8 results to 1968 on the basis of partial information), suggests some decrease in the low-end regressivity and increase in the high-end progressivity through time. Despite the presence of a few regressive elements—export duties on rubber and some import duties and excise taxes[8]—the Malaysian tax system, by all accounts, at least does not seriously worsen income distribution. Putting the conclusion more positively, it succeeds in raising, in a reasonably equitable manner, a rapidly growing amount of public revenue[9] which can then be spent in such a way as to improve the distribution of income and social consumption.

BENEFIT INCIDENCE

Methodology

Snodgrass (1974, 1975) conducted the first benefit incidence study for Peninsular Malaysia in conjunction with the tax incidence estimates discussed in the preceding section. Recently Meerman (1977, 1977a) has carried out detailed studies of benefit incidence for selected categories of government expenditure.

Although benefit incidence has been studied much less frequently than tax incidence the methodological problems which it poses are similar.

The same types of imputations must be made, on the same kind of assumptions and with the same kinds of questions raised.

In the Snodgrass study government outlays were first categorized as (1) purchases of goods and services, which is further broken down into (a) public consumption and (b) public investment; (2) transfer payments extended; (3) loan account payments; and (4) purchases of assets. Public consumption and investment were further subdivided using an activity code. The activity code plays two roles. First, it distinguishes between overhead expenditures which must be regarded as being consumed by, or invested on behalf of, the entire population indivisibly and expenditures which are allocable to particular beneficiaries. Thereafter, it subdivides the second category functionally.

The coding system employed is:

- I. Overhead expenditures
  - a. General administration
  - b. Defence
  - c. Internal security
- II. Allocable expenditures
  - A. Economic services
    1. Agriculture and rural development
    2. Mining
    3. Commerce and industry
    4. Transportation
    5. Communication
    6. Utilities
  - B. Social services
    1. Education and training
    2. Health and family planning
    3. Housing
    4. Others

This approach implicitly values government services at cost. No theoretical defence can be offered for this procedure, since there is no competitive market for the services involved, to validate the interpretation of cost of production as the market value of the service. However, there is no practical alternative to following here the precedent of all past studies.

The above paragraphs discuss the way that the government financial data were treated in the study. A separate set of questions concerns the definition and classification of beneficiaries.

Defining a beneficiary is even more complex than the analogous problem of defining a taxpayer. First of all, as noted earlier, many government expenditures are relatively pure public goods. These are consumed by the population as a whole and can be allocated to beneficiaries only on the basis of some arbitrary rule, such as equal amounts per capita or per dollar of income. Secondly, there is a phenomenon similar to tax shifting, in which a *secondary beneficiary* shares the benefits with the *primary beneficiary*. An example is a fertilizer subsidy, which benefits the farmer (the primary beneficiary) by raising his net income but may also benefit the consumer (the secondary beneficiary) through lower prices for farm produce. And thirdly, there are *indirect beneficiaries* of government expenditure. If the *direct beneficiary* is the person for whom the service is provided, the *indirect beneficiary* is the person or firm to whom the payment is made.[10] The latter category includes government employees, contractors and suppliers. In a really refined analysis, one could add all those who benefit from subsequent rounds of expenditure initiated by the first-round indirect beneficiaries. Their identity would depend on the expenditure patterns of the indirect beneficiaries and recipients in subsequent rounds. A rough indicator of this pattern would be provided by the location of the first-round indirect beneficiary, which could be different from that of the direct beneficiary.

In the midst of all this complexity, the study focused its main attention on direct primary beneficiaries, classified by ethnic group, region and income size group as described earlier.

Major Findings

The findings of Snodgrass (1974, 1975) with respect to the benefit incidence of public consumption, transfer payments and public investment in 1958 and 1968 are displayed in Tables 6.2 and 6.3, above.

In 1958 there was a strong positive correlation between the level of household income and the receipt of allocable *public consumption* services (Table 6.2). By 1968 the situation had changed considerably. The differential between high- and low-income households had narrowed, and the pattern in relation to income had become uniformly progressive.[11] This differential was evident in transportation, communication, utility, education, health, housing and other social services. It remained so, although reduced, in 1968.

This same differential is visible in the ethnic-group breakdowns (Table 6.3). The Malays received just 40 per cent of the allocable public consumption services in 1958. Although this represented a 7 per cent income gain for the Malays, compared with about 5 per cent for the non-Malays, the Malays were at a disadvantage in absolute terms. Significant improvement was however made by 1968. The estimate for that year is that Malays received 48 per cent of allocable consumption services. The amount of money budgeted for agriculture and rural development had increased substantially and the relative disadvantage of the Malays with respect to social services had been reduced. However, with 51 per cent of the population in 1968, the Malays still got less than a proportionate share of government services.[12]

A considerable volume of *transfer payments* flows through the Malaysian fiscal system each year. Transfer payments to residents of Peninsular Malaysia from the federal government (directly or through the states) and the EPF totalled $259 million in 1958, and had risen to $582 million by 1968. These transfers are of several kinds, as Table 6.4 shows. They have never been strongly redistributive.[13] Although the poorer ethnic groups and regions have tended to receive slightly lower transfer payment benefits than the richer, the broad trend has been

TABLE 6.4
TRANSFER PAYMENTS TO RESIDENTS
($ million)

	1958	*1968*
General grants to state governments	73.0	114.1
Educational grants	117.7	301.7
Rubber replanting contributions	37.5	28.6
Other agricultural subsidies	0.9	17.9
EPF benefits	12.1	68.9
Others	18.2	39.2
Total	259.4	582.4

toward per capita equality (see Table 6.3). Of course, this in itself implies some redistribution effect in relation to the unequal pre-transfer levels of income.

Perhaps the most important tool of fiscal redistribution has been *public investment*. The level of public investment was low in 1958.[14] Moreover, it, like public consumption, was biased against the Malays and low-income groups generally. This pattern no doubt reflected lingering colonial influences. In addition, a period of low rubber prices and severe depression in the tin market immediately after Independence dampened the urge to innovate. Not long thereafter, however, changes occurred which are evident in the data for 1968.

Chapter 3 discussed the efforts made during the early 1960s to break through implementation constraints and raise the level of development expenditure. These efforts led to a sharp rise in public investment. Even though there had been a period of stagnation in 1965–8, investment as measured in Table 6.2 was well over three times as great in 1968 as in 1958. While the volume rose, the pattern of investment was transformed. This transformation, which is shown in Table 6.5, involved very large increases in expenditure on rural economic projects, as well as provision of economic and social infrastructure in the rural areas, intended to bring levels of service closer to those enjoyed in the towns. The effect was dramatic. As shown in Table 6.3, the Malay share in public investment rose from under 40 per cent to over 60 per cent. Much of this shift will be reflected in time in the distribution of public consumption as well. At least in ethnic-group terms, it seems likely that the disparity in public consumption levels per head which existed in both 1958 and 1968 is well on the way to elimination, and possibly even reversal.

The overall conclusion of the Snodgrass study was as follows:

> Progressivity has increased markedly over the years. The increase has come, by and large, not through taxation but through expenditure.... Inequities in the distribution of public consumption have been reduced considerably, and the volume of transfer payments has risen. Perhaps most important of all, there has

TABLE 6.5
COMPOSITION OF PUBLIC INVESTMENT FINANCED BY THE FEDERAL GOVERNMENT

	1958		*1968*	
	$ million	*Per cent of total*	*$ million*	*Per cent of total*
I. Overhead expenditures	11.8	11.2	18.4	5.1
a. General administration	8.0	7.6	8.5	2.3
b. Defence[1]	—	—	—	—
c. Internal security	3.8	3.6	9.9	2.7
II. Allocable expenditures				
A. Economic services	68.5	64.9	232.0	63.9
1. Agriculture and rural development	9.6	9.1	139.3	38.4
2. Mining	0.1	0.1	0.2	0.1
3. Commerce and industry	—	—	3.6	1.0
4. Transportation	30.4	28.8	37.2	10.2
5. Communication	12.8	12.1	25.8	7.1
6. Utilities	15.6	14.8	25.9	7.1
B. Social Services	25.0	23.7	112.6	31.0
1. Education and training	16.1	15.3	47.7	13.1
2. Health and family planning	2.2	2.1	21.3	5.9
3. Housing	4.4	4.2	40.4	11.1
4. Others	2.3	2.2	3.2	0.9
Total	105.5	100.0	363.0	100.0

[1]All expenditure on defence is classified as public consumption.

been a sharp rise in expenditure on investment projects specifically aimed at low-income groups. These changes are more evident in the racial tabulations than in the size-group or regional tabulations. The reason for this is that the government during this period had a well-developed rationale, political impetus and program for redistribution of income along racial lines, while it did not have such a basis for redistribution among regions or from rich to poor generally. The advantages which low-income groups and states derived from fiscal changes in 1958–68 were mainly a by-product of the programs to redistribute income from non-Malays to Malays (Snodgrass, 1975, p. 283).

Although this conclusion was followed by a list of qualifications inherent in such a study (see also de Wulf, 1974), the work was criticized by Meerman (1975) on several grounds, among them the inferential way in which beneficiaries were identified and the use of arbitrarily allocated overhead expenditure items ('Public consumption II' and 'Public investment II' in Tables 6.2 and 6.3) to achieve a significant part of the allegedly redistributive effect of overall benefit incidence. Meerman sought to overcome these shortcomings in the study he undertook on behalf of the World Bank (Meerman, 1977, 1977a). This study abandoned the goal of comprehensiveness while sparing no effort to identify beneficiaries and cost out specific services provided in the areas which it did cover: agriculture, federal expenditures on rural development, education, health/family planning and pensions/gratuities. A sample survey was designed and carried out specifically for the purposes of the study. In this survey, the respondents' use of the public services was ascertained directly, along with classificatory characteristics such as their income, ethnicity, region and level of urbanization.

The summarized findings of the Meerman study are given in Table 6.6. As is evident there, the study found the pattern of public expenditures in 1974 to be strikingly pro-poor—even more so than the Snodgrass findings for 1968. Expenditures on the public expenditures covered in the study were greater on a per capita basis for Malays than for non-Malays and greater for rural residents than for urbanites. Somewhat

TABLE 6.6
DISTRIBUTION OF SELECTED PUBLIC EXPENDITURES, 1974

(1) *Beneficiary class*	(2) *Annual household income per capita*	(3) *Cost of charged benefits per capita*[1]	*(3) as a percentage of* (2)
Mean	969	128	13
Income quartiles			
1	234	109	50
2	428	133	31
3	621	131	21
4	958	128	13
5	2,620	142	5
Ethnic groups			
Malays	775	156	20
Chinese	1,244	90	7
Indians	911	109	12
Regions			
Selangor	1,714	110	6
Other	844	137	16
North	689	123	18
Level of Urbanization			
Metropolitan	2,028	126	6
Large urban	967	108	11
Small urban	879	115	13
Rural	696	138	20

Source: Meerman (1977, p. iii), adapted.

[1]Includes charged costs for education, medical care, agriculture and pensions.

more was spent on a per capita basis to benefit the highest quintile of income recipients, as compared to lower quintiles, but when benefits are expressed as a percentage of income the progressivity of the expenditure pattern is revealed to be dramatic, with charged benefits rising from 5 per cent of income in the highest quintile to 50 per cent in the lowest.

COMBINED INCIDENCE

Tables 6.2 and 6.3 contain a category called 'Net current balance'. This figure is the algebraic sum of three receipt items—taxes, payments for services and transfer payments received—and two outlay items—public consumption and transfer payments extended. It thus constitutes an indicator of the net redistributive impact of the fiscal system on particular segments of the population. (Public investment is left out of the calculation because it is essentially a provision for government services to be produced in the future and should not be lumped with the current provision of services.) As thus measured, the 1958 fiscal system as a whole was uniformly, if not very strongly, progressive. The regressivity of taxation at low income was more than offset by progressivity in expenditure. This overall progressivity had increased by 1968, although a shift from current deficit to current surplus (Table 6.2) kept the net benefit to the lowest income groups from increasing as much as the net extraction from the highest groups.

On balance, Malays are estimated to have gained $167 million through federal government current fiscal operations in 1958, while the non-Malays gave up about $24 million.[15] By 1958–68 the distribution of consumption services improved, the volume of transfer payments increased and new taxes were levied on the higher incomes. The net result was that the volume of redistribution had increased considerably by 1968, when more than $300 million was in effect transferred from the non-Malays to the Malays. This, in terms of Malaysian magnitudes, is income redistribution on a significant scale (about 3.5 per cent of GNP).

QUALIFICATIONS

Four major qualifications should be attached to the above conclusions:

1. All the studies reviewed deal solely with primary direct beneficiaries. The full effects of public expenditure are hard to assess. It is well known, for example, that many government projects which have rural Malays as direct beneficiaries have non-Malays (or, increasingly, well-placed urban Malays) as indirect beneficiaries in the form of contractors and suppliers. No attempt has been made to analyse this kind of situation.[16] More broadly, the many inter-dependencies in the economy have not been done justice here. If full account could be taken of secondary relationships, including effects on economic growth, an altered picture might emerge.

2. The studies are confined to redistribution through the fiscal system; redistribution through relative prices is ignored. Although it is less

important in Malaysia than in most other low-income countries Malaysia does possess examples of the second kind of redistribution, the most important of which—rice price support and protection of manufactured consumer goods—will be discussed below.

3. State and local governments have been excluded, except in the Snodgrass study in so far as they are financed by the federal government, and in the Andic study. The whole fiscal system may be slightly less progressive than the 80–85 per cent of it examined in my earlier study.

4. Perhaps the most important qualification relates to the use of the dollar as a *numéraire*. All the studies assume that a dollar given up in taxation by the private sector has the same value as a dollar spent by the public sector, and that this is true regardless of what the public sector spends the money on. But government outlays may yield less (or more) welfare than private spending, and the effects of public expenditure programmes vary widely. This is precisely the matter taken up in Chapters 7–9.

DEVELOPMENTS SINCE 1968

The political shocks and policy responses which have occurred since 1968 make it important to consider what changes in the redistributive pattern of the fiscal system may have occurred in later years. Unfortunately, this consideration can be carried out only impressionistically because of problems of data availability and comparability. Nevertheless, several important points can be made, based mainly on an examination of data on federal government finances for all of Malaysia;[17] these points can safely be assumed to apply, in the main, to the fiscal system of Peninsular Malaysia.

In its more activist post-1969 guise, the government has been taking an increasing share of GNP in the form of public-sector extractions. Consolidated government revenue rose from 22.7 per cent of Malaysian GNP in 1968 to 26.9 per cent in 1976, a jump from $2.29 billion to $6.75 billion in absolute terms.[18] This, of course, increases the government's ability to use the fiscal system as a means of redistribution if it so chooses.

These substantial revenue increases came about with no truly major changes in tax structure. Table 6.7 shows federal revenue by source in 1968–77. Most of the revenue increases shown in the Table resulted from increases in the tax base in either real or nominal terms. Significant[19] structural changes made through 1975 were:

1. Levy of some new exercises and imposition of a supplementary export duty on rubber in the 1970 budget;

2. Increase of the import surcharge from 2 per cent to 4 per cent in 1971, when the payroll tax was also abolished.

3. Introduction of a 5 per cent sales tax (later raised to 10 per cent on some luxuries) in 1972.

4. Introduction of an excess profits tax and a service tax on hotel

TABLE 6.7

FEDERAL GOVERNMENT CURRENT REVENUE, 1968–1977
($ million)

Year	*Income tax*	*Other direct taxes*	*Rubber export duty*	*Tin export duty*	*Other export duties*	*Import duties, excises, export surcharge*	*Licence fees*	*Other indirect taxes*	*Total taxes*	*Non-tax revenues*	*Total revenues*
1968	452	35	52	111	34	665	144	43	1,536	354	1,890
1969	500	39	117	122	40	708	157	47	1,730	361	2,091
1970	657	44	80	130	48	806	169	66	2,000	400	2,400
1971	687	26	50	127	54	889	176	72	2,081	337	2,418
1972	741	60	49	127	56	955	194	212	2,394	525	2,920
1973	838	52	233	130	74	1,153	224	342	3,045	357	3,402
1974	1,305	79	383	271	289	1,335	257	392	4,311	476	4,788
1975	1,926	95	121	195	309	1,251	241	438	4,576	541	5,117
1976	2,066	101	519	291	200	1,528	262	524	5,491	666	6,157
1977	2,791	155	557	441	392	1,835	298	601	7,070	689	7,760

Source: Ministry of Finance (1976, pp. xxx–xxxi; 1978, pp. xxiv–xxv).

rooms, restaurant food and entertainment, together with increased road taxes, in 1974.

5. A further increase in the import surcharge to 5 per cent, higher import duties, tighter provisions in the individual income tax and a new real property gains tax in 1975 (this was the largest tax package of the period, totalling $108 million in its estimated effect on annual revenues).

Otherwise, rate changes in 1968–75 were minor. Import duties were raised gradually between 1968 and 1972, cut as an inflation-relief measure in 1973 and then raised again in 1975.

The distributive impact of these rate changes can only be a matter for speculation, since detail on revenues and current information on income and consumption patterns are both lacking. Much of the additional tax revenue has come from export profits made on high commodity prices (e.g. rubber in 1973–4 and again in 1976) or soaring production (petroleum, palm oil). This, plus the progressive character of some of the tax rate changes just enumerated, might be taken as a hint of increasing progressivity.[20] On the other hand, the regressive export duty on rubber smallholders has not been modified or removed and the sales tax constitutes a potentially regressive new element in the tax picture.[21] On balance, therefore, one's guess would have to be that the pattern of tax incidence is much the same today as it was in 1968, or slightly more progressive at best.

In the current expenditure accounts for 1968–77 (Table 6.8) there are no pronounced trends toward a changing pattern of outlays. The major categories of allocable current outlays changed little as a percentage of the total, either individually or collectively, generally quadrupling over the nine-year period. Security, the major 'unallocable' expenditure of the incidence analysis, rose disproportionately up to 1975 before declining again. The distributive implications of rising unallocable expenditures are ambiguous.[22] There was a decline in transfer payments, which reduced one of the system's modestly progressive effects. Current expenditure, like revenue, rose relative to GNP in 1968–77. Thus, as far as one can tell from these aggregated statistics, expenditure incidence may have changed little in 1968–77.

It is development expenditure which most clearly reflects the changes in policy emphasis which occurred after 1969. As Table 6.9 shows, the total volume of spending increased five-fold (in current prices) between 1968 and 1977. Most expenditure categories shared in the increase, but the largest gains were registered by commerce and industry, once a minor category in the development budget but in the 1970s one of the largest areas of expenditure. Once again, then, the pattern of development expenditure gave the clearest indication of the direction in which the government was moving. However, the distributive implications of the increased volume and changing pattern of expenditure indicated by Table 6.9 cannot possibly be deduced from these gross statistics. Only by closer examination of the programmes concerned could one hope to learn much, and even then there would be many questions that can only be answered only as time goes by and as the programmes mature.

TABLE 6.8

FEDERAL GOVERNMENT CURRENT EXPENDITURE, 1968–1977

($ million)

Year	Education	Health	Other social services	Agriculture and rural development	Commerce & communication	General administration	Security	Grants to states	Other transfers	Debt service	Pensions	Total
1968	404	144	16	48	136	203	384	178	32	173	78	1,796
1969	439	139	25	54	147	191	418	189	25	193	110	1,930
1970	477	155	40	52	165	242	496	170	26	237	101	2,161
1971	536	209	33	61	135	262	592	153	42	278	97	2,398
1972	798	234	48	74	149	273	774	169	100	324	125	3,068
1973	805	257	47	56	150	410	904	170	11	413	118	3,341
1974	1,051	313	49	161	261	434	1,103	258	15	493	177	4,315
1975	1,158	361	126	112	246	479	1,314	272	44	619	169	4,900
1976	1,261	387	136	171	275	553	1,219	250	537	837	202	5,828
1977	1,750	532	185	180	312	763	1,517	274	740	960	185	7,398

Source: Ministry of Finance (1976, pp. xxxii–xxxiii; 1978, xxvi–xxvii).

TABLE 6.9
FEDERAL GOVERNMENT DEVELOPMENT EXPENDITURE, 1968–1977
($ million)

Year	*Education*	*Health*	*Other social services*	*Agriculture and rural development*	*Public utilities*	*Commerce and industry*	*Transportation*	*Communication*	*General administration*	*Security*	*Total*
1968	53	26	57	200	34	25	84	32	9	99	619
1969	43	18	53	198	14	39	73	52	20	105	615
1970	44	20	17	198	20	100	80	53	21	172	725
1971	86	23	37	235	31	260	148	29	19	217	1,085
1972	112	27	32	307	42	177	234	76	24	211	1,242
1973	142	34	24	334	49	180	184	39	32	110	1,128
1974	187	42	51	436	55	462	314	46	43	242	1,878
1975	212	57	59	506	118	223	486	65	196	229	2,151
1976	227	47	42	514	133	296	561	46	77	435	2,378
1977	274	44	134	591	250	417	652	219	166	470	3,217

Source: Ministry of Finance (1976, pp. xxxiv–xxxv; 1978, pp. xxvi–xxvii).

Finally, it should be noted that the government has been engaging in an increasing volume of lending outside the budget framework. Some of this lending is to state governments but more of it goes to public authorities and companies in which the government is participating. The volume of federal government net lending rose from $116 million in 1968 to $1,124 million in 1977 (Ministry of Finance, 1976, 1978). Much of the lending is connected with the new types of commercial and industrial venture.

CONCLUSIONS

The Malaysian fiscal system possesses a significant capacity for fiscal redistribution, which was used even before 1969 to redistribute private income and social consumption. As of 1968, quite a lot of the capacity for fiscal redistribution remained unused.[23] Information on how much more of it has been exploited in more recent years is unsatisfactory, although the increase in the size of the public sector relative to the economy as a whole and the rise in and re-allocation of development expenditure are unmistakable trends. One may safely conclude, therefore, that command over resources is not likely to be a major impediment to efforts to reduce economic inequality. The much more important question is the nature and effectiveness of the programmes in which the resources are to be used.

1. On the basis of the incidence studies which he surveyed, Jacob Meerman (1972, p. 38) concluded that *taxation* in low-income countries is only moderately progressive, if not distribution-neutral, but that increasing certain kinds of *expenditures* 'has been an effective device for decreasing income-concentration'. This latter conclusion was based on evidence which Meerman describes as 'tentative, weak and restricted'.

2. This fact is attributable partly to the open and organized structure of the economy, which makes tax collection easier, and partly to strong 'tax effort'. In a group of fifty-two low-income countries studied by Lotz and Morss (1967), Malaysia ranked fourth in tax revenues as a share of GNP. When allowance was made (through a multiple regression technique) for its relatively high GNP per capita and its openness, it ranked fifteenth.

3. The EPF has run large net surpluses and invested them almost entirely in government securities, so it has been an important source of public finance. EPF contributions are not generally regarded as taxes in Malaysia but are so treated here.

4. Between 1966 and 1975, federal revenues ranged between 82 per cent and 85 per cent of the consolidated total for the federal and state governments. During the same period the federal government also accounted for 87 to 91 per cent of current expenditure and between 70 and 77 per cent of development expenditure. Some of the federal spending consisted of the provision of financing for expenditures by the states. Including expenditures financed with federal government money, the states accounted for a steady 18–20 per cent of consolidated current expenditures. Together with the public authorities, they made up from 30 to 38 per cent of development expenditure (all figures based on Ministry of Finance, 1976, pp. xxvi–xxix, xliv–xlv). But development expenditure is largely financed by borrowing, which is strictly a federal prerogative. The fiscal powers of the states are thus severely limited. (Those of the local governments, which are excluded from the above statistics, are even more so.)

5. The regional analysis is not discussed here.

6. This is attributable partly to tax increases between 1958 and 1968 and partly to greater understatement of the income base in the later year. The income base in 1958 is estimated using the *HBS*, while the 1968 estimate relies on the *SRM/Ford survey*; see the discussion of the under-reporting of household income in Chapter 4, above.

7. Oddly, Andic (1977) reflects no recognition of the large discrepancies discussed in this paragraph.

8. Plus the implicit tax involved in the protection of domestic rice production. This is discussed in Chapter 7.

9. Increases in the tax base, the levying of new taxes and rate increases for existing ones (as well as improved enforcement in some cases) have steadily raised revenue as a percentage of GNP over the years. Consolidated government revenue was around 20 per cent of GNP in 1957 (Department of Statistics, n.d.—*c*. 1962, pp. 4, 7). During the 1960s it rose gradually. Faster increases have followed in the 1970s, culminating in a record figure of 28.4 per cent on a Malaysian-wide basis in 1975 (Ministry of Finance, 1976, pp. iv, xxvi). These totals all omit EPF contributions.

10. Some experts distinguish three kinds of incidence: tax, benefit and expenditure. Expenditure incidence is also sometimes referred to as procurement benefits. The terminology used here is intended to reflect the fact that there are actually two sets of beneficiaries of government expenditure programmes (direct and indirect), who, however, benefit in very different ways. It should be noted that the distinction between direct and indirect beneficiaries applies to public consumption and investment only. For transfer payments extended and (to the extent that there is any subsidy element involved) loan account payments and purchases of assets, the distinction is meaningless because there is no government service involved other than the payment itself.

11. Progressivity and regressivity, terms usually applied to taxation, have obvious parallel meanings in relation to expenditure. Note, however, that progressivity of expenditure (i.e., decreasing expenditure in relation to income as income rises) is consistent with higher expenditure per head at higher income levels. Parity in expenditure is a much more demanding criterion than progressivity. The progressivity referred to in the text is less evident in the per household tabulations of Table 6.2 than it would be in per capita data. In per capita terms, public consumption was probably less than twice as high in the highest income group as in the lowest.

12. These are the *facts* regarding the distribution of public services among ethnic groups; politically, of course, people's *perceptions* of what the distribution is may be more important than the actual facts. It is sometimes said that Malay perceptions emphasize the greater wealth of the Chinese, while Chinese perceptions emphasize the alleged slanting of public services to benefit the Malays. This generalization suggests that both groups manage to find cause for major dissatisfaction, yet one study of popular perceptions of the distribution of benefits from a particular development project reached a contrary conclusion. Montgomery and Katzman (1976) evaluated the Penang Water Supply Project financed by The Asian Development Bank and found that the public regarded the benefits as being more or less equally distributed among ethnic groups, even though in fact the lower-income Malay community was more likely to be excluded from the project altogether, or to use only the public standpipes, than were the generally better-off non-Malays.

13. Lai Ah Hoon (1968) analysed in detail the history of federal grants to the states up to 1963. She found that the impetus to use these grants for large redistributions to the poorer states was always overcome by the opposition of the richer states and the dominance of ethnic over regional interests.

14. 'Public Investment' was used loosely in the study to refer to total expenditure on investment projects. In general, it was impossible to remove land purchases and other non-investment elements from such expenditures. However, the vast majority of expenditures enumerated are really for investment goods. Investment was limited to physical assets; investment in human capital was treated as consumption expenditure.

15. The failure of Malay gains to equal non-Malay losses is of course attributable to the fact that the budget was not balanced in terms of the transactions enumerated here. Previous students of overall fiscal incidence (e.g. Gillespie, 1965) have worried about whether this apparent fiscal dividend was real or merely an indicator of inflationary fiscal policies. Since the Malaysian economy experienced virtual price stability in 1958–68, it seems legitimate to regard the dividend as a real one in this case.

16. To the extent that government attempts to favour Malays over non-Malays as government employees, contractors and suppliers succeed, Malays receive a larger share of the

indirect benefits of government expenditures than they would otherwise. However, non-Malays must have received by far the larger share in absolute terms, at least until very recently.

17. The main statistical source for this section is the *Economic Report 1976/77* (Ministry of Finance, 1976). Additional sources consulted include Budget Speeches, *Annual Reports* of Bank Negara Malaysia and *Economic Reports* for earlier years.

18. The source for this is the Treasury, 1974; and the Ministry of Finance, 1976. The percentage shares are lower than those cited earlier in the text because they exclude EPF contributions. They also refer to Malaysia as a whole, rather than just Peninsular Malaysia, but this probably makes little difference. The absolute figures are influenced by inflation, which became significant in 1973.

19. Defined as changes which were expected to affect annual revenue by $30 million or more.

20. However, income distribution may also have worsened during the 1973–4 boom. If so, the tax structure did not necessarily become more progressive relative to the changing income base.

21. The difficulties of the rubber smallholders, caused by the sudden collapse of boom prices during 1974, led to demonstrations in December of that year. The effect of the sales tax is difficult to determine *a priori*. Although sales taxes are generally regressive, the Malaysian tax has a large number of exemptions and its incidence is difficult to assess accurately in the absence of current data on consumption patterns.

22. One could argue that they are equally beneficial to all citizens; differentially beneficial according to ethnic group, income level or some other attribute; or not a benefit at all, but a 'cost of civilization', to use Kuznets's phrase. See Jacob Meerman's comment on my earlier article (Meerman, 1975) and my reply (Snodgrass, 1975a).

23. Five major ways of making the fiscal system more progressive were suggested in Snodgrass (1975):

'(1) The regressivity of taxation at low incomes could be eliminated by altering the taxation of consumption and reducing taxes on smallholder rubber production. Import duties, excises, and the new sales tax are regressive in effect; they would be less so if they exempted more items with low income elasticities and concentrated on those with higher elasticities. Rubber smallholders are discriminated against *vis-à-vis* both rubber estates and smallholders producing other crops.

(2) Somewhat greater progressivity at the high end of the income range could probably be obtained at little cost. Malaysia is fortunate to have an extractive sector which has a low supply elasticity and a high degree of foreign ownership, with, one suspects, little intention of reinvesting its substantial profits in Malaysia. It could be taxed more and probably not produce much less or draw down its capital much faster than it otherwise would. In general, company taxation (at 40% with a wide range of possible reliefs) is very moderate. However, taxation of employment—the EPF levy is 10%; the 2% payroll tax which existed in 1968 has been repealed but replaced by a workman's compensation levy—is alarmingly high in view of the unemployment problem.

(3) Efforts, now well advanced, to provide essentially equal public services to all parts of the population should make a major contribution to equity.

(4) Projects aimed at increasing the earning power of the poor are the most revolutionary of all, but only if they are well enough designed to achieve their objective' (Snodgrass, 1975, p. 284).

7 Rural Development Policies

> In Southeast Asia the Federation of Malaysia is unique in its modern development. All countries of the region, as indeed all new states of the world, have created national development plans and often new organizations to implement these plans. Of the countries, only the Federation of Malaysia and Singapore have achieved any success in their development programs. Malaysia and Singapore alone appear to have made serious and sustained efforts to translate their development programs into action.
>
> Ness, 1967, p. vii

ORIGINS AND RATIONALE OF THE PROGRAMME

THE rural economy of Malaysia divides rather neatly into three segments: the estates, export smallholders, and peasant producers (especially padi farmers) and fishermen producing for their own consumption or sale to domestic consumers. The first and second groups are distinguished from the third by the important technological fact that they are concerned with perennial tree crops. Otherwise there is much similarity between the second and third groups: each operates on a small scale, predominately through family enterprises, and each is overwhelmingly Malay.[1] Many individuals, in fact, keep a foot in each camp. The contrast between these two peasant sectors and the estates is of course enormous. The estates are generally owned by limited liability companies, either foreign or non-Malay, and operated using hired labour and management. By contrast to the export smallholders, they are typically much closer to the technological frontier of the best available trees and production methods.

Although this three-way division emphasizes the most important internal distinctions within the rural sector, there are grey areas. The official dividing line between the estates and smallholdings is arbitrary: rubber estates are defined as units of 100 acres or more under unified ownership and management, but there are many units of less than 100 acres that are more like estates than peasant smallholdings. Some of these are in fact estates which were legally subdivided by registration in various names, usually members of a family, in order to qualify for the larger replanting grants obtainable by smallholders. These medium-sized units, plus a few market gardens and poultry or livestock farms, represent a medium-scale capitalist segment of the rural economy.

Differences in living standards among these sectors have arisen as a result of the performance of their respective economic bases. In the early post-war period, the very survival of the natural rubber industry, then almost the sole base for both the estate and the smallholder sectors, was in doubt. The Depression, war and post-war Emergency, plus the sheer passage of time, had all contributed to the industry's deterioration, while the synthetic rubber industry, itself a child of World War II, offered unprecedented competitive challenge. Fortunately for Malaya, improved, high-productivity stock was available for replanting and by the early 1950s the government was firmly committed to the support of a massive replanting programme. This saved the estates, which had replanted two-thirds of their rubber acreage by 1962,[2] and in fact foreshadowed a long and impressive list of technological improvements which proved applicable to rubber and other tree crops, thus in time guaranteeing the continued prosperity of the estate sector. However, it was more difficult to apply these advances to the smallholder sector and of course they had no relevance at all to the peasant padi producers and fishermen, whose economic base was completely different. To do something for the smallholder, therefore, required devising means of diffusing available technologies to the smaller units, while for the padi growers and fishermen an entirely different set of technological improvements had to be first devised and then diffused.

Rural population growth continuously complicated the problem of rural development. In the early years of the Emergency a large number of rural Chinese, many of whom had fled the towns during the Japanese occupation, were resettled in 'new villages'. This massive relocation programme caused the rural population[3] to stagnate during the 1947–57 intercensal period (Table 7.1). However, the numbers of Malays and Indians residing in rural areas grew and after the mid-1950s the numbers of rural Chinese also increased. The dominant influence was of course the high rate of natural increase experienced from the early 1950s on. Since the Malays experienced both a high rate of natural increase and a low rate of rural–urban migration, their rural population growth was

TABLE 7.1

GROWTH OF RURAL POPULATION, 1947–1970

(thousands)

	Year	*Malays*	*Chinese*	*Indians*	*Others*	*Total*
Population in:	1947	2,153	1,074	352	29	3,608
	1957	2,522	619	409	49	3,599
	1970	3,665	874	513	33	5,085
Intercensal changes:	1947–57	+369	–455	+57	+20	–9
	1957–70	+1,143	+255	+105	–17	+1,486

Note: Discrepancies are attributable to rounding. 'Rural population' means population not residing in communities of 1,000 or more inhabitants.

the highest. More than a million Malays were added to the rural population in 1957–70, an increase of 45 per cent. Although there have been economic difficulties created for the other ethnic groups by rural population growth (especially the South Indian estate population, which has been squeezed between high rates of natural increase, on the one hand, and stagnant estate labour demand combined with limited job opportunities in other sectors, on the other hand), it is the Malays who have been hit hardest. Population growth clearly held back gains in income per capita for the rural Malays.

The phrase 'rural development', as used in Malaysia, connotes both direct productivity-rising programmes and efforts to improve infrastructure and social services for consumption as well as production purposes. The programme originated in the 1950s, close on the heels of the decisions to replant the rubber estates and relocate the rural Chinese.[4] With these conspicuous efforts to aid the predominantly non-Malay parts of the rural economy going on and Merdeka drawing near, the cry for the government to do something for the mass of rural Malays became irresistible. One important rationale was to lessen the inequality in the provision of infrastructure and social services which resulted from colonial biases. Although the existing systems of transportation, communication, power and (to a lesser extent) education and public health were good by colonial standards, the infrastructure was designed almost exclusively to serve the needs of the towns, estates and mines (especially the European-owned estates and mines), while good social services were available primarily to the populations dependent on these enterprises.

As time went by, the growing realization that rural advance was limited by the strength of the sector's economic base led to increased emphasis on productivity-raising projects. Beginning with the *First Malaysia Plan*, 1966–70 (*FMP*), rural development was thought of increasingly in the context of national development goals such as production growth, diversification and greater economic equality. In the *FMP* emphasis was given to efforts to increase production along both the intensive and the extensive margins. The hope was to narrow the rural–urban income gap, if possible, thereby assuring some diffusion of the benefits of economic growth, and perhaps also retarding to some extent the rural–urban migratory drift.

The origin of a 'rural development' policy—as opposed to an older emphasis on 'agricultural policy'—can be traced to the formation of RIDA in 1950. The mission of RIDA, and its successor MARA, has undergone continual change during the years. Its original role was very broadly defined as improving rural life through a variety of productive and welfare programmes. Innumerable difficulties were encountered, and RIDA/MARA ultimately was redefined, first as an authority to promote non-agricultural activities in rural areas, and later very largely as a training body to fit rural Malays for effective entry into the urban economy.

The formation of RIDA expressed a dissatisfaction, at least on the part of prominent Malay politicians, with the performance of traditional arms of the federal and state governments in satisfying the desires of the rural electorate to share in development. This dissatisfaction also led to the creation of the Federal Land Development Authority in 1956. FELDA concerned itself with the opening up and settlement of unused but cultivable land. Private land development, which had been rapid during the first three decades of the twentieth century, had virtually halted since 1930. Opposition to further alienation to foreign estate interests was adamant and Chinese land developers also faced formidable difficulties in obtaining the requisite approval from the state governments, which control land use under the federal Constitution. In these circumstances, the federal government took the initiative in a campaign to increase the planted area. Out of several programmes launched during the late 1950s, FELDA, quickly transformed from a co-ordinating body into an instrument for direct federal implementation of land development projects, proved to be a success and has expanded steadily up to the present day.

In 1959 RIDA, FELDA and other rural development activities were co-ordinated under a newly created Ministry of Rural Development. The persistence of ambiguities and unresolved power struggles is suggested by the subsequent fate of this Ministry. First renamed National and Rural Development, later simply National Development, it never gained responsibility for overall development planning. Important programmes affecting the rural areas remained under the aegis of the Ministries of Agriculture, Lands or even (in the case of rubber replanting) Commerce and Industry. Later, in a cabinet reshuffle, the Ministry was abolished and its functions distributed to other Ministries.

The highly political nature of rural development programmes made the distribution of functions among ministers a matter of great sensitivity. The Ministry of Rural Development was very much the creation of Deputy Prime Minister (later Prime Minister) Tun Abdul Razak. Successive Ministers of Agriculture were rivals with their opposite numbers for Rural (or National) Development for support among the rural Malays, if not indeed for leadership of UMNO itself.[5] These divisions of function and rivalries unavoidably led to co-ordination problems. 'Rural development' programmes have more consistently been aimed at benefiting the small-scale, overwhelmingly Malay smallholders, padi growers and fishermen than have 'agricultural policies', even though the latter are obviously of equal importance for rural welfare.

'Agricultural policies' have historical antecedents which were mentioned in Chapter 2. The first deviation from *laissez-faire*, as seen there, was the promotion of rice cultivation in the 1930s. The concern at the time was more one of maintaining the price of the wage good for the estate and mining sectors than of diversifying the economy or improving the status of the padi cultivators. Support of the rice industry was limited in the 1930s but after the War it grew apace. The main instrument was investment in drainage and irrigation facilities for areas which could be made suitable for padi cultivation—or, if already single-cropped with padi, suitable for double-cropping. Other elements were introduced into the programme in time.

Amazingly, action to reverse the colonial neglect of the rubber smallholder was slow to come in the post-Merdeka period.[6] Smallholders were included in the subsidized replanting programme inaugurated in the 1950s, and received larger grants per acre than the estates, but were subjected to strict conditions, with which many found it difficult to comply, if they were to qualify for actual receipt of the grant. As a result, replanting of the smallholdings proceeded much more slowly than that of the estates; for example, in 1965, when 80 per cent of estate rubber acreage had been replanted, the corresponding figure for smallholdings was only 50 per cent.[7] Income earned by smallholder families from rubber continued to be subject to much heavier taxation than applied to comparable incomes in any other part of the economy. The otherwise admirable Rubber Research Institute of Malaya (RRIM), which is financed by a cess on the exports of estates and smallholders alike, remained strongly under the influence of estate interests, although the attention which it devoted to the problems of smallholders did increase gradually through time and a Rubber Industry Smallholders Development Authority (RISDA) was established in 1972. Still more recently, the rubber smallholders have begun to mobilize their latent political power to push for more active government assistance.

Finally, the nature of Malaysian land policy should be noted. The major, indeed almost the sole, element of land policy has been the programme to develop jungle for new cultivation. Although the decision to emphasize expansion of the land base over rationalization of the use of presently cultivated land makes good economic sense, it may also be surmised that the choice has been influenced by political factors: political barriers to land development are less formidable than those impeding land reform. Action has been taken through the Malay Reservation enactments of nine of the eleven Peninsular states to halt the sale of land by Malays to non-Malays. This has prevented the polarization of landlord–tenant relationships along ethnic lines. It has not, however, prevented high and growing rates of tenancy on padi land in many parts of the country, land fragmentation through inheritance under Islamic law and other events which may be harmful to productivity and are certainly indicative of growing inequality. Efforts to curb tenancy abuses, beginning with the Padi Cultivators (Control Rents and Security of Tenure) Ordinance of 1955, have been marked by the lethargic enforcement characteristic of countries in which landlords wield significant political power.

The rationale for rural development policies, like virtually everything else in Malaysia, was affected by the events of 1969. The most important effect was to reduce the overall priority of rural development relative to industrialization/urbanization policies and education. Within rural development itself, the most noticeable change was toward more active intervention in rural markets for credit and produce. Thus, the activities of the Federal Agricultural Marketing Authority (FAMA, founded in 1965) and the agricultural bank, Bank Pertanian Malaysia (1969) were expanded and a National Padi and Rice Authority was created (1971).

Otherwise, the content of the rural development programme remained approximately as it was. Expenditure on drainage and irrigation facilities for padi declined as work on the giant Muda and Kemubu schemes was completed, while FELDA continued, under government urging, to accelerate its rate of land development and settlement.

One new theme which gained strength after 1969 was the planning of land development and other rural programmes in close relationship to plans for urban and other non-agricultural activities. A series of regional plans was drawn up, covering both 'opportunity' and 'problem' areas of the country. The 'opportunity' area plans, of which the large-scale development in the Jengka Triangle of Central Pahang was the first, started as nearly pure land-use plans and developed over a period of time into socio-economic plans for developing particular areas in accordance with national objectives. Perhaps the most ambitious of the plans, for the quarter-million acre Pahang Tenggara region, aims at creating an integrated urban–rural economy in the last large and promising but nearly empty segment of Peninsular Malaysia. The resulting East Coast urbanization, it is hoped, will support the entry of more Malays into urban pursuits.

The fundamental significance of these policy changes is that rural development programmes are no longer framed on the tacit assumption that underlay earlier programmes to raise first the welfare and later the productivity of the rural Malays: that these people not only were, but would indefinitely remain, overwhelmingly rural. In the new emphasis improvement of rural life and economic activity is not an end in itself but—ideally, at least—a way of preparing some rural Malays for intersectoral mobility and making interim improvements in the lives and incomes of those who will have to remain for some time in the rural areas as a result of the gradual nature of structural change.

This review of the purposes and rationale of rural development policies provides the framework which will be used to evaluate specific policies in the remainder of this chapter. This will be done under four headings: policies toward rubber and other perennials (with heavy emphasis on smallholders relative to estates); land development; policies toward rice and other annuals; and rural development policies. In each case the overall aim will be to determine, in so far as possible, what the actual contribution of rural development policies to the reduction of economic inequality (as defined in earlier chapters) has been and what their *potential* is.

POLICIES TOWARD RUBBER AND OTHER PERENNIALS

Malaya has been uniquely suited for the planting of tree crops by both ecology and history. Little else will grow very successfully on the hilly landscape which characterizes most of the Peninsula. The potential for both annual crops and pasturage is quite limited, but tree crops, which imitate the indigenous forest, are easily accommodated. Rubber in particular has proved a successful transplant and oil palm, coconut, tea, coffee and cocoa have all found smaller niches in the Malayan scene. History contributed to the compatibility of Malaya and natural rubber by providing a low population density which left ample space for the planting of rubber on previous forest land and sufficient political influence for British, Chinese and other investors to obtain title to the land. Before World War II the Malayan plantation economy was by no means unique (the Dutch in the Indies were technologically more advanced) but after the War, beginning with the massive replanting programme of the 1950s, a technological gap opened up between Malaysia and other natural rubber producers. This gap has probably widened through time, even though most of the technology developed in Malaysia is freely available to other producers. Technological improvement has not only kept Malaysia ahead of other producers of natural rubber but it has enabled the industry to withstand the long-dreaded inroads of synthetic rubber. Although synthetic's share in the world market has increased enormously since World War II, the production of natural rubber has not, as many feared, become unprofitable. Currently, with the cost of synthetic rubber subject to the influence of higher prices for petroleum, its main ingredient, the position of natural rubber looks stronger than it has for decades.

Rubber has been so important to Malaya and Malaysia throughout the twentieth century that it is sometimes thought to have diverted attention from other, possibly more promising opportunities. Like import substitution in rice, diversification of export crops has often been stated as a major policy objective.[8] The degree of emphasis on both has varied inversely with the perceived prospects of rubber and other current foreign exchange earners. In fact, Malaysia's superiority in the technology of growing and processing rubber may have assisted, rather than impeded, the development of other tree crops. The prime case in point is oil palm, a wild jungle product in West Africa which had been grown on a small scale in Malaya since the 1920s.

When fears for the survival of the natural rubber industry were at their height in the 1950s, oil palm emerged as the one alternative tree crop which was well enough established, through research and limited commercial plantings, to warrant significant substitution for rubber. A rubber price downswing in 1961 accelerated the planting of oil palms by estates in preference to replanted rubber. Subsequently, oil palm was adopted as the preferred crop for FELDA land development schemes where it was technically feasible. In later years, judgements about the relative merits of rubber and oil palm see-sawed as their relative prices changed.[9] Meanwhile, however, planting continued at a rapid rate and production of palm oil and kernels soared. When in 1970 the United Nations Food and Agriculture Organization urged Malaysia (in its World Indicative Plan for Agricultural Development) to cut back on its plans for further expansion of oil palm cultivation the government had the good sense to ignore this gratuitous advice.[10] As a result, oil palm producers and Malaysian foreign exchange reserves have benefited from enormous earnings gains produced by steeply climbing output and a generally elevated price level resulting from world shortages of competitive fats and oils.

The central problem of the natural rubber, coconut and oil palm industries, in terms of their impact on economic inequality, has been to diffuse technological improvements incorporated by the larger, more progressive estates to the smaller holdings. Some of these technological improvements have been embodied in improved varieties of trees, while others have related to better ways of tapping/harvesting and processing the crop. The main improvements which have been embodied in trees are the high-yielding rubber varieties (which were introduced in the 1950s and steadily improved thereafter) and the shift from rubber to oil palm. The main disembodied improvements have been the adoption of less frequent tapping systems, the introduction of chemical yield stimulants and the improvement of grading and packaging to produce a more uniform, valuable product.

Experience with each of these innovations will be reviewed briefly to determine the extent to which smallholders have been able to benefit.

High-yielding Varieties

The natural rubber industry, estates and smallholders alike, faced a 'replant or die' situation at the close of World War II. Although some progressive estates and a very few smallholders had begun to replant on their own initiative in the 1930s, the Depression, War and Emergency had combined to inhibit autonomous replanting to such an extent that active official intervention had become imperative. The first response to this need was the establishment of a Rubber Industry (Replanting) Board in 1952.[11] Two funds were created under this Board: Fund A, which was intended to help finance replanting by the estates, and Fund B, which was to provide a similar facility for the smallholders. A replanting cess of 4½ cents was levied on each pound of rubber exported, the proceeds of which were to be paid into Fund A and Fund B in proportion to the estimated shares of exports derived from estate and smallholder production respectively. Procedures for making payments from the two funds differed. The proceeds of Fund A were to be automatically refunded to all estates upon receipt of their production statistics, while the proceeds of Fund B were to be used to pay subsidies to those smallholders who actually replanted, under official supervision and according to various specified conditions.[12]

Two years after this programme was established, the Mudie Report (Malaya, 1954) reviewed its design and early operation and made several important recommendations. It found the financial resources thus made available for replanting inadequate for the task at hand (especially in view of the post-Korean War slump in rubber prices) and the discrimination against the smallholder objectionable. It therefore recommended that payments from Fund A be made conditional upon actual replanting or new planting by the estates and that the export duty on rubber be reduced to zero when the price fell below 60 cents per lb. so as to lessen its regressive impact on the smallholders.[13] The Report also recommended that steps to be taken to expand rubber acreage, in keeping with its prophetically optimistic view of the long-term prospects of replanted rubber.

The government, under pressure from the Rubber Producers' Council and badly in need of revenue, found itself unable either to impose a conditionally refundable cess on the estates or to grant relief from the export duty. Instead, it decided to underwrite the replanting drive by voting a $280 million subsidy from general revenue. At the same time, the export duty applicable at prices of 80 cents a lb. or more was increased. The combined effect of these two measures was that the government would lose revenue at prices below 80 cents and gain revenue at prices above that figure.[14]

Smallholder replanting grants were originally set at $400 per acre. To receive the grant, a cultivator must clear his land properly, replant using RRIM-approved materials and do an acceptable job of tending the plot until the trees became tappable. His efforts must be officially inspected at each stage, and the subsidy is only paid (in tranches) as the requisite approvals are granted. Many slips are possible in this sequence.[15]

Although the replanting grants pay most of the explicit costs of replanting, they do not cover the important implicit element of cost—the income forgone during the immaturity of the new trees. The importance of implicit costs as a deterrent to replanting varies inversely with size of holding. The owner of a few acres can less well afford to do without a given fraction of his holding for the six years or so it takes modern rubber trees to start yielding, but in fact he must usually forgo all of it, and even persuade his neighbours to co-operate, because small plots of new rubber will not grow healthily if they are surrounded by mature trees which cast a dense shade. Even when substantial increases in income are in prospect, the inadequacies of the rural capital market and the high effective interest rates which prevail can make replanting unattractive to the very small-scale producer. Unquestionably, this is the major reason why smallholder replanting has lagged far behind that of the estates.

Smallholders reacted sluggishly during the early years of the scheme (David Lim, 1973, pp. 224–5). A target of 500,000 acres, nearly one-third of total smallholder acreage, was set for the first six years (1953–8) but only 130,000 acres were in fact replanted during the first three years, despite the increase in the grant to $500 per acre in 1954. The grant was raised further, to $600, in 1956, and then to $750 (with an additional $50 per acre for holders of fewer than five acres) in 1960. These increases had the unintended effect of inducing the subdivision of some of the smaller estates into smallholdings (at least as a legal fiction), so as to qualify for the larger replanting grants.[16] They also brought about some acceleration of replanting by legitimate smallholders, so that by 1967 some 838,000 acres, nearly half of the total at the time the programme began, had been replanted. During the 1967–8 Economy Drive, however, a limit of 45,000 acres per year was imposed on smallholder replanting because Fund B's resources would not permit a larger programme and the government was unwilling to supplement those resources from general revenue.[17] In 1969 the ceiling was raised to 60,000 acres a year, but smallholders were reported by this time to be anxious to replant much larger areas.

Aside from the differences of treatment between the estates and the smallholdings, there have also been systematic, if unintended, differences among sub-groups of smallholders. Owners of larger plots, and plots which are more accessible to markets and therefore easier to intercrop during the immaturity period,[18] almost certainly have been much quicker to replant than owners of the smaller, more isolated holdings. Goering (1969) estimates that while two-thirds of all smallholding workers were Malays in 1962, smallholder acreage replanted during the 1953–66 period was 62 per cent Chinese-owned.

The Shift to Oil Palm

From a mere 100,000 acres during the 1950s, oil palm plantings took-off after 1960 and grew to 240,000 acres by 1965, 675,000 by 1970 and 1,324,000 by 1974. The main impetus behind this growth was the search of the estates for an alternative to replanted rubber—an impetus which was strongest during the recurring periods of gloom about the future prospects of natural rubber. Mainly as a result of oil palm's emergence as the one viable alternative to rubber, estate rubber acreage slipped from two million acres in the mid-1950s to 1.5 million in 1970.[19] Once its agronomic feasibility in large parts of the country had been demonstrated,[20] oil palm was seen to offer producers several important advantages compared to rubber. While its projected returns per acre varied with the fluctuating projections of world prices for palm oil and kernels,[21] they were at least likely to move in a different pattern from that of rubber. Thus, oil palm diversification provided advantages to large estates or estate groups. Moreover, oil palm matured faster (in three years, versus five to six for even the fastest varieties of rubber) and, in an era of unionized estate labour, had the important advantage of requiring lower labour inputs per acre. The principal disadvantage of oil palm is that the capital requirements of the processing plant are much greater. Palm fruit must be picked at just the right moment and processed expeditiously if the quality of the resulting palm oil is to be adequate. Processing cost is a larger share of total cost than for rubber, and managerial and minimum scale requirements are more stringent. An even larger scale of production is required for the efficient processing of palm kernels into palm kernel oil; the first plant for this purpose in Malaysia was not built until around 1970.

For these reasons, oil palm has been exclusively an estate crop, initially a product of the European estates.[22] Beginning in the early 1960s, however, ways were sought for smallholders to share in the growing boom. One possibility considered was the 'nucleus estate'. Under this approach, a state government would lease land to an estate group for oil palm cultivation, on the condition that the group would supervise the planting and cultivation of surrounding smallholdings and open its processing facilities to smallholder output. But nucleus estates planned for south-east Pahang failed when the lessees ignored the needs of the smallholders or, worse yet, neglected even to plant up their own acreage, instead contenting themselves with the extraction of valuable timber from the land leased to them. The only successful means of peasant participation in oil palm cultivation yet devised involves the establishment of publicly-owned estates. FELDA oil palm schemes are in effect estates—albeit worker-owned, although not worker-managed—and oil palm estates have also been set up by federal and state government agencies.

Less Frequent Tapping Systems

With collectively bargained wages rising and becoming more independent of the price of rubber, many estates abandoned the traditional daily tapping routine and started tapping only every second or third day.[23] The technology which makes this possible combines the plastic bag with an anti-coagulant which enables the latex to remain in a usable form for a longer period. This and other labour-saving devices (e.g. greater mechanization of latex collection) have brought about substantial reductions in the labour intensity of rubber production on the estates. Labour per unit of land fell from 14.9 workers per 100 acres in 1963 to 12.8 in 1972, while output per worker soared from 3,700 lb. to 7,600 lb. in the same period. Total employment actually fell by 90,000 (31 per cent) while production rose by 110,000 tons (46 per cent). Estate rubber production is highly routinized and price-inelastic, whereas smallholder output is more elastic and finely tuned to the benefits to the smallholder of tapping versus other uses of his time (or of hiring contract tappers, in the case of the medium-scale owners). The innovations described in this paragraph were particularly responsive to the circumstances of the estates.

Chemical Yield Stimulants

These are a very recent development whose implications are not yet fully defined. Originally applied to old trees which were about to be cut down, their use began to spread to younger trees in the late 1960s. At first it was thought that their effect was to speed the extraction of a given amount of latex from the tree, thus shortening tree life, but in time it became apparent that no reduction in tree life is necessarily implied if adequate fertilization is provided. Although experience is still limited, chemical yield stimulation would appear to be a remunerative technique, since the cost of the chemical and the extra fertilizer needed are low relative to the value of added production. Use of chemical yield stimulants has been limited primarily to the estates so far. Official policy has been to discourage their use by smallholders because of the alleged risks involved. In December 1974 their use was temporarily banned on estates as well (see below).

Improved Grading and Packaging

Traditionally, rubber was graded visually in the form of crepe or sheet. Smallholders usually sold their output as unsmoked sheet; subsequently, when it was smoked for export the amount of foreign matter present was so great that the rubber was graded RSS (Ribbed Smoked Sheet) 3. This low grading (most estate output qualified as RSS 1, which commands a premium of about 2 cents a lb. over RSS 3) reduced smallholder income and inspired several attempts to improve the processing of smallholder rubber (Barlow, Lim and Ong, 1969). A number of group processing centres were set up with private or RIDA/MARA financing. RIDA also built two large factories in the early 1960s but these lost money and were closed in 1965.

The processing issue became more important in the late 1960s, when the industry began to move toward the production of technically specified block rubbers, which would offer consumers the same convenience and predictable quality they were already receiving from synthetic rubber. An agreed system for classifying block rubber, the Standard Malaysia Rubber (SMR) scheme, was adopted in 1965 under RRIM sponsorship. Predictably, smallholders lagged behind the estates in production of SMR, although the closed ex-RIDA plants were reopened as block rubber factories under RRIM management and analyses (ibid., pp. 597–603) showed high rates of return to central processing facilities. Since its creation in 1972, the Rubber Industry Smallholder Development Authority (RISDA) has supervised the multiplication of such units.

The conclusion of this discussion of rubber must be that the smallholders have failed to reap anything like the full benefits of the industry's revitalization since World War II, despite gradually accelerating official efforts to assist them. Granted that the diffusion of new technology to thousands of small-scale producers poses formidable difficulties, there are several instances—especially before Merdeka, but also to some extent after—in which official policy favoured the estates. The effect has been to widen the productivity gap between the estates and the smallholdings (Table 7.2). This gap yawned ever wider during the 1950s, then stabilized in the 1960s. Post-war events have thus made a reality of the then-erroneous pre-war belief (Bauer, 1946, 1948, 1948a; Lim Teck Ghee, 1977) that the estates were substantially more productive than the smallholdings.

Although rubber smallholders form the largest single bloc of rural poor,[24] they showed few signs of effective political mobilization before December 1974. In that month, following a 74 per cent drop in rubber prices (from highly unusual boom levels), some of them engaged in 'hunger marches' in small towns in Kedah. After the marchers had received impassioned support from student demonstrators in Kuala Lumpur, the government announced a bold plan to restrict rubber output and particularly to raise the incomes of the smallholders (Pillai, 1974). The plan required the estates to remove from production for immediate replanting all land yielding less than 700 lb. per acre, to suspend the use of chemical yield stimulants and to reduce the frequency of tapping. The government itself undertook to stockpile rubber and endeavoured to compel private dealers to hold larger stocks as well. The

TABLE 7.2
OUTPUT PER ACRE ON ESTATES AND SMALLHOLDINGS, 1949–1973
(lb. per acre)

	Estates			*Smallholdings*	*Smallholder yield ÷ estate yield*[1]	
Period	*Yield per acre planted*	*Yield per mature acre*	*Yield per acre tapped*	*Yield per acre planted*	*A*	*B*
1950–4	389	451	481	365	.94	.81
1955–9	420	529	553	359	.85	.68
1960–4	516	722	751	305	.59	.42
1965–9	689	894	941	379	.55	.42
1970–3	972	1,148	1,186	543	.56	.46

Sources: P. O. Thomas and A. Fong Chu Chai (1968); *Monthly Statistical Bulletin of West Malaysia*, various issues; Department of Statistics (1975).
[1]A = Smallholder yield per acre planted ÷ estate yield per acre planted;
B = Smallholder yield per acre planted ÷ estate yield per mature acre.

intended effect of the measures was of course to raise prices by reducing estate output and increasing demand. In the wake of this unilateral effort to support the market,[25] the government sought the support of Indonesia and Thailand in a new international restriction scheme (Davenport, 1975). This effort, which was probably misguided,[26] now appears to have been abandoned, at least temporarily, as market prices have recovered. The entire campaign can be seen as having been forced on the government by the limited success of its past efforts to raise smallholder productivity.

Before leaving the subject of perennial crops, smallholdings which produce crops other than rubber may be noted. Such crops are minor—among them only coconut, with perhaps 35,000 cultivators and 440,000 acres planted in the late 1960s,[27] is really worth mentioning. Coconut has long been a smallholder crop of some importance in coastal areas with sandy soils. Estate acreage in Peninsular Malaysia fell from 80,000 in 1960 to 44,000 in 1974, mainly through replanting with oil palm.[28] Poverty among coconut smallholders, plagued by waterlogging and tree diseases, is similar to that among rubber smallholders.[29]

LAND DEVELOPMENT

The improvement in existing stands of rubber and other perennials just discussed has been an important, even dramatic, part of Malaysian agricultural development. But it is far from the whole story. Long ago Peter Bauer (1948, pp. 345–7) argued for new planting of rubber in the forest areas as an alternative to replanting in existing locations, since the smallholders in particular would then be assured some continuing income from the tapping of their old trees while the new ones matured and because many of their old stands were replanted in unsuitable locations anyhow. Although unwilling to alienate more land to foreign estate companies, Malayan and Malaysian governments have been well aware of the possibilities afforded by the existence of millions of acres of uncultivated land—many of them fully as cultivable as the land currently in use, except perhaps for less convenient access to markets.[30] With a growing rural population and limited opportunities for offtake of labour into non-agricultural activities, this land provided a marvellous chance to extend agricultural production outward along the extensive margin at much lower cost than other countries could attain.[31] To this economic attractiveness can be added the political appeal of land development: although anything to do with land is intensely political in the Malaysian context, the political barriers to the development of new areas, under acceptable institutional arrangements, have proven to be much less imposing than those facing efforts to reform ownership and tenancy arrangements in older cultivated areas.

The land development programme which began in the 1950s marked a kind of revival of the land rush which had characterized Malaya up to the early 1930s. In the earlier period, state governments had freely granted lands for export-crop production to Chinese and European entrepreneurs although they did, through the Malay Reservation Enactments, step in to protect existing Malay land from acquisition by non-Malays. Official sponsorship of land development had been limited to modest subsidization of colonization schemes intended to increase rice production, of which the Krian project in Perak (1904–29) was the outstanding pre-1930 example. The Depression accelerated the padi settlement schemes (development began at Sungai Manik in Lower Perak in 1932 and at Tanjong Karang, Selangor, in 1936) while other forms of legal land development came to a sudden halt. New rubber planting was banned as part of international output restriction, although illegal smallholder planting continued into the 1930s.

The political climate of the 1950s would permit land development only under some form of official sponsorship. It was assumed, probably correctly, that any resumption of free alienation along pre-war lines, even if efforts were made to limit it to Malays, would ultimately redound to the benefit of the Chinese. Malay-dominated governments in those states which had good land to alienate thus adopted a generally restrictive attitude. This held land development in check until, just before Merdeka, the federal government decided to take the initiative.

The most important action was the creation of the Federal Land Development Authority in 1956.[32] Originally it was thought that several different kinds of officially sponsored land development would occur under state auspices and that FELDA would help plan and finance, but not directly administer, a number of them (Malaya, 1956a). A variety of programmes did in fact emerge, as Table 7.3 shows. There were the state-sponsored *fringe alienation schemes*, which provided supplemental plots within walking or bicycling distance of home to owners of uneconomic holdings. There was *controlled alienation* of large land blocks

TABLE 7.3
LAND ALIENATION AND DEVELOPMENT
IN PENINSULAR MALAYSIA,
BY PROGRAMME, 1961–1970
('000 acres)

	Alienated		*Developed*	
	1961–5	*1966–70*	*1961–5*	*1966–70*
FELDA	176.1	132.1	119.3	179.0
Fringe alienation	128.5	11.3	115.6	11.7
Youth schemes	—	9.8	—	5.3
Controlled alienation	187.7	106.3	108.2	42.0
Public and joint-venture estates	121.8	101.0	21.8	30.3
Private estates	139.0	225.8	140.1	46.0
Block planting and state schemes	135.0	28.2	34.8	15.3
Total	888.1	614.5	539.8	329.6

Source: *Second Malaysia Plan* (1971, pp. 125–6).

to individual settlers by some state governments. There were plans for *public-sector or joint-venture estates* in some states, and even a limited amount of alienation to *private estates*. There was *block planting* under Fund B, which enabled groups of rubber smallholders to apply their replanting grants to new planting in more promising areas. Finally, there were some miscellaneous *state schemes* and, in the late 1960s, *youth schemes*.[33]

Of all these approaches to land development, FELDA was to prove the most successful. One reason FELDA succeeded while the others failed was that it was able to cope with the troublesome fact that the land with greatest unexploited agricultural potential, though extensive, was concentrated in a few states, mainly on the East Coast, while the populations with greatest land hunger were to be found in other West Coast states. The problems thus created became apparent in the very early years of the land development programme, when areas with settlement potential, and even lands available for fringe alienation, began to be exhausted in densely-populated areas of states like Kedah, Penang and Malacca. Obviously, really telling use of the land development opportunity would require significant inter-state movement of population. But this posed not only physical and social problems but also real conflicts of interest, since land is a state subject under the federal Constitution and all the states which possessed cultivable land were pledged, in greater or lesser degree, to its development for the benefit of their own citizens. Even FELDA could not overcome this difficulty as long as it merely planned and financed state projects. Perhaps it is just as well, then, that that conception came to early grief.

The very first of more than 100 FELDA schemes was Ayer Lanas, in Kelantan, where land clearing began in March 1957. Just two years later the voters of Kelantan rejected Alliance rule and elected a PMIP government intensely hostile to the federal government. A dispute soon broke out over the Ayer Lanas project, leading to the state government's repudiation of its debt to FELDA and initiating a controversy which was to last for many years.

The Ayer Lanas fiasco, plus less spectacular difficulties with other state governments, led to FELDA's conversion to a federally-implemented programme in 1960. Two years earlier, a National Land Council had been created as a forum in which the federal government could consult with the states and bring some pressure to bear on their land policies.

The assumption of direct federal control was the first step in the evolution of a standard method of operation for FELDA. The eventual achievement of this standard method provided the key to FELDA's success because it became a blueprint which could be followed over and over again, with only minor variations, by middle-level settlement administrators.

The standard FELDA pattern, as it evolved over time, can be described as follows. A plot of land is chosen, of requisite size,[34] fertility, topography, accessibility and freedom from more productive use potentials, such as mining. After road access to the land is provided, if necessary, the clearing of the land commences. This is done by contractors.[35] A town site is laid out and modest settler housing constructed. Soon afterwards the settlers, chosen from the rural poor on the basis of a point system,[36] move in and take over the work of tending the young rubber trees or oil palms.[37] At this stage they operate more like an estate work gang, under the close supervision of FELDA staff, than like smallholders. Each settler receives a quarter-acre house and garden plot, which he can tend as he chooses. He is also the presumptive owner of 8–10 acres of rubber land, or 10–14 acres of oil palm, but his rights to that land are somewhat theoretical until the crop matures.[38] In the meantime, he receives a subsistence allowance from FELDA in return for work performed. When the trees begin to bear, settlers in rubber schemes receive, by lot, their individual plots,[39] although they remain responsible for repayment to FELDA of a debt of $14,000–17,000.[40] Settlers in oil palm schemes never receive individual plots of land, only certificates representing an ownership share in the common venture; these schemes are run as worker-owned, but FELDA-managed, estates. In neither case is full title received until the settler's debt is paid in full (which may be ten to fifteen years or more). Even this title carries certain restrictions, the most important one being a prohibition on subdivision of plots.

This *modus operandi* is much less individualistic than any other form of land development known in Malaysia, or than FELDA was originally intended to be. It has been criticized for stifling settler initiative and fostering dependency. There is undoubtedly something to this criticism. Yet FELDA has opened 186 schemes, settled 37,435 families and planted 812,684 acres with rubber, oil palm, sugar-cane or cacao by 1976 (FELDA, 1976, p. 1). It is doubtful whether these achievements could have been possible without a standardized operating format using professional management. The 812,684 acres represent nearly a 50 per cent augmentation of the acreage which rubber smallholders cultivated in 1952, so FELDA's accomplishment is clearly a substantial one.

Expenditure on FELDA totalled $989 million by 1975. This averages $26,400 per family settled.[41] The Authority has often been criticized for lavishness in the quality and variety of services which it provides. Lower-cost forms of land development, based on lower income targets and encompassing less provision of publicly financed infrastructure, have been suggested repeatedly but never implemented by the federal government—largely because of the issues of interpersonal equity (between FELDA and other settlers) they would raise.[42] Although economies could be effected, the FELDA programme stands as an effective, and probably also efficient, use of public funds.[43]

The economic effects of the FELDA programme have never been analysed satisfactorily. By expanding the supply of cultivated land, it definitely keeps the average rural income above what it otherwise would be, and probably retards rural–urban migration as a result. Since most of its settlers were previously landless, or owners of very small plots, the programme probably frees up little land in the areas from which they migrated. Nor is it likely to have much effect on measured unemployment, since most of the settlers come from rural areas where outright unemployment is low; such effect on unemployment as it has probably comes through the inhibition of rural–urban migration. What the programme *does* do is facilitate the accommodation of natural increase in the rural population, although it is by no means able to do the whole job, since by the early 1970s rural natural increase was running about 150,000 a year while FELDA absorbed only 2,740 families—perhaps 14,800 individuals—per annum.[44]

FELDA started with an income target of $400 per family per month. Since this was nearly four times the median income level for rural Malay households in 1957–8, and doubtless represented an even bigger jump for the relatively disadvantaged families who were potential FELDA settlers, the target was an attractive one to the settlers and made good copy for government propagandists. But the $400 target was dependent on world commodity prices and could not be guaranteed. At times such as the 1967–8 and 1974–5 rubber price slumps, settler incomes fell to half or less of the target and discontent welled up. FELDA could do little more than ease the problem by deferring debt repayments.

The social and political effects of the FELDA programme are even more uncertain than its economic effects. Although the notion that FELDA is a productive programme, in which settlers work for their own benefit, has decisively won out over the view that it is a social welfare programme, the latter idea can never be totally banished from a programme which is run in such a paternalistic manner. Feelings of dependency are said to stifle initiative and bring about a tendency to blame the government for every setback, and there have been stories of heavy anti-government voting on some FELDA schemes. Yet there is little doubt that the FELDA programme is a bright spot in the rural scene. In a survey conducted among rural youths in Johore in 1970–1 (Government of Malaysia and State of Johor, 1971, pp. 32, 38), only the sons of FELDA settlers felt hopeful enough about rural life to tell the researchers that they wanted to pursue careers as farmers.

FELDA's success relative to other land development programmes may be gauged from the fact, seen in Table 7.3, that while just 20 per cent of land *alienated* in the early 1960s went to FELDA, as much as 54 per cent of the area *actually developed* during the second half of the decade was developed by FELDA. Other forms of land development for which there had been high hopes during the late 1950s and early 1960s had either

TABLE 7.4

GROWTH OF RURAL POPULATION AND CULTIVATED LAND IN PENINSULAR MALAYSIA, 1947–1970

	Area cultivated ('000 acres)		
Year	*Total*[1]	*Estates*[2]	*Other*
1947	5,307	2,103	3,204
1957	5,548	2,208	3,340
1970	7,144	2,164	4,980
	Rural population ('000)		
Year	*Total*[3]	*Estates*[4]	*Other*
1947	3,608	556	3,052
1957	3,599	601	2,998
1970	5,085	543	4,542
	Density (population per 100 acres)		
Year	*Total*	*Estates*	*Other*
1947	68	26	95
1957	65	27	90
1970	71	25	91

[1]*Sources*: *Monthly Statistical Bulletins*, various issues. Based on aggregation of areas under various crops and includes some double-counting, arising from the existence of intercropped areas, in 1947 and 1957. The total for 1970 is based on aerial surveys and is accurate; thus, any bias in the implied increase of acreage is downward.

[2]*Sources*: *Monthly Statistical Bulletins*, various issues; Thomas and Fong (1968, p. 18); Pee Teck Yew (1967, Vol. 1, Table 1.3). Includes rubber, oil palm and coconut estates only.

[3]From Table 7.1, above.

[4]Based on estate employment data given in *Monthly Statistical Bulletins*; employment in 1947 is estimated by extrapolating backward from 1951 (the first year of the data series), on the assumption of a constant labour–land ratio. The figures in our Table are intended to include dependants of estate workers and are calculated by doubling the employment figure. The low dependency rate is assumed because of the tendency on estates for men, women and often children as well to work. We cannot vouch either for its accuracy or for its constancy through time, but plausible alternative assumptions give similar results for the measure we are after here: the trend in population density, on and off the estates.

failed to materialize on the expected scale or had proven to be failures. The least successful programme was fringe alienation (Tunku Shamsul Bahrin, 1969), which was halted in the late 1960s. Other development programmes had mixed results. Controlled alienation to smallholders and alienation to private estates occurred in some states, despite strong political constraints;[45] in a number of cases, however, the land alienated was not developed. More and more, therefore, FELDA came to be the chosen instrument of land development. This trend was only mildly reversed in the 1970s when relatively minor forms of land development such as youth schemes emerged, interest in the concept of government estates increased and the Federal Land Consolidation and Rehabilitation Authority (FELCRA) and RISDA began to open FELDA-type Schemes.

Although there were failures, land development has, overall, been an important successful element in Malaysian rural development. As Table 7.4 shows, the total area cultivated was raised from about 5.3 million acres just after World War II to 7.1 million in 1970, with the great bulk of the increase occurring after Merdeka. This made it possible to accommodate 1.5 million additional rural residents in 1957–70 with no increase in the ratio of population to cultivated land—even though the estate sector contributed to the problem, rather than to its solution, by expelling labour. Although an increase in the land–man ratio would have been better, constancy is a major success compared to the nearly universal experience in low-income countries of rapidly rising rural population density.[46] Had efforts to raise output per unit of land been more successful, it would have permitted at least a modest rise in the average income of rural households.

Land development in Malaysia has been criticized for not raising the incomes of more people, for failing to teach more readily transferable modern skills and for encouraging dependency. But, given the surge of rural population and the distance Malaysia has to go before a large industrial work force is needed, the use of available land to create a halfway house for underemployed rural labour seems undeniably to have been a good thing. The only real question is how long to continue along the path now being followed.[47]

POLICIES TOWARD RICE AND OTHER ANNUALS

The preceding two sections of this chapter dealt with the principal *modern* agricultural occupations of Malaysia. By contrast, padi growing and fishing were the main economic activities in pre-colonial times. Individuals who are still pursuing these occupations during the second half of the twentieth century can therefore be regarded as having been left behind by the growth of other opportunities, and it is not surprising that their incomes are very low. There are two possible ways to remedy this situation: expand other activities sufficiently that labour can gradually be shifted out of traditional occupations, or else raise incomes *in situ* by modernizing them. It is the latter possibility which is considered here.

Rice cultivation received considerable attention in colonial times, particularly from 1930 on. Many colonial officials regarded padi cultivation as the traditional and proper occupation of Malays and a bulwark of social stability, which in turn supported continued colonial rule; it followed from this that Malays should be encouraged, even coerced if necessary, to grow padi, and that other ethnic groups should be excluded.[48] Although Malayan prosperity always depended on specialized production for the world market, the colonial régime's devotion to the principles of comparative advantage wavered at times of severe deterioration in the terms of trade. Then concern about the country's heavy dependence on imported foodstuffs, especially rice, became temporarily dominant. Partly because of the limited-government principles to which it subscribed and partly because it was precisely during export slumps that finances were most pinched, the colonial government's response to the perceived need to bolster rice production never matched its concern. Only after World War II, in a rapidly changing political environment, did a really serious programme to encourage food production get underway.

The post-war rice-production programme, which gained momentum from the approach of Independence in the late 1950s, had several elements. One major emphasis, which had had its beginnings in the founding of the Drainage and Irrigation Department (DID) in 1932, was public-sector investment to permit double-cropping of much of the existing rice area and some marginal extension of cultivated acreage. Another, dating from the late 1940s, was support of producer prices. Additional elements of the programme, which have been somewhat less important, include input subsidies, innovations in marketing and credit, tenancy reform and efforts to diffuse new seed varieties and other cultivational improvements through extension services. These efforts will be examined in turn, after which fishing and minor food crops will be briefly discussed. First, however, the padi-growing industry of Peninsular Malaysia will be quickly sketched.[49]

Padi growing at present is a diverse, transitional industry, in which some cultivators produce for the market along sophisticated profit-maximizing lines while others are more governed by habit and produce solely or mainly for the use of their own households, in which some have irrigation and can thus double-crop while others do not and must single-crop, in which net income varies by a factor of three among regions of the country but is everywhere low relative to incomes in other industries. One thing, however, is practically invariant: at least 95 per cent of padi cultivators are Malays.

The hilly Malay Peninsula lacks the broad plains, ideal for the cultivation of wet rice, of Burma and Thailand. The 300,000 or so[50] padi cultivators of Peninsular Malaysia can be divided roughly into two groups: those who work the 'rice bowl' areas of Kedah, Perlis, Kelantan, Province Wellesley, Krian district in northern Perak and Tanjong Karang in Selangor, and those who cultivate small pockets of land scattered throughout the remainder of the country. In general, cultivation is more efficient in the rice bowl areas. The marketed surplus, however, comes almost entirely from the areas of concentrated production on the West Coast; producers on the Kelantan plain, although highly specialized in rice production, have low productivity levels and consume two-thirds of the crop themselves.

The diversity of the industry in the late 1960s is underlined in Table 7.5, which gives descriptive statistics for three padi areas: Province Wellesley, Kelantan and Selangor. The first of these was a long-established double-cropping area,[51] in which cultivation practices were probably as advanced as anywhere in the country. Yields and marketed output were thus above the national average, and gross padi income was also relatively high, though not high enough to lift most padi-growing households above the poverty line. Like padi cultivators everywhere, Province Wellesley farmers relied on income from non-padi sources for a significant share of their total income.

Kelantan presented a sharp contrast to Province Wellesley. There farmers could raise only a single padi crop at the time the statistics were collected.[52] And the yield on this crop was very low, about half the

TABLE 7.5

CHARACTERISTICS OF PADI FARMS IN THREE GROWING AREAS, LATE 1960s

	Province Wellesley	*Kelantan*	*Malay farms*	*Selangor*	*Chinese farms*
Acreage planted ('000 acres):					
Main season, 1967–8	39	171		48	
Off season, 1968	36	14		43	
Average farm size (acres)	3.29	2.21	4.5		4.5
Average production/ farm (*gantangs*)[1]	2,735	476	2,695		3,826
Average yield (*gantangs*/acre)	462	215	408		554
Disposal of crop (%)					
Domestic consumption	27	69	20		18
Sales	57	6	57		76
Wages, rent, taxes and other	16	25	23		6
Imputed value of gross padi income ($)	1,504	262	1,469		2,104
Income from non-padi sources ($)	418	376	634		667

Sources: Acreage planted is from the *Monthly Statistical Bulletin* and refers to the entire state, including the small acreage on Penang Island in the case of Province Wellesley. Other data are cited by Huang (1971) and originate in surveys conducted by Selvadurai and others in 1968: Udhis Narksuasdi and S. Selvadurai (1968); Selvadurai and Ani bin Arope (1969); and Selvadurai, Ani and Nik Hassani bin Mohammad (1969). These data relate to samples of farms in Province Wellesley, the Kemubu area of Kelantan and the Tanjong Karang area of Selangor, in each case the dominant rice-producing area in the state.

[1]A *gantang* (gallon) is a volumetric unit; one *gantang* of padi weighs approximately 5.6 lb., and 400 *gantangs* are thus equivalent to one long ton.

national average, as a result of soil infertility and the absence of water control. The farmers were desperately poor, relying on non-padi income sources to keep their families from starvation.[53] One survey (cited by Huang, 1971, p. 4) found that 68 per cent of households even had to buy some rice during the year to supplement their own production.

Finally, there is the Tanjong Karang area of Selangor, which has already been discussed in Chapter 5. Here, unlike the other two areas, there are some Chinese, and a few Indian, padi farmers. Double-cropping had only recently been introduced in Tanjong Karang when the statistics shown in Table 7.5 were collected. Thus, yields of Malay farmers there were somewhat below those of their Province Wellesley compatriots at this time, although they undoubtedly have risen since. On the other hand, farmers in Tanjong Karang had greater opportunities to earn non-padi income and thus were better off overall than farmers in Province Wellesley. They also benefited from a larger average farm size than that of Province Wellesley—and much larger than the badly subdivided rice-growing areas of Kelantan.[54] Finally, as already noted in Chapter 5, Chinese farmers in Tanjong Karang out-produced their Malay neighbours and also bettered them in non-padi income.[55] With an average income level of about $2,000 per annum, they were among the very few padi growers in the country who could earn more than the median rural income level.[56]

Although a poor, low-productivity industry, padi has not been stagnant. As Tables 7.6 and 7.7 show, production rose by 150 per cent from the early 1950s to the early 1970s. Various government policies contributed to this rise, but the part played by off-season cropping (which accounted for 65 per cent of the increase in production) is obvious from a glance at the tables.

The provision of *drainage and irrigation facilities* is a natural function of government, and indeed has been theorized to be the main factor leading to the emergence of strong governments in Asian history (Wittfogel, 1957). This governmental role developed late in Malaya.[57] The first attempts to double-crop were made during the Japanese occupation.

TABLE 7.6
PADI PRODUCTION,
1951/2–1953/4 TO 1971/2–1973/4
(million gantangs)

	Wet padi			
	Main season	*Off season*	*Dry padi*	*Total*
1951/2–1953/4 average	259.8	2.2	5.1	267.1
1961/2–1963/4 average	344.6	21.9	11.6	378.2
1971/2–1973/4 average	401.6	263.3	5.8	670.7

Source: Selvadurai (1972); *Monthly Statistical Bulletins*. Selvadurai has corrected old data which understated production before 1961/2; these continue to be published uncorrected in the *Monthly Statistical Bulletins*.

TABLE 7.7

STATISTICS FOR MAIN- AND OFF-SEASON PADI, 1951/2–1953/4 TO 1971/2–1973/4

	Acreage planted ('000)	*Production (million gantangs)*	*Productivity (gantangs/acre)*
Main season			
1951/2–1953/4	790.3	259.8	329
1961/2–1963/4	879.6	344.6	392
1971/2–1973/4	907.7	401.6	442
Off-season			
1952–4	7.4	2.2	296
1962–4	51.4	21.9	426
1971–3	516.3	263.3	510

Source: Same as Table 7.6.

After the War the pre-war policy of building drainage and irrigation works in existing padi areas was resumed. Development expenditure for such facilities rose from $38.3 million in 1956–60 to $108.5 million in 1961–5, to a peak of $328.5 million in 1966–70, when the giant Muda and Kemubu schemes were constructed. By the end of 1970 the situation was as follows (Selvadurai, 1972, p. 59): out of 943,000 acres of padi land, about 620,000 acres (66 per cent of the total) had been provided with irrigation by the DID; of this area, 286,000 acres (30 per cent of the total) received enough water to permit double-cropping, while the remaining 334,000 got only enough water to single-crop effectively; finally, 323,000 acres of padi land were purely rain-fed or served only by traditional farmer-built water-retention and diversion systems.

Efficiency and equity issues have arisen in connexion with the expensive construction programme of the DID. To its credit, the DID was one of the first departments of the Malaysian government to employ cost/benefit analysis as a tool for selecting projects for implementation. Although there are limitations to its analyses,[58] the DID has generally been faithful to an efficiency-dictated strategy in which the projects with the highest benefit/cost ratios are implemented first. This led to falling benefit/cost ratios by the late 1960s, as irrigation gradually spread to all the concentrated padi-growing areas best suited to its use. Quite apart from the issue of whether investing hundreds of millions of dollars in rice cultivation had ever made sense in the first place, by 1970 nearly everyone was ready to agree that the limit of efficient expansion had been reached.

Working against the efficiency considerations, however, were questions of equity. With producer incomes so variable from area to area and dependent in large measure on governmental provision of drainage, irrigation and other facilities, the demand that all producing areas should receive what some had been given naturally arose. Although the government formally decided in 1970 to limit drainage and irrigation works construction to projects then underway, the pressure to make exceptions was great and the decision was later reversed.[59] The horizontal equity issue was present in all programmes to assist padi producers, but was perhaps greatest in connexion with drainage and irrigation because of the particular involvement of landowners as beneficiaries of this service. Most analyses suggest that, as gains resulting from improved water control are embodied in the land, the returns from them will accrue mainly to the owner of the land, and labour as a factor of production will benefit little.[60] Some, but only a little, of the landowner's added income would be expected to return to the government via irrigation water rates, which fall far short of covering the cost of the system. Since landowners probably have significant political influence through UMNO, the complaints of those of their number who are not yet served by drainage and irrigation facilities are a force to be reckoned with.

The other main pillar of padi policy is *price support*. In 1949, when the government dropped its post-war compulsory sales programme, it retained a Guaranteed Minimum Price (GMP) for padi as a production inducement. This price followed world prices, with a lag, in the early years. In 1952–4 it stood at $17 per picul,[61] a comparatively high level chosen to retard the flow of resources from rice to rubber during the Korean War boom. Then in 1954 the government precipitated a furor by abruptly cutting the GMP to $12 a picul. As Independence neared, the GMP crept back to $16, the level at which it has remained ever since.

Producer price support is financed indirectly by rice consumers. Imports are licensed, and recipients of licences are required also to purchase domestic rice from the government stockpile, in a ratio which is varied as a policy instrument. The trade then markets the resulting quantities of imported, generally high-quality, and domestic, generally inferior,[62] rice for what they will bring—usually losing money on the local rice and making it back, with a profit, on the imports.

Like drainage and irrigation investments, price support raises questions of efficiency and equity. The implications of the system received closer scrutiny as self-sufficiency was approached, implying that indirect financing of producer price support through import licensing might soon cease to be possible and that it might even prove necessary to dispose of surpluses through subsidized exports, American-fashion.[63] Although this concern led to the 1970 decision to halt new drainage and irrigation projects, it did not seriously threaten the $16 support level.

The distorting effects of price support become more apparent when the quality dimension is taken into account. The GMP applies to good, clean padi of not more than 13 per cent moisture, delivered to a rice mill. Since no distinction is made either among rice varieties or with respect to key features such as the percentage of broken grains, the government purchasing system naturally ends up with the lowest-quality part of the crop. Moreover, the incentive for farmers to plant the most desired varieties and take care to preserve the quality of the harvested crop is reduced. Since Malaysian consumers are quality-conscious and many can afford to pay more for the type of rice they want, the support system tends to encourage the production of rice that no one really wants and which must be retailed at a substantial discount. Although this problem has long been recognized,[64] the system has not yet been fine-tuned to take account of quality variations.

The marketing of padi and rice is a complex business, involving private, co-operative and official bodies. The farmer rarely delivers his padi to the mill door, so he seldom receives the full GMP for his crop.[65] Because the seasonal nature of the crop fails to match the year-round nature of his needs for consumption items and productive inputs, the padi farmer is perennially in need of credit. Like peasant agriculturalists elsewhere, he obtains the great bulk of this credit from middlemen.[66] Thus credit and marketing become intertwined, and seemingly simple questions such as what rate of interest is being paid on debt and what price is being obtained for the farmer's produce become surprisingly difficult to answer. As noted in Chapter 5, it is harder to reach a conclusion about the competitiveness of rice marketing than is the case for smallholder rubber. Padi growers clearly get some of the benefits of the GMP, but not all of them.

An important limitation of the GMP as an income-redistribution device has been analysed by Richard Goldman (1975). This is the fact that whereas the GMP augments the incomes of padi producers, an important low-income group, it also has a perversely redistributive effect through the implicit taxation of rice, the major staple consumption item in the household budget. The latter effect pervades Malaysian society, since all households consume a lot of rice. In 1957–8, low-income households (less than $150 a month) devoted an average 29 per cent of their budgets to it.[67] Goldman calculates that in 1965–72 the price of the low-quality rice which poorer households consume was 19 per cent higher than it would have been if imports had been permitted to come in freely at world prices.

Compared to the DID and GMP programmes, *input subsidies* and *extension services* have been relatively minor parts of the padi-industry support programme. Fertilizer has been subsidized, and since the effort to persuade farmers to adopt high-yielding seed varieties and double-cropping began use has also been made periodically of special demonstration areas, in which input packages have been distributed free to farmers. Since extension manpower has been chronically scarce, geographic concentration of services has often been adopted as preferable to a concentration of services has often been adopted as preferable to a thinly-spread extension service which falls short of adequacy everywhere. This is undoubtedly the best policy from the point of view of efficiency, although it again raises questions of horizontal equity.

Finally, the area of institutional reform in the padi industry encompasses questions of *marketing*, *credit* and *ownership and tenancy arrangements*. These are emotive, highly politicized issues which involve open conflicts between the interests of different groups of Malaysians. Because of their thorniness and because of the considerable uncertainty, previously noted, about the extent to which institutional barriers have actually inhibited production and lowered producer incomes—not to mention the question of what the government could do about it if they did—there was for a long time an extreme hesitancy to move in these three areas. More recently—mostly since, but in some instances shortly before, the 1969 watershed—the government has started to move more aggressively on the marketing and credit fronts.

The major figure in padi and rice marketing and milling has long been the Chinese dealer. Malayan and Malaysian governments could never be indifferent to allegations by the growers that the dealers are exploiting them. Over the years the government tried to exercise a modicum of control over the dealers and millers by licensing and inspecting them, by setting up a few government mills to compete with the private ones and by encouraging the formation of producer co-operatives. These actions were not enough, however, to stifle the growers' complaints, and visiting experts found from time to time that the marketing system was inadequate (Thomson, 1954; Biggs, 1964). Accordingly, the government, beginning in 1965, launched a major effort to reform the marketing system.

The institutions directing the reformed marketing system have been the Federal Agricultural Marketing Authority (FAMA) and, since its activation in January 1972, the National Padi and Rice Authority (known as the LPN, after its Malay initials). These bodies have inaugurated padi marketing schemes in all the major producing areas. The schemes involve the grant of purchasing monopolies either to licensed private dealers (who are purportedly closely regulated so as to assure that they live up to the terms of their licences), to co-operatives or to the LPN itself. The LPN backs up its regulatory authority with an extraordinary range of police powers.[68] All in all, the LPN appears to represent an aggressive, and probably expensive, effort to deal with a problem which is undoubtedly more political than economic.

The experience with *credit* has been similar to that with marketing. The majority of padi farmers are perpetually in debt, mainly to private retailers and wholesalers. The original government-sponsored alternative, the co-operative society, never made much of a dent on this state of affairs. In the late 1960s the introduction of double-cropping, with its augmented requirements for purchased inputs, lent increased urgency to the belief, already prevalent in some quarters, that something better had to be found. Thus a new credit network was formed, with Bank Pertanian Malaysia (created in 1969) at its apex and the newly created Farmers' Associations as its local credit centres. This new credit system began by lending only relatively small sums, but it is hoped that it will succeed—by virtue of professional management and business-like, fairly high-interest lending practices—where the co-operatives failed.[69]

Finally, there is the third type of institutional innovation, *land reform*. Compared to other Asian countries, little has been heard about land reform in Malaysia. This may be attributable partly to the smaller amount of tenancy and rural crowding and partly to the political power of the richer rural interests. Only in padi cultivation is tenancy of significant magnitude. About 40 per cent of padi lands are worked by tenants under some sort of arrangement, the main ones being fixed rent in cash, fixed rent in padi, crop-sharing or long-term lease. Perhaps a quarter of Peninsular Malaysia's 300,000 padi farmers lease all the land they cultivate; another quarter lease some of their land and own the rest; the remaining half cultivate only their own land.[70] Even in padi, therefore, the extent of tenancy is less than overwhelming.

There has been no serious discussion in Malaysia of land reform in the sense of acquiring land from larger owners for redistribution to smaller ones.[71] Instead, such concern as there has been has focused on questions of tenancy terms and land subdivision and fragmentation.

Efforts to protect tenant cultivators from exploitation by landlords began with the Padi Cultivators (Control of Rent and Security of Tenure) Ordinance 1955, which aimed at setting maximum rent levels for different classes of land and preventing precipitous evictions of tenants from their holdings. By official admission (Selvadurai, 1972, p. 29), the Act was totally ineffective, except to a limited extent in Kedah, the only state which made any effort to enforce it. Accordingly, after a long lag, Parliament passed another, similarly titled, Act in 1967. The 1967 Act repeated the provisions of the 1955 ordinance and added a requirement that tenancy agreements be made in writing for periods of not less than three years. Apparently the 1967 Act, like its predecessor, has been implemented selectively at best. Actually, the Act is only a piece of enabling legislation, since the federal Constitution specifies that such legislation becomes effective only after the state governments give it force in their own states. If the states do not move, nothing is done.[72]

Equity questions aside, there is evidence that the present tenure system is well adapted to promote efficient use of land. Huang (1971, pp. 81 ff; 1975) notes that fixed-rent systems (previously measured mainly in padi, but now primarily in cash) predominate in the principal producing areas, where yields are high and relatively predictable and most cultivators depend on commercial padi sales as their principal source of income. In more marginal producing areas, such as Kelantan and Malacca, share-cropping predominates. These variations, he notes, are consistent with efficiency and may be beneficial to both landlords and tenants. Tenants in the more dependable producing areas receive the incentive that is most valuable to them, namely the assurance that increments in production will accrue entirely to them,[73] while tenants in the marginal areas are induced to produce more by the landlords' willingness to share the substantial risk involved.

Tenancy is much more common in the highly productive areas such as Perlis, Kedah and Province Wellesley than in the marginal areas. Similarly, the better lands *within* padi-growing states are likely to be tenanted, while the poorer lands are owner-cultivated. This fact contributed to the surprising finding that productivity is actually higher on tenanted acreage than on cultivator-owned acreage.[74] No one has yet determined the effect of tenancy, or the differential effects of different forms of tenancy, on the productivity of land of given quality.[75]

The other land tenure condition which has caused concern is the continuous subdivision and fragmentation of padi land holdings through the operations of Islamic inheritance law. This body of law has contributed to steady decreases in the size of family holdings, as well as fragmentation (i.e. tendency for holdings to be made up of non-contiguous parcels) and joint ownership. The National Land Code of 1965 prohibits the subdivision of holdings of less than one acre, but how effectively it is being enforced is not clear.

In conclusion, padi industry support programmes have involved the expenditure of much larger sums, probably with less effect, than programmes to promote the welfare of the larger, though somewhat less poor, group of rubber smallholders. Since padi is inherently a low-productivity peasant industry, which will some day disappear from the Malaysian scene (or, to the extent it survives, radically alter its technology), one can easily question the wisdom of such an emphasis. The issue becomes even sharper when one considers the numerous (but never precisely enumerated) peasants who cultivate both rubber and padi. Although in world prices it is usually advantageous for them to devote themselves to rubber, government policy perversely draws them, even pushes them,[76] into padi.

The distortion thus introduced into the economy is not unrecognized in Malaysia but it has been countenanced for a variety of reasons. Increasingly in recent years the incomes of padi producers have been cited as the leading concern. The other major objective, national self-sufficiency in rice, may be consistent with the income distribution goal in so far as it is implemented through incentives to grow rice (e.g. the GMP) but is clearly inconsistent in so far as padi planters are excluded from more remunerative economic activities. In the longer run there must be better ways of redistributing income than by inducing the production of a large surplus of unwanted grades of padi, especially since the incentives involved may do little for the poorest farmers. In the shorter run there is undoubtedly a transitional role for the padi industry to play in an equity-oriented development strategy, but it must operate in tandem with effective programmes to move the marginal farmers out of the industry and on to better things.

Other parts of peasant agriculture are trivial relative to those discussed so far. Dry-land annual crops count for little. There are 100,000 acres or so of annual food crops (tapioca, sugar-cane, maize, vegetables, etc.) and about 160,000 acres of fruit cultivation (bananas and various tree crops), which supplement consumption and cash incomes in the *kampung*. Some other agricultural activities (market gardening, poultry and eggs, pig-raising, dairying), which tend to be more remunerative, are dominated by the Chinese (except for dairying and cattle-rearing, which is a traditional Indian occupation).

The remaining sizeable group of low-income rural residents is the *fishermen*, of whom there are about 70,000. Poverty among fishermen is comparable to that among rubber smallholders or padi cultivators.[77] As with padi farmers, there is considerable diversity within the group. This diversity has technological and geographical dimensions.

Malay fishermen have traditionally fished close to shore, using traps, unmechanized *prahus* and time-honoured styles of nets. Partly through the efforts of the Fisheries Division, the fleet has gradually become more mechanized over the years, permitting some extension of the effective fishing range.[78] However, the Malay fishermen and the Fisheries Division have been no match for the Chinese entrepreneurs who have outfitted motorized trawler fleets to fish the under-exploited off-shore waters. Trawling has reduced the incomes of traditional in-shore fishermen. As long as the trawlers remain off-shore there is little competition between the two groups, but in fact the line of demarcation has been a matter of constant dispute and, despite official efforts to keep them apart, small but violent 'fishing wars' have broken out from time to time.

The in-shore–off-shore competition has been confined to West Coast waters, where the fishing is best, if only because weather conditions permit fishing to be carried out at all times of the year. However, nearly half of the fishermen live on the East Coast. Their principal problem is the seasonal nature of their occupation. The north-east monsoon prohibits fishing on the East Coast for about six months of the year; it also limits alternative, shore-based, economic opportunities, always meagre in that region. It is therefore not surprising that East Coast fishermen are among the very poorest of poor Malaysians.

Government efforts to assist traditional fishermen have included subsidization of improved equipment, credit programmes, marketing schemes and improved fishing ports. A fisheries development authority (MAJUIKAN) was formed in 1971. FELDA has encouraged the resettlement of fishermen in rubber and oil palm schemes, although they naturally tend to make less satisfactory settlers than persons from agricultural backgrounds. Despite these programmes, the prescription for the traditional fisherman seems to be the same as that for the marginal padi farmer: some form of subsidization in the short run, followed by movement out of the industry as fast as circumstances permit.

GENERAL RURAL DEVELOPMENT POLICIES

The cropwise classification scheme used in preceding sections of this chapter reflects the tendency for rural poverty to be concentrated in a small number of crop specializations and for many of the policies intended to ameliorate that poverty to be crop-specific as well. However, this leaves out the general rural development programme. Launched by the Federation of Malaya at the time of Merdeka and pursued vigorously up to the outbreak of Confrontation in 1963, this programme had as its hallmarks in its early years the Red Books and the operations rooms, both of which aimed at effectively linking together the elements of the programme, from the *kampung* to the national level. Although some observers heralded the system as a participative revolution, local initiative in fact had influence primarily over minor rural development projects. These projects—village mosques, *suraus* (smaller prayer houses), markets, bicycle paths and so on—were spread thinly around the country, allowing each Alliance MP in a rural constituency and each Menteri Besar (state chief minister) to preside at frequent intervals over the opening of some new facility or other. No doubt there were economic benefits as well, although some of the new facilities deteriorated rapidly because of the lack of adequate provision for their operation and maintenance (for example, the Public Works Department would refuse to accept responsibility for maintaining a small bridge which had not been constructed to its specifications). In response to an increasing feeling that the programme was wasteful, expenditure on minor rural development projects was gradually curtailed during the mid- and late 1960s.

The more seriously beneficial parts of the rural development programme—and indeed the parts which have absorbed by far the largest amounts of expenditure—have been the physical and social infrastructural programmes.

A major emphasis of the early post-Merdeka years was the construction of rural roads. The World Bank mission of 1954 had commented on the contrast between the excellence of the main road network and the paucity of rural roads. Road construction under the First and Second Malayan Five-Year Plans and the First Malaysia Plan (600, 2,300, and 1,600 miles respectively) went far towards remedying this defect.[79] Secondary and tertiary road construction extended the effective range of the market and thereby conferred undoubted economic benefits upon rural residents. It also facilitated their integration into the main body of the emerging Malaysian society, for example by bringing them into contact with better schooling. The spread of the bicycle and, for the somewhat more prosperous, the motor scooter, complemented the increasing road links.

By and large, decisions on what extensions of the road network to undertake when have been based on economic criteria.[80] Much of the construction was dictated by the location of land development schemes. Politics did sometimes get the upper hand, for instance in the choice of which of several *kampungs* to link with the road network first.

Improved transportation linkages for the poor and relatively remote north-eastern states remained a vexing problem for years. Kelantan's links with the rest of Peninsular Malaysia consist of the small East Coast railway line and the indirect road linkage which also serves Trengganu and Pahang. A direct road connexion through northern Perak to Province Wellesley was not provided until the late 1970s.

Other types of physical infrastructure have been extended to rural areas somewhat more slowly than roads. Electricity supply has been provided by the autonomous National Electricity Board, operating on strict commercial principles. The NEB extends service as demand warrants, charging users a close approximation of the cost of serving them. Naturally this results in a slow rate of growth in rural areas—which are more thinly populated and have lower incomes, and are therefore more costly to serve—especially on the East Coast. As a partial offset to this tendency, the government appropriates money to the NEB each year to be used to offset the difference between cost and revenue in rural electrification. The sum involved is fairly small—only $3 million a year in 1966–1970, rising to $12 million in 1971–5.

Telephone and postal services are provided by federal government departments, which are less puristically commercial in their operating principles than the NEB. They have considerably extended their services since Merdeka but have not been oblivious to the high operating and maintenance costs involved in rural call boxes and small post offices.

Piped drinking water and water-borne sewerage are provided by the state governments, which have limited them mainly to the larger towns and only slowly extended them to the smaller communities and rural areas.

Finally, publicly-provided low-cost housing, an amenity so closely associated with development in neighbouring Singapore, has been provided to a much smaller extent in Malaysia. Singapore's politics are almost wholly urban, while Malaysia's are mainly rural. Malaysian public housing investment has tended to turn upward in years preceding general elections, as the government tries to make some kind of appeal to the urban electorate which so frequently votes for the opposition. Such an upturn occurred in 1968, when an attempt was made to provide rural and small-town as well as urban housing. The rural public housing projects, undertaken in great haste, were generally not very successful, and little was heard of them after the 1969 election.

Social services are also an important part of the rural development programme. These are discussed in Chapter 9 in the context of general policies related to inequality. However, in view of the strong urban bias which the education system and other social-service networks exhibited at the time of Merdeka, it is well to remember that their expansion almost inevitably implies improved service in the rural areas. For example, the achievement of near-universality of primary education during the late 1950s meant that for the first time rural youth had access to much the same type of schooling (despite significant differences in teacher training and experience, as well as in physical facilities) as their urban counterparts. This should have conferred economic benefits, since literacy and other basic skills acquired in primary school have economic value in either a rural or an urban environment (although by Merdeka primary schooling no longer carried much weight in the urban job market). The expansion of enrolment at the lower secondary level (years seven to nine) and introduction of a comprehensive curriculum in the mid-1960s effectively introduced secondary schooling into the smaller towns, where it became much more accessible to rural youth. (Parents could now frequently avoid the expense of boarding their student children, who, because of their prior primary schooling and the abolition of the Secondary School Entrance Examination, were much more likely to possess the necessary credentials for admittance.) Upper secondary education continued to be heavily concentrated in the larger towns, but the spread of schooling at the lower levels led to increased participation of students from rural backgrounds there, too. By the 1970s significant numbers of rural students began to appear in the universities and other third-level institutions. It was a long way from the colonial ideal of educating the son of a farmer to be a better farmer.

Experience with public health services was similar to that of education, although the rate of expansion of the service into the rural areas was less dramatic. Under the Second Malayan Five-Year Plan the Ministry of Health formulated a plan for blanketing the country with a network of curative facilities: regional health centres, smaller health sub-centres and rural midwives' clinics. Construction of the necessary physical facilities went into high gear in the early 1960s, quickly outrunning the Ministry's ability to provide the prescribed numbers of trained personnel. Thereafter the construction programme was slowed down and training programmes accelerated to achieve a better balance. Slowly, rural health services improved—although health services never received anything like the political and budgetary emphasis accorded to education. A study conducted in the early 1970s found use of the public health services to be laudably evenly spread across all strata of the population and regions of the country.[81]

The sharp declines which occurred in the crude death rate (from 16.3 per thousand of population in 1948, to 12.4 in 1957, to 6.4 in 1975), infant mortality rate (from 97 per thousand live births in 1951, to 76 in 1957, to 33 in 1975) and toddler mortality rate (from 10.7 per thousand 1–4 year-olds in 1957 to 3.1 in 1975) all attest to rising standards of nutrition and preventive medicine. Early studies, especially that of Burgess and Laidin (1950), demonstrated the existence of severe deficiencies in the diets and health conditions of poor rural residents. Although subsequent nutritional data are weak, the mortality statistics give good reason to believe that improvement has been substantial.

EVALUATION AND CONCLUSIONS

Taking a comprehensive view of the many different policies discussed in this chapter, one's overall evaluation of rural development policy must be positive but qualified. The *most* affirmative thing that can be said is that rural development is by no means the area of neglect and uniform failure in Malaysia that it is in so many low-income countries. A number of bold initiatives have been undertaken, many of them of real and constructive socio-economic substance and not just matters of political posturing. These initiatives have had their origins in the imperatives of ethnic politics and have achieved their reality through the government's substantial capacity for solid, pragmatic programme implementation. There is thus considerable basis for the praise which has been accorded Malaysian rural development efforts by so many outside observers.

This generally positive assessment is, however, subject to four major qualifications:

1. There have been a number of programme failures. For example, while FELDA succeeded the fringe alienation schemes did not. This is probably the least telling qualification, since a certain incidence of failure is an unavoidable concomitant of experimentation and the Malaysian

administration has usually been quick to abandon, or at least de-emphasize, the unsuccessful programmes and pour increasing shares of its resources into the more successful ones.

2. The devotion to inequality reduction as the major goal of rural development has been less than universal and unwavering. In a few key areas, notably rubber replanting and land policy in padi cultivation, deference has been paid to narrower economic interests which possess political influence. This led to some missed opportunities, notably to increase the productivity of rubber smallholders.

3. One major element of the programme, the promotion of rice production, has almost certainly been over-emphasized—at least to the extent that inequality reduction is the objective. Some significant fraction of the substantial resources devoted to the expansion of rice production surely could have contributed more to economic equality if it had been spent in other ways. The heavy emphasis on padi and the large extent to which the government is intervening in the markets for padi and rice also risk the creation of rigidities which will be expensive to maintain and difficult to eliminate in the future.

4. Finally, and most significantly, there is the limited impact of rural development policies on rural incomes. It was seen earlier (Table 4.8) that mean household income in rural areas rose by perhaps 18 per cent between 1957–8 and 1970, while urban mean income increased by at least 35 per cent, and that the distribution of income within the rural sector became markedly more unequal. The number of rural households living below the poverty line apparently increased. The obvious question, therefore, is what the successful rural development programmes have achieved.

As noted earlier, the programmes did facilitate the accommodation of a rapidly growing rural population (see Table 7.1) with no fall—indeed, with a modest rise—in average income. They might have increased more if they had not been subject to the limitations just enumerated, but they did at least achieve that. Moreover, they brought about very great improvements in several forms of social consumption which are not reflected in household income statistics: in education, public health services and a variety of amenities. They thus made rural life less grindingly difficult and brought the *kampung* into closer contact with the town. Whether they also did much to provide rural people with the requisites of satisfactory functioning in the urban setting—usable modern skills and values—is more doubtful.

The rural development programme thus can be seen largely as a holding programme, although this should not deprecate its importance. In particular, programmes that deal with those rural occupations which have the lowest potential productivity, such as padi cultivation and traditional in-shore fishing, can succeed only to the extent of temporarily buttressing income levels in industries which must eventually disappear, or change radically, as development proceeds. Their objective is merely to hang on until labour demand in more productive industries outruns rural population growth.[82] Other parts of the programme, such as those dealing with the cultivation of high-yielding rubber trees and oil palms, are more positively concerned with activities which will remain part of the modernizing Malaysian economy for the foreseeable future.

In political terms, the pre-1969 rural development programme was an exercise in constructive conservatism. By making the life of the rural Malays more comfortable, it hoped to head off both communal and class conflict. But since the programme inevitably contributed to the growth of awareness and ambition in the rural population, the desired contentment and placidity could not be maintained indefinitely. Discontent developed, coming to a head in 1969 and forcing a major shift in emphasis from rural development to urban activities.

1. At least, in terms of numbers of holdings and participants. Chapter 4 showed (p. 96) that although about two-thirds of rubber smallholdings are Malay-owned the smaller average size of Malay holdings reduces the Malay share in acreage to half or less. Padi cultivation is overwhelmingly Malay, as is fishing, except that the Chinese (and Japanese) have established a position in the more modern segment of the industry in recent years.

2. By 1962, 68 per cent of mature and immature rubber planted on estates consisted of high-yielding material (Department of Statistics, 1963a, p. 15). Thereafter, planting continued at a slower pace. By 1974 over 99 per cent of estate output came from high-yielding trees.

3. 'Rural population' here means population not residing in gazetted towns or villages of 1,000 or more inhabitants. The resettlement programme moved the rural Chinese into more than 200 'new villages'. All these communities were still relatively small in 1957. For this reason, one does not obtain a decline in the non-Malay rural population in 1947 if a higher urbanization cut-off point, such as 10,000, is used.

4. For a thorough analysis of the early years of the programme, see Ness (1967).

5. In 1963 Minister of Agriculture Aziz bin Ishak was forced to resign as the result of a power struggle with Tun Abdul Razak which was said ultimately to concern the choice of an heir apparent to then Prime Minister Tengku Abdul Rahman. Similarly, the decision in 1966 to replace co-operatives with farmers' associations as the chosen instrument for provision of credit, subsidy and technical assistance programmes for padi farmers was linked by observers to the political ambitions of Agriculture Minister Ghazali bin Jawi.

6. See Martin Rudner (1970a), who is somewhat more impressed by pre-1970 efforts to develop rubber smallholdings than I am. Rudner fails to bring out the contrast between the solicitous official concern for padi farmers and the comparative neglect of rubber smallholders.

7. *First Malaysia Plan 1966–1970* (1965, p. 99). These figures understate the gap between the estates and the truly small holdings, since replanting on smallholdings as officially defined (anything up to 100 acres) was concentrated on medium-sized holdings in the 25–99 acre range.

8. Diversification emerged as a major emphasis in policy statements at the time of the rubber industry's post-war survival crisis. Just what was to replace rubber was for a long time unclear. The hollowness of the concept prompted the government to bring in an expert consultant team to study technical possibilities for agricultural diversification, and means of realizing them, in 1962; see Karl Brandt, J. Norman Efferson and Don Paarlberg (1963). In subsequent years, as noted in the text, the only real diversification was provided by oil palm.

9. See Khoo Swee Joo (1964) for a good review of the oil palm industry up to that time but an unduly cautious assessment of its expansion prospects.

10. See United Nations Food and Agricultural Organization (1970, pp. 140–8). The Plan urged Malaysia to limit acreage to 225,000 hectares (about 556,000 acres) in 1975 and 400,000 hectares (988,000 acres) by 1985. Actual planted area had risen to 883,000 acres by 1972, when the ink on the FAO's Plan was hardly dry. Output, productivity and prices have all been running well above the FAO's projections.

11. Several writers have summarized and evaluated the rubber replanting drive and its application to smallholders in more detail than is provided here. See Lim Chong Yah (1961); J. M. F. Greenwood (1964); James C. Jackson (1964); Mohd. Noor bin Wahab and K. C. Arun (1969); Rudner (1970a); and David Lim (1973, pp. 217–18).

12. The cess 'was, therefore, an additional smallholders' replanting tax, and the estates were brought in only for administrative reasons. It would be administratively very difficult, if not impossible, to tax smallholders' rubber production alone through the export tax mechanism. The government's original intention to extend this tax to the estate sector was dropped on account of the strong opposition from estate interests, and the tax thus remained a smallholders' tax' (Lim Chong Yah, 1961, p. 46).

13. The Report urged that the export duty be regarded as a means of reducing excess purchasing power during commodity booms such as the Korean boom which had then recently ended, not as a revenue device.

14. For details, see Lim Chong Yah (1960, 1961).

15. For example, shortages of administrative personnel often led to delays. A significant number of smallholders, especially some of the poorest Chinese, have been unable to participate at all in the programme because they lack a clear title to the land they have been farming.

16. This displaced estate labourers, depriving them of legislated wages and social benefits. The problem led to an investigative committee, a study directed by Ungku Aziz (Malaya, 1963) and finally to anti-subdivision legislation.

17. The author's former colleague, T. J. Goering (1969) has calculated that payments by smallholders into Fund B from its inception through 1967 totalled $517 million, while the Fund's payments to smallholders amounted to $540 million. Thus the government at the time was reneging on its promise to subsidize smallholder replanting by up to $280 million.

18. Immature rubber may be intercropped (e.g. with vegetables or quick-growing trees like papaya); the profitability of doing so obviously varies with the marketability of the resulting produce. Mature rubber creates a dense shade which makes intercropping impossible.

19. The subdivision of rubber estates referred to earlier made a comparatively small contribution to the decline in acreage. Most of the decline occurred after 1963, when estate acreage in rubber was still 1,919,000, and is attributable to the shift to oil palm.

20. More demanding in terms of nutrients and water than rubber, oil palm was long thought to be suited only to limited coastal areas of the Peninsula. Field trials showed, however, that its limitations are in fact much less than had been believed.

21. While all commodity prices determined by free markets are difficult to predict, those of oil palm products are especially so because of the complex substitution relationships which exist among the many different fats and oils.

22. At Merdeka, the experimental oil palm stock of the College of Agriculture at Serdang was actually dispersed to various estate groups, in the belief that there could be no national advantage in oil palm experimentation because it was a European crop! Thus the key research work was conducted by the foreign estates, especially the Guthrie group. In 1969, when the Malaysian Agricultural Research Institute (MARDI) was founded, oil palm research was returned to official auspices, despite misgivings on the part of the estate interests.

23. This reduced estate costs, but it also contributed to unemployment and may well not have been beneficial in social terms (Donald R. Snodgrass, 1976, pp. 284–7).

24. A government study (Economic Planning Unit, 1975) based on data from the 1970 Post Enumeration Survey put the number of poverty households (defined as those in which income per member was $25 a month or less) in rural areas (plus urban-based agriculturalists) at 535,000. Of this total, rubber smallholders were estimated to number 176,000. Although the incidence of poverty among rubber smallholder households (50 per cent) was lower than the incidence among other groups such as padi cultivators (75 per cent) and fishermen (65 per cent), they accounted for the largest category of poverty households in the population.

25. This was not the first time the Malaysian government had attempted to support the world rubber market. It had also done so by buying rubber during the 1968 price slump (reportedly turning a profit by selling off the stocks thus acquired during the 1969 upturn) and for short periods thereafter.

26. C. P. Brown (1974) has shown, through a simulation study, that the Malaysian government could not conceivably possess sufficient resources to support the world rubber market for long unilaterally. With Indonesian and Thai co-operation (the three countries together account for 86 per cent of world natural rubber output) effective support for at least a few years becomes plausible, especially at a time when synthetic rubber producers are under severe cost pressures. Eventually, of course, the artificially elevated price will stimulate rubber planting in non-participating countries; natural rubber supply, which is rather inelastic in the short run, should prove to be highly elastic over a period long enough to permit new areas to be brought into production. Whether the whole scheme was in Malaysia's national interest is very doubtful, in my opinion. Malaysia was willing to bear most of the cost of an international buffer stock, and even if the Thais and Indonesians had co-operated fully it seems likely that output restrictions would have endangered Malaysia's large and growing technical advantage. The output restriction proposal appears to be a misapplication of the lessons learned in the generally successful International Tin Agreement.

27. *The Socio-Economic Sample Survey of Households* found 39,700 people to be employed primarily in coconut growing and processing in 1967–8; Ministry of Labour statistics put estate employment at this time (which should be deducted from the *SES* total) at about 4,500. Smallholder acreage statistics are weak, partly because of the prevalence of tiny, scattered holdings. The best source of information on coconut smallholdings is Selvadurai (1968).

28. There were evidently over 600,000 acres of coconut in Malaya in 1935, compared to less than 450,000 (estates plus smallholders) now. See International Bank for Reconstruction and Development (1955, p. 256).

29. The EPU study cited earlier (Economic Planning Unit, 1975) put the incidence of poverty among 32,000 coconut smallholder households in 1970 at 45 per cent.

30. An important aid to the land development programme has been extensive study of land use and capability. A study by P. C. Lee and W. P. Panton (1971, pp. 25–7, 35, 40) showed 7.7 million of Peninsular Malaysia's 32.5 million acres of land to be of high agricultural potential for a wide range of crops, while an additional 8.2 million acres were found to possess moderate potential for agricultural development with a restricted range of crops. Despite the extension of cultivated area by some 1.3 million acres in the preceding two decades, only 7.1 million acres out of the 15.9 million found suitable for agriculture were being cultivated in 1966–7. The major uncultivated areas of high or moderate potential were found to be located in Pahang, Johore, Trengganu, Kelantan and Perak (in order of extent).

31. For example, the government of Sri Lanka has been sponsoring land settlement schemes for many years, but the benefit/cost ratios that it has been able to achieve appear to be much lower than those of Malaysia and probably even negative. The fact that Sri Lanka's schemes have involved the provision of irrigation and the cultivation of rice while Malaysia's are for rainfed export crops explains much of the difference.

32. For accounts and analyses of various stages of FELDA's development, see M. C. Agarwal (1961); D. E. M. Fiennes (1962); Taib bin Haji Andak (1964, 1968); Amina H. Degani (1964, 1965); R. D. Hill (1965); Robert Ho (1965); R. Wikkramatileke (1965, 1972); Raja Muhammad Alias (1975); FELDA (1976).

33. A schematic presentation of all the public and private land development patterns extant in 1973 appears in Syed Hussain Wafa (1975, p. 165).

34. After some early experimentation, FELDA settled on scheme sizes of 3,000–3,500 acres for rubber and 5,000 acres for oil palm (the minimum scale required to feed a processing plant) as its standards. Some development of much larger areas was also undertaken, beginning with the Jengka Triangle project in the mid-1960s.

35. In 1958, very early in its experience, FELDA abandoned the customary practice of land clearing by the settlers themselves in the belief that it was too slow and resulted in inferior cultivations. Two years later responsibility for planting, maintenance of the new crop over its first few months and construction of settler housing was also given over to contractors.

36. Settler selection has been a controversial aspect of FELDA operations. There have been conflicts between the desire to choose individuals who are willing and able to contribute to the success of the scheme, on the one hand, and those who most 'need' the benefits of the scheme, on the other. The ideal settler has been defined as someone from an agricultural background who is landless and about 35 years old, has several children and is physi-

cally fit, enthusiastic and determined to work hard. Favouritism along political lines is also said to have influenced settler selection. A few early schemes included significant numbers of Chinese and Indian settlers but later schemes were almost entirely settled by Malays; a tabulation as of 1970 showed 94 per cent of the settlers on all FELDA schemes to be Malay (Wikkramatileke, 1972).

37. Early plans envisaged a variety of main crops and the creation of balanced agricultural communities, in which fruit, vegetables, livestock, poultry and freshwater fish culture would supplement income from the main crop. From the start, however, attention focused on the more remunerative main crop and subsidiary activities were all but ignored. Rubber and oil palm were the only main crops planted until the early 1970s, when a sugarcane scheme and a pilot cacao scheme were established.

38. Holding sizes were progressively increased as settler income targets were adjusted upward. Current allotments are at the high end of the ranges mentioned.

39. Settlers work in 'block groups' during the immaturity period and then receive randomly chosen lots from within the area in which they have been working.

40. The most recent settlers repay $17,000 at 6¼ per cent interest. Settler debt includes the cost of developing productive facilities and excludes FELDA administrative costs and the cost of social and economic infrastructure. Raja Muhammad Alias (1975, p. 20) reports the government's total cost as $28,000 per family. Loan repayment is geared to settler income, which is heavily dependent on the price of rubber or palm oil. Debt collection problems during the period of low prices in the early 1970s caused FELDA to contemplate a compulsory savings scheme.

41. This figure is subject to two major biases. On the one hand, only FELDA outlays are included; substantial expenditures by other federal agencies are excluded, as are costs incurred by the settlers themselves. On the other hand, not all costs incurred up to a given date, say 1975, are applicable to families settled by that date; some relate to families that will be settled in the future. The two biases work in opposite directions, but it is difficult to gauge their relative magnitudes.

42. One model frequently proposed for federal emulation is the Kelantan Land Development Authority. In KLDA schemes, settlers do their own clearing and planting, receiving much lower levels of public assistance and direction. These schemes have been generally successful, but they would not *necessarily* work in other parts of the country, since the Kelantanese peasants being settled are among the poorest, and also reputedly the most aggressive and enterprising, in the country. Nor are they even necessarily desirable, since they result in slower and lower-quality development (Dixon, 1977).

43. A formal benefit-cost analysis of the FELDA programme was undertaken by S. Singh (1965, 1968). Counting only direct production benefits and including all costs incurred by the Authority, government departments and (explicitly or implicitly) the settlers themselves, Singh obtained social benefit/cost ratios in the range of 1.2 to 2.4, depending on what price was assumed for rubber and how labour was valued. A questionable aspect of Singh's work was the low discount rates used: 6¾ per cent and 5½ per cent, respectively the rates paid on FELDA's early borrowings from the Colonial Development Corporation and the then current yield on long-term Malaysian government securities; an alternative would be the social opportunity cost of capital, which is thought to be around 10 per cent and would be a more acceptable rate to employ because all, or nearly all, of FELDA's financing would also be available for alternative projects. Nevertheless, he seems to have shown that, except under an exceptional combination of unfavourable assumptions, the FELDA programme is an efficient use of public funds. Singh's results were later replicated, with innumerable variations, by several writers. See, for example, Syed Hussain Wafa (1972, 1975), S. C. Lim (1972), Little and Tipping (1972) and Dixon (1977). Tan Bock Thiam (1975) summarizes and compares eight studies done on oil palm land development projects.

44. The Authority's target had been to settle 23,700 families in the five-year period 1971–5, while developing 55,000 acres per year (*Second Malaysia Plan 1971–1975*, 1971, p. 133). In fact, 82,400 acres were developed annually but only 13,700 families were settled in the five-year period (*Third Malaysia Plan 1976–1980*, 1976, p. 288).

45. Policies on land development varied widely among states. For an instructive comparison of Trengganu and Johore, see Dorothy Guyot (1971).

46. The data on rural population run only to 1970, but the development of just over one million acres of land in 1971–5 (*Third Malaysia Plan 1976–1980*, 1976, p. 302) should have made it possible *at least* to keep pace with rural population growth in the early 1970s.

47. In connexion with the large Pahang Tenggara area development project, extensive

analysis was made of rubber, oil palm and productive forestry as alternative uses of land. Although rubber was found to absorb much more labour per unit of land than forestry, the latter created far more linkages to the industrial and service sectors. Oil palm fell between the other two possibilities in both respects.

48. The view that Malays should only grow rice was voiced by A. S. Haynes, then Secretary of Agriculture, in a speech to the Legislative Council in 1933:

'The British in their duty as trusteeship for the Malay people demand that we administer the country on lines consistent with their welfare and happiness, not only for today but for the future ages. That end will be attained rather by building up a sturdy and thrifty peasantry living on the lands they own and living by the food they grow than by causing them to foresake the life of their fathers for the glamour of new ways . . . to abandon their rice fields for the new crops which they themselves cannot utilize and the market for which depends on world conditions beyond their orbit' (*Proceedings*, *Federated Malay States*, *1933*, 1934, p. 293; cited in Yukon Huang, 1971, p. 9).

It was also believed that only Malays should grow rice. Even in the Depression, when it wanted rice production to increase, the government resisted demands by Chinese and Indian spokesmen that their compatriots be allowed to plant padi. Only in 1939, when the approach of War made disruption of foreign rice supplies all but certain, did it yield. By then, of course, the Japanese invasion was less than two years away (Ding Eing Tan Soo Hai, 1963). After the War orthodoxy was re-established within the colonial administration. As late as 1962, decades after Malay smallholders began planting rubber, D. E. S. Fiennes (1962, p. 158) was to complain about opposition, 'perhaps connected with the cold baths and puritan upbringing of English public schools', to the idea 'that the farmer should grow the crop or crops which are most profitable . . .' in FELDA schemes:

'To grow rubber, the argument runs, is to incur the danger of committing the Malay farmer to the Chinese dealer and the untrusty vagaries of distant markets. There is, however, apparently something noble in plodding through the mud of a ricefield behind a buffalo in the hot sun, thus (with the help of a government subsidy on the price of rice) ensuring that the farmer has enough to eat, but equally that he does not have the price of a cinema or cabaret ticket in his pocket. Malaya now plans for rich farmers, even if unprotected from the temptations of wealth.'

49. S. Selvadurai (1972) provides the most convenient summary account. Other important general works are T. B. Wilson (1958); Robert Ho (1969); John T. Purcal (1971); Yukon Huang (1971); and Otto C. Doering III (1973). James C. Jackson (1972) succinctly describes the varied rice-growing environments of Peninsular Malaysia.

50. The number is from the 1967–8 *SES*. The exact number of padi cultivators is very hard to identify because of the seasonal nature of the work and the fact that many cultivators follow other occupations as well.

51. Double-cropping was introduced in Province Wellesley and a few other areas by the Japanese (Van Thean Kee, 1949).

52. The area surveyed is the site of the Kemubu drainage and irrigation scheme, since implemented.

53. Kelantan's relative isolation limits opportunities to earn income from non-padi sources compared to those which exist elsewhere. Even so, Kelantan farmers often earn more by planting tobacco and other crops in their dry fields during the off-season than from main-season padi (Dixon, 1971, 1971a).

54. A major force leading to fragmentation of padi holdings is Muslim inheritance laws, which prescribe that the deceased's property be divided among his heirs according to certain specified proportions. This accounts for the smaller farm size in areas which have been farmed longer.

55. Chinese also benefited by not having to pay *zakat*, which took 9 per cent of the crop in Province Wellesley, 6 per cent in Kelantan and 9 per cent in Selangor (Selvadurai, 1972, p. 37). This is a religious tax, originally intended for the relief of poverty, which is enforced in Malaya only on padi producers. The tax is levied on the actual producer of padi (e.g., a tenant rather than his landlord) and its incidence appears to be highly regressive. Older, orthodox farmers are said to be faithful in paying *zakat*, while some younger farmers are said to resist. *Zakat* is discussed by Wilson (1958) and Purcal (1971).

56. According to the survey, Chinese padi planters in Tanjong Karang average $2,771 in gross annual income (Table 7.5). Subtracting average outlays of $106 for purchased inputs and $626 for hired labour, their average net income was $2,039 per annum, or $170

a month. The SRM/Ford survey put rural median income in 1967–8 at $133 a month; the mean was $185.

57. The limited pre-1932 experience is discussed in D. C. Short and James C. Jackson (1971).

58. The DID used 'private', rather than 'social', benefit/cost analysis; that is, it did not shadow-price either the output or any of the inputs. The most obvious bias introduced, in terms of efficiency, is the failure to correct for the inflated domestic price of rice, which leads to overstatement of the net benefits of all DID projects in terms of world prices. Of course, it could be argued that this is not a bias but a distortion of efficiency prices introduced deliberately on distributive grounds. Other problems are the tendency to omit some costs and the difficulty of calculating in advance just what a project (especially a large and complex one) will cost. Doering (1973, pp. 89–125) carried out an *ex post* benefit/cost analysis of the Muda River project; he found a benefit/cost ratio of about one, compared to values of three or four obtained *ex ante* by consultants who analysed the project for World Bank financing.

59. Fears of the financial difficulties of subsidizing surplus production prompted the 1970 decision; renewed concern about the supply of imported rice during the 1972–3 world food crisis brought about its reversal.

60. Although these expectations have been borne out by empirical studies conducted elsewhere, an analysis of the Muda area carried out by Goldman and Squire (1977) gives contrary results. Through 1973, at least, Muda project benefits appear to have gone mainly to labour through increased employment and wage increases. Goldman and Squire attribute their results partly to the labour-using bias of the new rice technology and partly to limitations of available labour supply in the project area.

61. A picul is 133⅓ lb.; there are 16.8 piculs in a long ton.

62. The government purchasing system, as noted in the text below, discriminates insufficiently among qualities of rice and therefore tends to be offered the lower qualities, which are worth less than the GMP on the open market.

63. These issues are discussed in C. P. Brown (1973).

64. For instance by Brandt, Efferson and Paarlberg (1963, pp. 9–12).

65. An exception was the early 1970s' food crisis, in which the free-market purchase price for most grades of domestic rice moved above the GMP.

66. Huang (1971, p. 18) cites a 1966 finding that only 5 per cent of padi farmers had ever borrowed from a co-operative society, the only alternative to private lenders which then existed. Following the creation of an agricultural bank (Bank Pertanian Malaysia) and the formation of Farmers' Associations, this percentage has undoubtedly risen in the 1970s. It seems likely, however, that padi growers still satisfy the great majority of their credit needs from non-institutional sources.

67. Based on the *HBS*.

68. These powers, which are described by Brown (1973, pp. 173–4), are intended to strengthen the LPN's hand against powerful rice smugglers, who bring in rice illegally from Thailand so as to capitalize on the large internal market price differential between the two countries. However, Selvadurai (1972, p. 40) also mentions the existence of 'illegal padi buyers who buy directly from farmers and sell to the mills or to licensed buyers' in areas where a padi marketing scheme has been established. How such people can compete successfully with a programme which is supposed to offer the farmer a better deal is not made clear.

69. The Farmers' Associations were given authority over all agricultural production credit in 1968, leaving the co-operatives with responsibility only for crop processing and the supply of consumer goods. However, in 1970, when the length of time required to establish a full network of FAs began to be better appreciated, the right to run credit schemes in certain circumstances (with government help in areas where FAs had not yet been established, without it where they had) was restored to the co-operatives. See Selvadurai (1972, pp. 66–71); Ahmad Sarji (1975). Licensed private traders have also served as local credit centres in some cases. The emerging system is discussed in Millard Long (n.d.).

70. Selvadurai (1972, pp. 28–9). These data are from the 1960 Census of Agriculture and may no longer be accurate.

71. The statement also applies in a broader sense than is suggested here. The *real* potential for redistributing land obviously lies in the break-up of estates into smallholdings. Quite apart from the question of what the consequences of such a radical reorganization of

the rural economy would be, it is interesting to note that the possibility has seldom or never been raised (although the radical Malay party, Parti Rakyat, has repeatedly called for nationalization of foreign estates).

72. Additional reasons for the ineffectiveness of the 1955 Act were the failure to provide adequate enforcement machinery and the involved and time-consuming procedures specified for registering tenancy agreements. See Eldon D. Smith and Peter R. Goethals (1965).

73. Of course, fixed rents provide an incentive to tenants only over the period during which the amount of rent paid remains fixed. To the extent that landlords raise rents in the wake of increasing productivity, the incentive is lost.

74. Based on Census of Agriculture data. Smith and Goethals (1965), consultants brought in to study land tenure conditions, in particular the question of whether tenancy disincentives were likely to lead to under-utilization of the capacity to be created by the Muda River project, were forced by these findings to express agnosticism about the relationship between land tenure and productivity. However, they still came out in favour of more effective enforcement of conditions favourable to tenants, as well as for actual redistribution of ownership rights if supported by an adequate long-term credit programme. Apparently they believed that these measures would lead to more equitable distribution of an approximately constant amount of income.

75. However, see the interesting speculations by Huang (1975, pp. 709–16) on why productivity may be higher on tenanted than owned land of equal quality (and on share-cropped land than on the other forms of tenanted land).

76. Land titles specify the crop or crops which may be grown; most land suitable for wet rice cultivation is 'gazetted' *only* for padi.

77. According to the EPU study cited earlier (Economic Planning Unit, 1975), 65 per cent of fishermen's households fell below the poverty line in 1970. This percentage was exceeded only by padi cultivators, mixed agriculturalists and agricultural labourers. The classic analysis of East Coast fishing, comprehensive and authoritative although now somewhat dated, is Raymond Firth (1966).

78. According to Fisheries Division data, the share of powered boats rose from 26 per cent in 1957 to 82 per cent in 1976. See *Monthly Statistical Bulletins*.

79. *First Malaysia Plan 1966–1970* (1965, p. 141); *Second Malaysia Plan 1971–1975* (1971, p. 189). The length of the road network was 10,800 miles by 1970.

80. However, the PWD, into whose province road construction falls, has made less extensive use of benefit/cost analysis than has the DID. Formal analyses of this sort have been confined primarily to the larger, foreign-financed road projects.

81. Peter S. Heller (1974, 1975, 1976) surveyed the users of a sample of government hospitals and found that their socio-economic characteristics generally matched those of the population as a whole. However, his estimates of public health expenditure per capita by state do imply a rank correlation of + .4 with income per capita. *Private* health expenditures per head, as one would expect, are strongly correlated with income (rank correlation of + .8).

82. The government has been diffident about making a frontal attack on rural population growth through extension of the national family planning programme from the towns, where it began, into the rural areas. This obviously reflects the continuation among many Malays of ill-founded fears that the non-Malays could come to outnumber them in time.

8 Urban Development Policies

> ... the ability of the industrial sector to absorb labour has been grossly exaggerated and ... greater Malay participation in it has been restricted by a number of economic and institutional factors. However, the higher the rate of growth of the industrial output, the greater will be the absolute number of employment opportunities available to both the Malays and the non-Malays.
>
> David Lim, 1973, p. 246

THIS chapter complements the preceding one. While Chapter 7 discussed problems of economic inequality arising in the context of rural, mainly agricultural, economic activity, along with policies to deal with them, Chapter 8 does the same for urban, primarily industrial and commercial, activities.

DIMENSIONS OF URBAN (NON-AGRICULTURAL) DEVELOPMENT

Chapter 4 showed that urban household incomes average about twice as high, according to available statistics, as rural incomes. One can point to two obvious reasons why this is so: (1) Many of the most productive uses of labour take place in the towns, where the most rapidly growing industries are located. (2) The towns are a repository for accumulated wealth; the great bulk of property income flows there.

Traditionally, the urban areas of Peninsular Malaysia (along with the estates and mines) have been the natural habitat of the non-Malays, just as the *kampung* has been the domain of the Malays. In view of the wide gap between the two realms in terms of wealth and modernity, this ethnic bifurcation has become unacceptable to many Malays. They have therefore been pressing, with steadily increasing vigour, for a significant share of urban incomes and jobs, as well as a measure of control over urban economic life.

The traditional division of the economy along ethnic lines creates a fundamental difference between efforts to reduce economic inequality in rural areas and parallel efforts directed toward urban areas. Since the rural economy is already the domain of the Malays, and contains most of the poor, programmes intended to raise productivity there are almost automatically harmonious with the drive toward greater equality. Indeed, the phrase 'rural development' is often used to encompass both output and distribution objectives. But 'urban development' or 'industrial development' is usually interpreted to mean the growth of total non-agricultural income and employment, quite independent of the question of how these totals are to be shared. The crucial contribution which structural change must make both to raising national income and to improving its size distribution over the long run (i.e., in two decades or more) provides partial justification for this outlook. But it does not accommodate the political fact that greater Malay participation in the urban economy cannot wait for the long run. The question, then, is whether significant progress can be made in achieving more equitable sharing in the income, jobs, wealth and power generated by the urban sector, without jeopardizing the sector's role in the secular development process.

The most convenient way to review urban development policies is in sectoral terms, since this is how most of the statistics are organized. Urban development will therefore be regarded as essentially non-agricultural development—even though the two are not perfectly congruent. This chapter will survey the non-agricultural economy, industry by industry, analysing the three kinds of 'imbalance' identified by the Malaysian government and discussed in Chapter 4: imbalances in income, in employment and in the ownership and control of wealth.

Before proceeding to this survey, however, it is desirable to recall the state of the non-agricultural economy in the period leading up to Merdeka. As was seen in Chapter 2, European interests had staked out a limited number of highly profitable and otherwise congenial areas of operation—tin mining (especially dredging), banking, international trade, insurance. The Europeans also controlled the public sector, in which they practised some nominal and symbolic sharing of power with the Malay élite. This sector was small and limited in its functions. The rest of the non-agricultural economy—retail trade, road and water transportation, small manufacturing and repair establishments and a wide variety of services—was Chinese-dominated. In addition, as seen in Chapter 2, there were successful Chinese owned and managed enterprises in some of the European-dominated areas.

The Malay role in urban-based economic activity was not only very small but had suffered a clear-cut decline since pre-colonial times. Before British 'intervention' opened up the Peninsula in the 1870s, Malays performed most of the commercial, industrial and service roles which existed in their low-level agricultural economy. Village fairs were the principal setting for trade, the many rivers provided the main arteries of transportation and *kampung* handicrafts furnished most of the simple manufactures used in that society. Following intervention, these non-agricultural Malay activities went into retreat in the West Coast states, as factory-made imports replaced handicrafts and Chinese (and, to a lesser extent, Indian) traders took over commerce, right down to the level of the smallest retail shop. The old pattern persisted longer on the East Coast. George Maxwell, an elderly ex-civil servant writing in 1948, recalled the extent of Malay commerce which had existed in Kelantan and

Trengganu before those states came under British protection in 1909 (Maxwell, 1948). Returning years later, he found that the Chinese shop had all but supplanted the periodic markets to which rural Malay women would come to sell their agricultural produce and *kampung* handicrafts. The censuses bear out his memory, registering a steady decline in the number of Malay women traders.[1] Similarly, cottage and handicraft industries which had once employed significant numbers of people and significantly supplemented rural incomes—attap (woven roofing) making, mat weaving, jewellery making, handloom textile weaving, basket-making, sugar boiling and others—declined in the face of competition from factory-made substitutes. Some of these industries enjoyed a resurgence during the Japanese occupation but they melted away again as the flow of factory-made consumer goods resumed after the War.

Traditional Malay commerce and industry, as in many other societies, was largely women's work. The dominant economic activity, which the men followed and around which many social and cultural practices and beliefs revolved, was always agriculture, specifically rice cultivation. Yet trade and small-scale manufacturing played important subsidiary roles; and there can be little doubt that Malay society was made worse off by their decline.

What follows is an industry-by-industry survey of trends and policies.[2]

MANUFACTURING

Of all the non-agricultural industries, the most important is manufacturing. Malaya historically had a very small manufacturing sector, not only relative to the industrialized countries but even compared to other countries at the same general level of income per capita. Yet Malayan and Malaysian politicians and planners have always regarded manufacturing as a key section in their economic thinking. From the 1950s up to the 1969 watershed the sector was thought of principally as a leader in the process of economic growth and structural change. When reduction of inequality became the dominant goal the manufacturing sector remained important because of its close relationship to the various types of imbalance which the government pledged itself to correct, especially the imbalances in employment and in ownership and control of wealth.

In 1957 manufacturing accounted for only a few percentage points of the Federation of Malaya's GNP.[3] It employed 160,000 persons, including craftsmen and workers in handicrafts industries as well as factory workers. No particular effort had been made to develop manufacturing during colonial times, and neither the structure of the economy nor the policies which prevailed as Independence approached favoured its growth. Competing investments in extractive industries were exceptionally attractive, at least in normal times. There were few protective tariffs. Although a significant share of government revenue was raised from import duties, duty revenue was concentrated on a small number of products selected for their high revenue potential and/or because it was thought socially desirable to discourage their consumption (alcoholic beverages, tobacco and tobacco products). Industrial wages were higher than in other Asian countries because of the alternative forms of employment available. Power was expensive. All these factors militated against the spontaneous development of a significant manufacturing sector (Wheelwright, 1965).

Most of the manufacturing establishments which had been established despite these impediments (ignoring the handicraft industries mentioned earlier) were based on strong locational advantages relative to sites in distant Europe and North America. They all derived sizeable cost advantages from proximity either to the local market or to Malaya's primary exporting industries. The market-oriented group inclined strongly towards high-weight, low-value products such as bricks, beer, soft drinks, ice and lumber. It also included the traditional but retreating handicrafts, as well as still competitive trades such as tailoring, dressmaking and shoemaking. The export-related group consisted mainly of simple manipulations of local primary products to raise their value-to-weight ratios and make them more portable: the smoking of rubber, milling of coconut oil and so on. However, it also included tin smelting—a genuine large-scale, capital-intensive factory operation which it made sense to locate near the source of ore supply because of the enormous weight loss involved in the conversion of ore to ingots. Finally, a certain amount of local metal working was spawned by tin mining and by other industries such as railroading (Thoburn, 1977).

The politicians who assumed full control of the newly independent government of the Federation of Malaya in 1957, like their counterparts elsewhere, wanted to see their country develop a larger manufacturing sector. To further this desire, they took up the same array of tools which other countries have employed: tariff protection, direct tax concessions, development banking, subsidized provision of factory sites. The most promising manufacturing opportunities at the time appeared to lie in import substitution, since an exceptionally wide range of items was being imported and the local market, although small in terms of population, was relatively rich in terms of income per capita. As in so many other countries at that time, there was an exaggerated view of what manufacturing growth could accomplish in terms of foreign exchange savings and employment generation. Enthusiasm for hothouse manufacturing was tempered, however, by the realization (hammered home by the World Bank Report of 1955; see International Bank for Reconstruction and Development, 1955, pp. 119–28, 417–38) that the laws of comparative advantage had been good to Malaya in the past and could be abandoned only with peril in the post-Merdeka era. This realization saved Malaya from the excesses of price distortion to promote import substitution in which some other countries indulged.

To further the new industrialization policy, a Pioneer Industries Ordinance was enacted in 1958. This law authorized the Minister of Commerce and Industry to grant relief from the 40 per cent tax on company profits for periods ranging from two to five years depending on the size of the initial investment (projects of $250,000 or more were eligible for the five-year exemption).[4] Relief was allowed or disallowed in any particular case at the discretion of the Minister, based on general criteria laid down in the law.

The Pioneer Industries Ordinance set the pattern for manufacturing development in Peninsular Malaysia during the decade following its passage. In the first five years, 85 pioneer establishments were set up; after ten years (i.e. by 1968) the total was 146. Although pioneer firms still produced only 28 per cent of manufacturing value added in 1968 they had accounted for nearly half its growth in the preceding eight years.[5] They had also stamped the new manufacturing sector with some of its most prominent characteristics:

1. The pioneer firms were relatively capital intensive. Employment in them rose slowly, reaching only 22,652 full-time paid employees in 1968. Value added per full-time paid employee in that year was over $12,000, five times the average in the economy as a whole and three times the level prevailing in the industrial sector generally. Clearly the incentives given favoured the use of capital-intensive techniques.

2. The firms were predominantly foreign-owned; 70 per cent of value added in all pioneer establishments in 1968 came from the foreign-owned firms.[6] Pioneer firms thus swelled the already high foreign ownership share.

3. Pioneer establishments were heavily oriented toward the production of consumer goods for the domestic market.

4. They were geographically concentrated; 54 per cent of value added originated in Selangor and another 16 per cent from oil refineries in Negri Sembilan. Johore, Penang and Perak also had a stake in the programme but there was little or no pioneer industry on the East Coast, in the north-west or in Malacca.[7]

5. However, they did hire more Malays than other firms. Whereas non-pioneer manufacturing establishments included in the 1968 census averaged only 24 per cent Malays among their full-time paid employees, pioneer firms averaged 42 per cent and did so despite their tendency to cluster in areas where the population is predominantly non-Malay.[8] No doubt pioneer firms felt under greater pressure to comply with the vaguely specified ethnic employment guidelines than did other firms, and most of their Malay employees were in general in unskilled categories, but substantial income and training benefits must nevertheless have resulted.[9]

Although the pioneer industries thus became the leading edge of manufacturing development, it was not solely the tax relief afforded by the Ordinance that brought about this result. Other inducements also played a part, and at least one—tariff protection—was probably even more influential than relief from direct taxation.

The power to set (and set aside) tariffs resides with the Minister of Finance. Tariff advisory committees and boards have played a secondary role from time to time, as has the Federal Industrial Development Authority (FIDA) since its establishment in 1967. The tariff-setting power has perhaps been exercised in an even more discretionary way, with less clarity of overall guiding criteria, than the award of other investment incentives.[10] The general trend of effective protection, resulting both from tariffs and from the import quotas which began to be common in the late 1960s, was clearly up. Although one study (Power, 1971) found Malaysia's level of protection to be low relative to other developing countries in 1965, more recent work (Panchamukhi, 1972; Edwards, 1975; Economic Planning Unit, 1975a) confirms the later rise and even questions whether the level of protection was actually so low in 1965.

It is probable that tariff protection enabled a large number of new firms to compete successfully with imports and induced exporters of consumer goods to Malaysia to move at least a part of their manufacturing operation behind the tariff wall. Direct tax relief, by contrast, was demonstrably more selective in its impact.[11] Except perhaps for the broader, intangible attractions of Malaysia for private investors—stable government, low labour costs, receptive ideology—protection from foreign competition was undoubtedly the most potent inducement for manufacturing investment.

Other forms of official encouragement played a much smaller part. Malayan (later Malaysian) Development Finance, the development finance institution established in 1960 under World Bank tutelage as a source of long-term financing for relatively risky large investments, has in practice been run on rather cautious, conservative lines and thus has never become a major source of investment finance. Its lending programme grew slowly during the 1960s; the volume of loans outstanding at the end of 1968 amounted to only $47 million (Bank Negara Malaysia, 1969, pp. 27–8). An MIDF subsidiary, Malaysian Industrial Estates Ltd. (MIEL), constructed industrial estates in various parts of the country for the use of small manufacturing enterprises, as did several state governments. These industrial estates have tended to fill up rapidly when they were located in areas favoured by investors (Greater Kuala Lumpur, Province Wellesley, Johore Bahru) and very slowly when they were more out of the way. In neither case does the existence of the facility appear to have been a decisive factor in the investment decision.

Tempted by all these inducements, manufacturing value added grew at a high and rising rate, averaging 11 per cent per annum in 1960–8.[12] This made manufacturing easily the most dynamic sector of the economy, in accordance with the expectations of the 1950s. But the performance of the sector was much less satisfactory when measured against the economic equality objectives which took on increasing importance after 1969. This can be seen when the three dimensions of inequality discussed in Chapter 4—income, employment and ownership and control of wealth—are considered.

The development of manufacturing generated income for some Malaysians while costing other Malaysians some of their real disposable income. The 1968 Census of Manufacturing Industries gives a good idea of who received the income created by at least the larger manufacturing enterprises. The 9,000 units covered in the census had sales in excess of

$3 billion, with value added of $874 million. They employed 121,000 persons on a full-time paid basis, and an additional 9,000 part-time. Department of Statistics data suggest that 94 per cent of this work force was Malaysian and 27 per cent Malay. Salaries and wages paid during 1968 totalled $267 million, and thus averaged over $2,000 per employee per annum. The benefits to those who were able to obtain manufacturing jobs were thus substantial.

To what extent the latter, relatively small, group's gains were realized only at the expense of the much larger population of manufactured goods consumers, and of taxpayers as a group, is not very clear. One would expect protected import-substituting manufacturing growth to entail some increases in consumer prices. Yet all indications are that the prices consumers had to pay for manufactured goods rose very little during the 1960s. The official consumer price index rose an average of less than 1 per cent per annum, and although the index is probably biased downward and in any case measures only the average prices of all goods, from foreign as well as domestic sources, the fact remains that the discernible rise in the index which one might expect to see as a result of import substitution is decidedly absent.[13] Thus anyone who would claim that domestic manufacturing development in the 1960s significantly burdened the West Malaysian consumer would seem to have a case to prove.[14] There is more evidence, already noted, that the programme burdened the taxpayer by unnecessarily costing the government revenue which it presumably had to make up in other ways.

Only 6 per cent of the establishments covered by the 1968 Census of Manufacturing had majority foreign ownership. Yet these firms were so much larger, on average, than the domestically owned firms that they accounted for 47 per cent of gross sales, 48 per cent of the total value added and 52 per cent of non-labour value added (Department of Statistics, n.d., p. 38). One implication of these statistics is that a large, if not easily estimated, share of the non-labour income generated left the country for foreign pockets.[15] Another is that Malaysian ownership and control was at least as tenuous in this leading sector as in the longer-established parts of the economy—thanks in part to the Pioneer Industry Ordinance.[16]

The official attitude toward heavy foreign participation in the leading growth sector of the economy was consistently positive and tolerant prior to 1969. Foreign investors were generally thought to represent a source of capital, technology and business skill which had to be tapped if manufacturing was to keep growing rapidly. Implicit in Malay attitudes was the additional belief that the Malays themselves were not yet ready to manage large, modern businesses and that a degree of foreign domination was preferable to, because more manageable than, heavier reliance on Chinese enterprise. This created a temporary community of interests between Malay political leaders and international business (Golay, 1969). Although the government was simultaneously hailed for its enlightenment by enthusiasts of private enterprise (Freeman, 1968; Kasper, 1974) and excoriated for its retrograde behaviour by socialist and nationalist critics (Wheelwright, 1965; Sumitro, 1969; Anonymous, 1972), both groups sometimes failed to grasp the close relationship between the government's investment policy and transient domestic political expedients. This connexion was more evident to the government's numerous domestic (mainly non-Malay) critics, who, regardless of their ideological stripe, agreed that the role of foreigners should be much more sharply limited and that of Malaysians expanded accordingly.[17]

A very small start towards Malay ownership of a part of the new industrial sector was made through the practice of reserving a proportion (initially 10 per cent, later more) of each local stock issue for purchase by Malay individuals or Malay interests. A National Investment Company established in 1961 bought some of these shares, while others were purchased by Tabung Haji, a trust fund which held the accounts being built up by Muslims saving for an eventual pilgrimage to Mecca. MARA Unit Trusts Sdn. Bhd., founded in 1967, helped to market some of these reserved shares to individual Malays in unit trust (mutual fund) form. A Malay stock exchange was set up in 1970 to enhance the value of reserved stock by making it easier for Malays to trade shares among themselves. All these measures together, however, were tiny in scale relative to the widening scope of modern industry in the country.

The most significant contribution of manufacturing growth before 1969 to improve ethnic balance in the economy was made in the area of employment. In 1957 there had been 160,000 workers employed in manufacturing, of whom some 30,000 were Malay.[18] Roughly one-third of the Malays worked in the declining handicraft industries rather than the newer part of the sector. A decade later, when total manufacturing employment had risen to 232,000, Malay employment was 60,000. Malays had thus raised their share from 19 per cent to 26 per cent in a decade, no mean feat despite the fact that the jobs gained were mostly among the lower-paid and less-skilled positions. The value of this accomplishment to the Malay community was limited, however, by the slowness of growth in total manufacturing employment. While value added in the sector rose by more than 10 per cent a year, employment grew by less than 4 per cent per annum. So even though Malays probably filled more than 40 per cent of the new jobs created, this amounted to only 30,000 or so jobs in all.

Although governments before 1969 saw little immediate role for Malays in manufacturing beyond that of employee, they did not of course subscribe to the view that the Malays would be predominantly rural and agricultural forever. They reconciled these two opinions by thinking in terms of a gradual development of Malay entrepreneurship, moving from trading into manufacturing and from small-scale enterprises to larger ones, much as the Chinese had done before except that in the case of the Malays official assistance and encouragement would accelerate the process. The main instrument of this effort, which Wheelwright (1965) scornfully characterizes as 'synthetic capitalism', was to be RIDA/MARA.

From the mid-1950s onwards RIDA's purview was defined as

Bumiputra participation in all sectors other than agriculture, fishing and livestock. Under this mandate it tried to promote Malay-owned and managed small- and medium-sized businesses in manufacturing, trade, construction and some services. Its programme included (1) direct operation of a limited number of enterprises by RIDA/MARA itself; (2) small loans to Malay entrepreneurs; and (3) technical and commercial advice to Malay businesses. Although the Authority had an unassailably high political priority, the sums allocated to it remained relatively small throughout the 1960s. Government subventions (excluding funds for training programmes which are discussed in Chapter 9) totalled only $10 million in the 1961–5 plan period and $51 million in 1966–70. That they were not larger was largely a result of MARA's inability to spend greater sums effectively.

As a semi-autonomous Authority, RIDA/MARA has always operated somewhat to one side of other government programmes. Political influence in its day-to-day operations has probably been much greater than is the case in government departments. In what can only be regarded as a confusion between means and ends, RIDA/MARA has always been staffed almost entirely by Malays; since until recently very few Malays possessed the skills and experience needed for the effective conduct of its business, the sacrifice of potential non-Malay inputs has been costly. Not surprisingly, there have been many problems.[19] The default rate on loans has reportedly been high, but this is not the most telling performance indicator. More damaging is the small number of viable enterprises created by a programme in which such high hopes were placed. Chee Peng Lim (1974), in his comprehensive study of small manufacturing enterprises in Peninsular Malaysia, found the Malay position in 1969 to be scarcely stronger in the smaller type of firm than in the larger corporate enterprises. Despite nearly two decades of RIDA/MARA, over 90 per cent of small industry chief executives were found to be Chinese; only 7 per cent were Malay, and many of these were to be found in the traditional activity of batik manufacturing. The Malay share of small-industry employment was found to be 24.4 per cent, close to the figure for manufacturing employment as a whole.

One is forced to conclude that RIDA/MARA failed to effect any significant change in the ethnic composition of ownership and control in manufacturing (nor in the non-agricultural sectors generally, although there are some exceptions). No formula was ever found which would have permitted MARA to turn out Malay businessmen on a mass scale, the way FELDA has created agricultural smallholders. As dissatisfaction with existing trends mounted during the late 1960s, therefore, demands for other programmes to aid Malay business became more insistent.[20]

Although it might seem otherwise to outside observers, Malay businessmen and would-be businessmen have consistently regarded lack of capital as the biggest barrier to their success. As early as the 1950s plans were afoot to found a Malay bank, not only as a source of funds for Malay borrowers but also as a means of tapping rural savings and of giving some Malays practical experience in banking, which they totally lacked at the time. This bank, initially called Bank Ra'ayat (People's Bank) and subsequently re-labelled Bank Bumiputra, was established under government sponsorship in the early 1960s. In its early years, however, it behaved much like any other profit-oriented commercial bank, doing nothing special to mobilize the savings of the Malay peasants and making far more loans to the more credit-worthy Chinese, Indian and foreign enterprises than to Malay. Meanwhile, the national development finance company, MIDF, as noted earlier, remained small and conservative in its operations, thus having little influence on industrial finance in general and still less on Malay participation in particular.

Such commercial and technical advice as has been available to Malay entrepreneurs has come mainly through the Advisory Services Division of RIDA/MARA, a small, indifferently staffed unit with only a very limited capacity to help. There is also a National Productivity Centre (NPC), sponsored by the Ministry of Labour, which provides advice as well as conducts industrial training programmes. However, the NPC (at least before 1969) tended to work closely with the existing structure of small industry and made no effort to change that structure.

A different approach to getting Malays into manufacturing, which was talked about occasionally but never seriously attempted, would have involved policies to disperse industry to the more backward areas of the country. There is no doubt that the percentage of Malays employed by manufacturing enterprises tends to be higher in areas with more heavily Malay populations.[21] There are probably also more Malay-owned and operated firms in those areas. But the new pioneer firms were highly concentrated in the more developed areas, particularly in Selangor. There were two possible ways to reverse this trend. One was to offer systematic incentives for firms to locate in the poorer states of the North-west and East Coast. This kind of measure, which was in fact enacted in the early 1970s, might well have been ineffective in view of the main strong centripetal influences on locational decisions. The alternative was direct efforts by the state and federal governments, through integrated regional development schemes and the state economic development corporations (SEDCs), to create industrial complexes in promising locations in the less developed states. This approach, which gained momentum after 1969, is probably the more promising of the two.

All that has been described up to this point has been significantly affected by the events of 1969. Several different reactions to the shocks of that year are evident in the field of industrial policy. Two prompt and significant reactions, which pulled in opposite directions, were the establishment in June 1969 of the Capital Investment Committee (CIC) and the founding of PERNAS in September of the same year.

The CIC, which was chaired by sometime Minister of Finance Tun Tan Siew Sin,[22] tried to make the existing industrial policy work better by improving its administration.[23] It achieved a considerable measure of success in this regard. Private fixed investment, which had been practically stagnant from 1967 to 1969, rose sharply in 1970 and 1971. The number of pioneer and ex-pioneer establishments in production jumped from 146 at the end of 1968 to 288 four years later. Value added by pioneer firms did not grow commensurately because of the start-up lag, but total manufacturing value added continued to rise at 10–15 per cent a year and value added in pioneer firms at 15–20 per cent.[24] The success of the CIC's efforts to revive industrial investment and maintain output growth hard on the heels of severe civil strife is remarkable, but it was purchased at the price of accentuation of some of the less attractive features of pre-1969 industrialization. These included continued heavy reliance on foreign capital and increasing protection of the domestic market. The tendency for pioneer enterprises to be capital intensive also persisted, although more was done to encourage labour-using export industries to locate in Malaysia through the promotional efforts (spearheaded by the Penang state government) which brought a number of electronics assembly plants into the country, through the establishment of duty-free export processing zones in several locations and through the award of labour utilization tax relief, as provided for in the amended Investment Incentive Act.

Despite the CIC's efforts, the old approach to industrialization rapidly lost credibility in the post-1969 political atmosphere. The clamour of the small but growing group of Malay businessmen and would-be businessmen, which had been building up throughout the 1960s (Muzaffar, 1977), could be disregarded no longer. More had to be done to promote Malay participation, particularly after the government became committed to the 30 per cent ownership and control target in early 1970. But would the 'more' consist of expanded efforts to bring into existence more private, inevitably small, Malay enterprises or would the government step in more actively to own and manage larger enterprises on behalf of the Malays? Characteristically, the Malaysian government chose to follow both courses, trying both to invigorate and expand the old entrepreneurial development programmes and to do much more to affect the ownership and control of large-scale enterprises, especially new ones.

Existing agencies with functions relevant to Malay business promotion got much more money, and more pressure to achieve, after 1969 (Table 8.1). MARA's original budget allocation for 1971–5 was $73 million; this was increased to $183 million in the *Mid-Term Review of the Second Malaysia Plan 1971–1975* (1973, pp. 153–67). MIDF, MIEL, Bank Bumiputra and the NPC, none of which had done much for Malay business in the past, were all constrained to do more in the future. Finally, new agencies (an Urban Development Authority, UDA, in 1971; a Credit Guarantee Corporation, CGC, in 1972) were formed to assist in new ways while existing agencies were assigned new functions (e.g. MIDF set up a Bumiputra Assistance Unit).

The first indication of extensive public-sector direct involvement in industry and commerce was the founding of PERNAS in late 1969. PERNAS and its many subsidiaries have so far formed the main instrument of publicly-sponsored enterprise,[25] but they have not been the sole instrument, as is indicated by the activities of the SEDCs and the formation of other corporations—such as PETRONAS, the national petroleum corporation, founded in 1974. The mushrooming growth of the Plan allocation for commerce and industry, traditionally very small because of the reliance on private enterprise to develop this part of the economy, suggests just how fast these two types of programme have expanded in the past few years. Compared to actual public development expenditure of $137 million in this sector in 1966–70, the original SMP (formulated during the early stages of post-1969 programme development) allocated four times as much money, $565 million. Less than three years later, the allocation had doubled again, soaring to $1,160 million (Table 8.1).

TABLE 8.1
PUBLIC DEVELOPMENT EXPENDITURE FOR COMMERCE AND INDUSTRY IN PENINSULAR MALAYSIA, 1966–1980
($ million)

Programme	*1966–70 Actual*	*1971–5 Original allocation*	*1971–5 Revised allocation*	*1971–5 Actual*	*1976–80 Original allocation*
PERNAS	10.0	100.0	150.0	150.0	200.0
MARA	50.9	73.0	183.4	205.3	315.0
SEDCs	—	45.6	150.0	190.5	368.8
Industrial estates	19.3	4.4	22.8	18.0	—
UDA	—	100.0	160.0	182.1	200.0
MIDF	16.0	100.0	100.0	100.0	—
Malaysian Rubber Development Corporation	2.6	35.0	50.0	60.6	132.9
Malaysian International Shipping Corporation	10.1	46.0	107.0	113.0	11.0
Other economic enterprises[1]	7.3	45.1	95.9	233.7	120.9
Tourism	0.4	10.0	9.4		
FIDA	3.4	—	—	29.1	52.0
NISIR, SIM, NPC[2]	0.3	5.5	15.0		
Selangor government	—	—	100.0	260.0	—
PETRONAS	—	—	—	10.0	—
Contribution to Bumiputra Investment Fund	—	—	—	—	200.0
Others	16.7	—	16.1	—	0.3
Total[3]	137.0	564.6	1,159.6	1,552.3	1,600.9

Sources: Columns 1 and 2: *Second Malaysia Plan 1971–1975* (1971, p. 69).
Column 3: *Mid-Term Review of the Second Malaysia Plan 1971–1975* (1973, p. 99).
Columns 4 and 5: *Third Malaysia Plan 1976–1980* (1976, p. 240).

[1]Includes FIMA (Food Industries of Malaysia Sdn. Bhd.), Bank Pembangunan, Malaysian Shipyard and Engineering, and others.

[2]National Institute of Scientific and Industrial Research; Standards Institute of Malaysia; National Productivity Centre.

[3]Discrepancies between components and totals are attributable to rounding.

When the Third Malaysia Plan was published in early 1976 it was revealed that actual public development in 1971–5 had been $1,552 million, and that an additional $1,601 million was allocated for use in 1976–80.

The broader policies adopted since 1970 are harder to evaluate than the pre-1970 policies discussed previously. The time period over which results might become evident is still relatively short; many of the institutions and programmes involved are still quite new and some of them have been little reported in public documents. What follows, therefore, is heavily dependent on judgement and interpretation.

One clear change since 1970 is that the supply of capital to Malay entrepreneurs and would-be entrepreneurs has increased substantially. MARA lending, which had been running at around one thousand loans and a few million dollars per year during most of the 1960s, shot up to nearly 6,500 loans and $26 million by 1974.[26] Meanwhile, MIDF, through its Bumiputra Assistance Unit, has stepped up its meagre lending to Malays. Its affiliate, MIEL, has liberalized mortgage terms for Malay firms purchasing its factories and instituted a rental scheme for small firms which cannot meet the down payment requirement for factory purchase. Similarly, Bank Bumiputra found ways to lend more money to Malay firms (39 per cent of cumulative lending through 1975) and joint ventures in which Malays are involved (14 per cent).[27] Less is known about UDA, which is much more oriented towards urban commerce and real estate development than towards manufacturing in any case.

Another significant development affecting capital supply has been the creation of the CGC, which went into business in early 1973. The potential of this programme, which partially indemnifies commercial banks from default risk on approved small business loans,[28] lies in its ability to harness the loan evaluation and supervision capacities of the commercial banks, thus sidestepping a major constraint on the part of MARA and other public lending agencies. By 1975 the CGC had guaranteed loans worth $302 million, 42 per cent of which by value went to Malays. Some 11 per cent of CGC lending in 1974 was for small-scale manufacturing; other sectors borrowing significant amounts included commerce (25 per cent), construction (14 per cent) and agriculture (10 per cent). Banks were pushed to raise small business loans covered by the CGC programme to a minimum amount equivalent to 10 per cent of their savings deposits. In response to these pressures, some commercial banks probably classified as CGC loans a certain amount of lending which they would have done anyway, even without the guarantees.[29]

Added together, the post-1969 activities of MARA, MIDF, MIEL, UDA, Bank Bumiputra and the CGC constitute a tremendous continuing increase in the supply of capital to Malay business. But capital availability is not a sufficient condition of small business success, as experience in many countries has shown. Particularly when the borrowers have had scant business experience, assistance in using capital effectively is also required.[30] Malaysian programmes of technical assistance to small business have not been conspicuously successful, either before or since 1969.

Small business advisory services, as noted earlier, are provided mainly by MARA and the NPC. Neither agency has proclaimed any major expansion or new departure in the last few years. The only publicized expansion of advisory capacity was the establishment of MIDF Industrial Consultants Sdn. Bhd. (MIDFIC) in 1971. Like its parent, MIDF, MIDFIC seems to have concentrated its services on medium-to-large enterprises, though it is also reported to have done some work for small firms, including some owned and managed by Malays.

While one cannot write off 'synthetic capitalism' as a total failure—Popenoe (1970) found, even before the post-1969 push, that most of the Malay entrepreneurs whom he studied had benefited from one or more government assistance programmes—the best guess is that its progress has continued to be slow despite the intensified efforts made since 1970. At the root of its problems, perhaps, is the fundamental dilemma posed by Popenoe: how can one foster private initiative through programmes which intrinsically involve dependence on the government? While the dampening of incentives referred to here may be an inescapable feature of entrepreneurial development programmes,[31] the fact remains that nascent businessmen must get their experience somehow. If they are not surviving without protection or assistance, then some form of support may be needed for some period of time. But little comfort can be taken from this rationale, since it is clear enough that Malay private business failed to make significant progress between 31 August 1957 and 13 May 1969. It is hardly surprising, therefore, that—without ever really announcing that it was doing so—the government gradually moved towards adoption of Wheelwright's preferred alternative, public ownership.

Public corporations are not a new phenomenon in the Malaysian economy.[32] Autonomous, business-like bodies had been created for a variety of purposes in the past. Frequently the rationale was to give undivided attention, free of the bureaucratic restraints which characterize government proper, to the accomplishment of some task which has been recognized as important. Most of the tasks so recognized in the past, and some recent ones as well, have nothing to do with ethnic economic balance. The Malayan Railway and National Electricity Board have long been run as public corporations,[33] and such later additions as the Malaysian Airline System, the Malaysian International Shipping Corporation and Food Industries of Malaysia Sdn. Bhd. share with them the characteristic of having been formed to provide a specific service under public control with no particular reference to ethnicity. What is new, therefore, is not the existence of public enterprise but its use as a tool for dealing with the problem of ethnic imbalances.

Despite their newness, public enterprises concerned with ethnic imbalance have grown to be of significant size in just a few years. This is shown in Table 8.2, which presents valuable data assembled by M. C. Puthucheary (1977).

TABLE 8.2
DATA ON PUBLICLY-SPONSORED ENTERPRISES IN COMMERCE AND INDUSTRY, *c*. 1977
(Companies in which Parent has Interest)

Parent enterprise	*Wholly owned companies*	*Partly owned companies* *Equity 50 per cent or more*	*Partly owned companies* *Equity less than 50 per cent*	*Total number of companies*	*Total amount invested ($ million)*
MARA	15	13	6	34	47.9
UDA	2	50	25	77	81.4
PERNAS	12	20	14	46	116.3
SEDCs	23	72	39	134	197.7
Total	52	155	84	291	443.3[1]

Source: M. C. Puthucheary (1977, pp. 10–11); information on numbers of companies based on data from the Ministry of Public Enterprise for MARA, UDA and the SEDCs and on Chopra (1977, p. 59) for PERNAS; information on capital invested based on 'information received from interviews, annual reports, etc.'

[1]Total investment by the parent enterprises in companies having total paid-up capital of $733.6 million.

The principal instrument for central government-sponsored Malay penetration into the world of big business has been the Perbadanan Nasional (National Corporation), called PERNAS.[34] Founded only a few weeks after the 1969 riots, PERNAS has functioned primarily as a holding company, spawning a growing number of operating subsidiaries and associates in a wide range of fields. Among the many activities of its subsidiaries have been major construction projects undertaken for the government, off-shore tin mining, urban property development, import–export trade, wholesaling to Malay retailers, insurance and investment services. The associated companies are joint ventures, mostly with foreign partners, in which PERNAS participates. These include the Kuala Lumpur Hilton Hotel, a Goodyear tyre plant, a cement plant, a container shipper and an electronics factory. As of 1975, PERNAS was said to possess eight major wholly-owned subsidiaries with total paid-up capital in excess of $100 million; associated companies and subsidiaries of subsidiaries accounted for nearly $380 million in additional equity, including amounts invested by joint-venture partners (*Third Malaysia Plan 1976–1980*, 1976, pp. 195–6).

The state governments' role in industrial development has been a persistent issue. Just as the federal government requires co-operation from the states in matters which the Constitution assigns as state powers (e.g. use of land and natural resources), in a federal-power area such as industrialization the relationship is reversed and the states can do only what the centre permits. Prior to 1969, this consisted mostly of building industrial estates and hoping that businesses would come along to occupy them. Even before the New Economic Policy, however, most state governments had formed a State Economic Development Corporation (the names vary slightly from state to state but they can be referred to collectively as SEDCs) as an instrument of direct participation in business, mainly real estate development. (The Trengganu SEDC was a pace setter in commercial agriculture when it established an oil palm estate in the late 1960s.) The scope of the SEDCs was limited by a constraint on their financial capacity: like their parents, the state governments, they could not borrow abroad without Treasury approval. Federal officials generally regarded this as just as well, since they feared the mal-coordination, ill-conceived projects and corruption which might result from unrestrained SEDC activities.

After 1969 the constraints were eased and the SEDCs were allowed to flower, much as state land development schemes had bloomed a decade before. A wide range of projects emerged. By the end of 1972 the SEDCs had reportedly established four wholly-owned manufacturing enterprises, with capital of $1.4 million, and had supplied 29 per cent of the $70 million capital of 25 joint ventures (Thillainathan, 1976a, p. 60). By the mid-1970s, however, there were signs that the pendulum was beginning to swing back the other way, as Deputy Prime Minister and newly-appointed Minister of Coordination of Public Corporation Hussein Onn publicly criticized the managers of the SEDCs, saying that some of them 'want to build their own empires and fortunes and seem to forget teamwork'.[35]

What can be said about the success of Malaysia's post-1969 policy to win a place for the Malays in owning and managing the manufacturing sector, and modern economic activities generally? To take the most positive and striking conclusion first, it is obvious that, in contrast to the years of effort to develop Malay small business, publicly-sponsored enterprise has been dramatically successful in achieving the main goal of beginning to carve out a sizeable Malay share in parts of the economy where Malays had no place before. In just a few years it has altered the face of the economy far more than RIDA and MARA were able to do in two decades of effort. It is obvious that a major and irreversible change has occurred.

The other side of the picture, of course, concerns the effects of the New Economic Policy (NEP) on the operations of the traditional business groups. Both Chinese and foreign investors have had reasons to worry, not only about the effects of policy changes already announced but about what further changes might be in the offing. One question left open when the NEP was first announced was whose share was to fall to make room for the rise of the Malay share in corporate assets from 2 per cent in 1970 to 30 per cent by 1990. This issue was clarified in 1973, when it was stated that it is the foreign share which will fall, leaving the 1990 target proportions as 30 per cent Malay, 30 per cent non-Malay Malaysian and 40 per cent foreign. Since a substantial growth in total share capital (11.5 per cent a year in constant prices) is anticipated by government planners, there is room for significant growth in the absolute holdings of all three groups. The plan frame envisages that non-Malay

Malaysians can see their assets grow by about 12 per cent per annum, and even the foreigners can enjoy 8 per cent growth, while Malay holdings grow by some 28 per cent a year to reach the target of 30 per cent of the total by 1990, according to the projections (*Mid-Term Review of the Second Malaysia Plan 1971–1975*, 1973, pp. 80–8).

Despite this clarification of the target, considerable concern about how the strategy will be implemented persists in business circles. A major cause of worry has been the Industrial Coordination Act (ICA), passed in 1975. This Act 'to provide for the coordination and orderly development of manufacturing activities in Malaysia' makes the conduct of medium- and large-scale manufacturing enterprise subject to licence.[36] Criteria for granting licences and conditions which may be imposed when licences are granted are not stated in the Act,[37] but government pronouncements indicate that a wide range of matters may be involved: location, marketing arrangements, equity structure, employment structure, use of local professional services. Government spokesmen have stated that immediate compliance with all conditions will not be expected, that non-Malay employees are not to be fired or distribution networks necessarily changed overnight. However, compliance over a 'reasonable period of time', accompanied by long-term plans to achieve the conditions specified, is expected.[38]

The ICA is widely regarded as having had a stifling effect on private investment, not only in manufacturing but in the economy generally. The problem, one suspects, is not so much that the Act assures implementation of the NEP at the enterprise level as that it introduces so much uncertainty into business planning, thus constituting a 'classic example of a disincentive against which all forms of incentive appear unattractive' (Chee Peng Lim, 1977, p. 13). At least partly because of the ICA, both private investment and value added in manufacturing abruptly stopped growing in 1975 and have continued to be disappointingly sluggish during the early part of the Third Malaysia Plan period. It is probably not fair, however, to attribute the slowdown entirely to the NEP and ICA; other factors, such as slow growth of world trade and uncertainty about the political future of South-East Asia, have also contributed to it.[39]

The ICA is surely not the last word on how the NEP will be implemented in the manufacturing sector. Malaysian policy-makers are concerned about the lagging growth just referred to and, as in the past, are likely to make pragmatic policy adjustments in an effort to reconcile their various objectives. Looking to the longer run, however, there are at least three major strategic issues which deserve to be raised.

The first of these issues is the ultimate devolution to individual Malays of the assets being accumulated on their behalf of the various public and quasi-public bodies. Although such devolution is a proclaimed government intention, a student of nationalized industries in various countries would surely predict that it will never happen. Public corporations, like all institutions, tend to become interest groups working for their own preservation. And the financial interest of any government favours retaining indefinitely any enterprises which are profitable and returning to private hands only those which have failed. Since private interests do not want unsuccessful enterprises either (certainly not at the inflated valuations which governments tend to place on them so as to avoid book losses), few nationalized firms ever revert to private hands. Another problem is the terms on which the transfer would be made. There are two major alternatives, with intermediate possibilities. To the extent that individual Malays are to pay for these shares, they must have the wherewithal to do so. Payment of full market value for the assets would mean that no inter-communal wealth transfer would be involved, and that the problem of income disparity would have to be largely solved *by some other means* over the coming decade if the Malays were to become wealthy enough to buy up 30 per cent of the economy. The alternative is to subsidize the transfer, or even make it an outright gift. The higher the subsidy element the larger the inter-communal wealth transfer—but also, one would suppose, the greater the resentment of the non-Malays—would be. There might also be deleterious incentive effects on the Malays, as discussed earlier.

The government is reported to be taking the devolution issue seriously, perhaps because it believes that the electorate will ultimately insist on receiving individul share certificates, refusing to tolerate indefinitely a vague system of trusteeship (Fred R. von der Mehden, 1975, pp. 259–61). The presumption seems to be that these shares will be purchased by individual Malays, not given to them. How the purchase price will be determined remains to be seen.

A second major question relates to the political economy of publicly-sponsored enterprise. The businesses held in trust for the Malay community as a whole are in fact managed by members of the Malay élite. The new tycoons who make up the top layer of this élite are drawn from high social status groups; most are ex-civil servants and several are members of royalty. Although appointed by the political authorities, they have the opportunity to acquire substantial financial resources and operating autonomy. This creates several dangers. One is large-scale corruption. Another is the use of wealth and power to 'buy' a political following. Yet a third is the possibility that the policy will spawn an industrial empire which will eventually become uncontrollable by political authority, as happened with General Ibnu Sutowo's PERTAMINA in Indonesia. However, Malaysia is not Indonesia, being smaller and less riddled by fissiparous divisions of power, so this last danger, at least, is perhaps not great.

A final related and possibly more worrying concern is whether publicly-sponsored enterprise will be used to aggrandize the Malay élite as a whole, as opposed to the individual members of it. Certainly it is true that while the new enterprises will provide jobs for only a tiny fraction of the Malay labour force they could offer a significant way of 'taking care of' the swelling flow of educated Malays, which has already exceeded the absorptive capacity of the public sector, the traditional employer of educated Malays. One can picture the continued steady growth of a Malay middle class, dependent on the activities of public corporations which do little or nothing to benefit the padi farmer, rubber smallholder or fisherman.[40]

Much of the foregoing has related not just to manufacturing but to the entire modern sector. It was discussed in the context of manufacturing because that is the most important industry in the modern sector. The remainder of this chapter touches on problems and policies specific to other non-agricultural industries.

MINING

Mining has traditionally meant tin mining, an industry in which Chinese and European business styles have met in open competition over a long period. Other minerals have been of incidental importance, although the development of a petroleum industry in very recent times does betoken major changes in a long-established pattern.

Although it can tolerate a variety of technologies, mining differs from export agriculture in being inhospitable to very small-scale producers.[41] The Malays have lacked the capital and business experience to penetrate the industry, and even the Malaysian Chinese have only recently established a stake in its highly capital-intensive dredging segment. The Malays have long possessed a potential entrée into the industry, in the form of their control of tin-bearing lands located in Malay Reservations and of off-shore areas where mining is becoming feasible as exploration proceeds, technology improves and prices rise to meet the higher cost of off-shore mining. Development of these two types of mining area has proceeded slowly to date, but as the older part of the industry stabilizes as a result of reserve depletion and these new mines come on stream, the Malay share in industry employment, which has been only about one-fifth, may rise.

Petroleum is a long-established industry in South-East Asia but the upsurge of worldwide exploration which has occurred in the past fifteen years has given it a new lease of life. Within the present-day borders of Malaysia the only older wells are those of the Miri field in Sarawak, which goes back to the 1920s. Off-shore prospecting began in Brunei waters in the early 1960s and spread to Sarawak thereafter. Strikes were achieved in both places. During the late 1960s, off-shore areas of Peninsular Malaysia—first the East Coast, then the West—were leased to international oil companies for exploration and development. In 1973 strikes were announced off the East Coast and off Sabah in East Malaysia. At about the same time the government began pressing the concessionaires to sign production-sharing agreements which altered concession terms to be more favourable to Malaysia. This move, which foreshadowed still bolder initiatives to come, was undoubtedly influenced both by the example of the Middle Eastern oil countries' success in gaining larger shares of the earnings from oil taken from their territories and by the increasing value of the resource as OPEC forced up its world price. The Indonesian experience also influenced Malaysian thinking, which culminated with the formation of PETRONAS in 1974 and the freezing of all existing contracts in the following year. The latter move led to a stalemate which was broken in 1976 but left a residue of distrust, not only in oil circles but among foreign businessmen generally.[42]

The recent experience with oil and gas (which was discovered off the East Coast in 1974) illustrates the particular determination of the Malaysian government to secure national, Malay-administered, control over the newer industries. It would appear that the strategy (as opposed to the 1974–6 tactics) is well conceived. The Malaysian oil and gas resource, while small by Middle Eastern (or even Indonesian) standards, appears to be a considerable one for a smallish country: the most optimistic forecasts (made before the recent disruption of the industry's development) predicted output of as much as 500,000 barrels a day of high-grade, low-sulphur crude by 1980.[43] Although that target now may not be reached on schedule, Malaysia does seem likely at some point to gain considerable national income from oil and gas.[44] A more problematic question is how much of the income generated through the public corporation will become available for general public sector use, as opposed to being sequestered by PETRONAS for use in its own, not necessarily economic or socially desirable, projects.[45]

COMMERCE

Whereas petroleum is a brand-new industry in Peninsular Malaysia, commerce is as old as civilization. It is regarded as important not as a leading sector but as a training ground for small-scale business enterprise. The paucity of Malays in trading and financial activities is believed not only to hamper the development of Malay business generally but also to exacerbate the resentment felt by the mass of poor Malays as a result of their dealings with non-Malay retailers, wholesalers and moneylenders.

Efforts made through small business lending by RIDA/MARA have done little to increase Malay participation in commerce. According to EPU estimates (*Mid-Term Review of the Second Malaysia Plan 1971–1975*, 1973, p. 77), commerce ranked seventh out of the eight major sectors of the economy in terms of Malay share in employment in 1970. Malay shops have tended to remain small and specialized while general trading, even in areas with a primarily Malay population, has been conducted mainly by Chinese, with limited Indian participation.

When Malays did open trading establishments, often with official assistance, difficulties were usually encountered. Ironically, even Malay customers frequently preferred non-Malay shops, since their prices tended to be lower and, being better capitalized, they were more willing to extend credit. Social obligations may make it hard for Malay merchants to maintain business-like relations with their customers; some fledgling Malay retailers have reportedly been ruined by 'purchases' made on 'credit' which they can neither refuse nor collect without violating social norms. Limiting commercial relations to non-Malays, whom it is socially acceptable to malign and cheat if possible, has long been the natural order of things from the viewpoint of the ordinary Malay.[46]

It is from this unpromising base that aggressive steps have been taken to increase Malay participation in commerce in the 1970s through the activities of UDA, PERNAS and the SEDCs.

UDA has constructed or acquired choice urban sites, which they could not otherwise obtain, for Malay retailers, particularly in Kuala Lumpur. It is not clear, however, that site availability was a major constraint, or what the overall results have been.

PERNAS has used its preferred position to move into new areas of export–import trade as they open up. One early opportunity was the execution of bilateral trading agreements with the various Communist countries with which Malaysia established diplomatic and commercial relations soon after PERNAS was formed. Considerable friction, understandably, was caused by PERNAS's efforts to take over trade with the People's Republic of China, with which diplomatic relations were established on 1 June 1974 (although trade had been going on through third countries for many years).[47] Reportedly, PERNAS had also toyed with the idea of persuading the government to enact a system of import quotas, a share of which would be reserved for PERNAS and other Malay importers, for distribution to Malay retailers.[48] However, no such system has materialized so far.

One reason for PERNAS's interest in large-scale international trading is that control of supplies at the wholesale level can be used to promote Malay retailing. Whether PERNAS will be any more successful at the latter venture than MARA has been remains to be seen. In March 1974, it announced the establishment, in joint venture with a British concern, of a system of wholesale depots intended to sell to Malay retailers, on a cash basis, goods purchased at low bulk rates. An extension service to help retailers use the facility was also planned.[49]

Several SEDCs have also entered the trading field, apparently with the idea of aiding retailers who could not operate under the 'cash and carry' rules of PERNAS and to provide a more fully articulated trading network (M. C. Puthucheary, 1977, p. 13).

Besides wholesale and retail trade, the commercial sector also includes banking and other financial services, insurance and real estate. Companies operating in these industries have traditionally been either Chinese or foreign. Most Chinese banks have been Singapore-based, reflecting that city's traditional role as the financial centre for the whole Malaysian area. In recent years Malaysia-based banks, with government encouragement, have gained a larger share of the market. All banks have been pressed to hire more Malays. Recently they have been urged to open Bumiputra lending departments, where 'sympathetic' (i.e. Malay) staff would make it easier for Malay borrowers to approach the banks, with which they have had few dealings in the past.

Besides urging existing banks to change their ways of doing business, the government has profoundly influenced banking in Malaysia by establishing a large public-sector role in the banking industry. Four new banks have been created: Bank Bumiputra, which has grown to become one of the largest commercial banks in the country, Bank Rakyat (the apex bank of the co-operative credit system), Bank Pertanian Malaysia (the agricultural bank at the apex of the rural credit structure run largely through the Farmers' Organizations) and Bank Pembangunan (a development bank founded to lend exclusively to Malay enterprises). In addition, the government has acquired interest in 'at least three other commercial banks' (M. C. Puthucheary, 1977, p. 15), including Malayan Banking Corporation, the largest domestically controlled bank operating in the country. Finally, there are now twelve merchant banks in the country, ten of which are partly owned by some publicly-sponsored enterprise (ibid.).

All the foregoing discussion, however, concerns only the formally organized segment of the capital market. Small businesses, to say nothing of farmers, still have little to do with the organized market. Even Chinese-owned small business generates most of its own funds internally and obtains what loan funds it uses primarily from business associates and family contacts. Malay entry as employees, owners and managers of formal capital market institutions is thus of value partly for the direct experience it entails and partly for its impact on the flow of capital funding to large-scale enterprise but it has much less relevance to the smaller-scale units.

CONSTRUCTION

Construction is an industry of small firms which Chinese enterprise has made very much its own. Traditionally, nearly all building in Malaysia has been done by Chinese construction firms, employing Chinese male craftsmen to do the skilled jobs and Chinese labourers, frequently women, for the unskilled. With the growth of public-sector investments in the early 1960s the government attempted to encourage the formation and growth of Malay construction firms. The main instrument of this policy was a 5 per cent bidding preference on the smaller construction contracts (there were hardly any Malay firms qualified to bid for the larger contracts). This policy spawned a number of small-scale Malay and joint-venture contracting firms (some reportedly of the 'Ali-Baba' variety), but these appear to have won only a tiny share of public-sector construction contracts, to say nothing of private construction.

Chinese construction contractors hired few non-Chinese. Among eight major industry groups, construction ranked dead last in 1970 in percentage of Malays hired and first in percentage of Chinese.[50] As in other fields, the post-1969 period has seen some Malay penetration of the industry through large firms. Thus Pernas Construction Sdn. Bhd. and similar companies established by some of the SEDCs have entered the industry as the first large-scale Malay construction companies. Although their place in the industry as a whole remains minor, they have taken over some of the larger public-sector construction projects. In addition, the government has pressed its efforts to promote participation in the industry by small-scale Malay firms. Recently a provision was announced whereby Bumiputra contractors can receive an advance equivalent to 10 per cent of the project's cost on signing a public sector construction contract.

TRANSPORTATION

As noted in Chapter 2, the dominant transportation mode in Malaysia, once water and subsequently rail, is now road. Road transportation enjoys the distinction of having been the first non-agricultural industry in which increased Malay participation was sought as a policy objective. This policy dates back as far as 1954 (Federal Legislative Council, 1954, 1955). Why road transportation was picked as a target for this kind of policy at such an early date is somewhat obscure, but it seems likely that official licensing of taxis, buses and trucks, which began in the 1930s, both provided the statistics which demonstrated the scantiness of Malay involvement and implicated the government as a contributor to the situation, leading to pressure to increase the Malay role.

During the early 1950s the Malays held only a small share of taxi licences—about 10 per cent in early 1952, raised to nearly 20 per cent when the number of licences was increased above pre-war levels in 1952–3 (Federal Legislative Council, 1955, pp. 6–7)—and played hardly any role at all in bus and hauling services. The new policy changed this situation by favouring Malays in the issuance of taxi and common carrier hauling licences and by promoting the formation of Malay bus companies. RIDA/MARA joined in the last element of the programme by establishing rural bus lines, some of which were subsequently sold off to Malay companies.

The success of this early effort to increase Malay participation in a non-agricultural industry was somewhat mixed. On the positive side, one can point to the fact that the Malay share in road transportation industry employment rose from 28 per cent in 1947 to 35 per cent in 1967.[51] On the negative side, there is the extent of purely nominal compliance (for example, *sub rosa* leasing of Malay-licensed taxis to non-Malays) and the inefficiencies introduced into transportation services. There is no doubt that the numbers of licensed taxis and common-hauler trucks have increased less than they would have in the absence of the restrictive licensing policy, while substitute vehicles such as private cars (some of which are used as 'pirate taxis') and trucks licensed only to carry the owner's goods have grown correspondingly faster. On balance, the policy would not seem to have been very successful in reconciling social goals.

OTHER SECTORS

Rather than any of the activities discussed in early sections of this chapter, it has been public-sector service occupations such as public administration, education, the army and the police that have served historically as the principal points of entry for Malays into the urban economy. Taken together, government and community services[52] accounted for a massive

77 per cent of the net additional to non-agricultural jobs for Malays in 1947–57 and a still significant 40 per cent in the following decade. Thus, at least in terms of employment imbalance, the government's own hiring policy was of comparable significance to all its efforts to influence what happened in the private sector put together.

One might speculate about the broader effects of this massive public-sector hiring programme, which created 78,000 jobs for Malays in 1947–57 and another 76,000 in 1957–67. Although work in the public sector involves considerable learning of both specific skills and general attitudes and disciplines which are potentially transferable to the private sector, the amount of such transfer has been quite limited in practice. No doubt there are some drivers and mechanics, and also some engineers and architects, employed in the private sector who learned their trade or sharpened their skills in government employment. For Malays in particular, however, the transfer did not come easily, even when identical or very similar skills were involved. Before 1969, private-sector employment always meant entry into an alien atmosphere, dominated by non-Malays, and one that offered less security and prestige, from the Malay viewpoint, than could be had in the government.

Preferential hiring in public-sector employment has been an active political issue, and one about which there has been some misunderstanding. The 1957 Constitution granted the Yang Dipertuan Agung the power to establish quotas specifying the proportion of jobs in various branches of the public services which must be filled by Malays. Several such quotas have in fact been established, the best-known of which is the ratio of four Malays to one non-Malay in the Malaysian Administrative and Diplomatic Service, MADS (formerly the Malayan Civil Service). Among the commonly misunderstood facts relating to the quota system are the following:

1. The four-to-one ratio applies only to the small, élite MADS, where it originally represented an advance for the non-Malays, since they had previously been altogether excluded;[53]
2. Only a few other services have any quotas at all;[54]
3. Most government jobs, including all junior civilian positions and senior posts in nearly all the specialized services (education, health, agriculture, etc.) are not affected by quotas;
4. The majority of senior federal officers are in fact non-Malays.[55]

All of this is somewhat beside the point, however, since what really matters is not so much the presence or absence of formal quotas but what *de facto* hiring policy has been. Examination of the highly imperfect statistics on government employment indicates that although there are large numbers of non-Malays employed in the public sector new job openings have been allocated predominantly to Malays.

In 1947–57, when, as noted above, Malays gained 78,000 jobs in government and community services, Chinese and Indians gained 37,500. During the succeeding decade, when Malay employment in these industries rose by 76,000, Chinese and Indian employment increased by 44,900. During the first ten years of independence, the Malay share went from 57 per cent to 67 per cent in government services, from 47 to 53 per cent in education services and from 33 per cent to 45 per cent in health services.

The principal restraint on this growth in Malay employment was the lack of suitably qualified Malay candidates for many of the more highly skilled jobs. It is this supply situation which largely explains the high percentage of non-Malays in senior positions, especially in the technical and professional services. During the first five years of independence, when Malayanization was proceeding rapidly, the Malay share in senior posts not held by Europeans actually went down as non-Malays were hired in large numbers to replace departing expatriates and to staff expanding programmes.[56] By 1968 more Malays were receiving the education required to get top-level jobs and the percentage of Malays in the various specialized services was going up; however, Malays still held only 37.4 per cent of senior federal government positions, compared to 35.9 per cent for the Chinese and 23.2 per cent for the Indians (Tilman, 1964, pp. 73–6; Gibbons and Zakaria, 1971; Esman, 1972, pp. 76–7).

As noted earlier, the shortage of Malay talent often posed a dilemma when insistence on hiring Malays, doggedly adhered to even when no qualified Malays were available, led to serious delays in important development programmes—often, ironically, programmes designed to benefit the Malays themselves. It is thus clear that government employment, though a powerful tool for Malay advancement, has been overused at times.

The pressure to use government job openings as a means of advancing Malays increased after 1969. Still greater use of an already over-used instrument could have caused severe distortions, if it were not for the fact that the supply of trained Malay manpower was growing more rapidly by this time. The supply of university-trained Malay generalists, in fact, threatened to outrun demand, until the government's move toward direct participation in business gave a new boost to demand growth.[57]

With Malays preferred in the public sector, private professional practice and professional employment with private firms remained non-Malay domains. The government's only action in this area so far has been to insist that many more Malays be trained in such university faculties as medicine, engineering and science.

Thousands of humble people continued to be employed in the more mundane occupations in the service sector—in hotels, restaurants, domestic service. Such jobs, once held predominantly by Chinese males, then largely by Chinese females, are now being taken increasingly by Malays and Indians. In the hotel industry, where recent growth opened up sizeable new employment opportunities, MARA and other agencies have sought to train Malays for increased participation. In the past, the predominantly Chinese ownership and management structure has impeded Malay entry. It is partly for this reason that government-sponsored corporations have entered into joint ventures such as the one which involved PERNAS in the Kuala Lumpur Hilton Hotel.

CONCLUSIONS

The non-agricultural, urban-based industries are unquestionably the spearhead of economic growth, in Malaysia as elsewhere. Policies directed toward greater equality of income distribution, employment and ownership and control in this sector therefore raise serious questions of consistency between growth and equity objectives.

Malaysian policies toward the sector can be divided quite definitely into their pre- and post-1969 variants. Before 1969 the growth of the sector was actively promoted by the government through inducements which transferred income to foreign and domestic capitalists. Ironically, these inducements appear in many cases not to have been very effective in promoting growth. One result of this policy was the creation of jobs which provided above-average incomes and valuable learning experiences for ordinary workers, but the number of jobs created was not large. In the hope of furthering this pattern of development, pre-1969 governments did not press hard for employment quotas, other than in the public sector. Nor did they object to the existing ownership and control pattern; indeed, they strengthened it by their inducements.

Thus the pre-1969 policies receive rather low marks when judged by post-1969 criteria. And even by their own lights they do not do so well. Industrial growth in Peninsular Malaysia, although substantial, was probably well below potential. This is suggested by the significantly superior performance of other small East and South-East Asian countries, notably next-door Singapore. Several of the touted inducement policies, especially the Pioneer Industries programme, appear to have contributed little to industrial growth in Malaysia. While these policies could have been improved, even from the viewpoint of economic growth alone, their shortcomings probably did not constitute the most important impediment to investment and growth. A larger stumbling block was probably the uncertainties produced by Malaysia's continuing internal political problems (and to a lesser extent external problems such as Communist activities and Indonesian confrontation).

The post-1969 policies have made a much bolder attack on the inequality in ownership and control of wealth, as well as (less dramatically) employment. The weapons now being used, especially publicly-sponsored enterprise, are potent ones. Significant results are to be expected, although there are questions (discussed above) about the extent to which these results will actually constitute redistribution in an élite-to-mass sense, as opposed to assumption of greater power by the Malay élite at the expense of foreign and non-Malay domestic capitalists.

The other major question is how much loss in growth momentum will accompany efforts to effect major changes in the ownership and control pattern. Some loss would appear to be inevitable. The traditional entrepreneurial groups are clearly far more experienced and capable, at this stage, than any expertise the government can bring to bear. By circumscribing the role of the private entrepreneur, how can one expect any result other than decelerated investment growth? This seemingly compelling conclusion probably holds in so far as domestic, mainly Chinese, entrepreneurs are concerned. Despite the frequently reported assurances that Malay gains will not be achieved at the expense of non-Malay losses, it is clear that, at the margin, opportunities will be lost as government-favoured bodies take up activities which would otherwise be left to purely private entrepreneurs. How great this loss will be is still an unsettled issue. Obviously Malaysia today is far from being a socialized economy; the remaining opportunities for private economic activity are very great, and in fact still constitute by far the greater part of the non-agricultural economy.

Where foreign enterprise is concerned, the government's problems appear to be more tactical than strategic. If it is correct that investment was held down before 1969 by uncertainty about domestic politics, then resolution of that uncertainty could conceivably be a positive inducement to investment, even though the direction in which uncertainty was resolved was in itself unfavourable to the interests of foreign business.[58] Corporations which find themselves unable to tolerate the degree of involvement by government-sponsored bodies which is now a virtual requirement for doing business in Malaysia will simply stay away. However, Malaysia has many business attractions and its stipulations are not particularly odious compared to those of many other countries, so many international corporations—conceivably even more than in the earlier, freer but more ambiguous period—should still be interested. For this to be so, however, will require that the government avoid tactical blunders of the type committed in its dealings with the oil companies in 1974–5.

If the foregoing analysis is correct, Malaysia's problem *vis-à-vis* foreign capital may be less that of being shunned by investors than that of achieving the desired ownership proportions by 1990 in the face of continued investment by foreigners in the Malaysian economy. The growth versus equity problem arises not so much in that context as in that of relations between the domestic interest groups. Chinese capital appears to be much less resigned to the post-1969 formula than is foreign capital. Unless some way is found to harness at least a substantial part of the Chinese vitality in economic pursuits which has played such an important part in Malayan development, then the threat of significant lost growth opportunities is very real.

1. The number of Malay women reported to be following commercial occupations in what is now Peninsular Malaysia fell from 9,559 in 1921 to 8,013 in 1931, 7,909 in 1947 and 7,478 in 1957. In all years such employment was heavily concentrated in Kelantan and Trengganu, as the impenetration of Chinese commerce into other states predates the censuses.

2. For a comparable survey, covering the period up to the mid-1960s, see Frank H. Golay (1969).

3. The pioneering national accounts compiled by Dorothy Walters (1963, p. 4) put manufacturing and construction together at only 5.2 per cent of GDP (in 1959 prices) in 1957. This is surely too low, but even by 1960, when the official national accounts begin

and after some Merdeka-inspired investment had taken place, the share was only 8.5 per cent. The 10 per cent mark was not reached until 1965.

4. Later, the required minimum investment for a five-year exemption was raised to $1 million.

5. The first statistic in this sentence refers to Malaysia as a whole, while the second refers to Peninsular Malaysia only. However, this makes little difference since there was very little manufacturing, pioneer or otherwise, in Sabah and Sarawak. See *Census of Manufacturing Industries West Malaysia 1968* (Department of Statistics, n.d., pp. 226–30); these statistics include ex-pioneers as well as firms currently holding pioneer status. Total value added in manufacturing is from Department of Statistics (1972) and from Treasury (1974, p. vii).

6. See *Census of Manufacturing... 1968* (Department of Statistics, n.d., p. 229). The shares were 30 per cent Malaysian, 23 per cent British, 15 per cent American, 8 per cent Singaporean, 1 per cent Japanese and 23 per cent other foreign.

7. (ibid., p. 226.) More precisely, three states—Kedah, Kelantan and Malacca—had only one small establishment apiece, while three others—Perlis, Pahang and Trengganu—had none at all.

8. *Source*: Department of Statistics. However, pioneer establishments appear to have been no more prone to hire Malays than other firms which increased their work forces in 1957–67; see pp. 8–15.

9. For a comprehensive evaluation of the economic, political and social impacts of the Pioneer Industries programme, see Marc Merrill Lindenberg (1973).

10. At one point, Finance Minister Tun Tan Siew Sin, as quoted in local newspapers, seemed to be saying that enough protection would be provided to ensure the profitability of *any* venture which investors wished to establish in Malaysia.

11. Studies conducted at the Economic Planning Unit by T. K. Osgood show that tax revenue forgone as a result of the first decade of operation of the Pioneer Industries programme was very heavily concentrated in a few companies; many other pioneer firms received little or no tax benefit. Thus, unless investors' expectations were substantially different from their experience, it would appear that only a few firms received large enough profit boosts from pioneer status to make their investments profitable if they would not have been so without the tax holiday. Moreover, most of those whose investment decision might have turned on receipt of pioneer status received much greater benefits than the minimum required to induce them to invest.

12. There are no reliable data for 1957–9. The average annual growth rate for 1960–8, as calculated from the official national accounts, is 11.2 per cent. The statistics are in current prices, but the Malaysian economy was practically inflation-free during this period.

13. Malaysian consumer prices rose less than prices in industrial countries during the 1960s. One theory of how this could be so is that Malaysia gradually offset the effects of world inflation by shifting from high-cost sources of its imports, such as the United Kingdom and other European countries, to lower-cost sources such as Japan and China. The same compensating device could have offset upward price pressures resulting from substitution of local production for imports generally.

14. The circumstances of *East* Malaysian consumers were significantly different, since they faced very low import duties at the time of their incorporation into Malaysia, and thus very rapid increases as their tariff structures were gradually harmonized with that of Peninsular Malaysia.

15. Charles Hirschman (1971a) and Marc Merrill Lindenberg (1973) both found that foreign-owned manufacturing firms had much lower re-investment rates in the late 1960s than did domestically-owned manufacturing firms.

16. There was a general rule that pioneer firms should have 51 per cent local ownership. However, the system was not run by general rules and large and/or numerous exceptions were evidently made to this one.

17. The best-known critique is J. J. Puthucheary (1960). Puthucheary argued from a socialist point of view, but some of his arguments have been echoed repeatedly in public statements by Chinese businessmen associated with the Chambers of Commerce and the MCA. The attitudes of the latter group have been understandably ambivalent, since while they would prefer a great role for domestic investors *vis-à-vis* foreign investors they also have a stake in the maintenance of liberal policies towards private enterprise in general. An excellent recent restatement of the Puthucheary thesis is Tan Tat-wai (1977).

18. These numbers are derived from estimates made by the author, based on examination of a number of statistical sources. The main sources are the 1947 and 1957 population censuses and the 1967–8 socio-economic sample survey of households.

19. RIDA/MARA has frequently been regarded as above rational planning and evaluation; criticism of it has sometimes been equated with disloyalty. I know of no objective statement of its cumulated achievements and failures over a period of years, although there are published Annual Reports for some individual years. The generalizations in this paragraph are therefore based on impressions rather than solid evidence.

20. There was also dissatisfaction with other aspects of the industrialization programme. A new Investment Incentives Act, incorporating the previous Pioneer Industries legislation and adding an investment credit and several incentives to encourage exports, was passed in 1968. Later, provisions were added for extending the tax-exempt status of firms which expanded employment by certain percentages and for encouraging the location of new enterprises in 'development areas' outside the principal regions of manufacturing concentration.

21. In 1957 the Malay share of manufacturing employment was 50 per cent in the low-income, heavily Malay states of the North-west and East Coast (Kedah, Perlis, Kelantan, Trengganu and Pahang), while in the remainder of the country it was only 11 per cent (based on the population census). Much of the Malay employment in the poorer region was of the handicraft or cottage industry variety, but even in factory industry the regional differential persisted. Firms covered by the 1968 Census of Manufacturing Industries (Department of Statistics, n.d.) hired 41 per cent Malays in the five poorest states and only 25 per cent in the other six.

22. Tun (a title awarded in 1967) Tan Siew Sin became Finance Minister and President of the MCA in 1959 and served in that capacity until his sudden resignation in May 1969. He resumed the Finance portfolio in 1971 and held it until his retirement from politics in April 1974. Like his predecessor, Tun H. S. Lee, he stood for integrity, fiscal conservatism and the interests of business. With Tun Tan's retirement the MCA lost its grip on the important Finance portfolio, which has been held by a series of UMNO Ministers since 1974.

23. It also reviewed existing industrialization policy and proposed incentives for labour intensity and dispersal of industries referred to in footnote 20, above. The pamphlet titled *A New Industrial Development Strategy*, issued by FIDA in July 1969, gives a good summary of industrialization policy as enunciated by the CIC. It makes no mention of ethnic employment quotas, ownership share targets, public enterprise or other key elements of the soon-to-be proclaimed New Economic Policy.

24. The statistics on numbers of pioneer firms and value added originate from FIDA and refer to all of Malaysia.

25. Legally, PERNAS is a private corporation; that is, it was formed under regular corporate law, not by special enactment. But it is government-owned and sponsored, run mainly by ex-civil servants and heavily dependent on government actions for its success.

26. *Source*: Economic Planning Unit. Of course, MARA did not just lend for manufacturing projects; only 8 per cent of its cumulative lending in 1966–70 was for manufacturing. More important areas of lending were construction (32 per cent), transportation (27 per cent) and commerce (18 per cent); agricultural machinery purchases also accounted for 8 per cent of the total.

27. *Source*: *Third Malaysia Plan 1976–1980* (1976, p. 193). Again, the lending is not just for manufacturing. Lending to Bumiputra firms during 1974 was reportedly allocated as follows: agriculture 9 per cent, mining 1 per cent, manufacturing and construction together 28 per cent, general commerce 5 per cent and 'miscellaneous projects' (the composition of this large residual is not specified) 57 per cent (*Source*: EPU).

28. The guarantee applies to 60 per cent of the value of CGC-approved commercial bank loans to individuals, partnerships, co-operatives, associations and companies whose paid-up capital and reserves do not exceed $100,000 (initially, lower limits were specified). Lending is at 9 per cent, a rate which has been equal to or less than the prime lending rate for most of the period since the scheme began.

29. The presence of so many Malay borrowers in the statistics, when Malays have borrowed so little from the banking system in the past, might lead one to conclude that a large proportion of CGC lending must have been genuinely additional. This conclusion is risky, however, because the entire CGC programme is only a tiny fraction of total bank lending. For comparison, Malaysian commercial banks had $5.7 billion outstanding in loans and

advances at the end of 1975 (Bank Negara Malaysia, 1976, p. 62).

30. Just how much, and what kind, of assistance is a matter of debate. Most small-business programmes have tried to provide a wide variety of support services, as recommended by the standard reference on the subject (Staley and Morse, 1965). These programmes have tended to be expensive per small business created. Harvard psychologist David McClelland argues that a more effective and economical approach would involve identifying a small number of individuals with high entrepreneurial potential and giving them only a short course of motivational and management training. See McClelland and David G. Winter (1969).

31. I say *may be* because the McClelland-type programmes referred to in footnote 30 claim to be able to do the job without continued dependence of the entrepreneur on any sort of official assistance.

32. The scope of public enterprise in Malaysia has been surveyed by Hamlin Robinson (1973), Abdul Rahim Mohd. Said (1974), R. Thillainathan (1975, 1976a, 1976b), Tan Sri Dato Abdullah bin Ayub (1976) and Clifford Herbert (1976). For a cogent critique and some recent data which are not available elsewhere, see M. C. Puthucheary (1977).

33. Here, as elsewhere in the text, I gloss over differences in the legal form of publicly-sponsored enterprises; such differences have no importance for the discussion here.

34. 'PERNAS' is an example of the Indonesian-style acronym, formerly little used in Malaysia, which has become popular in the last few years. The use of such imitative terminology for public corporations (PETRONAS is another example) is suggestive of the influence which Indonesian experience with nationalization, once derided by Malaysia, has had in recent years.

35. *Straits Times* (Singapore), 11 September 1974, p. 10.

36. Firms with less than $250,000 in shareholders' funds and less than 25 full-time workers are exempted.

37. Clause 4, Section 4 states that, 'The Minister, in issuing a licence, may impose such conditions as he may think fit.'

38. See Chee Peng Lim (1977, pp. 9–16), on whose discussion this paragraph is based.

39. On the other hand, prices of Malaysia's principal commodity exports were generally high in 1975–7. In the past, even immediately after the 1969 riots, strong export earnings have invariably led to increases in private investment after a short lag.

40. A critical evaluation of the New Economic Policy might hold that in fact it has nothing at all to do with equality but is concerned with the expropriation of one élite by another. This seems a harsh judgement, since there continue to be government programmes aimed at benefiting poor Malays and even where publicly-sponsored enterprise is concerned there has not yet been enough experience to tell which way things will go. All I would say is that the public enterprise programme runs a risk of being captured by the élite and used for its own purposes. Only the responsiveness of the political system to popular interests will prevent this danger from being realized (see Chapter 10, below).

41. The Malayan equivalent of old-fashioned gold panning by individual prospectors is 'dulang washing', a process whereby 'tin tailings' (the mine effluvia) are panned to extract small quantities of ore missed by the initial separation process. Dulang washing is a very marginal occupation, followed mainly by children and old people.

42. The contracts were frozen in an attempt to force the companies to accept a system of 'management shares', which would have given PETRONAS a voice in their management without having to make any investment. PETRONAS also sought control of all downstream operations. When the companies refused to accede, the government backed down, dropping both demands and reducing the tax rate on the industry from 50 to 45 per cent. The initiative had been heavy-handed and ill-timed, in the sense that the industry was not yet well enough established to give the government much bargaining power and there was ample scope for employing the companies' prospecting resources elsewhere. It undoubtedly heightened businessmen's suspicions of government intentions and caused more sinister interpretations to be put upon the Industrial Coordination Act of 1975 than otherwise would have been the case (Chee Peng Lim, 1977, pp. 6–9).

43. Primary Industries Minister Taib Mahmud predicted in July 1974 that Malaysia would be producing 200,000 barrels a day by 1977 and exporting 400,000–500,000 barrels by 1980. See *Straits Times* (Singapore), 25 July 1974, p. 4.

44. Already in 1975 petroleum exports (estimated at $853 million) exceeded all other commodities in value, except for rubber, tin and timber. By 1980 petroleum is expected to top all products except rubber (*Third Malaysia Plan 1976–1980*, 1976, pp. 117–18).

45. The dangers inherent in PETRONAS are illustrated by Indonesia's experience with PERTAMINA and by the Minister of Primary Indusries' statement (in the interview cited in footnote 43, above) that PETRONAS would establish a petro-chemical complex, very probably an uneconomic project in the Malaysian context. The legislation does provide, however, for regular payments to both the federal and the state governments.

46. See Peter J. Wilson (1967, pp. 17–31) for a good description of this attitude.

47. Although the original aim seemed to be to monopolize the China trade, complaints from the established traders and pressure from the People's Republic itself caused PERNAS to backpedal to the position that it is only trying to exclude traders who are nationals of third countries (i.e., Hong Kong and Singapore). See statement by PERNAS General Manager Wan Hamid, *Straits Times* (Singapore), 11 October 1974, p. 11.

48. Such a system, known as the 'Benteng System', was attempted unsuccessfully in Indonesia in the early 1950s.

49. *Straits Times* (Singapore), 9 March 1974, p. 9.

50. The EPU estimated that the industry's labour force was 72.1 per cent Chinese, 21.7 per cent Malay and 6.0 per cent Indian. See *Mid-Term Review of the Second Malaysia Plan 1971–1975* (1973, p. 77).

51. Author's estimate; see footnote 18, above.

52. Government services include public administration, military and police; community services consist of education, health, religion and a few minor categories. The former group consists entirely of public service employees and the latter mainly so. The data are derived from the author's employment estimates.

53. Non-Malays began to be admitted to the MCS in 1952, apparently as a means of cementing the loyalty of Chinese and Indian citizens during the Emergency.

54. Five services had quotas in 1972. These were the MADS, then called the Home and Foreign Service (four-to-one), the Judicial and Legal Service (three-to-one), the Customs Service (three-to-one) and the armed forces. The armed forces quota, the size of which is not disclosed 'for security reasons', extends to the rank and file. All the other quotas apply to senior positions only. See Tan Sri Mohamed Suffian bin Hashim (1972, p. 251).

As this list suggests, the main purpose of the quota system is probably not so much jobs as control of government programmes and policies. The MADS is crucial in this regard, since it staffs key positions in the ministries to which the various departments, staffed by the specialized services, report. This arrangement creates some tension between generalists and specialists, who are often Malays and non-Malays respectively. For discussion of these and related administrative issues, see Milton J. Esman (1972, pp. 67–108).

55. At least, this was still true as of 1 November 1974, when Malays constituted 36.0 per cent of all government employees in the management and professional group (formerly Division One) and 48.3 per cent in the executive and semi-professional groups (formerly Division Two). See Ahmad Nordin (1975).

56. The Malay share in *total* senior positions increased, but the Chinese and Indian shares increased more. Tilman (1964, pp. 70–2) gives the following figures:

	1957		*1962*	
Expatriates	1,687	(61 per cent)	409	(14 per cent)
Malays	390	(14 per cent)	850	(29 per cent)
Chinese	366	(13 per cent)	987	(34 per cent)
Indians	191	(7 per cent)	462	(16 per cent)
Others	127	(5 per cent)	194	(7 per cent)
Total	2,761		2,902	

57. The New Economic Policy has in fact led to reshuffling of the occupational hierarchy among Malay public servants. Whereas general administrative work was once

preferred, there is now a great demand for positions in the new publicly supported enterprises, and for the business education which is regarded as a stepping stone to such jobs.

58. This seemingly paradoxical phenomenon may be what is being referred to in a *New York Times* article of 30 August 1975 (pp. 1, 6), which reports the overthrow in a military coup of Peru's leftist nationalist President General Juan Velasco Alvaredo. The article states that conservative critics of the ex-President, while criticizing him for being 'antibusiness, Marxist and totalitarian . . . grudgingly concede that [his] Government has attracted more foreign private investment than any of its predecessors'.

9 Education and Other General Policies

> ... as the days go by we are beginning to achieve more and more bumiputra participation in our economy ... bumiputra participation ... means active, efficient and purposeful practice by those of you who have been lucky enough to attend this College, and have acquired knowledge and skills with which you are now equipped, so that you can play a positive part in the commercial and industrial life of our country. As more and more of you graduate from this College and take your rightful place in the economic development of our country, the happier I and all true Malaysians become. . . .
>
> Tun Abdul Razak, in Morais, 1969, p. 466

INTRODUCTION

THE two preceding chapters reviewed efforts to reduce ethnically correlated economic inequality through programmes aimed at the rural and urban sectors respectively. While these two categories might appear to be exhaustive where earned income is concerned, there is in fact a third category of what might be called general policies. Into this grouping fall any policies which aim to reduce inequality by making Malay labour more productive, irrespective of the sectors in which the beneficiaries work or the areas in which they live. This is the category to be discussed in the present chapter.

By far the most important type of general policy—certainly in terms of the emphasis which Malaysians place on it, and probably in terms of its intrinsic potential as well—is education. The term is used here in its broad, modern sense to mean all forms of learning and not just that which occurs in schools.[1] Thus, the discussion encompasses not only *formal education*, which takes place in institutions called schools, but also *non-formal education* (learning which occurs in institutions other than schools, e.g. vocational training courses, apprenticeship programmes, adult education classes) and *informal education* (learning which takes place outside institutions, e.g. the process of learning by experience from one's work or from life in general).

Other general policies which merit consideration as potential instruments of inequality redressal, even though they have not been seriously so considered in Malaysia itself, are health services, family planning, public housing and social welfare services. These will be discussed in a later part of this chapter.

EDUCATION

Pre-World War II Background

Governments' educational policy objectives usually derive from their fundamental social, political and economic aims. Compared to both the American administration in the Philippines and the Dutch régime in the Indies, British colonialism in Malaya prior to World War II lacked a clear long-run political objective. It was explicitly aimed neither at the preparation of the indigenous population for eventual self-government nor at the systematic and indefinite suppression of independence ambitions. Instead, the British governed pragmatically, focusing their attention on immediate problems, allowing things to happen and intervening only when a threat to British interests was perceived.

Formal education spread much more slowly in Malaya than in the Philippines (Koh Eng Kiat, 1965). Much of what happened occurred through private rather than government initiative. No unified system emerged, probably because any common system instituted before World War II would have had to have been based on English as the medium of instruction, and this would have been unacceptable to the colonial authorities, who repeatedly voiced fears of the disruptive potentials of English-speaking Asians. Thus, while some education in English was provided both its amount and access to it were strictly limited. The Chinese were left to go their own way, while the government tried to assure that the major remaining elements of society—Malay aristocrats, Malay peasants and Indian estate labourers—received the kinds of education that would fit them to play the roles assigned to them in the colonial scheme of things.

Some idea of the impact of pre-World War II educational development can be gained through a brief review of the educational opportunities open to the children of each of the major ethnic groups.[2]

Malays could provide their sons with a Koranic education in the Arabic language, aimed at achieving the ability to recite the Muslim holy texts. This traditional schooling was provided by officials of the *kampung* mosques or by Muslim scholars who took in pupils as boarders. The learning thus provided was narrowly circumscribed and of hardly any practical use—in a traditional, let alone a modernizing, society.

In the 1870s the Straits Settlements government inaugurated the only form of free public education made available in Malaya before World War II. This was primary schooling in the Malay medium.[3] Although anyone could attend these schools, in practice their enrolment was nearly all Malay. The system spread in time to the FMS and was still gradually penetrating the Unfederated States (except Johore, which was reasonably well covered) when the War intervened. The government Malay schools aimed, in four years, to teach their pupils to read and write in both the *Rumi* and the *Jawi* versions of Malay,[4] to do simple arithmetic and to master a few rudiments of geography. The modesty of the effort can be judged from the length of the school day, which was two hours in the first three years and four hours in the fourth.

A famous statement of purpose by the FMS government held that the aim of Malay education

> . . . is not to turn out a few well-educated youths, nor yet numbers of less well-educated boys; rather it is to improve the bulk of the people and to make the son of the fisherman or peasant a more intelligent fisherman or peasant than his father had been, and a man whose education will enable him to understand how his own lot in life fits in with the scheme of life around him.[5]

The objective was carefully regulated modernization of the Malay community: the next generation, like the last, was to be made up of peasants and fishermen,[6] but they were to be 'better' (more productive? happier?) peasants and fishermen than their fathers had been. The progressive aspects of the system included the secularization of education, gradual improvements in curriculum and the system's spread (despite recurrent problems of inadequate budget and insufficient teacher supply) to enrolment of 57,000 by 1938.[7] The system failed, however, to prepare the Malays to cope with rapid changes occurring all around them. 'Education to the Chinese and Indians was chiefly a key to economic advancement or else a means of preserving their own culture, and Malay education did neither' (Silcock, 1964, pp. 208–9). Many Malays realized, as did their Chinese and Indian contemporaries, that the most promising road to economic advancement lay through entry into what Radcliffe (1970) calls the 'colonial domain'. They hoped that Malay-medium education would help their sons make this transition, but since the system was explicitly designed *not* to be used for this purpose it is not surprising that such ambitions were usually frustrated.[8]

In time colonial officials woke up to the fact that their educational prescription was helping to hold the Malays back while other communities advanced. Most injurious were the failure of primary education in Malay to lead to any form of post-primary schooling and the sparseness of Malay enrolment in English-language schools.

Although the very earliest English-medium schools were secular,[9] the main thrust of pre-1900 educational development was provided by Christian missionary groups. Fear of conversion prevented many Malay parents from sending their children to mission schools. Moreover, the policy of protecting the Islamic religion, which was adopted in the 1870s and strictly maintained throughout the colonial era, discouraged the missionaries from establishing schools in predominantly Muslim areas. Thus it is not surprising that Malay enrolment in English-medium schools remained small.[10]

One school started for the specific purpose of educating Malays in English was the residential Malay College at Kuala Kangsar, founded in 1905. Up to 1920 this 'Malay Eton' enrolled only sons of the royalty and chiefs. Later, a 50 per cent quota for commoners was established. Like Malay-medium schooling for the masses, the Malay College was intended to bring about limited and carefully controlled change. It accentuated the stratification of Malay society by preparing a small, élite segment of Malays to participate in the administration of the country.[11]

A somewhat broader channel for Malay entry into English-medium education was opened up later on, in the form of Special Malay Classes in English secondary schools. These classes, which were free, ran for two years and enabled students who had completed the four-year Malay curriculum to make the jump to the English stream. Although all major English-medium schools provided such classes, these schools were all located in urban areas. Despite government scholarships and hostels built for the exclusive use of Malays, the economic barrier was insuperable for most Malay families. Still, by 1941 there were 5,200 Malays enrolled in government and aided English schools.

Colonial officials often complained about lack of interest in schooling among Malay parents, or even of outright opposition to secular education. It would appear, however, that where boys were concerned such resistance essentially died out by World War I. Acceptance of formal education for girls came more slowly; even in 1938 less than 30 per cent of the pupils enrolled in Malay-medium schools were girls.

Despite this evidence of slowness to accept the value of formal education (or at least of the form of education that was offered), analysis carried out by Charles Hirschman (1972) suggests that it was lack of opportunity, not weakness of social demand, which principally constrained the spread of education among Malays during the colonial period. His conclusion gains credence from the continual complaints of education officials that their budgets were always the first to be cut in any of the periodic retrenchment exercises in which the colonial governments so frequently indulged.

Chinese, like Malays, were educated both in their own language and in English. Provision of Chinese vernacular education was not regarded as a necessary or proper function of the colonial government.[12] The demographic structure of early Chinese communities kept the number of school-age children relatively small. As clusters of children developed, the Chinese community organized itself to provide a rudimentary form of schooling. Run by teachers from China and sponsored by a trade guild, ancestral association or well-off individual, these schools were at first conducted in the dialect of the group concerned (Cantonese, Hokkien, Hailam, etc.). After the Chinese Revolution of 1911, the use of *Kuo-yu*, the Chinese National Language, became standard. Loh (1970, p. 46) comments that the extent of this self-help school system was never recorded in colonial administrative reports, although the fact that it was considerable was occasionally noted.

It was the resurgence of pan-Chinese nationalism after 1911 that finally attracted administrative attention to Chinese-medium education. The new government claimed sovereignty over ethnic Chinese everywhere, and this claim gained substance from the intense feeling most overseas Chinese had for their culture and homeland. As Purcell (1967, p. 229) puts it, 'it was clear that the [Malayan] Governments could not leave uncontrolled a system of education turning out boys and girls who were to all intents and purposes members of a foreign State, owing no duty to the country they lived in. . . .' There was also, he notes almost as an afterthought, a welfare argument for standardizing the diverse and frequently low-quality Chinese-medium schools. Legislation to register and control Chinese schools and teachers was introduced in 1920; a system of modest grants-in-aid was inaugurated three years later. Conceding that the original motive for control was political, Purcell (1967, pp. 230–2) notes that efforts were made during the 1920s and 1930s in the SS, FMS and Johore to remedy the deficiencies of Chinese schools with respect to textbooks, buildings, teaching methods and sanitation.

The system of control and subsidization of Chinese schools got a cool reception from the Chinese community itself; the number of schools receiving government assistance rose slowly.[13] The system did nothing to promote the objectives sought by the community through Chinese-language schooling. As Silcock (1964, p. 211) notes, primary education in Chinese was of little economic value (except perhaps in the handling of money), but it was an aid in preserving a Chinese cultural and political orientation. Although the government attempted no frontal assault on this orientation, it did impose limitations in the name of preventing subversion. Private Chinese-language secondary schools, which developed in time, prepared students for clerical and managerial posts in Chinese businesses. Until 1949 they also opened the way to higher education in China, although the resulting degrees were generally not recognized in Malaya.

Besides formal schooling, the Chinese community also provided its members with various types of non-formal and informal education intended to fit them for particular socio-economic roles within the community's self-contained structure. Although no one has fully traced the nature and impact of these forms of education, they have clearly been of importance for the economic advance of the Malayan Chinese community.

Like other ethnic groups, the Chinese also had opportunities to be educated in English. Through some combination of superior opportunity and greater alacrity in seizing what opportunity there was, the Chinese made much more extensive use of this facility than did the Malays and Indians. As early as 1901, 60 per cent of English-school enrolment in the Straits Settlements (and there was hardly any English education anywhere else) was Chinese.[14] During the twentieth century both the number of school-age Chinese and parental interest in English education soared. By 1938 there were 62,000 students in English-medium primary and secondary schools, 80 per cent of whom were Chinese (Ministry of Education, 1968, pp. 33–45; Cheeseman, 1955, p. 38).

Unquestionably the main motive behind this rapid growth of Chinese participation in English-medium education was economic. A basic education in English prepared one for a clerkship in the government or a European-owned business. Increasingly, as time went by, it also opened up opportunities for further education.[15] In the early part of this century many Chinese parents withdrew their sons from school as soon as they had achieved a rudimentary command of English, since this was enough to get a relatively well-paid job. Later, as employment standards rose, more students were permitted to finish the course.

The opportunity to benefit from English-language education was not open exclusively to Chinese. Why, then, was the Chinese response disproportionate to that of the other communities? There are several reasons for believing that the Chinese were in a better position to respond than either the Malays or the Indians. Their tolerant, often syncretic religious outlook obviated the suspicion of missionary education which proved so large a barrier in the case of the Malays. More important factors, however, were proximity and income level. The geographical distribution of the Chinese population accorded well with the distribution of English-medium schools, which were all urban and more prevalent in the Straits Settlements than the Malay States (the Unfederated States, except Johore, had none at all). And the somewhat better-off Chinese families were better able to bear the several kinds of cost which accompanied English-language education than were most Malay and Indian families. Even though tuition, and often board as well, were paid for Malays, minor explicit costs and the implicit cost of losing a potential income-earner added up to an excessive burden for most Malay households. Indeed, the majority of *Chinese* children remained in vernacular schools up to World War II, in part no doubt because of their lower cost.

Like the Malays (although for different reasons), the Chinese were at first reluctant to send their daughters to school. However, a minimum of primary schooling became standard for Chinese girls around World War I, long before any substantial fraction of Malay girls was enrolled.

Not only did more Chinese than Malay children enrol in English-medium schools, they also performed better once they got there and stayed in school longer. This had a significant effect on the relative positions of the two groups up to World War II.

Most *Indians*, including all the estate labourers, faced very limited educational opportunities. An FMS enactment of 1912 and a similar law passed later in the SS required that a vernacular school be provided by any estate on which there were ten or more school-age children. These schools, which taught in Tamil or another South Indian language, were of notoriously poor quality. The teachers, usually untrained, were generally brought in from India. Pupils in estate schools were strongly discouraged from studying English or entering English-medium schools. There was no link system to facilitate transfer to the English stream, such as was provided for the Malays. The whole system seems to have been aimed at assuring that estate workers' children remained on the estate.

Two-thirds of the Indian-medium schools were located on estates. The rest catered to other Indian populations, including those in the towns. Urban residents of Indian origin could also send their children to English-medium schools if they could afford to do so.

Specialized and higher education developed slowly during the pre-war period. Although the 'vocational fallacy' (see P. J. Foster, 1966) was pursued as vigorously in Malaya as in other colonies (the first unsuccessful trade school opened in 1816, the second in 1853), two significant occupation-oriented training institutions were successfully developed before World War II: the Agricultural School (later College and now University) at Serdang and the Technical College (now University) in Kuala Lumpur. Pre-war higher education was limited to a Medical School and Raffles College, both located in Singapore.

To summarize the pre-war situation, different ethnic groups faced different educational opportunities. Although the Malays were nominally favoured by being given the largest share of public educational expenditure, it was the Chinese who were best able to benefit from the structure of opportunities offered.

The results of colonial educational development can be assessed in Tables 9.1 and 9.2. Drawing on information on the educational attainments of various age cohorts which was collected in the 1957 census, these Tables provide a general idea of patterns of school attendance during various periods ranging from the late nineteenth century up to the 1950s.[16] Table 9.1 shows the percentages of various age cohorts who received one or more years of primary schooling. It shows that prevalences of 90 per cent or more came in only after World War II, and then only for males. Around World War I just over half of Malay boys were getting any formal schooling at all, compared to two-thirds of Indian boys and 80 per cent of Chinese. At the turn of the century the ratio was one-fifth for Malays, one-half for Chinese. Girls have lagged far behind throughout. Few girls went to school before World War I. Despite growth in female enrolment during the 1920s, the gap between boys and girls widened until some time in the 1930s. Major gains were made after World War II but the gap was not really closed until after Merdeka.

Table 9.2 provides similar information on the prevalence of seven years or more of schooling. Notable points in this Table are the relatively strong showing of the Indian community and the educational inferiority of the Malays, which is much greater relative to the other communities than it was in Table 9.1. The latter finding may reflect the severely

TABLE 9.1

PERCENTAGES OF AGE COHORTS WITH SOME SCHOOLING, 1957

Age in 1957	*Approximate year of school entry*	*Males*			*Females*		
		Malays	*Chinese*	*Indians*	*Malays*	*Chinese*	*Indians*
10–14	1949–53	91	94	92	72	77	70
15–19	1944–8	85	92	90	53	70	58
20–24	1939–43	76	88	87	35	54	44
25–34	1929–38	68	85	85	23	40	39
35–44	1919–28	57	80	67	10	24	17
45–54	1909–18	45	69	53	4	12	9
55–64	1899–1908	35	59	44	2	5	8
65+	before 1899	21	48	39	1	3	8

Source: H. Fell (1960, pp. 87–90).

TABLE 9.2

PERCENTAGES OF AGE COHORTS WITH POST-PRIMARY SCHOOLING, 1957

Age in 1957	*Approximate year of primary school completion*	*Males*			*Females*		
		Malays	*Chinese*	*Indians*	*Malays*	*Chinese*	*Indians*
15–19	1950–4	23	32	34	8	17	14
20–24	1945–9	14	23	24	3	10	10
25–34	1935–44	9	20	25	1	7	9
35–44	1925–34	9	22	19	4	5	4
45–54	1915–24	6	14	14	—	2	3
55–64	1905–14	3	10	12	—	1	2
65+	before 1905	2	8	11	—	—	2

Source: H. Fell (1960, pp. 87–90).

limited access from Malay-medium primary education to post-primary schooling which has been discussed.

World War II to Merdeka

Although British control continued for a dozen years after the defeat of Japan, the War brought fundamental political changes which had profound effects on education. From the régime's point of view, the major change was that eventual democratic self-government had been conceded; education now had to be altered so as to enhance the ability of the diverse Malayan peoples to live together in peace. Representatives of the Malay, Chinese and Indian communities took an increasing part in educational policy-making during this period. In this role they were subject to conflicting pressures. On the one hand, they had to demonstrate their concern for the vital and deeply felt interests of their constituents (especially protection of the group's cultural identity and opportunities for individual advancement). On the other hand, they had to prove to the British that they could effect workable compromises among themselves, since this was a condition of Independence. In this increasingly politicized atmosphere, education became a major subject of controversy.

One result of the changed political environment was to revive discussion of the possibility of a unified national system of education. Although there was some sentiment for English as the basis of a unified system, it was far too late for that solution. Silcock (1964, p. 215) analyses the ruling political considerations as follows:

> The English educated Malays could capture power only by coming to terms with the Chinese. Having a majority of the electorate, as well as a greater participation in the British system of government, they had superior bargaining power and they realized that emphasis on English education would favor the urban non-Malays. They could not, however, press for a completely Malay system of education without alienating the essential minimum of Chinese support. As a

... mixed system with gradual pressure toward Malay as a national language was introduced.

The development of that 'mixed system with gradual pressure toward Malay as a national language' is best traced by means of a series of landmark committee reports. The first of these was the Barnes Report (Malaya, 1951). Asked to examine the Malay-medium schools, related teacher training and 'the steps necessary to advance the education of Malays in English', the British and Malay members of the Barnes Committee felt compelled to get into broader issues of the educational system as a whole and the place of the Malay community in society. From these far-ranging deliberations emerged a proposal for comprehensive reform of primary education. The Committee proposed a single inter-racial type of school, the 'national school'. It would have provided six years of free bilingual (Malay and English) education for all 6–12-year-olds. Community participation in the schools would be encouraged and the system would be administered and partially financed by local educational authorities. The new system would be sufficiently attractive, the Committee hoped, that the other communities would in time be enticed to send their children to national schools.

What the Barnes Committee aimed at, therefore, was nothing less than eventual achievement of the elusive goal of educational unification, based on Malay–English bilingualism. But it was not to be.

> This idea was proposed twenty years too late. The rise of nationalism in Malaya had the effect of making all communities very sensitive to anything which could be interpreted as an attack on their language and culture. The National School idea was so interpreted by the Chinese and Indians and the scheme was modified to allow the teaching of Chinese and Tamil to the children of those races, who would thus be faced with the task of making themselves tri-lingual . . .
>
> (Dartford, 1957, pp. 36–7).

Countervailing the pressures exerted by and on behalf of the Barnes Committee were the claims and fears of the Chinese community. Two experts commissioned to survey the state of Chinese education and make recommendations produced a report which reflected Chinese desires to safeguard their separate cultural identity.[17] The authors of this report urged that support for Chinese-medium schooling be continued indefinitely, with any unification of the educational system to be achieved through long-run evolution. They denied that Chinese education was inherently subversive and pointed out that, in the absence of anything that could truly be called Malayan culture, 'Malayanization' was interpreted by many Chinese to mean coercion to become more like Malays.

Although the government at first moved to adopt the Barnes proposals, embodying them in the Education Ordinance of 1952, it soon pulled back from their immediate implementation. It is not clear how much Chinese objections had to do with this hesitation, but the main cause appears to have been financial. As rubber and tin prices plunged from their 1951 peaks the Treasury pronounced itself unable to finance the creation of a national system of primary education. A committee set up to break the impasse recommended more gradual movement toward unification (Malaya, 1954a).

Momentum toward unification quickly picked up again when Alliance Ministers were appointed after the 1955 elections. Another committee, chaired by Minister of Education Dato Abdul Razak bin Dato Hussein, was appointed. Its report (Malaya, 1956b), popularly known as the Razak Report, was the most influential of all the education committee reports. The Razak Report cited two major desiderata: a place in primary school for every child and a unified educational system which would promote national unity and consciousness. The former goal it saw as readily attainable; the latter would take time. For the immediate future, the Report prescribed two kinds of primary schools: 'Standard Schools', which would teach in the national language, and 'Standard-type Schools', which would use English, Tamil or *Kuo-yu* as their language medium but follow the same Ministry-prescribed curriculum as the Standard Schools. Malay would be a required subject in Standard-type Schools, and English in all schools. Tamil or *Kuo-yu* would be taught as a subject in any school in which the parents of fifteen or more pupils requested that this be done. Government financial support was to be provided to any school which agreed to follow this pattern. Similarly, the Report recommended that there be two types of assisted secondary schools: 'National Schools', in which Malay would be the medium of instruction and English a compulsory subject, and 'National-type Schools' which would use the English or *Kuo-yu* medium and teach Malay and English as required subjects.

Since Independence

The Razak Report set a pattern for development of the school system in succeeding years. Like many compromises effected in difficult situations, it failed to satisfy zealots on either side. Some Chinese groups (especially the self-interested Chinese-medium teachers, but also many Chinese guilds and associations) saw the Report as the first step in a gradual but insidious process of desinification (Margaret Roff, 1967; K. J. Ratnam, 1965, pp. 126–41). On the Malay side the opposite fear was expressed: that the Report conceded too much to multilingualism and failed to specify definite steps for achieving educational unification based on the Malay medium. These fears prompted the appointment of yet another study group, the Rahman Talib Committee, which was to review progress under the Razak Report (which had been implemented through the Education Ordinance of 1957) and make additional recommendations if necessary (Malaya, 1960).

Meanwhile, primary enrolments were completing their surge toward near-universality. As Table 9.3 shows, there were already four times as many primary-level pupils in 1956 as there had been before World War II. Some time around 1960 the spread of primary schooling reached the approximate dimensions which it has retained ever since: 95 per cent or more of children age six-plus enter school; with subsequent drop-outs, the enrolment ratio over the entire six-year span of primary schooling averages about 90 per cent.

The most rapid post-war enrolment growth occurred in the Malay and English streams. The high growth rate for the Malay schools reflects the extension of primary schooling to previously deprived groups, especially rural Malay girls. The growth of English-medium primary education had different origins. It testifies to the increasing opportunities for socio-economic mobility outside the bounds which had been traditional for each of the ethnic groups, to the utility of English language competence as an aid to such mobility and to the growing desire to proceed on from primary school to secondary education, which was still conducted mainly in English.

Once near-universality in primary enrolments had been attained, it was inevitable that a boom in the 'social demand' for secondary schooling should follow. Secondary schools (conducted in English and, to a lesser

TABLE 9.3

SCHOOL ENROLMENT BY LEVEL AND LANGUAGE MEDIUM, 1938–1974[1]
(thousands)

Year	*Language medium*				
	Malay	*English*	*Chinese*	*Tamil*	*Total*
		Primary			
1938	57	42	86	26	211
1947	171	57	190	35	453
1956	392	136	291	48	867
1962	501	230	362	64	1,160
1968	607	310	373	82	1,372
1974	942	62	470	80	1,555
		Secondary (academic)			
1938	—	20	3	*	24
1947	—	13	3	*	17
1956	3	59	27	*	89
1962	13	152	34	—	200
1968	136	334	20	—	490
1974	255	428	22	—	706

Year	*Higher*			
	Teacher training[2]	*University degree courses*[3]	*Other*[4]	*Total*
1938	—	—	*	*
1947	—	—	*	*
1956	1	—	*	1
1962	7	1	1	10
1968	6	6	3	14
1974	6	14	14	33

TABLE 9.3 (continued)

Year	*Vocational schools*[5]	*Other Further education*[6]	*Adult education*[7]
1938	⋆	—	—
1947	⋆	—	—
1956	1	—	—
1962	9	41	234
1968	10	27	223
1974	21	20	65

Source: Ministry of Education (1968, 1970, 1976, 1978).
Notes: — = Nil.
⋆ = Less than 500.

[1]Includes government, assisted and private schools in all categories.

[2]Includes teacher training colleges and centres.

[3]The University of Malaya first enrolled students at its Kuala Lumpur campus in 1959. The 1974 total also includes four recently created universities: Universiti Sains (University of Science), Universiti Kebangsaan (National University), University of Agriculture (formerly the Agriculture College) and the University of Technology (formerly the Technical College).

[4]Includes the College of Agriculture (1938–68), MARA College (later MARA Institute of Technology) (1956–74), Technical College (1956–68), Ungku Omar Polytechnic (1973) and Tunku Abdul Rahman College (1974). In 1974, includes diploma courses offered at the universities of Agriculture and Science.

[5]Includes schools variously characterized as technical schools, trade schools or vocational schools, both public and private, mostly at the secondary level.

[6]Consists of a variety of courses conducted in urban areas by the Ministry of Education.

[7]Literacy classes in Malay, conducted since 1961 by the Ministry of Rural Development and its successors and by the Ministry (later Board) of National Unity.

extent, Chinese) continued to be concentrated in urban areas, to charge fees and to be entered by means of a competitive examination, the Malayan Secondary Schools Entrance Examination (MSSEE). Despite greatly expanded use of devices such as remove classes, scholarships and hostels, the number of Malays, especially rural Malays, who gained entry to them remained relatively small.[18] With the number completing primary schooling rising rapidly (Standard Six enrolment tripled between 1956 and 1961), the pressure to provide more secondary places, especially for Malays, built up. This led to the provision of special Malay-medium classes in English-medium secondary schools in 1956, and then, in 1964, to the creation for the first time of secondary schools teaching in the Malay medium. Another momentous step was taken in 1960 when, on the recommendation of the Rahman Talib Committee, public support for secondary education was restricted to schools teaching in either Malay (the national language) or English (which remained an official language until 1967). This severely crimped the growth of Chinese-medium education at the secondary level. By contrast, English-medium secondary enrolments boomed, in part because of transfers from the Chinese-medium schools.

Even non-Malays were finding access to secondary education difficult, since only 30–40 per cent of those completing Primary Six were admitted to the three-year Lower Secondary programme.[19] In March 1964 the government eased the pressure by abolishing the MSSEE and prescribing a system of comprehensive education to which all students would be automatically promoted after completing primary school, effective the following January.

Like the Barnes recommendation thirteen years earlier, the decision to universalize lower secondary schooling met with financial objections. In the more politicized post-Merdeka atmosphere the Treasury was no longer strong enough to have the plan set aside but it did succeed in retarding its implementation, stretching out the schedule for providing new places to would-be secondary students. As late as 1968 the enrolment ratio at the lower secondary level was estimated by the Ministry of Education to be only 54 per cent.[20]

The Treasury's remonstrances are easily understood when the data shown in Table 9.4 are studied. The spread of the educational system, rapid growth in the school-going age cohorts and introduction of new services such as secondary schooling in Malay had combined to create heavy financial demands. Qualified teachers, Malay-language teaching materials and other needed inputs were also in short supply.

Another danger posed by the 1964 decision was increased youth unemployment. Although one reason cited for the introduction of the comprehensive schools was the immediate job market relief which three more years of universal education would provide, there was good reason to fear that the decision would on balance contribute to the growing unemployment problem rather than to its solution. And, indeed, labour market surveys did register a rise in already high rates of youth unemployment between 1962 and 1967–8.

Following a progression which has become familiar from the experience of so many other countries, growing educational outputs from the lower secondary level now created 'social demand' for places at higher levels. Upper-secondary schools were valued primarily as channels to the university and other third-level educational institutions. After its late start, domestic higher education began to expand rapidly during the late 1960s. Although there had been no local university before 1959 and only one up to 1970, by 1973 there were five, two of which had emerged from 'college' status (see footnote 3 to Table 9.3). Although a large number of Malaysian students still studied abroad, local third-level enrolment had reached 31,529 by 1975 (*Third Malaysia Plan 1976–1980*, 1976, p. 387).

Like secondary enrolment before it, the expansion of tertiary education posed issues of access and language medium. The University of Malaya taught in English (at first exclusively, then primarily, into the 1970s). This naturally tilted its enrolment toward those parts of the population which were receiving the most and best English-medium secondary schooling. As late as the 1963–4 academic year, University of Malaya enrolment was only 21 per cent Malay, while Chinese made up 60 per cent and Indians and others the remaining 19 per cent.[21] From

TABLE 9.4
FEDERAL GOVERNMENT EDUCATIONAL EXPENDITURES, 1957–1977

Year	*Amount ($ million)* *Recurrent*	*Development*	*Total as percentage of:* *Federal government total expenditure*	*GNP*	*$/capita*
		Federation of Malaya			
1957	123	13	14.2	2.9	22
1958	135	15	15.2	3.3	23
1959	150	9	16.2	3.1	24
1960	165	14	18.0	3.2	26
1961	184	27	17.5	3.7	30
1962	219	43	18.5	4.4	36
1963	237	46	16.4	4.4	37
1964	283	44	15.0	4.8	38
		Malaysia			
1965	334	67	18.9	4.6	43
1966	360	63	18.6	4.5	43
1967	403	52	18.8	4.7	45
1968	404	53	18.9	4.5	44
1969	439	43	18.9	4.4	45
1970	477	44	18.1	4.3	48
1971	536	86	17.9	5.0	56
1972	798	112	21.1	6.7	79
1973	805	142	21.2	5.3	81
1974	1,051	187	20.0	5.7	103
1975	1,158	212	19.4	6.3	111
1976	1,261	227	18.1	5.5	118
1977	1,750	274	19.1	6.6	156

Sources: For 1957–64, primarily Ministry of Education (1968, p. 109); for 1965–77, from Treasury (1974) and Ministry of Finance (1976, 1978).

that level, the Malay share of total enrolment was pushed up year by year in the late 1960s, reaching 40 per cent by 1970–1. This rise was supported by the admission, beginning in 1965, of students from the Malay medium.[22] As the Malay share in total enrolment rose, concern shifted to the paucity of Malay students in many specialized Faculties of the University. More than 80 per cent of Malay students were registered in the Arts Faculty and (after its inauguration in 1966) the Faculty of Economics and Administration. Fewer than 20 per cent enrolled in the Faculties of Science, Engineering, Agriculture, Education and Medicine. This skewed enrolment pattern resulted from a combination of demand and supply factors. On the demand side, it appears that what most Malay students wanted was simply a university degree (particularly an honours degree)[23] in any field of specialization, since this was the requirement for obtaining the most sought-after government jobs. They therefore gravitated toward the least demanding courses of study, most notoriously to the Malay Studies specialization within the Arts Faculty. At the same time, the supply of Malay candidates possessing reasonable qualifications for study in the scientific and technical faculties was very small. Malays were much less likely to have received adequate preparation in science and mathematics than were non-Malays. The deficiency was especially great for students from the Malay-medium schools, where science and mathematics teaching tended to be abysmal because of the inexperience of the teachers and shortage of Malay-language texts. By the early 1970s the scientific and technical faculties of the University of Malaya were inaugurating remedial programmes to help larger numbers of Malay students overcome these difficulties.

After 1970 the admission of Malays to places in third-level institutions was accelerated, so that by 1975 they were more than proportionately represented: Malays formed 71.3 per cent of total third-level enrolment in that year and 65.1 per cent of enrolment in degree courses.[24] Much of this enrolment growth is attributable to the increase in the number of higher educational institutions which has been mentioned. Nearly 30 per cent of Malay degree candidates in 1975 were enrolled in the Universiti Kebangsaan (National University), which was created to provide a full university curriculum in the Malay medium. Two other new universities, Universiti Pertanian Malaysia (Agriculture University) and Universiti Teknologi Malaysia (Technology University), also had heavily Malay student bodies in 1975. The remaining new university—Universiti Sains (the Science University, originally called the University of Penang)—had a student body which was somewhat less than half comprised of Malays, as was that of the University of Malaya.

One critical change in the system of formal education was not considered by any committee but simply announced on the night of 11 July 1969, by the Minister of Education.[25] It was that English-medium schools would be converted to the Malay medium one grade at a time, beginning with Standard One in 1970. Following this schedule, the conversion was to be completed at the primary level by 1975 and reach the *Sijil Rendah Pelajaran* (the national examination taken after Form III, formerly called the Lower Certificate of Education) in 1978, the *Sijil Pelajaran Malaysia* (taken after Form V; formerly the Malaysia Certificate of Education) in 1980 and the *Sijil Tinggi Persekolahan* (the Higher School Certificate, taken after two years of Form VI for purposes of university admission) in 1982. However, a 'pass' in Bahasa Malaysia became a necessary condition for passing the Sijil Pelajaran Malaysia right away, in 1970. The Minister's announcement implied universities and other institutions of higher education would have to teach in Malay from 1983 on.

The Minister's pre-emptive announcement essentially completed the conversion to a unified system of education based on the Malay medium. Although it permitted the continuation of primary education in Chinese and Tamil, as well as privately-financed secondary schooling in the Chinese medium, these forms of education were dead ends, which failed to prepare students either for any form of further education available or officially recognized in Malaysia or for employment other than in

TABLE 9.5

ENROLMENT RATES FOR YOUTHS AGED 15 BY ETHNIC GROUP, URBANIZATION AND SOCIO-ECONOMIC STATUS, 1972

Socio-economic status	*Urban*				*Rural*			
	Malay	*Chinese*	*Indian*	*Total*	*Malay*	*Chinese*	*Indian*	*Total*
High	88	59	77	67	67	53	54	63
Medium	54	39	47	43	28	30	28	28
Low	27	22	21	22	14	18	16	15
Total	63	42	42	47	28	31	22	28

Source: *Dropout Report* (Ministry of Education, 1973, p. 21). The overall averages were, by ethnic group, Malays 45 per cent, Chinese 47 and Indians 39; by socio-economic status, High 66 per cent, Medium 34 and Low 17. The comparable rates at age 11 for the three major ethnic groups were Malays 90 per cent, Chinese 89 and Indians 79.

small-scale ethnic businesses. The main road which non-Malays had been taking to higher socio-economic status, the English-medium schools, was shut off. This provoked consternation among middle-class Chinese and Indians. While many conformed to the new policy, some of those who could afford to do so sent their children abroad to be educated in English and a few were even prompted to emigrate to countries such as Singapore, Canada and Australia.[26] Some transferred their children to Chinese-medium primary schools (Table 9.3).[27] Although the government could change the principal language medium in education, it could do much less about either the economic and social advantages which English-speaking people continue to enjoy or the tendency of most Malaysians to regard Malay-medium schooling as inferior.[28]

By the early 1970s enrolment ratios had been substantially equalized among ethnic groups (Table 9.5); even gaps between the sexes had been reduced considerably (Table 9.6). However, very large differentials among social classes persisted, especially at the secondary level (Table 9.5), as children from poorer households were frequently forced to drop

TABLE 9.6

ENROLMENT RATES BY LEVEL OF EDUCATION AND SEX, 1972

(per cent of age cohorts)

Level	*Age group*	*Males*	*Females*	*Total*
Primary	6–11	94.0	89.1	91.6
Lower secondary	12–14	69.4	51.9	60.8
Upper secondary	15–16	28.2	19.7	24.0
Post-secondary	17–18	6.0	3.6	4.8
University	19–24	1.7	0.7	1.2

Source: Ministry of Education, Educational Planning and Research Division.

out of school before completing nine, or in some cases even six, years of education (Ministry of Education, 1973).

Effect of Education on Economic Inequality

Evaluation of the effect of education on economic inequality in Malaysia is an important and difficult task. It is important because education probably has some major impact on economic inequality; certainly Malaysians and their government have consistently assumed that it does. But it is also difficult because education's effects on society are multiple and complex, and scholars have been unable to agree, despite extensive study and discussion in recent years, about which effects are most important. There are at least four theories of education which might be applied in the evaluation. Their major premises can be stated as follows:

1. Education is primarily of *political* importance; it carries great symbolic weight, hinting to society as a whole of overall modernization and to particular ethnic groups of their own importance, or lack of it, relative to other groups. As one of the most easily established of modern institutions (at least in terms of appearances) education is inevitably accorded great importance by governments which want to be regarded as modernizing forces.

2. Education is primarily of *vocational* importance. There are different levels and types of education, each designed to prepare students for different types of work. Moreover, education is the unique method—or at least one important method—of preparing people for particular vocations. Therefore, it is important to anticipate national needs for different occupational skills and to regulate educational outputs so as to avoid both shortages and surpluses.

3. Education is primarily a process of *human capital formation*. Through the accumulation of economically useful learning, a resource is built up which can be used in the labour market to earn higher returns for the individual and make larger contributions to society. In contrast to Theory No. 2, human capital is thought of as widely usable in a variety of settings and not tied to specific vocations.

4. Education is primarily a *screening* device. Its role is not so much to transform people as to select those who will be assigned to different socio-economic levels. It may do this passively, as a mere transmitter of socio-economic status from one generation to another, or it may intervene more actively to select the most meritorious, somehow defined. As an adjunct to the selection function, it also *socializes* students, teaching future members of élites to think like élites and future non-élites to accept compliantly their subordinate roles in society.[29]

Each of these theories has something to offer to an interpretation of the Malaysian experience. The importance of the political explanation is supported by the prominence of the language medium question in the running debate on educational policy. None of the other three theories of education comes close to explaining this prominence. The government, supported by voluminous expert opinion, has consistently argued that school system integration was a necessary step toward breaking down communal barriers and building up national consciousness and unity. The problem has been that steps toward unification have often been divisive in their immediate effects. Language medium unification implies the choice of a particular medium of instruction and it is Malay, the language of one of the communal groups, that has been chosen. This approach of promoting unity by requiring all groups to adhere to Malay symbols, values and practices is a consistent one, despite its built-in difficulties.[30] Surely the reason for this seemingly perverse approach is that a policy such as the one announced on 11 July 1969, serves as a means of reassuring the Malay community, which has furnished the largest and most consistent bloc of political support to all governments since Independence, that its interests are being placed uppermost.

That the language medium policy is an important means of symbolic reassurance to the Malays is suggested by its use in 1969, when the government's confidence in Malay support was most severely shaken.[31] What, however, are the economic and social implications of the policy? Critics of the government's language policy, and of its hasty implementation, frequently cite the probable costs in terms of economic growth involved in the downgrading of English, the world's principal medium for transmitting new ideas across national boundaries. They contrast Malaysia with pragmatic Singapore, where English is being given more, not less, prominence. These critics have an undoubted point, although it is difficult to gauge its quantitative importance. To the extent that Theories 2 and 3 are valid, the whole society will suffer as a result of the additional barrier placed in the way of acquisition of valuable ideas and skills.[32] It may be, of course, that Malays will suffer less than non-Malays. On the other hand, it is likely that after a few years of experience in Malay-medium schooling Chinese and Indian students will be able to bring to bear the same kind of attributes which stood them in good competitive stead in English-medium education. It is also worth noting that one institution which has been strongly wedded to the idea of vocationally oriented schooling for Malays, the MARA Institute of Technology, has used English as its medium of instruction. This realistic response to the continuing importance of English in the most modern parts of the Malaysian economy has drawn fire from some Malay politicians, who evidently lay primary stress on the political objectives of educational policy.

In the mid-1960s, when the *vocational theory of education* commanded more support than it does today, the Malaysian government attempted to measure its future manpower requirements and plan the expansion of secondary and higher education accordingly. Based on an employer survey and the ideas of manpower planning prevalent at the time,[33] the First Malaysia Plan, published in 1965 just after the decision to implement the comprehensive schools scheme, called for rapid expansion of upper secondary and tertiary schooling. A much larger stock of middle- and high-level manpower was thought to be needed, since the country was still fairly heavily dependent on expatriates for technical and managerial posts and since the 'experience of somewhat more advanced nations suggests that, in the long run, the stock of such personnel must increase by at least double the rate of increase of employment generally' (*First Malaysia Plan 1966–1970*, 1965, p. 85). Because there was still a severe taper in the educational pyramid at the upper secondary level (that is, between the recently expanded lower secondary schools and the growing but still small third-level institutions), the Plan proposed that technical and vocational education be very substantially expanded as a means of providing better preparation for the job market for those who would not be able to go on to more schooling.[34] This recommendation, which was endorsed by a subsequent World Bank mission, preceded findings (I. Lourdesamy, 1962; Robert W. McMeekin, Jr., 1973) that existing vocational schools were expensive failures, attended only by those who could not gain admission to academic upper secondary schools and offering little that was valued in the job market. Fortunately, the Plan was never implemented.

Although subjected to strong challenges from the human capital and screening theories, the vocational theory of education has refused to die in Malaysia. People have continued to regard particular forms of education as necessary preparation for the performance of particular economic functions. A new manpower survey was carried out in the early 1970s; the obvious rationale was to obtain a precise measure of future openings in various professional and sub-professional fields, so that appropriate numbers of Malays could be put through the requisite courses to assure that attainment of the government's targets for Malay representation in high-level employment would not be impeded on the supply side. In fact, the vocational theory of education and the 'manpower requirements' planning techniques derived from it overstate the importance of unique links between education and occupation. It can be shown both that most jobs can be performed by persons not specifically trained for them (at least, in schools) and that many individuals educated for a particular economic role do not in fact play that role in later life. Yet the survival of the vocational theory is not surprising, if only because it leads to the same conclusions as the *screening view of education*, discussed below. In one sense, it makes no difference whether a particular form of education is necessary for the performance of a specific type of work or not: if a government, professional association or private employer requires that form of education as a prerequisite to employment, then it is indeed necessary from the viewpoint of the prospective employee, even if it is irrelevant from the social point of view. Those concerned with masking the rather nakedly political aspects of the screening process may choose to clothe their justifications in the vocational theory of education.

The human capital theory, which assumes that education has general rather than occupation-specific economic value, has also been applied to Malaysia. In a 1973 study, O. D. Hoerr calculated private and social rates of return to different levels of education.[35] These estimates showed education to be a good investment for society only at the secondary level. Estimated returns to primary education were low, mainly because of the relatively small income advantage which primary school leavers enjoyed over the unschooled; returns to higher education were also found to be low, despite a wide income gap between graduates and secondary school leavers, because of the substantial cost of providing higher education. In private terms, all forms of education were reasonably attractive investments. (This last finding is consistent with the strong 'social demand' for education noted earlier, in that education does apparently pay from the individual point of view.)

Hoerr's study could be taken to support the First Malaysia Plan's view that more middle-level manpower was needed, although it could hardly be used to justify further massive investments in higher education. Yet the very survey data on which the study was based showed that young people, who were now increasingly educated at least up to lower secondary school, were having a harder and harder time finding jobs.[36] Through unemployment, the labour market seemed to belie the very valuation which it placed on secondary education through the incomes which it paid.[37]

Although he tried to draw policy conclusions about the effects of education on particular social and ethnic groups, Hoerr was handicapped in this regard by the fact that his data were not coded either by ethnic group or by medium of instruction.[38] Even if he had had such data, however, his ability to draw these kinds of conclusions would have been constrained by well-known limitations of the analytical technique which he employed: (1) its assumption (which other theories contradict) that incomes associated with particular levels of education (or some arbitrary fraction of them) are caused by education's effect on productivity, valued through competitive labour markets; (2) its inability to estimate the amount of expansion or contraction needed at various levels of education; and (3) its silence on the issue of possible qualitative improvements in schooling.

The last of these points, at least, is addressed by a different technique of analysis, the 'educational production function'. In a 1972 Ph.D. dissertation,[39] Harold Beebout tried to measure the contributions of a number of factors to academic success at the upper secondary school level (see Table 9.7). Academic success was measured by a student's score on the Malaysia Certificate of Education (MCE) examination, taken upon completion of upper secondary school. As might be expected, a large part of the variation in MCE scores was predicted by scores on the Lower Certificate of Education examination which the students had taken on entering the upper secondary level. Somewhat surprisingly, however, this 'carry-over' effect was less pronounced for Malay-medium students than for English-medium students. Like the authors of earlier educational production function studies, Beebout found that most school inputs have a negligible effect on student performance. Here again, however, there was a contrast between the English-medium, where no input variations seemed to have much effect, and the Malay-medium, where teacher quality made a discernible mark on student results.[40] This suggested that academic performance in the Malay stream, although then inferior to that of the English stream,[41] did have the potential of being

TABLE 9.7

DETERMINANTS OF EXAMINATION PERFORMANCE BY UPPER SECONDARY SCHOOL STUDENTS, 1970[1]

Variable	*Malay medium* b_i	σb_i	β_i	*English medium* b_i	σb_i	β_i
Constant term	−6.47	(2.26)		−26.32	(2.07)	
Student's background						
LCE score (C)	.817	(.017)	.633	1.16	(.016)	.699
Out-of-school factors						
Non-Malay (B)	N.S.			3.09	(2.53)	.120
Medium percentage of farmer fathers (B)	7.28	(1.11)	.399	N.S.		
High percentage of farmer fathers (B)	4.18	(1.10)	.231	N.S.		
Fringe school location (B)	−1.68	(.493)	−.089	N.S.		
Rural school location (B)	.304	(.530)	.015	N.S.		
Boarding school (B)	N.S.			.405	(.302)	.015
School inputs						
S1: Percentage of graduate teachers (C)	.345	(.050)	.875	.012	(.014)	.025
Untrained teachers (B)	−2.02	(.319)	−.115	−3.26	(.569)	−.058
S3: Years of teaching experience (C)	.407	(.106)	.078	.219	(.084)	.048
(S1) × (S3) (C)	−.060	(.008)	−.906	−.004	(.002)	−.063
Class size (B)	−.150	(.038)	−.070	.027	(.030)	.010
High teacher motivation (B)	.521	(.293)	.031	N.S.		
Frequent library use (B)	.049	(.005)	.161	.019	(.005)	.042
Medium building age (B)	2.10	(2.74)	.123	−2.21	(.905)	−.095
Old building (B)	.883	(.539)	.036	−1.86	(.946)	−.081
Conditioning factors						
Girls' school (B)	1.63	(.706)	.070	2.09	(.346)	.086
Co-educational school (B)	.597	(.549)	.030	1.32	(.408)	.057
Double session (B)	−1.01	(.289)	−.060	.113	(.248)	.005
Size of school (C)	−.004	(.001)	−.099	.0003	(.001)	.004
Science major (B)	−4.01	(1.88)	−.026	5.07	(.328)	.152
R^2	——	.555	——	——	.647	——
$F_{.001}$		2.27			2.50	

Source: Beebout (1972, p. 166).

[1]The Table presents the results of regression equations in which the test scores of 3,180 Malay-medium students and 3,870 English-medium students, received upon completion of upper secondary schooling (i.e. on the Malaysia Certificate of Education examination), are 'explained' as a function of their incoming (Lower Certificate of Education) test scores and a number of other variables. The 'other variables' are categorized as out-of-school factors, school inputs and conditioning factors. Variables are either binary (B) or continuous (C). The b_i's can be interpreted as additional points on the MCE resulting from a unit increase in a continuous variable or from the presence of a binary variable. For each binary variable, one possible outcome is omitted (e.g. the Table lists Non-Malay but not Malay). The ob_i's are standard errors. The B_i's express the effect on the dependent variable of a variation of one standard deviation in the independent variable; this compares the impact of the various independent variables in a manner which is independent of the units in which they are measured. 'N.S.' indicates that the variable was omitted from the equation because there was insufficient variation in the observation.

significantly improved through judiciously chosen investments.[42] And, although most studies conducted in other countries have shown a low correlation between examination scores and future earnings, Beebout's findings probably have some economic significance because of the link between examination scores and admission to higher education.

The last comment recalls the fundamental issue of just what the economic function of the Malaysian school system is. The analytical techniques designed by economists—manpower requirements, international comparison, rate of return—are all based on a presumption that schooling makes people more productive. What is more, they tend to regard education as a linear process which occurs prior to labour force entry and can be measured in terms of years spent in school. In other words, these techniques analyse *schooling* rather than *education*. From this perspective, a two-pronged critique has been directed toward all these techniques: on the one hand, it maintains that much economically valuable education takes place outside the schools, in other types of institutions, on the job, in the community; on the other hand, it contends that schools, especially post-primary schools, may actually be socially and economically dysfunctional. How does this two-pronged critique apply to Malaysia?

Recent discussion has emphasized non-formal education as a means of raising productivity and incomes, especially among lower income groups (Coombs and Ahmed, 1974). Malaysia has had numerous programmes of non-formal education, although they are much harder than the formal education programme to describe and measure (in terms of enrolment, budget, etc.) because of their diversity and lack of administrative centralization. Vocation-oriented training courses and apprenticeship programmes have been conducted by the Ministry of Labour and Manpower, adult literary programmes by the Ministry of National and Rural Development, farmer training courses by the federal Ministry of Agriculture and state Agriculture Departments and specialized programmes for their own staffs by many other government departments. The volume of such activity has been far from inconsiderable, even though these programmes have had much less political push behind them than has formal schooling. Weaknesses of such training programmes have included their sometime failure to match occupational needs and their tendency to leave the ethnic structure of employment untouched (i.e., they train the workers who are already in an industry). Overcoming the latter weakness is a principal objective of the training programmes of MARA. Although there is little evaluative material available on the results of MARA training, large sums of money have been spent on it,[43] and at least in some cases (e.g., the MARA Institute of Technology and its predecessors) one gets the impression that the expenditure has had reasonably good effect. Still, a large amount of economically valuable education continues to take place on the job. So far the government has not intervened effectively in this area. Proposals to provide incentives for employers to offer more socially and economically useful on-the-job training have been made but not acted upon.

The possible dysfunctionality of formal education is a controversial issue, if only because so many people have a vested interest in defending the system. The notion that high rates of unemployment among young people who have received relatively large amounts of schooling are in any way caused by education has been vigorously attacked by Alan Wilson (1972, 1972a). Yet many would subscribe to three propositions put forward by R. P. Dore:

> First, in late developing societies schools and universities are likely to be more qualification-oriented than education-oriented.... Second, educational investment which is investment in qualification-producing institutions may hinder rather than promote economic growth. Third, the extent to which these propositions apply is very much dependent on each country's cultural and educational traditions...
>
> (Dore, 1972–3, p. 493; see also Dore, 1976).

In the article in which these propositions are stated, Dore examines the educational traditions of Sri Lanka and Japan. Although each country suffers from what he regards as excessive qualification-consciousness, Japan has developed rapidly and Sri Lanka has not, in part (Dore thinks) because Japan escaped the most pernicious effects of qualification-orientedness by never having been colonized and by establishing a firmer base of primary education before undertaking post-primary schooling on a large scale (Dore, 1972–3, pp. 503–4). Malaysia, needless to say, more closely resembles Sri Lanka than Japan. Among Malaysians there is widespread adherence to the *selection theory* of post-primary education, whereby 'qualification is the merely instrumental *use* of learning, not to do, but just to be' (Dore, 1972–3, p. 492). As a means of selecting a small colonial or immediately post-colonial élite to occupy the top one or two percentiles of the social and occupational scales, qualification-oriented schooling was a feasible (if arbitrary and expensive) method. As a means of training much larger percentages of each age cohort, most of whom will occupy less exalted positions on the socio-economic ladder, it makes very little sense at all. This is not necessarily to endorse radical proposals that formal schooling be abandoned altogether. As Dore puts it in the title of another of his papers, 'Deschool? Try Using the Schools for Education First.'[44] Unfortunately, the dominating attention which has been given to the ethnicity-inspired issue of language medium in education and the partially class-inspired issue of who receives the prized higher qualifications have led to a situation in which little serious attention is being given to considering how that might be done.[45]

Regardless of what view one takes of education's economic role, there are grounds for concern over whether the results of the government's language medium and Malay-sponsorship policies will be greater national unity or disunity. Studies by Bock, Takei and Nash (Bock, 1971; Takei, 1971; Takei, Bock and Saunders, 1973; Nash, 1972) suggest that during the early 1970s Malay and Chinese students were coming to hope for much the same things out of schooling, that each group saw the existing system as disproportionately benefiting the other and that inter-group competition and resentment were being stimulated. Bock (1971, pp. 232–312) found both Malay and Chinese students enrolled in ethnically heterogeneous secondary schools to be significantly more alienated than their counterparts in ethnically homogeneous schools. Contrary to the old stereotype of Malays as unambitious, Malay students seemed to have at least as high socio-economic aspirations as their Chinese contemporaries; moreover, they had a *greater* expectation of being able to satisfy these aspirations, largely through the schooling received as a result of government sponsorship (Takei, Bock and Saunders, 1973, pp. 13–14). It is clear that educational unification, quite apart from the complicating issues of language medium and ethnic sponsorship, contributes to a convergence of values and aspirations. But this tends to replace the old pattern of ethnic occupational specialization with heightened inter-group competition for the same kinds of jobs. This in turn can increase ethnic tensions and cause disunity rather than its converse. Of course, the strain can be eased through rapid expansion of the supply of desirable jobs. But the problem cannot be solved by this means alone, since the likelihood is that secondary and tertiary education will expand faster than *any* conceivable rate of increase in the number of jobs traditionally held by those who possess relatively high 'qualifications'. For this reason, if for no other, one wishes that more attention were being paid to the problem of making Malaysian education more economically useful in a variety of occupations.

What effect, then, *does* Malaysian education have on economic inequality? On the basis of the preceding discussion, it seems reasonably safe to suggest the following conclusions.

1. Colonial education policies worked to the economic disadvantage of the mass of Malays and, as at least half-consciously intended by its framers, to the detriment of Malay social and political development and the creation of any kind of national feeling across the ethnic groups. It was restrictive in its coverage, especially at the higher levels.

2. Beginning a few years before Independence, the drives to expand and unify the school system became highly politicized and dominated by the language medium issue.

3. As the system expanded and moved toward unification on the basis of Malay as the medium of instruction, the urban, mainly Chinese, population continued to derive the most economic advantage from schooling.

4. However, prodded by its Malay constituents, the government gradually expanded the system of Malay sponsorship to the point at which ethnic enrolment ratios have now essentially been equalized, and even in some cases (domestic higher education) skewed in favour of Malays.

5. Educational quality is surely suffering to some degree in the language medium conversion.

6. Malaysian education remains highly qualification-oriented and most citizens and government officials rightly regard it primarily as a system for selecting new members of the élite and near-élite, rather than a means of acquiring learning which is of intrinsic economic worth—or non-economic worth, for that matter.

7. Almost unnoticed, a number of training programmes have been developed which teach useful skills to low-income workers and farmers; non-formal education has not been emphasized as a matter of national policy, and one suspects that more could be done, to the benefit of both GNP and the incomes of the poor.

HEALTH AND FAMILY PLANNING

Turning one's attention from education to health, one quickly senses a transition from a stormy sea of controversy to something resembling a placid millpond. Whereas education has been close to the centre of the political stage for nearly three decades, health has been relatively neglected by citizens, politicians and analysts alike. It is hard to understand why this is so, unless one resorts to the rather cynical explanation that health improvement primarily benefits the relatively inarticulate poor, while educational policy lies much closer to the interests of the more vocal and powerful élites and would-be élites. Malaysian policy-makers have sometimes regarded health services as an 'amenity'—that is, a desirable addition to the range of goods and services consumed but not a contributor to production or otherwise of fundamental importance. Yet a case can be made that better health, like better education, increases productivity and contributes to the formation of human capital.[46] Since it renders this contribution disproportionately to the poor, the argument further suggests that appropriate health policies, like appropriate education policies, offer an opportunity simultaneously to promote both the growth objective and the equity objective.

This section surveys health and family planning conditions and policies in Peninsular Malaysia in an attempt to determine the validity of this thesis about the potentials of health policy. Because of the novelty of this question in the Malaysian setting (i.e., the paucity of relevant statistics and prior studies), the question is harder to answer than it should be.

Paradoxically, there is little doubt that the *colonial* government regarded health services as an investment, which raised the productivity of labour employed in the estates, mines and other modern economic enterprises. This belief is evident in policy statements of the time[47] and, still more eloquently, in the pattern of services provided. Health services were provided first in the principal administrative centres and then in the other West Coast towns and the main estate and mining areas, where health conditions had been abominable.[48] The East Coast states and the Unfederated States generally (with the usual exception of Johore) were much more sparsely provided with health facilities and personnel. Large parts of the rural Malay population, as well as many lower-class Chinese and Indians, were felt virtually untouched by Western medicine or sanitation and totally dependent on their respective traditional practices, remedies and healers. Although there are no reliable pre-World War II statistics on mortality and morbidity, it is probable that wide East Coast–West Coast and rural–urban differentials in health conditions prevailed in this period. Despite their proclaimed concern for the welfare of the traditional Malay economy, British authorities did little to ameliorate the complex of malnutrition and ill health which Ungku Aziz (1964) has stressed as a major cause of rural poverty. Still, Malayan health conditions at their worst were above the level which prevailed in many parts of Asia. Famine and, to a lesser extent, epidemic were generally avoided through the relative prosperity of the country and the development of its transport system.

It is only after World War II that solid evidence of health conditions in Malaya began to become available. The admirable study conducted by R. C. Burgess and Laidin bin Alang Musa (1950) under the auspices of the Institute for Medical Research clearly and thoroughly defined the health, dietary and living conditions of three groups of low-income Malayans: Malay smallholders and fishermen and Indian estate labourers. It revealed significant health problems, notably widespread anaemia, caused in large part by worm infestation, and kwashiorkor, resulting in the 'dejected and lifeless' appearance of many Malay children. Although the Indian labourers had suffered greater deprivation during the Japanese occupation (because unlike the Malays, they customarily grew little of their own food), their diet was markedly superior in calories and nutrients to that of the Malays. Unlike the Malays, the Indians consumed significant quantities of legumes and even some milk.

The inferiority of the Malay diet, which was judged inadequate for the maintenance of good health, was ascribed by Burgess and Laidin partly to traditional food practices and beliefs and partly to rural Malay poverty. Among the injurious food beliefs cited were the preference for highly milled rice, the general avoidance of pulses and green vegetables, the limitation of a new mother's diet to rice and fish for a period of 44 days following the delivery and the taboo regarding consumption of fish (the main source of protein) by newly weaned children. The poverty of the Malay groups surveyed was extreme. Among the smallholders food accounted for 75–85 per cent of the total consumption expenditure (including consumption of own produce); among the fishermen food accounted for two-thirds of total outlays.

The health conditions defined by Burgess and Laidin, while somewhat less extreme than those prevailing in many other Asian areas, were sufficiently bad to prompt speculation that they were not merely a result of rural poverty but also a major cause of it.[49]

There have been only a few comparable subsequent studies. In 1957–8 Florence A. Thomson carried out a nutritional study of infants in a poor area of rural Perak (Thomson, 1960) which revealed continued serious malnutrition of toddlers. Later studies were conducted by a WHO expert (MacArthur, 1962),[50] an American team (U.S. Interdepartmental Committee for Nutrition for National Defence, 1964), a pair of CARE/MEDICO doctors (Chappel and Janowitz, 1965) and two nutritionists from the Institute for Medical Research (Chong and Lim, 1975). The last of these studies, covering Malay pre-school children surveyed between 1969 and 1972, found 'significant malnutrition' in 44 per cent of cases examined in Ulu Trengganu (a remote area), 24 per cent in Kuala

Trengganu (an East Coast state capital), 16 per cent in Kuala Langat (a West Coast town), 10 per cent among army dependants and none at all among a group of upper-income Malays (Chong and Lim, 1975, p. 22). Children between the ages of one and three were found to be most affected.

TABLE 9.8

VITAL STATISTICS, 1948–1976[1]

	Births	*Deaths*	*Natural increase*	*Infant deaths per 1,000 live births*	*Toddler deaths per 1,000 1–4-year-olds*
	per 1,000 population				
			Malays		
1948–50	40.8	18.4	22.4	112	n.a.
1951–3	45.5	15.8	29.7	102	n.a.
1954–6	47.0	14.3	32.7	97	n.a.
1957–9	46.2	13.3	32.9	94	13
1960–2	43.6	11.1	32.5	80	11
1963–5	41.2	9.5	31.7	64	9
1966–8	39.5	8.4	31.1	53	7
1969–71	36.1	7.6	28.5	47	6
1972–4	34.6	6.8	27.8	42	4
1975–6	33.7	6.4	27.3	36	4
			Chinese		
1948–50	43.4	12.6	30.8	70	n.a.
1951–3	43.1	12.0	31.1	71	n.a.
1954–6	42.5	9.3	33.2	53	n.a.
1957–9	40.6	8.7	31.9	46	6
1960–2	38.4	7.6	30.8	37	5
1963–5	36.4	7.1	29.3	33	3
1966–8	34.3	6.8	27.5	30	3
1969–71	32.0	6.6	25.4	28	2
1972–4	29.8	6.4	23.4	27	2
1975–6	28.7	5.9	22.8	23	1
			Indians		
1948–50	46.7	13.0	33.7	97	n.a.
1951–3	46.6	12.8	33.8	101	n.a.
1954–6	47.6	10.3	37.3	78	n.a.
1957–9	47.5	10.1	37.4	71	8
1960–2	44.4	9.0	35.4	59	7
1963–5	41.4	8.7	32.7	52	5
1966–8	38.1	9.0	29.1	52	5
1969–71	33.3	8.7	24.6	48	4
1972–4	30.8	8.2	22.6	44	4
1975–6	30.5	8.3	22.2	38	3

TABLE 9.8 (continued)

	Births	Deaths	Natural increase	Infant deaths per 1,000 live births	Toddler deaths per 1,000 1–4-year-olds
	per 1,000 population				
			Total population		
1948–50	42.3	15.5	26.8	93	n.a.
1951–3	44.5	13.9	30.6	90	n.a.
1954–6	45.1	11.9	33.2	79	n.a.
1957–9	44.1	11.1	33.0	74	9
1960–2	41.7	9.5	32.2	63	8
1963–5	39.4	8.5	30.9	52	6
1966–8	37.3	7.9	29.4	45	5
1969–71	34.3	7.3	27.0	41	4
1972–4	32.4	6.8	25.6	37	3
1975–6	31.5	6.3	25.2	32	3

Source: *Monthly Statistical Bulletin*, various issues.

Note: n.a. = not available.

[1]These official statistics are believed to have become nearly complete by the late 1950s (see text footnote 52). Selected instances of rising birth and death rates up to 1957–9 are probably explained by improving coverage. Death rate declines in the pre-Independence period are probably understated for the same reason.

Although there have been few studies of nutritional status among non-Malays it seems likely that their position is far superior to that of Malays from the lower income groups, especially those living in the more out-of-the way areas.[51]

It is probable that the nutritional status of most groups has improved substantially since World War II. The best evidence of this comes not from nutritional studies but from the officially compiled vital statistics (Table 9.8). These statistics, which have been generally reliable since the mid-1950s,[52] reveal a 'demographic transition' in which a rapidly falling crude death rate is followed, with a lag of several years, by a more slowly falling birth rate. This produces a period of rapid natural increase, which lasts until the 'bottoming out' of the death rate and eventual beginning of birth rate decline combine to bring about a retardation of natural increase. Compared to some other countries, this period of very fast population growth was fairly brief in Peninsular Malaysia. The rate of natural increase remained above 3 per cent for about fifteen years, roughly from 1950 to 1965. Since then fertility has begun to decline among all ethnic groups,[53] bringing down the rate of natural increase. Even the rates which have prevailed since 1965—the current rate is about 2.5 per cent—may quite properly be regarded as very high, however.

Besides showing these trends, Table 9.8 also reveals a familiar cross-section pattern of inter-ethnic group differentials in death rates. Until the late 1960s, Malays consistently had the worst (highest) death rates, Chinese the best (lowest); Indians were in between. In the last decade, however, Malay death rates have fallen below those of the Indians. The changes which have occurred in these rates over the years appear to be related to pre- and post-Independence policies. Up to the late 1950s the Chinese were the main beneficiaries of improving health conditions; death rates for both Malays and Indians became higher relative to those of the Chinese during this period.[54] The probable reason is that improvements in health services and sanitation were concentrated in the towns during this period and the Chinese, already the most urbanized ethnic group, were becoming even more so as a result of Emergency-related resettlement. After Merdeka, with the new emphasis on rural development, Malay death rates fell faster than those of the Chinese (which had reached exceedingly low levels in any case). Indians, who were less likely to be the beneficiaries of new health-related services, experienced much slower improvements in mortality, so that by the late 1960s their death rates were no longer below those of the Malays. Both the Malays and Indians have continued to be at a significant disadvantage relative to the Chinese.[55]

Part of the difference in death rates among ethnic groups is attributable to differences in residential patterns. The poorer states of the East Coast and North-east had much higher death rates than other parts of the country in the 1960s, especially for Malays. By the mid-1970s, however, these interstate mortality differentials had been substantially reduced.[56]

Statistics on morbidity and cause of death are less satisfactory than those on mortality. It has been said that developed and underdeveloped countries can be distinguished from each other by their disease patterns. Hospital admission statistics for Peninsular Malaysia reveal a pattern generally characteristic of an underdeveloped country—with its prevalence of birth complications, skin diseases, gastro-intestinal difficulties and infectious diseases—although there are signs of transition to the developed-country pattern in which heart and cardio-vascular diseases and cancer predominate. Accidents, always a leading cause of hospital admission in Peninsular Malaysia, have recently accounted for an increasing percentage of admissions, presumably because of the rapidly growing use of motor vehicles.

There has been little evaluation of the contributions public sector activities may have made to reduce morbidity and mortality in the recent past, or of the part they might play in bringing about further declines in the future. However, little analysis was required to see that extension of preventive and curative services to the rural population probably offered a high potential, and this was seized upon as a policy emphasis at about the time of Merdeka. The Malayan Second Five-Year Plan allocated $145 million to the development of health facilities in 1961–5. Greatest propaganda emphasis was given to the goal of 'eventually . . . establish[ing] a network of health units serving the entire rural population. A long step forward towards this goal will be taken during 1961–5 with the establishment of 37 main rural health centres, 148 sub-centres and 652 midwives clinics. These facilities will provide additional medical and health services to more than 2 million of the rural population' (*Second Five-Year Plan 1961–1965*, 1961, p. 47). However, considerably more money was earmarked for the expansion of existing urban facilities and construction of new ones.[57]

The 1961–5 construction programme was substantially implemented,[58] but greater problems were encountered in staffing the newly created facilities. Medical personnel were in short supply despite recently accelerated training programmes, nearly all were non-Malays and most preferred the more comfortable and (for doctors who could consult privately) more lucrative life of the towns. These problems were eased in time through training and by efforts to bring significant numbers of Malays into the medical services for the first time.[59]

The Malayan Second Five-Year Plan was the last plan to emphasize expansion of the medical services. The First Malaysia Plan (1966–70), in which development outlays for health were targeted at a level ($150 million) only slightly higher than in the preceding five years and rural health service outlays were reduced in view of the difficulty of staffing the facilities already built, ushered in a period of consolidation. This continued into the 1970s, as the Second Malaysia Plan provided only $171 million for health services, most of it ($113 million) for new hospitals, improvements, extensions and equipment. Operating expenditures for health services, meanwhile, grew at, or just below, the growth rate of total government spending. In 1965 they amounted to $116 million, or 7.5 per cent of the operating budget; a decade later, the figures were $361 million and 7.4 per cent (Treasury, 1975, pp. xxxiv–xxxv; Ministry of Finance, 1976, pp. xxxii–xxxiii).

Despite the lack of urgency accorded to the improvement of health services, Peter Heller, in his recent research on the use of such services by various elements of the population (Heller, 1974, 1975, 1976), finds much to commend in Malaysia, as compared to other developing countries. According to his findings, users of government hospitals roughly matched the general population with respect to ethnicity and income, although there was a tendency in some areas for hospital in-patients to be better off than the general population. By state, the distribution of expenditures in 1973 was found to be as shown in Table 9.9. Taking into account causes of variation in expenditure levels such as centralized facilities which may be used by residents of several states and construction projects which happened to be going on in particular locations in 1973, the interstate variance in government health expenditures per capita is remarkably small. Private medical expenditures are much more unequally distributed, but since they make up only one-quarter of the total their overall effect is not great.

It can thus be seen that much, though not all, of the colonial pro-urban and West Coast bias has been eliminated from the pattern of health services provided. Relative to other countries, Malaysia is still somewhat under-endowed with doctors and (to a lesser extent) hospital beds, but it is well supplied with non-physician primary health workers.[60] Although there is really no evidence to support the proposition, one would think that renewed dedication to closing the regional and

TABLE 9.9

DISTRIBUTION OF HEALTH EXPENDITURE BY STATE, 1973

State	*Expenditure ($ million)* Government	Private[2]	Total	*Expenditure per head*[1] *($)* Government	Private	Total
Selangor	38.9	25.6	64.5	22	15	37
Negri Sembilan	13.8	2.5	16.3	27	5	31
Penang	15.8	8.1	24.0	19	10	28
Perlis	3.3	0.4	3.7	25	3	28
Pahang	12.9	1.6	14.5	24	3	27
Malacca	8.7	1.4	10.1	20	3	23
Johore	22.1	6.1	28.1	16	4	20
Perak	24.9	8.8	33.7	15	5	20
Trengganu	6.8	0.6	7.3	15	1	17
Kelantan	9.7	1.1	10.8	13	2	15
Kedah	12.4	1.9	14.3	12	2	14
Peninsular Malaysia	176.3[3]	58.0	234.3[3]	19[3]	6	25[3]

Sources: Peter Heller (1974); R. Chander (1971).

[1]Based on assumed population in each state 8 per cent greater than that found in the 1970 census.

[2]Includes incomes of private doctors, dentists and maternity homes. Traditional practitioners are excluded.

[3]Includes $7 million of central Ministry expenditures which was not allocable by state.

rural–urban gaps in health services and conditions—and this would have to include sewerage and water supply improvements,[61] which are the responsibilities of state and local governments—would significantly improve the welfare of the poor, as well as their ability to participate in society as workers, students and citizens.

Another way that Malaysian households could perhaps improve their material welfare is by having fewer children, thereby reducing the burden of dependency. Levels of fertility and the crude birth rate have been falling for some time in Malaysia, as in other East and South-East Asian countries. Singapore's birth rate underwent a sharp decline during the late 1950s and 1960s, and the birth rate among Malaysian Chinese followed a similar trend (Table 9.8). Fertility among Malays and Indians began to fall soon thereafter, but as late as 1970 both the Malays and Indians were still at higher fertility levels than the Chinese.[62]

The causes of the 'demographic transition' from high to low fertility rates are complex and far from fully understood.[63] Many regard it as inevitable result of development, but the 'developmentalist' solution is an unacceptably gradualist one for those who are deeply concerned about high present and prospective population densities in many parts of the world. Many who seek a quicker solution to the problem of global overpopulation put their faith in family planning programmes. Privately-sponsored family planning programmes appeared in Singapore and urban

Malaya at about the same time as the birth rate began to decline, although the causal relationship between the two events is unclear. Under the urgings of a number of concerned citizens, supported by international foundations, the Malaysian government established a National Family Planning Board in 1966. The Board has been instrumental in making contraceptive materials (especially the Pill, which has been emphasized from the start) more widely available over the past decade. Working mainly in urban areas, it established a promising record of achievement in its early years. Thereafter, despite an announced campaign to move into the rural areas (through field-level integration with the rural health service of the Ministry of Health), progress fell off.[64]

The unimpressive record of family planning in Malaysia is largely attributable to the government's understandable reluctance to force contraception on the rural Malays, many of whom still prefer large families.[65] In addition, however, the programme has been weakened by the lingering notion that the Malays must breed rapidly so as to avoid being outnumbered and thus subjugated by the non-Malays. Fallacious as this idea is—the Malays cannot now be outnumbered by the non-Malays, as Chapter 2 demonstrated, and their power relative to the non-Malays is not primarily dependent on numbers in any case—it retains a grip on many Malay minds.

Although they may be concerned about the future size of their community relative to the Chinese and Indians, few Malays are likely to base their family size decisions on such grand political considerations. More likely, they decide on the basis of more personal factors, such as calculations of the benefits and costs of children, the customs of their society and their ability to achieve their desired family size given the contraceptive possibilities available to them and their knowledge of how to use them.[66] It seems probable both that smaller families will benefit Malay economic advance as more and more families move away from dependence on family farms and fishing and that smaller Malay families will in fact emerge *pari passu* with that occupational shift.

OTHER GENERAL POLICIES

Education and health are not the only types of 'general policies' which could contribute to a reduction in economic inequality in Malaysia, although they are the major ones. Others include old age and survivors' insurance, workmen's compensation, public housing and social welfare institutions. All these policies, which are normally considered trappings of the modern welfare state and are generally absent or underdeveloped in low-income countries, have been introduced in some guise in Malaysia. The Employees Provident Fund, a compulsory savings scheme which is of limited value as a social welfare benefit because it lacks an insurance feature,[67] was introduced in the 1950s and expanded steadily, enrolling nearly 2.9 million members by the end of 1975.[68] Workmen's compensation (called 'social security' in Malaysia) was introduced in 1971. Public housing has been constructed in Peninsular Malaysian towns since the 1950s. Generally regarded as a sop to the urban Chinese electorate, it has been pursued with an ambivalence which reflects the lesser importance of that electorate in Malaysia, as compared to Singapore, where public housing became a major plank in the government's political platform. Social welfare institutions have existed since colonial times. They cater to the needs of particular disadvantaged groups, such as lepers, orphans and the physically and mentally handicapped.

None of these programmes does much to alleviate economic inequality of the kind with which this study is concerned. This is because they are aimed either at individual cases of hardship (workmen's compensation, social welfare institutions) or at groups which, while not the best off in Malaysian society, are not the poorest either (the EPF, public housing). Moreover, it can also be said that as a group they deal with particular, relatively minor manifestations of economic inequality rather than more general cases and causes. Thus, despite Ungku Aziz's pleas that such benefits—as well as minimum wage laws, legal standards on hours and working conditions—be extended to the rural areas,[69] it is almost certainly just as well that they have not been. The probable result would be large amounts of unproductive expenditure, a mass of complex and virtually unenforceable legislation and considerable disincentives to efficient resource allocation.

CONCLUSIONS

It is hard to reach conclusions that cover the whole area of 'general policies'. To the extent that such policies can increase the income-earning capacity of the less well off, they have an appeal derived from their generality: less intrusion into social and economic process is required to provide people with better education, health and other services which may then help them to earn higher incomes than if the government has to intervene in the income-earning process itself. But the extent and nature of the causal link from the provision of education and health services to the earning of income is difficult to establish. Perhaps the best defence of education and health programmes is that they are desirable in their own right, both from society's viewpoint and from that of the individual. Since everybody wants them, it is best to provide them in relatively equal amounts, if only for the sake of equity in the provision of the services themselves. This principle does not provide guidance on the share of society's resources to allocate to such services, but it does say something about how to distribute the amount that is provided.

Finally, a word of warning. In view of the difficulty of determining the effects on income of education, health and other social services there is no rational basis for expecting massive economic inequality of the type which Malaysia exhibits (or which the United States reveals in terms of black–white income differentials) can be eliminated through the use of general policies alone. It would be convenient to think that they could, but there is little evidence to support such a belief. While too little may have been expected of health and family planning, it would appear that Malaysia, in common with other countries, tends to expect too much of formal education.[70]

1. Malaysian bureaucratic usage defines education as that which comes under the Ministry of Education. Similar activities carried out or supervised by other ministries are referred to as training.

2. Useful surveys of pre-war education include D. D. Chelliah (1960); H. R. Cheeseman (1955); T. H. Silcock (1964); and Philip Loh Fook-Seng (1970, 1975).

3. Besides the sources cited in the preceding note, see also G. P. Dartford (1957) and David James Radcliffe (1970).

4. The Malay language can be written in a modified Arabic script (*Jawi*, i.e., 'Javanese') or in Roman characters (*Rumi*). In the twentieth century *Rumi* has become dominant, since that alphabet makes the language more accessible to those who know English or another European language.

5. This well-known credo first appeared in the FMS government's *Annual Report* for 1920 and was widely propagated through its quotation by George Maxwell in a paper given at a meeting of the Royal Colonial Institute in 1927.

6. The Perak Report for 1896 (quoted by Loh, 1975, p. 17) reported with satisfaction that a survey of former pupils in Malay schools showed their occupational distribution to be similar to that of Malays in general.

7. The figure is for assisted Malay-medium primary schools in the area of the future Federation of Malaya. See Ministry of Education (1968, p. 32).

8. Although Cheeseman (1955, p. 35) characterizes the statement in the Barnes Report of 1951 that 'many Malay parents have almost lost their hope in the Malay schools' as 'a bitter blow', Loh (1970, p. 118) cites a 1926 commission report which asserted that many Malays even then regarded Malay-medium education as useless and therefore wanted education in English for their children. This Report, which was ignored, recommended the establishment of Malay secondary schools, coupled with greater use of Malay in the government so as to create more jobs for educated Malay-speakers.

9. The Penang Free School was founded in 1816 by an East India Company chaplain. 'Free' (i.e., open-to-all but tuition-charging) schools were also open in Malacca in 1826 and Singapore in 1834. The first English school outside the Straits Settlements was the Victoria Institution in Kuala Lumpur, which was not founded until 1893.

10. English-medium boys' schools in the Straits Settlements enrolled 7,600 pupils in 1901, only 400 (5 per cent) of whom were Malays. This can be compared with 55 per cent Malays in the corresponding school-age population as revealed in the 1901 population census. See Loh (1975, p. 51).

11. The Malay Administrative Service, founded in 1910, admitted very small numbers of Malays, all aristocrats. Loh (1970, p. 66) says that the number taken averaged three or four a year up to 1927. Small numbers of Malays were also recruited into technician and clerk positions in Railway, the Survey Department and Posts and Telegraphs during the late 1920s (Loh, 1975, p. 86).

12. 'In the context of a then largely transient population characterized demographically by an abnormally small proportion of families and children... and socially and economically set apart as mining or urban communities headed by powerful headmen of the distinct dialect groups through whom control by the British Resident was largely exercised, the British approach to Chinese education [before 1900], not surprisingly, was laissez-faire, regarding it as a Chinese affair best left in Chinese hands. Crucial political and social implications that came to be associated with Chinese education in the Malay States and other overseas Chinese populated areas in Southeast Asia belong to a different period...' (Loh, 1970, pp. 46–7).

13. Cheeseman (1955, p. 37) says that while all Chinese schools registered only one-third ever applied for grants. School inspectors were regarded not as educators but as censors and policemen.

14. See footnote 10, above.

15. 'English education provided direct access to positions in the clerical service; it also provided access, even before World War II, to many types of supplementary training in subordinate positions. Firms trained their better clerks for junior executive positions, especially where a knowledge of local dialects was an advantage. But they normally excluded them—mainly by cultural barriers and by mistrust—from the senior executive positions.' (Silcock, 1964, p. 211.)

16. The Tables only approximate historical enrolment ratios, since they exclude those who died or emigrated after receiving schooling in Malaya and include those who immigrated to Malaya after receiving schooling elsewhere. These distortions are probably of insignificant magnitude, except for the oldest cohorts of Chinese and Indians. For more extensive analysis using the same data, see Hirschman (1972).

17. The experts were William Fenn, an American educator, and Wu Teh-Yao, a United Nations official. Their report was published as Fenn and Wu (1951). For a strong statement of similar views, see Wolfgang Franke (1965).

18. The 1957 census showed the percentage of 15–19-year-olds who were students to be 19 for Malays, 21 for Indians and 33 for Chinese.

19. The lower figure appears in the *First Malaysia Plan 1966–1970* (1965, p. 167). Enrolment in Form I averaged 38 per cent of Standard 6 enrolment in the preceding year, although the existence of remove classes and the possibility of grade repetition make it hard to interpret this statistic.

20. See Ministry of Education (1970, p. 4). By 1972 the estimated ratio had risen to 61 per cent (unpublished Ministry data).

21. See the Majid Report (Malaysia, 1971a, pp. 32–3), which is also the source for the other figures cited in this paragraph.

22. Thirty-one Malay-medium students were admitted in 1965. By 1970–1 the number of undergraduates from the Malay medium had reached 1,050, out of total enrolment of 7,777. See the Majid Report (Malaysia, 1971a, p. 48). This group had difficulties in integrating with the rest of the student population, as a result of factors such as the language gap (English remained the normal means of communication for the other students) and differences in socio-economic status. (These problems are discussed in the Majid Report.) They also contributed to political ferment on the campus, culminating in the major demonstrations of December 1974. These demonstrations were suppressed by government force and led directly to the 1975 amendments of the Universities and University Colleges Act of 1971, which clamped down on political activities on campus.

23. Malaysian universities follow British practice by distinguishing between 'honours' and 'pass' degrees. Honours degrees are further divided between first and second class.

24. Malays were very heavily involved (85 per cent of total enrolment) in non-degree ('diploma' and 'certificate') courses offered by the Agriculture University, Technology University, MARA Institute of Technology, Ungku Omar Polytechnic and University of Malaya. See *Third Malaysia Plan 1976–1980*, 1976, p. 401. They undoubtedly continued to be under-represented in the substantial amount of tertiary education which took place overseas.

25. The Minister in this period, Dato Haji Abdul Rahman Ya'akub, was widely regarded as a Malay 'ultra'. There were rumours at the time that his announcement was a unilateral, pre-emptive move, taken in the confident belief that subsequent retraction would be politically impossible.

26. A 1971–2 controversy over whether the Bahasa Malaysia requirement in the *Sijil Pelajaran Malaysia* was being used to discriminate against non-Malays heightened the fears which prompted non-conforming reactions. It is worth noting that some members of the Malay élite also sent their children abroad for schooling. Michael Wattleworth, in an unpublished paper on language and education in Malaysia, compares such people to middle-class American liberals who believe in school integration but guiltily send their children to suburban schools, where they are expected to get a better education and thus a better start in life. I am indebted to Wattleworth for letting me read his excellent discussion of the language question. For another discussion of the language question and other 'nation-building' issues in Malaysian education, see Chai Hon-Chan (1977).

27. By 1978 the high shares of Malays in the government universities and lack of outlets for Chinese-medium students led to a campaign for the establishment of a private university which would teach in Chinese. The government refused to allow this university

to be set up, preferring (according to recent reports) to increase once more the proportion of Chinese students admitted to existing universities.

28. Fears of a decline in educational quality with the conversion to Malay had some objective basis, particularly as the Ministry was caught unawares by the 1969 decision and was by no means prepared to meet the demand for Malay-speaking teachers and Malay-language texts. Although the phased nature of the conversion should have given the Ministry time to catch up, efforts to prepare teachers in a new language, translate textual materials and take other steps to implement the change have reportedly continued to lag.

29. The recent literature on the economic effects of education in low-income countries is voluminous. Useful critical surveys include Mark Blaug (1972, 1973); Surjit S. Bhalla (1973); and John Simmons (1974).

30. For a penetrating analysis of the policy's internal contradictions, see R. S. Milne (1970).

31. For an interpretation of the twists and turns of educational policy as a series of symbolic threats and reassurances to the Malay and non-Malay communities, veering first one way and then the other as political circumstances warranted, see Stephen A. Douglas (1970).

32. The height of this barrier will of course depend on how efficiently the language conversion is managed.

33. The survey was taken in 1963. 'The ideas of manpower planning prevalent at the time' refers to manpower requirements forecasting (see Herbert S. Parnes, 1962) and the international comparisons approach (see Frederic Harbison and Charles A. Meyers, 1964).

34. According to the Plan (*First Malaysia Plan 1966–1970*, 1965, p. 83), 306 students completed upper secondary technical education and 460 finished the vocational course in 1965. By 1970 these numbers were projected to rise to 4,180 and 8,590 respectively.

35. For those unfamiliar with this type of analysis, it may be noted that rate of return calculations involve a comparison between the additional income a person might be expected to earn over his or her working life as a result of receiving a particular level of education and the cost of that education. 'Private' rates of return take account only of those costs borne by the student's family, principally any fees involved and the income forgone by remaining in school. 'Social' rates of return also allow for costs borne by the government.

36. Measured unemployment rates for 15–19-year-olds rose from 17.3 per cent in 1962 to 21.5 per cent in 1967/8; for 20–24-year-olds, the increase was from 8.8 per cent to 11.0 per cent. For a fuller discussion of labour market trends and their relationship to education, see Donald R. Snodgrass (1976).

37. Theoretically, there are two possible ways of resolving this seeming contradiction. One is that the labour market was not in equilibrium at the time the data were collected. Since the numbers of secondary school leavers entering the labour market in the late 1960s was large compared to the number of such people already in the market, this has probably been the case. The other possibility is that the earnings of at least some of those with secondary and higher education were not competitively determined but were somehow maintained at above-market rates through job rationing. This phenomenon was probably also present, although its importance is hard to assess.

38. Some recent studies carried out for other countries have found rates of return to particular types of education to be very different for persons of different socio-economic origins. See, for example, Jean-Pierre Jallade (1977).

39. Harold Seymour Beebout (1972). For a review of the 'educational production function' technique and findings reached through its application to low-income countries, see Leigh Alexander and John Simmons (1975).

40. Beebout (1972, p. 173) comments that the relationship between teacher qualifications and MCE results is genuinely causal and not just associative, because there is a low correlation between LCE scores and teacher qualifications.

41. Although the mean incoming test score was the same (76 out of 100) for students in both language streams, the outgoing test score was lower for the Malay stream (58 versus 67).

42. Beebout costed potential system improvements and then worked out their cost-effectiveness. He found teacher-training investments to reduce the percentage of untrained teachers to be highly cost-effective. Expenditures to raise the percentage of graduate teachers in schools in which that percentage was below average were also found to be

cost-effective, as were outlays to reduce class size and double sessions in the Malay medium. The provision of boarding schools was found to be a bad investment in these terms.

43. According to the *Second Malaysia Plan 1971–1975* (1971, p. 231), $73 million was spent developing MARA's education and training programmes in 1966–70. This constituted 22 per cent of total public development expenditure for education and training during the period. In 1971–5 considerably larger amounts and percentages ($190 million, 28 per cent of the total) were recorded; see *Third Malaysia Plan 1976–1980* (1976, p. 405).

44. Dore (1975). The reference is of course to Ivan Illych and his proposals for 'deschooling society'.

45. Dore's ideas on how it might be done are summarized in the following passage:

'Let everyone have, as soon as it can be afforded, nine to ten years of general education—to learn basic literacy and numeracy, to learn those things about his nation's history and working of its institutions that all citizens need to know and the elementary canons of ethics and of aesthetic enjoyment that all human beings need to know.

Get selection for first jobs by and large over with by 16 or 17, not only for manual jobs, but also for the professional occupations which now recruit graduates. Civil service administrators would start off as clerks and executive officers, teachers as pupil teachers, future engineers as craftsmen and trainee technicians, doctors as medical assistants, and those in the ability ranges (in some developing countries, the less able sixty or even seventy per cent) whom the economy gives no real alternative but to be farmers and fishermen would discover the fact before they invested several years of heartache in trying to escape that fate.' (Dore, 1975, p. 62.)

The selection required in such a system could be made by some combination of aptitude testing and lotteries (Dore, 1975, pp. 63–6).

46. For a summary of current thinking about health and development, see World Bank (1975).

47. In 1904 the Medical Adviser to the Colonial Office declared that,

'Apart from humanitarian considerations, the Colonial Office had come to recognize the fact that a main difficulty in the successful working of our tropical colonies lay in the health factor, that deaths, invalidings and inefficiency from local diseases burdened the revenues, interfered with the continuity of administration, repressed the energy of the population and diverted funds which otherwise might have been invested profitably in remunerative public works.'

See Chai Hon-Chan (1964, p. 210). Pages 197–225 of Chai's book provide a good account of the development of health services and medical research in the 1896–1909 period.

48. Out of a group of 87 Chinese tin miners who opened up the Kuala Lumpur area in 1857, 59 died (presumably of malaria) within a month of their arrival (Gullick, 1956, p. 14). This lugubrious experience was repeated many times in a period in which vast areas of jungle were being cleared and nothing was known about the epidemiology of the disease.

49. Burgess and Laidin, 1950, pp. 11–12, 59:

'The whole question of the occurrence of [kwashiorkor] in Malaya requires further investigation. That it occurs, there can be little doubt, but it would appear to be a less pronounced clinical entity than that described in Africa and elsewhere.... There may be considerable irreversible damage resulting from an attack of the disease and this may be an important factor in the production of the apathy and general low standard of efficiency to be found in certain communities living at a low level.... [The traditional dietary habits and beliefs cited above] are all of importance not only from the health aspect but also from the economic point of view. The lowered state of health results in apathy and low productivity with consequent lower income and a vicious cycle is set up.'

50. I have been unable to locate a copy of this study.

51. For a good description of the current state of nutrition in Peninsular Malaysia, see Y. H. Chong (1976).

52. Saw Swee Hock (1964) estimated that under-registration of births declined from about 13 per cent in 1947 to 8 per cent in 1957, while Cho Lee Jay (1969) estimated that by the following decade birth registration had become virtually complete. Finally, Charles Hirschman (1971) investigated the under-registration of deaths, concluding that it was in the range of 5 to 15 per cent.

53. Marital fertility fell first among Chinese and Indians, and subsequently among Malays. There was also a rise in the average age of first marriage for women. See Saw Swee

Hock (1966); Cho Lee Jay, James A. Palmore and Lyle Saunders (1968); and Palmore, Ramesh Chander and Dorothy Z. Fernandez (1975).

54. The data, all derived from Table 9.8, on which this and other statements in this paragraph are based, are as follows:

	Malay/Chinese ratio		*Indian/Chinese ratio*	
	CDR	*IDR*	*CDR*	*IDR*
1948–50	1.46	1.60	1.03	1.39
1957–9	1.53	2.04	1.16	1.54
1966–8	1.24	1.77	1.32	1.73
1972–4	1.06	1.56	1.28	1.63
1975–6	1.08	1.57	1.41	1.65

	Average annual improvement (%)					
	Malays		*Chinese*		*Indians*	
	CDR	*IDR*	*CDR*	*IDR*	*CDR*	*IDR*
1948–50 to 1957–9	4	2	4	5	3	3
1957–9 to 1975–6	10	12	5	9	3	8

55. This disadvantage is understated by the crude death rate because the Chinese population contains much larger percentages of older people than do the Malay and Indian populations. The infant and toddler death rates, on the other hand, overstate the differences in overall mortality, since age-specific death rates for Malays and Indians are much closer to those of the Chinese after the age of ten than before. For comprehensive data for 1966, see Cho Lee Jay (1969a). For a detailed analysis of mortality trends and patterns among Malays, see Zainal Aznam Yusof and Khairuddin Yusof (1974).

56. Based on the official vital statistics for 1967 and 1974 (Department of Statistics, n.d., 1976). An earlier analysis of interstate mortality differences by Saw Swee Hock (1965) noted that crude death rates and infant mortality per state were correlated with literacy; with the ratios of doctors, nurses and hospital beds to population; and with urbanization. Saw did not disaggregate by ethnic group, so he missed the fact that the interstate variations he studied involved primarily Malays, affecting Chinese and Indians to a much smaller extent.

57. While $40 million was provided for rural health services a sum of $74 million was allocated to improve existing hospitals and build new ones in Kuala Lumpur, Seremban and Klang (*Second Five-Year Plan 1961–1965*, 1961, p. 52).

58. The achievement was reported to be 31 main health centres, 132 sub-centres and 645 midwives clinics (cf. preceding paragraph). See *First Malaysia Plan 1966–1970* (1965, p. 174).

59. Between 1958 and 1970 the number of registered doctors increased by 156 per cent, nurses by 231 per cent and assistant nurses by 220 per cent. For an interesting study of Malay nurses, see Stuart W. Gardner (1975, pp. 193–202).

60. Out of 80 developing countries listed by the World Bank (1975, pp. 78–9), Malaysia ranks 30th in physicians per 10,000 of population and 19th in hospital beds; however, her ranking with respect to non-physician primary health workers is 6th. (For comparison, Malaysia ranks 14th among these 80 countries in GNP per capita.) Although there has continued to be official concern about the shortage of doctors, leading to contract hiring of doctors from abroad, these statistics can be regarded as generally satisfactory. Many of the countries with which Malaysia is being compared here have probably over-invested in training physicians, relative to other, much less costly, health workers.

61. The following data on sanitary conditions by level of urbanization were revealed by the 1970 census:

	Source of water supply (%)			
	Piped	*Wells/pumps*	*Rivers*	*Other*
Metropolitan	90	9	0	1
Large urban	71	26	1	1
Small urban	62	35	2	2
Rural	32	54	8	5

	Toilet facilities (%)			
	Metropolitan	*Large urban*	*Small urban*	*Rural*
Adequate	95	85	83	60
Flush	52	29	16	10
Bucket	35	38	46	5
Pit	8	18	21	44
Inadequate	5	15	17	30
Over rivers	3	4	6	10
None	2	11	10	20

Source: R. Chander (1973, pp. 76–7).

62. Palmore, Chander and Fernandez (1975, pp. 74–6) give the following statistics for 1970:

	Gross reproduction rate	*Total fertility rate*
Malays	2.56	5,150
Chinese	2.34	4,745
Indians	2.42	4,920

63. The literature is vast, but the interested reader might start with Dudley Kirk (1971) and Michael S. Teitelbaum (1975).

64. According to the NFPB's *Annual Report* for 1972, new acceptors numbered 75,000 in 1968 (the first full year of operation); 71,000 in 1969; 56,000 in 1970; 55,000 in 1971; and 56,000 in 1972. Together with some 20,000 1967 acceptors, this makes a total of 333,000. The target of 600,000 acceptors by 1975, set early in the programme's life, was reduced to 535,000 in 1973 but actual acceptors by 1975 (including those enrolled by private programmes) totalled only 433,000 (*Third Malaysia Plan 1976–1980* (1976, p. 412). A longer-term and more fundamental target is to reduce the rate of natural increase to 2 per cent by 1985; whether this is attained is of course only partially a question of the success or failure of the official family planning programme.

65. Early acceptors tended to be urban, non-Malay and somewhat better educated than the average. However, all these biases were reduced in time. In 1971, according to unpublished NFPB statistics, Malays for the first time constituted a majority of new acceptors. While the greater representativeness of the later acceptors is heartening, it must be remembered that at the time the number of new acceptors per year was falling (instead of rising, as targeted).

66. Between 1966–7 and 1970 the number of children desired by rural women dropped fairly sharply for all age groups, according to surveys (Palmore, Chander and Fernandez, 1975, p. 72). Contraceptive use rose several-fold but still involved only a small proportion of rural women (peak use was found to be in the 25–34-year age range, where 16 per cent of women were current users and 27 per cent had used contraception at some time).

67. Under the EPF, employees make contributions which are matched by their employers. The money goes into a fund, which earns interest. At retirement the entire fund, with accumulated interest, is paid to the member as a lump sum.

68. Bank Negara Malaysia (1976, p. 84). Contributors' balances had reached $4.1 billion by this time, 96 per cent of which sum was invested in government securities.

69. Ungku Abdul Aziz (1969). Ungku Aziz further elaborated these proposals at the time the New Economic Policy was being formulated in 1970–1.

70. For an analysis of the distorting effects of Malay sponsorship in higher education which brings out the limitations of educational policy as a tool for reducing economic inequality related to ethnicity, see Wang, Chan Bee-Lan (1977).

10 Conclusions

> The NEP was political in its origins; its launching was prompted by desire to avoid a repetition of the political events of May 1969. . . . The implementation of the NEP, as determined by the government, is heavy with political implications. The unintended consequences of its implementation are less easy to discern, but are equally certain to affect the future shape of politics in Malaysia.
>
> Milne, 1976, p. 26

THREE basic tasks remain to be performed in this concluding chapter. The simplest of these is to pick up earlier threads of the historical narrative to obtain a brief, unified account of important changes during the early years of the NEP period. The second and hardest job is to assess, on the basis of the limited experience so far and the analysis of underlying forces which has been undertaken, the feasibility of the NEP in both economic and political terms. The final task is to spell out the lessons for other developing countries of the Malaysian experience.

THE EARLY NEP PERIOD

Political developments following the restoration of Parliamentary government and publication of the SMP in early 1971 have seen the Alliance pattern re-established, but with significant changes compared to earlier times. Contrary to predictions that a Malay dictatorship would be set up, non-Malay participation in government resumed, although the power of UMNO within the Alliance had clearly been enhanced. Because of the preponderance of central government power under the Constitution—and because of the availability of the ultimate power, so recently exercised, to amend or suspend the Constitution—opposition state governments in Penang and Kelantan (as well as former opposition members of the coalition government in Sarawak) were motivated to come to terms with the centre. This weakened and split the opposition, leading in time to the formation of a broader alliance, first a 'National Government' and then a 'National Front' (*Barisan Nasional*), which contested the 1974 elections. The National Front brought together, besides the original three Alliance parties, Parti Islam (the former PMIP), the Gerakan, the PPP, the Sabah Alliance and the Sarawak coalition. Somehow settling its seat-allocation problems (between Malays and non-Malays, but also between UMNO and Parti Islam, on the one hand, and among the MCA, MIC, Gerakan and PPP, on the other), it swept through the 1974 elections, taking 135 of the 154 seats in the federal parliament and controlling all 13 state governments (Pillay, 1975).

Since the 1974 elections two major political problems have been evident: the extent of Chinese (and Indian) participation in political decision-making and leadership succession within UMNO and the Malay community generally.

With the reconciliation (which later proved to be temporary) of UMNO–Parti Islam differences, the Barisan Nasional achieved a clean sweep of Malay-dominated constituencies in 1974 in the face of nominal left-wing opposition. The MCA and MIC also did considerably better than they had in 1969 but lost power in the distribution of portfolios which followed the election. The critical event was the passing of the Finance portfolio into Malay hands following the retirement of Tun Tan Siew Sin. The Gerakan and PPP did less well as components of the Barisan Nasional than they had as foci of anti-government discontent in 1969. Opposition voting in Peninsular Malaysia now centred on the DAP. This pattern became accentuated in the elections of July 1978, when the Barisan Nasional further increased its Parliamentary majority, Parti Islam (which had left the Barisan in 1977) lost ground and the DAP emerged with increased strength as the sole non-Malay focused opposition party in Peninsular Malaysia. Clearly this voting pattern reduces the chance of constructive Chinese influence on high-level policies and further enhances the dominance of UMNO. Although UMNO may derive some enjoyment from being able to deal with several weak Chinese parties, it could well be argued that in the long run Malay as well as Chinese interests are probably furthered by meaningful Chinese participation in the councils of state.

The UMNO leadership issue has been especially prominent since the unexpected death of Tun Abdul Razak in January 1976 and his succession by former Deputy Prime Minister Datuk Hussein Onn. Datuk Hussein's administration has so far avoided chauvinism, following Tun Razak's example of simultaneous support for Malay economic advancement and considerable liberalism toward non-Malay interests. Indeed, the Third Malaysia Plan, published a few months after Tun Razak's death, fairly explicitly increased the emphasis on the race-blind poverty alleviation aspects of the New Economic Policy. Although challenged and regarded as shaky at times, Datuk Hussein has gradually strengthened his position. In July 1978 he received a renewed mandate from the electorate, and in the following month he regularized his position as head of UMNO.

The last two general elections, in 1974 and 1978, were both held before the latest date permitted by the Constitution,[1] reportedly to take advantage of favourable economic conditions. In general, the Malaysian economy has performed well in the 1970s. The worldwide surge of inflation in 1972–4 hurt Malaysia by raising the prices of imports (most spectacularly oil, of course) and bringing about significant internal price increases for the first time in memory.[2] But these difficulties were more than offset by sharp increases in export prices. Rubber prices more than doubled from early 1972 to late 1973, while palm oil and timber prices also climbed sharply. Tin prices moved more slowly, but eventually joined the surge as well. The subsequent drop in rubber prices caused discontent in early 1974, as noted in Chapter 7, but prices have since recovered and the portents for commodity prices (especially natural rubber, which competes with oil-based synthetics) appear to be more favourable in the post-oil embargo world than they had been for some time previously.

An important indicator of how Chinese and foreign business groups are reacting to government economic policies has always been the performance of private investment. When all is well, a surge in export earnings is followed, with a lag of about one year, by an upswing in private investment. This occurred in 1973–4, when private fixed investment climbed sharply in response to growing export receipts. Thereafter, there were two years of stagnation while export earnings declined in 1975 and then began to grow rapidly once more in 1976. The investment response to this most recent export surge has been a matter of debate. The government's estimates for 1977 (Ministry of Finance, 1978, p. vi) show a 17 per cent increase in private fixed investment but even this strong one-year growth leaves private investment below the 1974 level, even in nominal terms. Whether the ambitious 16.7 per cent average annual rate (in real terms) established in the *Third Malaysia Plan 1976–1980* (1976, p. 116) can be attained remains subject to doubt. There is little doubt that both foreign and ethnic Chinese investors have had their fears aroused by the passage of the Petroleum Development Act and Industrial Coordination Act, as discussed in Chapter 8, above.[3] The question is how much effect these fears will have on their investment behaviour and on future economic growth.

Notwithstanding such difficulties Malaysian economic growth since 1970 has been considerably more rapid than in the preceding decade. By official estimation, national income per capita in current prices more than doubled in 1970–7, rising from $1,093 to $2,297 (Ministry of Finance, 1977, 1978). Deflating by the consumer price index, this works out to a rise of 37.8 per cent in real terms, or 4.7 per cent a year on average over the period. Taking into account effective revaluations of the *ringgit vis-à-vis* the US dollar, Malaysia's GNP per capita had risen to the neighbourhood of US$830 by 1976 (World Bank, 1978, p. 16). Post-1970 economic growth has thus greatly exceeded Malaysian economic growth in the 1960s.

The obvious question raised by this strong performance in terms of average income measures is what trends in the various forms of inequality and poverty have accompanied the faster overall growth. The inadequacy of published data, which makes this question hard to answer, was noted in Chapter 4. One's overall impression, however, is that in some areas progress has been rapid, while in others it has been slow or even non-existent.

The shift of priority attention from rural development to urban, non-agricultural concerns involved in the NEP could have brought about further worsening for the income distribution. As noted in Chapter 4, direct sample survey evidence exists but has not been released to the public and is said to be mutually contradictory. Partial indications suggest some further rise in inequality since 1970.

On the other hand (see Chapter 4), ethnic imbalances in ownership and control have clearly been reduced significantly since 1970. Although it is logical to suppose that economic growth could have been impeded, this is hard to prove statistically. Value added in manufacturing, perhaps the sector in which 'restructuring' has been pushed most vigorously, grew at 14.8 per cent a year in 1970–7 in constant prices—considerably faster than its growth in the pre-NEP period.

As seen in Chapter 4, official estimates indicate that the number and percentage of poor households in Peninsular Malaysia fell between 1970 and 1978. Further declines to 768,300 poor households and 33.8 per cent of the total are projected for 1980. The fate of particular poverty groups will depend both on government programmes and on other factors affecting their income-earning capacities. Thus, both differential programme possibilities and exogenous factors such as high rubber prices, on the one hand, and the drought currently afflicting northern padi-growing areas, on the other, may be responsible for the fact that the TMP projects a much sharper decline in poverty among rubber smallholders in 1975–80 than among padi farmers.

It can be seen that while areas of uncertainty exist development under the NEP compares favourably to development before the NEP by virtually any criteria. This finding would hardly be anticipated if one's expectations were based on press reports which have stressed difficulties and dissent associated with the NEP.

TABLE 10.1

COMPARISON OF OUTLINE PERSPECTIVE PLAN TARGETS AND OUTCOMES FOR 1975

Measure	*Target*	*Outcome*
Gross Domestic Product in 1970 prices	$14,509 million	$15,315 million
Manufacturing value added as per cent of GDP	18.0	14.3
Manufacturing employment as per cent of total	12.2	10.1
Total share capital (Peninsular Malaysia)	$ 8,663 million	$ 9,890.1 million
Malay share capital (Peninsular Malaysia)	$ 779.7 million	$768.1 million
Malay share capital as per cent of total	9.0	7.8

Sources: *Mid-Term Review of the Second Malaysia Plan 1971–1975* (1973, pp. 68, 70, 82, 84); *Third Malaysia Plan 1976–1980* (1976, pp. 12, 86, 140).

It is true that a less favourable verdict is reached if one evaluates progress under the NEP relative to the ambitious goals set in the Outline Perspective Plan. The original version of this Plan, published in the *Mid-Term Review of the Second Malaysia Plan 1971–1975* (1973, pp. 61–94) specified interim (i.e., 1975, 1980 and 1985) targets for only a few measures, in other cases defining only the ultimate target for 1990.[4] From the limited data available one can derive the comparisons shown in Table 10.1. These show that aggregate output growth in 1970–5 exceeded the target, despite slower structural change than projected. (As in the past, Malaysia had been helped by external trends more favourable than the planners' assumptions.) Total share capital had grown more rapidly than projected and holdings by Malays and Malay interests, despite rapid growth from a small base, had fallen slightly short of the ambitious targets specified. Interim targets for changes in employment structure were not specified in the original version of the Outline Perspective Plan, but this has been one of the areas of most rapid change.

Relative to interim NEP targets, therefore, development performance since 1970 could best be described as mixed. Change has been in the prescribed direction and of substantial magnitude, but not always up to the quantitative targets defined.

ECONOMIC FEASIBILITY OF THE NEP

The second of the three questions which this concluding chapter takes up is the feasibility of the NEP. This section discusses economic feasibility, while the following one reviews important political issues which will influence what actually happens between now and 1990.

The feasibility of the NEP has been discussed at length in the annual Malaysian Economic Congresses sponsored by the Malaysian Economic Association. Most of the discussion has concerned the logical consistency of the plan frame. One of the government technicians most deeply involved in the construction of that plan frame has defended it as both consistent and feasible (C. L. Robless, 1975), but academic critics (Basil Moore, 1975; R. Thillainathan, 1970, 1974, 1976) have pointed to alleged inconsistencies and a journalist (Philip Bowring, 1978) has recently published an account of current implementation difficulties which gives the impression that the 1990 targets are becoming increasingly unlikely to be reached as time goes by.

In relation to the employment balance target, academic critics have shown that attaining an ethnically balanced employment structure in a particular industry or occupational group becomes more difficult (1) the less rapidly total employment in the industry or occupational group is growing, (2) the smaller is the initial representation of the under-represented ethnic group and (3) the shorter is the time allowed for the change to take place. The issue is whether the specified targets can be reached without depriving any current job holders of their positions. Although hypothetical examples can be developed in which attainment of ethnic balance subject to this constraint becomes impossible, adoption of the twenty-year time perspection actually taken in the NEP permits enough natural labour force attrition to make the targets fairly comfortably attainable. Of course, to the extent that interim targets (for 1975, 1980, etc.) are not fully attained, then the magnitude of the task to be accomplished in the remainder of the period will be increased, conceivably even to the point of unattainability. From the perspective of the present, however, the conclusion must be that attainment of the employment balance targets by 1990 is not infeasible in the mathematical sense.

More significant questions of consistency and feasibility arise in a broader context. The interaction between the rate of economic growth and the supply of qualified Malay manpower has been identified as a possible source of difficulty by Moore (1975). If the number of qualified Malays is not adequate to attain the targets specified for higher-level positions, he points out, it will come down to a choice among (1) leaving the slots vacant, (2) filling them with under-qualified Malays or (3) hiring non-Malays instead. The first two responses would reduce the rate of economic growth through the operation of a manpower constraint, setting in train a negative feedback mechanism through slower growth of *total* employment, while the third alternative would mean abandoning the plan. As Moore has specified the problem, implicitly assuming that academic qualifications are what really counts for productivity purposes, this does not appear to be a very serious problem. As Chapter 9 has noted, the share of Malay enrolment in domestic institutions of higher education has risen very rapidly during the 1970s. In a broader sense, however, the problem could be important: to the extent that productivity in fact depends not on formal education but on learning on the job or in other out-of-school settings, the time available may not be adequate. Since so little is known about what really makes people more productive, it is very hard to say whether this is actually the case.

One major feasibility problem in relation to employment balance has not been highlighted by the critics. For higher Malay employment shares in the high income, high-skill industries and occupational groups to be attained, it is logically necessary for the shares of Chinese and Indian employment in some of the lower-income, less-skilled segments of the economy to register compensatory increases.[5] The Outline Perspective Plan (*Mid-Term Review of the Second Malaysia Plan 1971–1975*, 1973, p. 79) in fact specifies that the Chinese employment share should rise in three industries (agriculture, utilities and services) between 1970 and 1990, while the Indian share is projected to increase in no fewer than five of the eight major industries, one of which, again, is agriculture.

These compensating movements of Chinese and Indian labour seem exceedingly unlikely to occur, at least in the absence of highly coercive policy measures. Having made the significant advances up the socio-economic ladder documented in Chapters 2 and 4, the Chinese are unlikely to return voluntarily to agricultural or low-skill service occupations. Nor is there any evident mechanism whereby Indian employment could be increased significantly in all industries other than utilities, transport and services.[6] For this reason, rather than any of the reasons discussed earlier, it seems probable that the employment structure in 1990 will differ significantly, in one way or another, from that postulated in the Outline Perspective Plan. Either the absolute and relative targets for Malay employment will not be met in all cases, or, if they are, it will be at the cost of higher unemployment rates for Chinese and Indians than for Malays (this would be contrary to the Plan's assumptions but in line with experience in 1970–5) and/or emigration of non-Malays so as to increase the Malay share in the labour force.

Consistency and feasibility problems associated with the 30 per cent Malay ownership and control target have already been discussed in Chapter 7. The utter impossibility of individual Malays amassing enough wealth to purchase a 30 per cent share of corporate sector by 1990 has been noted by many commentators. Recognition of the need for some form of trusteeship if the 30 per cent target is to be achieved brings the question of the efficiency of public sector enterprise to the fore. Unless a reasonably high standard of performance can be achieved by these enterprises, the dilemma of whether to let the ownership share target slip or to insist on it and risk a much lower rate of output growth, which would endanger nearly all the targets of the NEP, will very quickly arise. The limited experience and still more limited information on the performance of public enterprise reviewed in Chapter 7 give little basis for guessing how soon this dilemma is likely to arise, but the possibility that it could come up in the next few years is too obvious to be ignored.

This completes the discussion of the economic feasibility of the New Economic Policy. I conclude that the plan frame published by the government contains no obvious logical or mathematical inconsistencies, so the NEP is in this sense feasible. There are nevertheless serious economic questions, just discussed, relating to the plausibility of building up a public enterprise sector large enough and efficient enough to permit the simultaneous achievement of the Plan's growth target and its Malay ownership and control target.

Other factors will, of course, influence Malaysia's economic future. No assessment has been made here of exogenous influences on economic growth. However, the Outline Perspective Plan's projected 1970–1990 real growth rate of 7.8 per cent does not seem notionally to be too far out of line with past experience, considering the wealth of still unexploited growth opportunities and assuming a relatively favourable world economic environment.[7] Serious questions can be raised, however, about the political economy of the NEP.

POLITICS OF THE NEP

The quotation at the head of this chapter pointed up the fundamentally political nature of the NEP. As a product of Malaysia's complex blend of ethnic- and class-based politics, the NEP's outcome will be heavily influenced by political developments in the country between now and 1990. Any projection therefore depends in part on analysis of how the political system works in relation to economic policy.[8]

The most prominent feature of Malaysian politics is its emphasis on expressing the interests of ethnic groups. Political scientists used to think that the political importance of ethnicity would decline in time as modernization gave people new roles which would gradually become more important to them than their communal identification. Clifford Geertz (1963) termed this process the 'integrative revolution'. But recent thinking has tended to refute this view. Based on studies of politics in low-income countries, as well as in richer countries (Glazer and Moynihan, 1970), the new consensus stresses the persistence of ethnicity. In fact, it has been argued (Melson and Wolpe, 1970), the development process is more likely to heighten than to dispel communal self-identification and competition. As communal groups develop at different rates and along different lines, new social cleavages are created (e.g., in occupational pattern or educational achievement), coinciding with and thus reinforcing the older distinctions which formed the original basis of communalism.

Melson and Wolpe do not contend that the boundary lines of communalism are immutable. On the contrary, they posit a process of 'communal transformation', in which (1) communal groups expand to include other groups with whom some basis for identification exists and which can serve as useful allies, (2) increased internal differentiation of communal groups along socio-economic and ideological lines take place, and (3) traditional group ties and perspectives are 'deparochialized' (i.e., focused on new, urban and national, horizons). The net result is a multiplication of social identities in which communalism is modified but not supplanted—and very possibly is even strengthened. Something like this has clearly been happening in Malaysia.

Fascination with communal groups and the interactions among them has often led political scientists to give too little attention to internal structure and group leadership. Although ethnic groups such as the Malays, Chinese and Indians of Malaysia have considerable internal coherence, especially if a common external threat is present, they are not socially or politically homogeneous. Groups must have leaders, and if the group is to compete effectively with other groups that leadership must be competent. In most newly independent countries political leadership has first been assumed by individuals who occupied the top rungs of the social ladder before Independence and served as leaders in dealings with the colonial régime. If for some reason this inherited leadership falters, leadership challenges are likely. In Malaysia, the succession of new generations to élite positions has generally been carefully managed. There has been change but few successful leadership challenges.

Leaders in a system of ethnic politics must relate simultaneously to the other communal groups and to their own constituents. They must in effect balance one of these considerations against the other. If under pressure from constituents, they will act vigorously to promote the interests of the group *vis-a-vis* other groups (or at a minimum to seem to be doing so) and publicize their devotion to the communal good among the mass membership of the community. If however the leaders are relatively secure in their positions, then the pressure to further mass communal interests is reduced and the opportunity to further their own self-interest expanded. In these circumstances the leadership of the dominant community may proceed more actively to promote its own narrower interests, perhaps behind a smokescreen of propaganda designed to convince its mass following that it is its interests which are really being advanced. Another possibility in this situation is that the leadership élites of some or all of the communal groups will collude to further their mutual interests and deceive all their constituencies simultaneously. It is this situation which opens up the possibility of class-oriented politics directed toward overturning élites in general, although a more probable outcome is independent leadership struggles within the various ethnic groups.

Those familiar with Malaysian politics can easily particularize aspects of this general description. The pre-1969 Alliance Party was a collaboration of communal élites, who were repeatedly challenged with the charge that class interests were being served better than community interests. After May 1969 Tengku Abdul Rahman's leadership of UMNO was aggressively attacked by a group of 'Young Turks'. Characteristically, the attack was repelled and the rebels cast out of the party. In time, however, the Tengku retired, the rebels were readmitted to the fold and eventually came to occupy positions of respect and authority. Another successful leadership transition had been made.

Similarly, the Barisan Nasional represents an effort to recast the pre-1969 system of inter-communal coalition politics through élite co-operation into a form which will be viable in the new political environment. This effort, too, has been generally successful. But the political environment *has* changed, and no precise recreation of the pre-1969 Alliance is possible. Certainly the most important change is that increasing education, improved communication and other social changes have led to much greater articulation of broader group interests than existed a decade ago. The middle class—i.e., those just below élite status—have increased enormously in numbers, as shown in Chapter 4, and in ability to express themselves and press the government to act in their favour. It appears to have been this kind of change within the Malay community which forced the more aggressive use of Malay political power after 1970 to further the economic interests of Malays, especially middle-class Malays or those with ambitions to be middle-class.

Out of this political perspective comes a question which will have an important bearing on the outcome of the NEP: in whose interests, basically, will economic policy be made in the years to come? At some risk of over-simplification, three main possibilities can be specified:

1. economic policy will be used mainly to promote the interests of the Malay community as a whole;
2. it will be used primarily to promote the interests of the Malay élite and middle class;

3. it will be used to promote the interests of the élites of all ethnic groups.

The first of these three alternatives would be regarded as the most favourable outcome by many. Since most of the poor are Malay it would be close to an anti-poverty strategy, deviating from a strict anti-poverty approach only to the extent that the government failed to pay as much attention to the needs of poor Chinese and Indians as it did to those of poor Malays. If it is impelled by this kind of political motivation, the NEP could yet disprove the assertions of many social theorists that a non-revolutionary government cannot and will not significantly redistribute income and wealth.

The second alternative is the nightmare scenario of many non-Malays and some outside observers. What is there, they ask, to prevent the Malay élite from turning the NEP into an exercise in self-enrichment, in which government power is used to expropriate wealth, power and opportunities from the non-Malays and foreigners? And what is there to force the élite to share such gains with the Malay masses? If this interpretation is correct, the NEP will not turn out to be a redistribution programme at all, except in the sense that it involves redistribution from one élite to another.

The third alternative is a variant which might appeal to Marxists and others who regard class as the fundamental basis for social and political conflict and ethnicity as a false issue created by colonialism. This view would predict that a new system of élite collaboration will be worked out, no doubt with ethnic group shares altered from their pre-1969 sizes, and the system will continue to work for the benefit of the élites and middle class. Any broader redistribution or genuine anti-poverty drive would be regarded as impossible in the absence of social revolution by those holding this view.

Which of these scenarios is most likely to obtain during the period of the NEP? My own belief is that while each scenario has an element of truth in it the 'nightmare scenario' is not likely to prevail and that the NEP is likely in practice to contain many of the liberal elements suggested by scenario one. This belief is based on the following two propositions:

1. Ethnicity will continue to be the main basis for politics; as in the past, Malay élites will have to appeal for support to their constituents; also as in the past, they will do this in large part by promoting the constituents' economic interests.

2. A degree of liberality will continue to be extended to Chinese and Indian Malaysians, as well as to international business; this is necessary because the economic contributions of these groups are essential if the 'redistribution with growth' strategy is to be implemented successfully.[9]

What the foregoing amounts to is a judgement that, despite the realignment and redistribution of power which it has experienced, the Malaysian political system is still characterized by pragmatism. This implies that the New Economic Policy was necessary to set the nation on a new course but that the actual navigation of that course will be adjusted as necessary to avoid rocks and shoals encountered along the way.

This is not to say that things will be as they were. Malaysian politics have changed in response to changing circumstances, becoming more nationalistic, both in the sense of more aggressively pro-Malaysian and in the sense of being more aggressively pro-Malay. Harry G. Johnson (1965) noted that economic nationalism (1) fosters activities selected for their symbolic value in terms of 'national identity'; (2) promotes activities offering prestigious jobs for the middle class and/or educated; (3) favours extensive use of public enterprise, largely for the purpose of controlling jobs; (4) tends to emphasize the production of psychic income in the form of nationalistic satisfaction, at the cost of material income; and (5) tends to redistribute material income from the lower class toward the middle class, particularly the educated middle class. In conclusion, Johnson commented that:

> Even though nationalism may involve a substantial redistribution of real income toward the middle class at the expense of the mass population, this redistribution may perform a necessary function in the early stages of forming a nation, in the sense that the existence of a middle class may be a prerequisite of a stable society and democratic government. In other words, an investment in the creation of a middle class, financed by resources extracted from the mass of the population by nationalistic policies, may be the essential preliminary to the construction of a viable national state . . .
>
> (Johnson, 1965, p. 185).

In my view, Malaysia reflects some elements of Johnson's 'theoretical model of economic nationalism', but it differs from it in the sense that the prevailing pattern of ethnic politics is likely to provide somewhat fewer benefits for the multi-ethnic class élite that Johnson suggests and somewhat more benefits for the low-income Malay masses. Obviously, the political ethos of Malaysia is very different from that of a revolutionary state, but I believe that the principal lesson of the Malaysian experience is that significant redistribution can be achieved through the operations of practical ethnic politics.

LESSONS FOR OTHER DEVELOPING COUNTRIES

The major lesson of the Malaysian case has just been enunciated. Redistribution of income, wealth, power and opportunity does not happen unless there is political motivation to bring it about. Although social revolution which overturns the class structure is rightly stressed as a potential source of such motivation, the operation of ethnic politics on behalf of a politically dominant but economically weak community provides an important (and neglected) alternative source. Although the Malaysian government has not been willing to employ all the tools of redistributive policy which a revolutionary government would bring to bear—for example, it has not seriously tackled the question of land reform—it has been able to develop programmes which have brought about certain forms of redistribution and, under the New Economic Policy, to launch still more ambitious redistributive programmes. In closing, I will recapitulate my judgements of how effective the various parts of the policy package have been, and go on to comment on what other developing countries could learn from the Malaysian case.

Before 1970, the government devoted substantial resources to the rural sector and left the urban, industrial economy mainly to the private sector. Even though the size distribution of income worsened in this period as a dualistic pattern of development worked itself out, there were significant redistributive achievements. The drainage and irrigation, land development and padi price support programmes propped up rural incomes, which were subject to unfavourable price and demographic influences and would have dropped further if these programmes had not been undertaken. Of course, more could have been done, notably to improve the diffusion of new tree crop technologies to smallholders. Very great advances were made in improving the coverage of social service distribution networks, thus raising the level of material welfare. What doomed the pre-1970 system was not that it was a failure in its redistributive efforts but that social change overtook it, forcing new priorities, and thus a new development strategy, on the government.

The main lesson of the pre-1970 experience is that a government which avoids urban bias (Michael Lipton, 1977) and re-allocates resources to the rural sector, *and which has significant amounts of resources to re-allocate and a relatively promising environment in which to spend them*, can do a lot to improve the distribution of welfare. Public services are much easier to affect than earned incomes, particularly if existing asset holdings are not to be significantly realigned. To make this strategy work, the government must have a relatively productive sector from which to extract a surplus—in Malaysia it was export agriculture and mining—and it must find ways for the public sector to spend relatively effectively. Ironically, if it succeeds in all this, it will probably find that eventually its generally successful strategy is rejected by the growing, urban-oriented middle class.

Malaysia's post-1970 strategy has both greater potentials and greater dangers than the pre-1970 strategy. While retaining the moderate adherence to 'redistribution with growth' (see Hollis Chenery *et al.*, 1974), it radically attacks the traditional division of the economy into separate ethnic spheres on behalf of the growing, ambitious Malay middle class. What the outcome will be is a matter of intense interest on which no one can pronounce authoritatively. It will depend on factors such as the degree of political competition which survives in Malaysia, the speed with which productive Malay human resources can be developed and the efficiency of the large public enterprise sector which is rapidly being created. Whatever happens, Malaysia and its New Economic Policy can certainly be seen as an example of the 'new meaning of development'—stressing greater national self-reliance and cultural awareness as well as redistribution of income, wealth and power—which is now beginning to gain international recognition (Dudley Seers, 1977).

1. The Constitution specifies five years as the maximum interval between elections. Since the Constitution was suspended from May 1969 to February 1971, the August 1974 election could have been postponed until February 1975. By the same token, the next election could have been called for any time up to August 1979.

2. The official consumer price index measured rises of 10.5 per cent in 1973 and 17.4 per cent in 1974, after which the rate of inflation fell back to levels (2–6 per cent) only slightly higher than had been traditional before the price level readjustment. See Ministry of Finance (1977, pp. xlviii–xlix).

3. See, for example, the expressions of concern published in *The New York Times* for 5 September 1977 (pp. 22–3) and *Asiaweek* for 17 March 1978 (pp. 39–40).

4. The Outline Perspective Plan was more fully specified in the *Third Malaysia Plan 1976–1980* (1976, pp. 51–90), but this is of no value for the present purpose, which is to compare 1970–5 achievements with previously set targets.

5. This would not necessarily be true if the Malay share of the labour force rose or if high rates of unemployment emerged for Chinese and Indians. In fact, however, the Outline Perspective Plan calls for little increase in the Malay share of labour force (from 51.5 per cent to 52.5 per cent) from 1970 to 1990 and equal unemployment rates (at 3.4 per cent) for all three ethnic groups in the terminal year.

6. Of course, the government could, if it chose, press employers to hire more Indians, just as it presses them to hire more Malays. At times the *Third Malaysia Plan* seems to suggest that this will be done. But there is no sign yet that it is actually happening, and the political weakness of the Indian community makes one sceptical that it will happen in the future.

7. Real GNP growth in 1970–5 averaged 7.4 per cent (*TMP*, 1976, p. 12). As noted in the text, this was faster growth than had occurred in the 1960s. In 1975–8 the average growth rate was reported to be 8.5 per cent (*MTR–TMP*, 1979, p. 6).

8. Useful surveys of Malaysian politics include Means (1970) and Milne and Mauzy (1978).

9. As suggested several times previously, I am less optimistic about the future of the Indian community than about that of the Chinese. The Indians have less to offer which is complementary to what the Malays can do for themselves and more which is directly competitive.

Glossary

British Malaya: Used before World War II to refer to the entire area of British influence in and around the Malay Peninsula.

Ceylonese: A person who identifies himself as such, usually a person who was born in Sri Lanka or whose ancestors came from there. See also *Indian*.

Chinese: A person who identifies himself as such, usually a person who was born in China or whose ancestors came from China.

East Malaysia: See *Malaysia*.

European: In Malaysian usage, includes North Americans and Australasians as well as those actually native to European countries.

Federated Malay States (FMS) (1895–1941): A federation (for purposes of administrative efficiency) comprising the four central states of Perak, Selangor, Negri Sembilan and Pahang.

Federation of Malaya (1948–63): Included the eleven states of Perlis, Kedah, Kelantan, Perak, Penang, Trengganu, Pahang, Selangor, Negri Sembilan, Malacca and Johore. Granted self-government in 1956 and full independence in 1957. The same land area was included in the predecessor *Malayan Union* and was called the *States of Malaya* in 1963–6, *West Malaysia* in 1966–73 and *Peninsular Malaysia* from 1973 on.

Indian: A person who identifies himself as such, usually a person who was born in, or whose ancestors came from, present-day India, Pakistan or Bangladesh. The small Ceylonese minority, once careful to distinguish itself from the Indians, is now gradually merging into the Indian community.

Malay: Defined in Article 160(2) of the Malaysian Constitution as 'a person who professes the Muslim religion, habitually speaks Malay [and] conforms to Malay custom . . .'. There is also a complicated residence clause which excludes most Indonesians who came to Malaya/Malaysia or Singapore after Merdeka Day (31 August 1957) but includes earlier immigrants from Indonesia. See Tan Sri Mohamed Suffian bin Hashim (1972, pp. 247–9). Before Independence 'Malay' was sometimes used to refer only to those whose recent ancestors lived on the Malay Peninsula, while more recent arrivals from the Archipelago were known as 'other Malaysians'.

Malay States: Used before World War II to refer to states which had existed before the Europeans came and continued to have Malay rulers under British indirect rule. Includes the four states ceded by Thailand in 1909 and sometimes also the two predominantly ethnic Malay states (Yala and Patani) which remain under Thai rule.

Malaya: Ambiguous. Its more usual meaning is Peninsular Malaysia plus Singapore, but it is sometimes used to refer to the Federation of Malaya. The term has no official meaning and seems to be dropping gradually from general use as well.

Malayan Union (1946–8): Unitary state installed by Britain after World War II and abandoned under pressure. Its area was the same as that of the *Federation of Malaya*.

Malaysia: Currently, denotes the present country, comprising the eleven states formerly in the Federation of Malaya, now collectively termed Peninsular Malaysia, and the Borneo states of Sabah and Sarawak. Singapore was also a part of Malaysia in 1963–5. Formerly, used occasionally to denote the entire area populated by the Malay peoples, i.e., Malaya, Indonesia, Brunei, the Philippines and Southern Thailand.

Malaysian: In contemporary usage, a citizen of Malaysia, regardless of ethnicity. Before Independence, the term was sometimes used to refer to the broad ethnic group to which the Malays of the Malay Peninsula belong (see *Malay*).

Other Malaysians: See *Malay*.

'Others': An official category used to describe individuals

who do not belong to any of Malaysia's three major 'races'. The 'others' include significant numbers of Thai, Ceylonese, Eurasians, Malayan aborigines, Japanese and 'Europeans'.

Peninsular Malaysia: See *Malaysia*. The main area of interest in this study.

States of Malaya (1963–6): Used briefly to denote the area called the *Federation of Malaya* previously and *West Malaysia* and *Peninsular Malaysia* subsequently.

Straits Settlements (SS) (1826–1941): Penang, Malacca and Singapore, plus, at times, additional small enclaves and islands administered as part of the SS.

Unfederated Malay States (UMS): Used informally before World War II to refer to the five Malay states (Perlis, Kedah, Kelantan, Trengganu and Johore) which were under British protection but not part of the FMS.

West Malaysia: See *Malaysia*.

Bibliography

Abdul Aziz, Ungku (1957), 'Facts and Fallacies on the Malay Economy', *The Straits Times*, 28 February–5 March.

______(1962), 'Facts and Fallacies About the Malay Economy, in Retrospect with New Footnotes', *Ekonomi* 3 (December), 6–30.

______(1964), 'Poverty and Rural Development', *Kajian Ekonomi Malaysia* 1, no. 1 (June), 70–105.

______(1965), 'Poverty, Proteins and Disguised Starvation', *Kajian Ekonomi Malaysia* 2, no. 1 (June), 7–48.

______(1967), 'Cooperation and National Development', *Kajian Ekonomi Malaysia* 4, no. 1 (June), 20–9.

______(1969), 'Wage, Fiscal, Social Security Policies and Institutional Change as Means of Redistributing Income in Developing Countries', in Anthony B. Smith (ed.), *Wage Policy Issues in Economic Development* (New York, St. Martin's Press).

Abdul Rahim Mohd. Said (1974), 'Public Enterprises in Malaysia—A General Survey', *Development Forum* 4: 2, 1–17.

Abdul Rahman, Tengku (1969), *May 13. Before and After* (Kuala Lumpur, Utusan Melayu Press).

Abdullah bin Ayub, Tan Sri Dato (1976), 'Public Enterprise in Malaysia', *UMBC Economic Review* 12: 2, 26–36.

Agarwal, M. C. (1961), 'Some Agro-Economic Aspects of Land Settlement in the FLDA Financed Schemes', mimeographed (Kuala Lumpur, Department of Economics, University of Malaya).

Ahmad Nordin (1975), Letter to the Editor, *Far Eastern Economic Review* 87, no. 5 (31 January), 6.

Ahmad Sarji (1975), 'Re-Structuring of Rural Institutions for Agricultural and Rural Development in Malaysia', paper presented at Second Malaysian Economic Convention, Kuala Lumpur, 26–30 March.

Alexander, Leigh and Simmons, John (1975), 'The Determinants of School Achievement in Developing Countries: The Production Function', Working Paper No. 201, World Bank (March).

Allen, G. C. and Donnithorne, Audrey G. (1962), *Western Enterprise in Indonesia and Malaya* (London, Allen and Unwin).

Allen, James de V. (1967), *The Malayan Union* (New Haven, Monograph Series No. 10, Southeast Asia Studies, Yale University).

Anand, Sudhir (1973), 'The Size Distribution of Income in Malaysia', mimeographed (Washington, Development Research Center, World Bank).

ANDIC, FUAT M. (1977), 'Poverty and Tax Incidence in West Malaysia', *Public Finance Quarterly* 5, no. 3 (July), 329–50.

ANONYMOUS (1972), 'Planning in a Volunteer Colony', *Economic and Political Weekly* (22 January), 149–52.

ARASARATNAM, SINNAPPAH (1970), *Indians in Malaysia and Singapore* (Kuala Lumpur, Oxford University Press).

AZIZ YASSIN, A. (1966), 'The Role of the Federal Marketing Authority in the Development of Agriculture in Malaysia', *Malaysian Management Review* 1, no. 2 (December), 12–22.

BANK NEGARA MALAYSIA (1969), *Annual Report and Statement of Accounts 1968* (Kuala Lumpur).

——— (1976), *Annual Report and Statement of Accounts 1975* (Kuala Lumpur).

BARLOW, COLIN (1978), *The Natural Rubber Industry: Its Development, Technology and Economy in Malaysia* (Kuala Lumpur, Oxford University Press).

BARLOW, COLIN AND LIM SOW CHING (1965), *A Report on the Survey of Malay Group Processing Centres, 1964* (Kuala Lumpur, Rubber Research Institute of Malaya).

BARLOW, COLIN, LIM POH LOH AND ONG YONG (1969), 'Assessment of Smallholders' Central Processing and Marketing Schemes', *Journal of the Rubber Research Institute of Malaya* 21: Fifth Part, 592–603.

BASTIN, JOHN AND WINKS, ROBIN W. (1966), *Malaysia. Selected Historical Readings* (Kuala Lumpur, Oxford University Press).

BAUER, P. T. (1946), 'The Working of Rubber Regulation', *Economic Journal* 56, no. 223 (September), 391–414.

——— (1948), *The Rubber Industry. A Study in Competition and Monopoly* (Cambridge, Mass., Harvard University Press).

——— (1948a), *Report on a Visit to the Rubber Growing Smallholdings of Malaya* (London, H.M.S.O.).

BECKER, GARY S. (1957), *The Economics of Discrimination* (Chicago, University of Chicago Press).

BECKFORD, GEORGE L. (1972), *Persistent Poverty. Underdevelopment in Plantation Economies of the Third World* (New York, Oxford University Press).

BEEBOUT, HAROLD SEYMOUR (1972), 'The Production Surface for Academic Achievement: An Economic Study of Malaysian Secondary Schools', Ph.D. dissertation, University of Wisconsin, Madison.

BHALLA, SURJIT S. (1973), 'The Education–Income Connection—An Investigative Report', Discussion Paper No. 40, Research Program in Economic Development, Woodrow Wilson School, Princeton University (October).

BIGGS, H. C. (1964), *Report on the Marketing of Agricultural and Other Rural Produce in Malaysia* (London, Department of Technical Cooperation).

BIRD, RICHARD M. AND DE WULF, LUC HENRY (1973), 'Taxation and Income Distribution in Latin America: A Critical Review of Empirical Studies', *I.M.F. Staff Papers* 20, No. 3 (November), 639–82.

BLAUG, MARK (1972), *An Introduction to the Economics of Education* (Harmondsworth, Middlesex, Penguin Books).

______ (1973), *Education and the Employment Problem in Developing Countries* (Geneva, International Labour Office).

BLYTHE, W. L. (1947), 'Historical Sketch of Chinese Labor in Malaya', *Journal of the Malayan Branch of the Royal Asiatic Society* 20, Part I (June), 64–114.

BLYTHE, WILFRED (1960), *The Impact of Secret Societies in Malaya* (New York, Oxford University Press).

BOCK, JOHN CHARLES (1971), 'Education and Nation-Building in Malaysia. A Study of Institutional Effect in 34 Schools', Ph.D. dissertation, Stanford University.

BOTTOMLEY, A. (1964), 'Monopoly Profit as a Determinant of Interest Rates in Underdeveloped Rural Areas', *Oxford Economic Papers* N. S. 16, no. 3 (October), 431–7.

BOWRING, PHILIP (1978), 'Malaysia 1990: Sums Get Tougher', *Far Eastern Economic Review* 90, no. 2 (13 January), 42–7.

BRANDT, KARL, EFFERSON, J. NORMAN AND PAARLBERG, DON (1963), *Policies and Measures Leading Toward Greater Diversification of the Agricultural Economy of the Federation of Malaya* (Kuala Lumpur, Government Printer).

BRODE, JOHN (1969), *The Process of Modernization. An Annotated Bibliography on the Sociocultural Aspects of Modernization (with a Foreword by Alex Inkeles)* (Cambridge, Harvard University Press).

BROWN, C. P. (1973), 'Rice Price Stabilization and Support in Malaysia', *The Developing Economies* 11: 3 (June), 164–83; reprinted in David Lim (ed.), *Readings on Malaysian Economic Development* (Kuala Lumpur, Oxford University Press), (1975), 97–110.

______ (1974), 'International Commodity Control Through National Buffer Stocks: A Case Study of Natural Rubber', *Journal of Development Studies* 10, no. 2 (January), 188–212.

BURGESS, R. C. AND LAIDIN BIN ALANG MUSA (1950), *A Report on the State of Health, the Diet and the Economic Conditions of Groups of People in the Lower Income Levels in Malaya*, Report No. 13 (Kuala Lumpur, Institute for Medical Research).

CADY, JOHN F. (1964), *Southeast Asia: Its Historical Development* (New York, McGraw-Hill).

CHAI HON-CHAN (1964), *The Development of British Malaya 1896–1909* (Kuala Lumpur, Oxford University Press).

______ (1971), 'Apprenticeship and Entrepreneurs in Malaysia', paper presented at Conference on Manpower Problems in East and South-East Asia, Singapore, 22–28 May.

______ (1977), *Education and Nation-Building in Plural Societies: the West Malaysian Experience*, Development Studies Centre Monograph No. 6 (Canberra, Australian National University).

CHANDER, R. (1971), *1970 Population and Housing Census of Malaysia. Field Count Summary* (Kuala Lumpur, Department of Statistics).

______ (1972), *1970 Population and Housing Census of Malaysia. Com-*

munity Groups (Kuala Lumpur, Department of Statistics).

______(1973), *1970 Population and Housing Census of Malaysia. West Malaysia Census of Housing, 1970. Final Report* (Kuala Lumpur, Department of Statistics).

CHAPPEL, JOHN NELSON AND JANOWITZ, EDWARD R. (1965), 'Health Survey on a Rural Malay Population, F.L.D.A., Sungai Tekan, Pahang', *Medical Journal of Malaya* 19: 3 (March), 191–200.

CHEE PENG LIM (1974), *Survey of Small-Scale Industries in Peninsular Malaysia*, mimeographed, University of Malaya.

______(1977), 'An Analysis of the Government's Industrial Policy in Malaysia with Special Reference to the Petroleum Development Act 1974 and the Industrial Coordination Act 1975', paper presented at the Fourth Malaysian Economic Convention, Kuala Lumpur, 19–21 May.

CHEE, STEPHEN AND KHOO SIEW MUN (eds.), (1975), *Malaysian Economic Development and Policies* (Kuala Lumpur, Malaysian Economic Association).

CHEESEMAN, H. R. (1955), 'Education in Malaya, 1900–1941', *Malayan Historical Journal* 2: 1 (July), 30–47.

CHELLIAH, D. D. (1960), *A Short History of the Educational Policy of the Straits Settlements, 1800–1925*, 2nd ed. (Singapore, Kiat).

CHENERY, HOLLIS, *et al.* (1974), *Redistribution with Growth* (London, Oxford University Press for the World Bank and the Institute of Development Studies, University of Sussex).

CHENG SIOK HWA (1969), 'The Rice Industry of Malaya: A Historical Survey', *Journal of the Malaysian Branch of the Royal Asiatic Society* 42, Part 2 (December), 130–44.

CHO LEE JAY (1969), *Estimates of Fertility for West Malaysia (1957–1967)*, Research Paper No. 3 (Kuala Lumpur, Department of Statistics).

______(1969a), *Life Tables for West Malaysia 1966*, Research Paper No. 2 (Kuala Lumpur, Department of Statistics).

CHO LEE JAY, PALMORE, JAMES A. AND SAUNDERS, LYLE (1968), 'Recent Fertility Trends in West Malaysia', *Demography* 5: 2, 732–44.

CHONG, Y. H. (1976), 'Aspects of Ecology of Food and Nutrition in Peninsular Malaysia', *Environmental Child Health* (October), 239–56.

CHONG, Y. H. AND LIM, RUTH K. H. (1975), 'The Prevalence of Malnutrition amongst Malay Pre-School Children—Comparative Assessment by Anthropometric Indicators', *Environmental Child Health* (February), 19–22.

CHOPRA, PAN (1977), 'The Dynamic World of PERNAS: Business plus Philosophy', *Asian Finance* (April–May).

CHOU, K. R. (ed.) (1960), *Savings in the Malayan Economy*, 13 vols., mimeographed (Singapore, Department of Economics, University of Malaya).

CHOUDHRY, N. S. (1970), *Socio-Economic Sample Survey of Households—Malaysia 1967–68. Employment and Unemployment, West Malaysia* (Kuala Lumpur, Department of Statistics).

CLINE, WILLIAM R. (1975), 'Distribution and Development. A Survey of Literature', *Journal of Development Economics* 1, 359–400.

COOMBS, PHILIP H. AND AHMED, MANZOOR (1974), *Attacking Rural Poverty. How Nonformal Education Can Help* (Baltimore, Johns Hopkins University Press for the World Bank).

COURTENAY, P. P. (1972), *A Geography of Trade and Development in Malaya* (London, G. Bell and Sons).

COWAN, C. D. (1961), *Nineteenth Century Malaya. The Origins of British Colonial Control* (London, Oxford University Press).

DARTFORD, G. P. (1957), 'Problems of Malay Education', *Oversea Education* 29: 1 (April), 33–7.

DAVENPORT, ANDREW (1975), 'Rubber Producers: Agreement in Sight', *Far Eastern Economic Review* 87, no. 11 (14 March), 51.

DEGANI, AMINA H. (1964), 'The Land Development Authority: An Economic Necessity?' *Malayan Economic Review* 9: 2 (October), 75–82.

_____ (1965), 'Reply' [to R. D. Hill], *Malayan Economic Review* 10: 1 (April), 120–1.

DEL TUFO, M. V. (1949), *Malaya. A Report on the 1947 Census of Population* (London, Crown Agents).

DEPARTMENT OF INLAND REVENUE (1960), *Annual Report . . . 1958* (Kuala Lumpur, Government Press).

_____ (1961), *Annual Report . . . 1959* (Kuala Lumpur, Government Press).

_____ (1974), *Annual Report . . . 1971* (Kuala Lumpur, Government Press).

_____ (1976), *Annual Report . . . 1973* (Kuala Lumpur, Government Press).

DEPARTMENT OF STATISTICS (n.d.–*c*. 1960–1), *The Household Budget Survey of the Federation of Malaya 1957–58* (Kuala Lumpur).

_____ (*c*. 1962), *National Accounts of the Federation of Malaya 1955–1960* (Kuala Lumpur).

_____ (1963), *Report on Employment, Unemployment and Under-Employment 1962* (Kuala Lumpur).

_____ (1963a), *Rubber Statistics Handbook 1962* (Kuala Lumpur).

_____ (1966), *Report on Employment and Unemployment in Metropolitan Towns* (Kuala Lumpur).

_____ (1967), *Rubber Statistics Handbook 1966* (Kuala Lumpur).

_____ (1969), *Report on the Financial Survey of Limited Companies Malaysia 1967* (Kuala Lumpur).

_____ (n.d.–*c*. 1969), *Vital Statistics West Malaysia 1967* (Kuala Lumpur).

_____ (n.d.–*c*. 1970), *Census of Manufacturing Industries West Malaysia 1968* (Kuala Lumpur).

_____ (1971), *Interim Report on Family Survey. West Malaysia* (Kuala Lumpur).

_____ (1971a), *National Accounts of West Malaysia 1960–1967* (Kuala Lumpur).

______ (1972), *National Accounts of West Malaysia 1960–1968* (Kuala Lumpur).

______ (1974), *Socio-Economic Sample Survey of Households—Malaysia 1967–68. Household Amenities and Conveniences West Malaysia* (Kuala Lumpur).

______ (1975), *Rubber Statistics Handbook Malaysia 1973* (Kuala Lumpur).

______ (1976), *Vital Statistics Peninsular Malaysia 1974* (Kuala Lumpur).

DE WULF, LUC (1974), 'Do Public Expenditures Reduce Inequality?', *Finance and Development* 11, No. 31 (September): 20–3.

DIXON, JOHN A. (1971), *Groundnut Production in the Kemubu Scheme Area* (Kota Bharu, Ranchangan Pengayeran Kemubu).

______ (1971a), *Tobacco Production in the Kemubu Scheme Area* (Kota Bharu, Ranchangan Pengayeran Kemubu).

______ (1977), *Some Economic Aspects of Rural to Rural Migration and Land Settlement in East Asia*, Ph.D. dissertation, Harvard University.

DOERING, OTTO CHARLES III (1973), 'Malaysian Rice Policy and the Muda River Irrigation Project', unpublished Ph.D. dissertation, Cornell University.

DORE, R. P. (1972–3), 'The Importance of Educational Traditions: Japan and Elsewhere', *Pacific Affairs* 45: 4 (Winter), 491–507.

______ (1975), 'Deschool? Try Using the Schools for Education First: The Educational Impasse in the Developing World', in John Simmons (ed.), (1975), 50–69.

______ (1976), *The Diploma Disease. Education, Qualification and Development* (Berkeley and Los Angeles, University of California Press).

DOUGLAS, STEPHEN A. (1970), 'The Symbolic Uses of Educational Policy in Malaysia', paper presented at the Interdisciplinary Conference on Processes of Change in Contemporary Asia, Urbana, Illinois (November).

DRABBLE, JOHN (1973), *Rubber in Malaya 1876–1922* (Kuala Lumpur, Oxford University Press).

DRUMMOND, STUART AND HAWKINS, DAVID (1970), 'The Malaysian Elections of 1969: An Analysis of the Campaign and the Results', *Asian Survey* 10 (April), 320–35.

ECONOMIC PLANNING UNIT (1975), 'Survey of Rural Poverty', mimeographed.

______ (1975a), 'Effective Protection and Industrialization Policies. Report on a Research Project', mimeographed (April).

EDWARDS, CHRISTOPHER (1975), 'Protection, Profits and Policy—An Analysis of Industrialization in Malaysia', Ph.D. dissertation, University of East Anglia.

EDWARDS, C. T. (1970), *Public Finances in Malaya and Singapore* (Canberra, Australian National University Press).

ENG KIAT KOH (1965), 'American Educational Policy in the Philippines and the British Policy in Malaya, 1898–1935', *Comparative Education Review* 9, No. 2 (June), 139–46.

ESMAN, MILTON J. (1972), *Administration and Development in Malaysia* (Ithaca, Cornell University Press).

FEDERAL LAND DEVELOPMENT AUTHORITY (1976), 'FELDA and its Activities', mimeographed.

FEDERAL LEGISLATIVE COUNCIL (1954), *Malay Participation in the Road Transport Industry*, Council Paper No. 17 of 1954 (Kuala Lumpur, Government Printer).

FEI, JOHN C. H., RANIS, GUSTAV, AND KUO, SHIRLEY W. (1975), 'Growth and the Family Distribution of Income by Factor Components: The Case of Taiwan', Discussion Paper No. 223, Economic Growth Center, Yale University (March).

FELL, H. (1960), *1957 Population Census of the Federation of Malaya. Report No. 14 (Final Report—Summary Tables for the Federation, with General Comments on the Census)* (Kuala Lumpur, Department of Statistics).

FENN, WILLIAM AND WU TEH-YAO (1951), *Chinese Schools and the Education of Chinese Malayans. The Report of a Mission Invited by the Federation Government to Study the Problem of the Education of Chinese in Malaya* (Kuala Lumpur, Government Printer).

FIENNES, D. E. M. (1957), *Report on Rural and Industrial Development Authority, 1950–1955* (Kuala Lumpur, Government Press).

______ (1962), 'The Malayan Federal Land Development Authority', *Journal of Local Administration Overseas* 1: 3 (July): 156–63.

First Malaysia Plan 1966–1970 (1965), (Kuala Lumpur, Government Press).

FIRTH, RAYMOND (1966), *Malay Fishermen. Their Peasant Economy*, 2nd ed. (London, Routledge and Kegan Paul).

FISK, E. K. (1961), 'Productivity and Income from Rubber in an Established Malay Reservation', *Malayan Economic Review* 6 (April), 209–25; reprinted in E. K. Fisk, *Studies in the Rural Economy of South-East Asia* (Singapore, Eastern Universities Press), (1964), 50–63.

______ (1962), 'Special Development Problems of a Plural Society', *Economic Record* 38 (June): 209–25; reprinted in Fisk (1964): 88–108.

______ (1964), *Studies in the Rural Economy of South-East Asia* (Singapore, Eastern Universities Press).

FOSTER, P. J. (1966), 'The Vocational School Fallacy in Development Planning', in C. A. Anderson and M. J. Bowman (eds.), *Education and Economic Development* (Chicago, Aldine), 142–63.

FRANKE, WOLFGANG (1965), 'Problems of Chinese Education in Singapore and Malaya', *Ministry of Education Journal* 2: 2 (December), 182–93.

FREEDMAN, MAURICE (1959), 'The Handling of Money: A Note on the Background of the Economic Sophistication of the Overseas Chinese', *Man* 59, 64–5; reprinted in T. H. Silcock (ed.), *Readings in Malayan Economics* (Singapore, Eastern Universities Press), (1961), 38–42.

______ (1960), 'The Growth of a Plural Society in Malaya', *Pacific Affairs* 33, No. 2 (June), 158–68.

FREEMAN, ROGER A. (1968), *Socialism and Private Enterprise in Equatorial Asia* (Stanford, California, Stanford University Press).

FURNIVALL, J. S. (1939), *Netherlands India. A Study of Plural Economy* (Cambridge, England, The University Press).

——— (1948), *Colonial Policy and Practice: A Comparative Study of Burma and Netherlands India* (New York, New York University Press).

GARDNER, STUART W. (1975), 'Ethnicity and Work: Occupational Distribution in an Urban Multi-ethnic Setting—George Town, Penang, West Malaysia', Ph.D. dissertation, University of California, Berkeley.

GATES, WILLIAM B. JR., GOERING, THEODORE J., AND KEARE, DOUGLAS H. (1967), 'The Role of Land in the Economic Development of West Malaysia, 1966–1985', mimeographed.

GEERTZ, CLIFFORD (1963), 'The Integrative Revolution. Primordial Sentiments and Civil Politics in the New States', in Geertz (ed.), *Old Societies and New States* (Glencoe, Illinois, The Free Press).

GIBBONS, DAVID S. AND ZAKARIA HAJI AHMAD (1971), 'Politics and Selection for the Higher Civil Service in New States. The Malaysian Example', *Journal of Comparative Administration* 3: 3 (November), 330–48.

GILLESPIE, W. IRWIN (1965), 'Effect of Public Expenditures on the Distribution of Income', in Richard A. Musgrave (ed.), *Essays in Fiscal Federalism* (Washington, The Brookings Institution).

GLAZER, NATHAN AND MOYNIHAN, DANIEL PATRICK (1970), *Beyond the Melting Pot. The Negroes, Puerto Ricans, Jews, Italians and Irish of New York City* (Cambridge, Mass., M.I.T. Press).

GOERING, T. J. (1969), 'Some Thoughts on Rubber and the Replanting/New Planting Programs', unpublished memorandum.

GOH KENG SWEE (1958), 'Entrepreneurship in a Plural Economy', *Malayan Economic Review* 3, No. 1 (April), 1–17.

GOLAY, FRANK H. (1969), 'Malaya', in Golay *et al.* (eds.), *Underdevelopment and Economic Nationalism in Southeast Asia* (Ithaca, Cornell University Press), 341–89.

GOLDMAN, RICHARD (1975), 'Staple Food Self-Sufficiency and the Distributive Impact of Malaysian Rice Policy', *Food Research Institute Studies* 14: 3, 251–93.

GOLDMAN, RICHARD H. AND SQUIRE, LYN (1977), 'Technical Change, Labor Use and Income Distribution in the Muda Irrigation Project', mimeographed (Harvard University and World Bank).

GOVERNMENT OF MALAYSIA AND STATE OF JOHOR (1971), *Johor Tenggah and Tanjong Penggarang Regional Master Plan. Supporting Volume 4. Sociology.*

GREENWOOD, J. M. F. (1964), 'Rubber Smallholdings in the Federation of Malaya', *Journal of Tropical Geography* 18 (August), 81–100.

GROVES, H. E. (1964), *The Constitution of Malaysia* (Singapore, Malaysia Publications).

GULLICK, J. M. (1956), *The Story of Early Kuala Lumpur* (Singapore, Donald Moore).

——— (1965), *Indigenous Political Systems of Western Malaya* (London, The Athlone Press).

——— (1969), *Malaysia* (New York, Praeger Publishers).

GUYOT, DOROTHY (1971), 'The Politics of Land: Comparative Development in Two States of Malaysia', *Pacific Affairs* 44: 3 (Fall), 368–89.

GUYOT, JAMES F. (1968), 'The Two Cultures and Malaysia's Development Revolution', paper presented at Association for Asian Studies annual meetings, Philadelphia, 24 March.

HAGEN, EVERETT E. (1962), *On the Theory of Social Change. How Economic Growth Begins* (Homewood, Ill., The Dorsey Press).

HALL, D. G. E. (1968), *A History of South-East Asia*, 3rd ed. (London, Macmillan).

HANNA, WILLARD A. (1964), *The Formation of Malaysia. New Factor in World Politics* (New York, American Universities Field Staff).

HARBERGER, ARNOLD C. (1962), 'The Incidence of the Corporate Income Tax', *Journal of Political Economy* 52 (June): 215–40.

HARBISON, FREDERIC AND MYERS, CHARLES A. (1964), *Education, Manpower and Economic Growth* (New York, McGraw-Hill).

HARRISON, BRIAN (1963), *A Short History of South-East Asia*, 2nd ed. (London, Macmillan).

HEALEY, DEREK T. (1972), 'Development Policy: New Thinking About an Interpretation', *Journal of Economic Literature* 10, No. 3 (September), 757–97.

HELLER, PETER S. (1974), 'An Analysis of the Cost and Utilization of the Health Services of Peninsular Malaysia', unpublished paper.

——— (1975), 'Issues in the Costing of Public Sector Outputs. The Public Medical Services of Malaysia', World Bank Staff Working Paper No. 207 (Washington, June).

——— (1976), 'A Model of the Demand for Medical and Health Services in West Malaysia', Discussion Paper No. 62, Center for Research on Economic Development, University of Michigan (October).

HERBERT, CLIFFORD (1976), 'The Organization and Management of the Public Enterprises in Malaysia', in International Legal Center (ed.), *Law and Public Enterprise in Asia* (New York, Praeger).

HIGH COMMISSIONER'S OFFICE (1950), *Draft Development Plan of the Federation of Malaya* (Kuala Lumpur, Government Press).

HILL, R. D. (1965), 'Comment' [on Degani (1964)], *Malayan Economic Review* 10: 1 (April), 116–19.

HIRSCHMAN, ALBERT O. (1973), 'The Changing Tolerance for Income Inequality in the Course of Economic Development', with a mathematical appendix by Michael Rothschild, *Quarterly Journal of Economics* 87, No. 4 (November), 544–66.

HIRSCHMAN, CHARLES (1971), 'Evaluation of Mortality Bias in the Vital Statistics of West Malaysia', mimeographed (Department of Statistics), (January).

——— (1971a), 'Ownership and Control in the Manufacturing Sector of West Malaysia', *UMBC Economic Review* 7: 1, 21–30.

——— (1972), 'Educational Patterns in Colonial Malaya', *Comparative Educational Review* 16, No. 3 (October), 486–502.

——— (1974), 'Economic Progress in Malaysia: How Widely Has It Been Shared?' *UMBC Economic Review* 10, No. 2, 1–10.

——— (1974a), *Estimates of the Inter-Censal Population by Sex, Community and Age-Group, Peninsular Malaysia (1957–1970)*, Research Paper No. 9 (Kuala Lumpur, Department of Statistics).

——— (1975), *Ethnic and Social Stratification in Peninsular Malaysia* (Washington, American Sociological Association).

HIRSCHMAN, CHARLES (1976), 'Recent Urbanization Trends in Peninsular Malaysia', paper read at Population Association of America Meetings (Montreal, April).

HIRSCHMAN, CHARLES AND SINGH, HARBANS (1975), 'Urbanization and Net Migration to Urban and Rural Areas, Peninsular Malaysia, 1957–1970', unpublished draft.

HO, ROBERT (1969), 'Rice Production in Malaya. A Review of Problems and Prospects', *Journal of Tropical Geography* 29 (December), 21–32.

——— (1975), 'Land Settlement Projects in Malaya: An Assessment of the Role of the Federal Land Development Authority', *Journal of Tropical Geography* 20 (June), 1–15.

HOERR, O. D. (1973), 'Education, Income and Equity in Malaysia', *Economic Development and Cultural Change* 21: 2 (January), 247–73; reprinted in David Lim (ed.), *Readings on Malaysian Economic Development* (Kuala Lumpur, Oxford University Press), (1975), 292–308.

HOLLISTER, ROBINSON G. (n.d.), Manuscript on poverty.

HUANG, YUKON (1971), 'The Economics of Paddy Production in Malaya: an Economy in Transition', Ph.D. dissertation, Princeton University.

——— (1974), 'The Behavior of Indigenous and Non-Indigenous Farmers: A Case Study', *Journal of Development Studies* 10, No. 2 (January), 175–87.

——— (1975), 'Tenancy Patterns, Productivity and Rentals in Malaysia', *Economic Development and Cultural Change* 23: 4 (July), 703–18.

——— (1976), 'Backward-Bending Supply Curves and Behaviour of Subsistence Farmers', *Journal of Development Studies*, 12, No. 3 (April), 191–211.

HUQ, MAHBUB UL (1972), 'A New Perspective on Development', in Andrew E. Rice (ed.), *Development for the 70's: Jobs and Justice*, papers from the 12th World Conference of the Society for International Development (Dobbs Ferry, New York, Oceana Publications), 60–68.

HUSSAIN WAFA, SYED (1972), 'Land Development Strategies in Malaysia: An Empirical Study', Ph.D. dissertation, Food Research Institute, Stanford University; also available as Occasional Paper No. 2, Malaysian Centre for Development Studies (1974).

——— (1975), 'Strategies in Land Development in Malaysia', in Stephen Chee and Khoo Siew Mun (eds.), *Malaysian Economic*

Development and Policies (Kuala Lumpur, Malaysian Economic Association), 158–93.

INKELES, ALEX AND SMITH, DAVID H. (1974), *Becoming Modern. Individual Change in Six Developing Countries* (Cambridge, Mass., Harvard University Press).

INTERNATIONAL BANK FOR RECONSTRUCTION AND DEVELOPMENT (1955), *The Economic Development of Malaya* (Baltimore, Johns Hopkins University Press).

JACKSON, JAMES C. (1964), 'Smallholding Cultivation of Cash Crops', in Wang Gungwu (ed.), *Malaysia: A Survey* (Singapore, Donald Moore Books), 246–73.

______ (1968), *Planters and Speculators. Chinese and European Agricultural Enterprise in Malaya 1786–1921* (Kuala Lumpur, University of Malaya Press).

______ (1972), 'Rice Cultivation in West Malaysia: Relationships between Culture History, Customary Practices and Recent Developments', *Journal of the Malaysian Branch of the Royal Asiatic Society* 45, Part II, 76–96.

JACKSON, R. N. (1961), *Immigrant Labor and the Development of Malaya* (Kuala Lumpur, Government Press).

JALLADE, JEAN-PIERRE (1977), 'Basic Education and Income Inequality in Brazil: The Long-term View', World Bank Staff Working Paper No. 268 (June).

JOHNSON, HARRY G. (1965), 'A Theoretical Model of Economic Nationalism in New and Developing States', *Political Science Quarterly* 80, No. 2 (June), 169–85.

KASPER, WOLFGANG E. (1974), *Malaysia. A Study in Successful Economic Development* (Washington, American Enterprise Institute for Public Policy Research).

KEESING, DONALD B. (1972), 'Causes and Implications of Growing Inequality of Income within Developing Countries', Research Memorandum No. 227, Stanford Research Center in Economic Growth.

KENNEDY, JOSEPH (1970), *A History of Malaya* (London, Macmillan).

KHOO SWEE JOO (1964), 'The Malaysian Oil Palm Industry', *Kajian Ekonomi Malaysia* 1: 1, 1–13.

KIRK, DUDLEY (1971), 'A New Demographic Transition?', in Roger Revelle, *et al.* (eds.), *Rapid Population Growth. Consequences and Policy Implications* (Baltimore, Johns Hopkins University Press for the National Academy of Sciences).

KNORR, KLAUS (1945), *Tin under Control* (Palo Alto, Stanford University Press).

______ (1954a), *World Rubber and Its Regulation* (Palo Alto, Stanford University Press).

KNOWLES, L. C. A. (1924), *The Economic Development of the British Overseas Empire* (London, George Routledge and Sons).

KUZNETS, SIMON (1955), 'Economic Growth and Income Inequality', *American Economic Review* 65, No. 1 (March), 1–28.

______ (1963), 'Quantitative Aspects of the Economic Growth of

Nations: VIII. Distribution of Income by Size', *Economic Development and Cultural Change*, No. 2, Part II (January).

______ (1975), 'Demographic Components in Size Distributions of Income', in *Income Distribution, Employment and Economic Development in Southeast and East Asia*, Vol. II (Tokyo, The Japan Economic Research Center; Manila, The Council for Asian Manpower Studies).

LAI AH HOON (1968), 'Problems of Federal Finance in Plural Societies: Case Studies of Malaya and Singapore', Ph.D. dissertation, University of York.

______ (1975), 'Problems of Federal Finance in the Malaysian Plural Society', in David Lim (ed.), *Readings on Malaysian Economic Development* (Kuala Lumpur, Oxford University Press), 399–407.

LAMB, ALASTAIR (1964), 'Early History', in Wang Gungwu (ed.), *Malaysia: A Survey* (Singapore, Donald Moore Books).

LEE, E. L. H. (1975), 'Income Distribution in a Developing Economy: A Case Study of West Malaysia', D. Phil. thesis, Oxford University.

______ (1977), 'Rural Poverty in West Malaysia, 1957–70', in International Labour Office, *Poverty and Landlessness in Rural Asia* (Geneva).

LEE HOCK LOCK (1971), *Household Saving in West Malaysia and the Problem of Financing Economic Development*, Monograph Series on Malaysian Economic Affairs No. 1 (Kuala Lumpur, University of Malaya Press).

LEE, P. C. AND PANTON, W. P. (1971), *First Malaysia Plan Land Capability Classification Report* (Kuala Lumpur, Government Printer).

LEVIN, JONATHAN V. (1960), *The Export Economies. Their Pattern of Development in Historical Perspective* (Cambridge, Mass., Harvard University Press).

LEWIS, OSCAR (1968), 'The Culture of Poverty', in Daniel P. Moynihan (ed.), *On Understanding Poverty. Perspectives from the Social Sciences* (New York, Basic Books), 187–200.

LIGHT, IVAN H. (1972), *Ethnic Enterprise in America: Business and Welfare among Chinese, Japanese, and Blacks* (Berkeley, University of California Press).

LIM CHONG YAH (1960), 'Export Taxes on Rubber in Malaya—A Survey of Post-War Development', *Malayan Economic Review* 5: 2 (October), 46–58.

______ (1961), 'The Malayan Rubber Replanting Taxes', *Malayan Economic Review* 6: 2 (October), 43–52.

______ (1967), *Economic Development of Modern Malaya* (Kuala Lumpur, Oxford University Press).

LIM, DAVID (1973), *Economic Growth and Development in West Malaysia 1947–1970* (Kuala Lumpur, Oxford University Press).

______ (1975), *Readings on Malaysian Economic Development* (Kuala Lumpur, Oxford University Press).

LIM LIN LEAN (1974), 'The Pattern of Income Distribution in West Malaysia, 1957–1970', World Employment Programme Research Working Paper, mimeographed (Geneva, International Labour Office).

LIM SOW CHING (1968), *A Study of the Marketing of Smallholders' Rubber at the First Trade Level in Selangor* (Kuala Lumpur, Rubber Research Institute of Malaya).

——— (1972), *Land Development Schemes in West Malaysia: A Study of Benefits and Costs*, Ph.D. dissertation, Australian National University.

LIM TECK GHEE (1977), *Peasants and their Agricultural Economy in Colonial Malaya 1874–1941* (Kuala Lumpur, Oxford University Press).

LINDENBERG, MARC MERRILL (1973), 'Foreign and Domestic Investment in the Pioneer Industry Program, Malaysia 1965–70, Political, Economic, and Social Impacts', Ph.D. dissertation, University of Southern California.

LIPTON, MICHAEL (1977), *Why Poor People Stay Poor. Urban Bias in World Development* (Cambridge, Mass., Harvard University Press).

LITTLE, I. M. D. AND TIPPING, D. G. (1972), *A Social Cost Benefit Analysis of the Kulai Oil Palm Estate* (Paris, Organisation for Economic Cooperation and Development).

LOH FOOK-SENG, PHILIP (1969), *The Malay States 1877–1895* (Kuala Lumpur, Oxford University Press).

——— (1970), 'British Educational Strategy in the Malay States', Ph.D. dissertation, Stanford University.

——— (1975), *Seeds of Separatism: Educational Policy in Malaya 1874–1970* (Kuala Lumpur, Oxford University Press).

LONG, MILLARD F. (1968), 'Interest Rates and the Structure of Agricultural Credit Markets', *Oxford Economic Papers* N.S. 20, No. 2 (July), 275–88.

——— (n.d.), 'Credit for Small Farmers: Indonesia, Malaysia, Thailand', mimeographed (Harvard University).

LOTZ, JØRGEN AND MORSS, ELLIOTT R. (1967), 'Measuring "Tax Effort" in Developing Countries', *I.M.F. Staff Papers* 14 (November), 478–99.

LOURDESAMY, I. (1972), 'The Vocational School Program in Malaysia: A Study in Effective Development Administration', Ph.D. dissertation, University of Pittsburgh.

MACARTHUR, A. M. (1962), 'Malaya—12: Assignment Report June 1958—November 1959' (Manila, World Health Organization).

MAHATHIR BIN MOHAMAD (1970), *The Malay Dilemma* (Singapore, Donald Moore for Asia Pacific Press).

MALAYA (1951), *Report of the Committee on Malay Education* ['Barnes Report'] (Kuala Lumpur, Government Press).

——— (1954), *Report of the Mission of Enquiry into the Rubber Industry of Malaya* ['Mudie Report'] (Kuala Lumpur, Government Press).

——— (1954a), *Report of the Special Committee to Consider Ways and Means of Implementing the Policy Outlined in the Education Ordinance 1952*, Council Paper No. 67 of 1954 (Kuala Lumpur, Government Press).

——— (1956), *A Plan of Development for Malaya 1956–60* (Kuala Lumpur, Government Press).

——— (1956a), *Report of the Working Party Set up to Consider the*

Development of New Areas for Land Settlement in the Federation of Malaya (Kuala Lumpur, Government Printer).

______ (1956b), *Report of the Education Committee* ['Razak Report'], Council Paper No. 21 of 1956 (Kuala Lumpur, Government Press).

______ (1960), *Report of the Education Review Committee 1960* ['Rahman Talib Report'] (Kuala Lumpur, Government Press).

______ (1963), *Report of the Subdivision of Estates Committee* (Kuala Lumpur, Government Press).

MALAYSIA (1971), *Towards National Harmony* (Kuala Lumpur, Government Press).

______ (1971a), *Report of the Committee Appointed by the National Operations Council to Study Campus Life of Students of the University of Malaya* ['Majid Report'] (Kuala Lumpur, Government Press).

MALAYSIA AGREEMENT (1963), *Malaysia, Agreement Concluded between the Federation of Malaya, United Kingdom of Great Britain and Northern Ireland, North Borneo, Sarawak and Singapore* (Kuala Lumpur, Government Press).

MARTIN, EDWIN M. (1970), *1970 Review. Development Assistance, Efforts and Policies of the Members of the Development Assistance Committee* (Paris, Organisation for Economic Cooperation and Development).

MAXWELL, GEORGE (1948), 'The Malay in Commerce', *United Empire* 39, no. 1 (January–February), 36–9.

MCCLELLAND, DAVID C. (1961), *The Achieving Society* (Princeton, N. J., D. Van Nostrand Company).

MCCLELLAND AND WINTER, DAVID G. (1969), *Motivating Economic Achievement* (New York, The Free Press).

MCGEE, T. G. (1962), 'The Malayan General Elections of 1959: A Study in Political Geography', *Journal of Tropical Geography* 16 (October), 70–99.

______ (1964), 'Population: A Preliminary Analysis', in Wang Gungwu (ed.), *Malaysia: A Survey* (Singapore, Donald Moore Books).

MCLURE, CHARLES E. JR. (1971), 'The Theory of Tax Incidence with Imperfect Factor Mobility', *Finanzarchiv* 30, 27–48.

______ (1971a), 'The Theory of Expenditure Incidence', *Finanzarchiv* 30: 432–53.

______ (1972), 'The Incidence of Taxation in West Malaysia', *Malayan Economic Review* 17, no. 2 (October), 66–98.

MCMEEKIN, ROBERT W. JR (1973), 'Analysis of Educational Expenditure Decisions in Developing Countries', Ph.D. dissertation, Harvard University.

MCNAMARA, ROBERT S. (1972), *Address to the Board of Governors of the World Bank Group* (Washington), (25 September).

MEANS, GORDON P. (1970), *Malaysian Politics* (London, University of London Press).

______ (1972), ' "Special Rights" as a Strategy for Development', *Comparative Politics* 5, no. 1 (October), 29–61.

MEERMAN, JACOB (1972), *Fiscal Incidence in Empirical Studies of Income*

Distribution in Poor Countries, A. I. D. Discussion Paper No. 25 (Washington, U.S. Agency for International Development).

_____ (1975), 'Income Redistribution in West Malaysia and Recent Empirical Work on Budget Incidence: A Comment', *Public Finance* 30, no. 1, 131–5.

_____ (1977), 'Meeting Basic Needs in Malaysia: A Summary of Findings', mimeographed (World Bank).

_____ (1977a), *The Distribution of Public Expenditure in Malaysia*, ms.

MELSON, ROBERT AND WOLPE, HOWARD (1970), 'Modernization and the Politics of Communalism: A Theoretical Perspective', *American Political Science Review* 64 (December), 1112–30.

MIDDLEBROOK, S. M. (1951), 'Yap Ah Loy', *Journal of the Malayan Branch of the Royal Asiatic Society* 24, Part 2 (July).

Mid-Term Review of the Second Malaysia Plan 1971–1975 (1973), (Kuala Lumpur, Government Press).

Mid-Term Review of the Third Malaysia Plan 1976–1980 (1979), (Kuala Lumpur, Government Press).

MILLS, L. A. (1966), *British Malaya 1824–67* (reprinted Kuala Lumpur, Oxford University Press).

MILNE, R. S. (1967), *Government and Politics in Malaysia* (Boston, Houghton Mifflin).

_____ (1970), '"National Ideology" and Nation-Building in Malaysia', *Asian Survey* 10: 7 (July), 563–73.

_____ (1976), 'The Politics of Malaysia's New Economic Policy', *Pacific Affairs* 49, no. 2 (Summer), 235–62.

_____ AND MAUZY, DIANE K. (1978), *Politics and Government in Malaysia* (Vancouver, University of British Columbia Press).

MINISTRY OF EDUCATION (1968), *Educational Statistics of Malaysia 1938 to 1967* (Kuala Lumpur, Dewan Bahasa dan Pustaka).

_____ (1970), *Educational Statistics of Malaysia 1968* (Kuala Lumpur, Dewan Bahasa dan Pustaka).

_____ (1973), *Lapuran Jawatankuasa di atas Kajian Pendapat mengenai Pelajaran dan Masyarakat* (*Lapuran Keciciran*) ['Dropout Report'] (Kuala Lumpur, Ministry of Education).

_____ (1976), *Educational Statistics of Malaysia 1973* (Kuala Lumpur, Government Printer).

_____ (1978), *Educational Statistics of Malaysia 1974/1975* (Kuala Lumpur, Government Printer).

MINISTRY OF FINANCE (1976), *Economic Report 1976/77* (Kuala Lumpur).

_____ (1977), *Economic Report 1977/78* (Kuala Lumpur).

_____ (1978), *Economic Report 1978/79* (Kuala Lumpur).

MOHAMED NOORDIN SOPIEE (1974), *From Malayan Union to Separation. Political Unification in the Malaysia Region, 1945–65* (Kuala Lumpur, University of Malaya Press).

MOHAMED SUFFIAN BIN HASHIM, TAN SRI (1972), *An Introduction to the Constitution of Malaysia* (Kuala Lumpur, Government Press).

MOHD. NOOR BIN WAHAB and ARUN, K. C. (1969), 'Smallholdings in

West Malaysia', *Journal of the Rubber Research Institute of Malaya* 21: Fifth Part, 581–91.

MONTGOMERY, JOHN AND KATZMAN, MARTIN (1976), 'Cui Bono? Measuring Income–Redistributing Effects of Capital Projects', mimeographed (Harvard University).

MOORE, BASIL J. (n.d.), 'Ownership and Employment: A Penang Micro-Study', mimeographed (Universiti Sains Malaysia).

——— (1975), 'Restructuring Society', mimeographed (Penang, School of Comparative Social Sciences, Universiti Sains Malaysia), (February).

MORAIS, J. VICTOR (ed.), (1969), *Strategy for Action: The Selected Speeches of Tun Haji Abdul Razak bin Dato Hussein Al-Haj* (Kuala Lumpur, Government Press).

MOYNIHAN, DANIEL P. (ed.), (1968), *On Understanding Poverty. Perspectives from the Social Sciences* (New York, Basic Books).

MUHAMMAD ALIAS, RAJA (1975), 'Pioneering into the Interior. The Malaysian Experience', mimeographed, FELDA (October).

MUZAFFAR, CHANDRA (1977), 'Some Political Perspectives on the New Economic Policy', paper presented to the Fourth Malaysian Economic Convention, Kuala Lumpur, 19–21 May.

MYINT, HLA (1967), 'The Inward and Outward Looking Countries of Southeast Asia', *Malayan Economic Review* 12, no. 1 (April), 1–13.

NAGATA, JUDITH A. (1975), 'Perceptions of Social Inequality in Malaysia', *Contributions to Asian Studies* 7, 113–36.

NARKSWASDI, UDHIS AND SELVADURAI, S. (1968), *Economic Survey of Padi Production in West Malaysia* (Kuala Lumpur, Ministry of Agriculture and Co-operatives).

NASH, MANNING (1972), 'Ethnicity, Centrality and Education in Pasir Mas, Kelantan', *Comparative Education Review* 16: 1 (February), 4–15.

NATHAN, J. E. (1922), *The Census of British Malaya 1921* (London, Waterlow and Sons).

NATIONAL FAMILY PLANNING BOARD (1968), *Report on West Malaysian Family Survey, 1966–67* (Kuala Lumpur).

NATIONAL OPERATIONS COUNCIL (1969), *The May 13 Tragedy* (Kuala Lumpur).

NESS, GAYL D. (1967), *Bureaucracy and Rural Development in Malaysia* (Berkeley, University of California Press).

NEWELL, WILLIAM H. (1962), *Treacherous River. A Study of Rural Chinese in North Malaya* (Kuala Lumpur, University of Malaya Press).

OSBORNE, MILTON E. (1964), *Singapore and Malaysia*, Data Paper No. 53, Southeast Asia Program (Ithaca, Cornell University).

OSHIMA, HARRY T. (1970), 'Income Inequality and Economic Growth. The Postwar Experience of Asian Countries', *Malayan Economic Review* 15, no. 2 (October), 7–41.

PALMORE, JAMES A., CHANDER, RAMESH AND FERNANDEZ, DOROTHY Z. (1975), 'The Demographic Situation in Malaysia', in John Kantner and Lee McCaffrey (eds.), *Population and Development in Southeast*

Asia (Lexington, Mass., Lexington Books), 57–82.

PANCHAMUKHI, V. R. (1972), 'Effective Protection and Intraregional Trade: A Case Study of Malaysia', paper presented to ECAFE Meeting of the Eighth Group of Experts on Programming Techniques: Intraregional Trade Projections; Effective Tariff Protection; and Income Distribution, Bangkok, January.

PARKINSON, BRIEN K. (1967), 'Non-Economic Factors in the Economic Retardation of the Rural Malays', *Modern Asian Studies* 1, no. 1: 31–46; reprinted in David Lim (ed.), *Readings on Malaysian Economic Development* (Kuala Lumpur, Oxford University Press), (1975), 332–40.

——— (1968), 'The Economic Retardation of the Malays—A Rejoinder', *Modern Asian Studies* 2, no. 3, 267–72; reprinted in David Lim (ed.), *Readings on Malaysian Economic Development* (Kuala Lumpur, Oxford University Press), (1975).

PARKINSON, C. NORTHCOTE (1964), *British Intervention in Malaya 1867–1877* (Kuala Lumpur, University of Malaya Press).

PARMER, J. NORMAN (1960), *Colonial Labour Policy and Administration: A History of Labor in the Rubber Plantation Industry in Malaya, c. 1910–41* (Locust Valley, New York, J. J. Augustin for the Association for Asian Studies).

PARNES, HERBERT S. (1962), *Forecasting Educational Needs for Social and Economic Development* (Paris, Organisation for Economic Co-operation and Development).

PAUKERT, FELIX (1973), 'Income Distribution at Different Levels of Development: A Survey of Evidence', *International Labour Review* 108, nos. 2–3 (August–September), 97–125.

PEE TECK YEW (1967), *A Statistical Source Book on Malayan Agriculture*, 2 Vols. (Kuala Lumpur, Faculty of Agriculture, University of Malaya).

PERKINS, DWIGHT H. (1975), 'Introduction. The Persistence of the Past', in Perkins (ed.), *China's Modern Economy in Historical Perspective* (Stanford, California, Stanford University Press), 1–18.

PILLAI, M. G. G. (1974), 'Seeking Support for Rubber', *Far Eastern Economic Review* 86, no. 49 (13 December 1974), 48–9.

PILLAY, CHANDRASEKARAN (1975), *The 1974 General Elections in Malaysia: A Post Mortem*, Occasional Paper of the Institute of Southeast Asian Studies (Singapore).

POPENOE, OLIVER (1970), 'Malay Entrepreneurs. An Analysis of the Social Backgrounds, Careers and Attitudes of Leading Malay Businessmen in West Malaysia', Ph.D. dissertation, London School of Economics.

PORTES, ALEJANDRO (1973), 'Modernity and Development: A Critique', *Studies in Comparative International Development* 8, no. 3 (Fall), 247–79.

POUNTNEY, A. M. (1911), *The Census of the Federated Malay States 1911* (London, H.M.S.O.).

POWER, JOHN (1971), 'The Structure of Protection in West Malaysia', in

Bela Balassa *et al.*, *The Structure of Protection in Developing Countries* (Baltimore, Johns Hopkins University Press), 203–22.

Proceedings, Federated Malay States, 1933 (1934), (Kuala Lumpur, Government Printer).

PROVENCHER, RONALD (1971), *Two Malay Worlds: Interaction in Urban and Rural Settings*, Research Monograph No. 4 (Berkeley, Center for South and Southeast Asia Studies, University of California).

PURCAL, JOHN T. (1971), *Rice Economy. A Case Study of Four Villages in West Malaysia* (Kuala Lumpur, University of Malaya).

PURCELL, VICTOR (1947), 'Chinese Settlement in Malacca', *Journal of the Malayan Branch of the Royal Asiatic Society* 20, Part I (June), 115–25.

——— (1965), *The Chinese in Southeast Asia*, 2nd ed. (London, Oxford University Press).

——— (1967), *The Chinese in Malaya* (Kuala Lumpur, Oxford University Press).

PUTHUCHEARY, JAMES J. (1960), *Ownership and Control in the Malayan Economy* (Singapore, Eastern Universities Press).

PUTHUCHEARY, M. C. (1977), 'Public Enterprise and the Creation of a Bumiputra Entrepreneurial Community', paper presented at the Fourth Malaysian Economic Convention, Kuala Lumpur, 19–21 May.

RADCLIFFE, DAVID JAMES (1970), 'Education and Cultural Change among the Malays 1900–1940', Ph.D. dissertation, University of Wisconsin, Madison.

RATNAM, K. J. (1965), *Communalism and the Political Process in Malaya* (Kuala Lumpur, University of Malaya Press).

RATNAM, K. J. AND MILNE, R. S. (1967), *The Malayan Parliamentary Election of 1964* (Singapore, University of Malaya Press).

REID, ANTHONY (1969), 'The Kuala Lumpur Riots and the Malaysian Political System', *Australian Outlook* 23 (December), 258–78.

Report of the Rice Cultivation Committee (1932), F.M.S. Council Paper No. 24 (Kuala Lumpur, Government Printer).

ROBINSON, HAMLIN (1973), 'Public Corporations in Malaysia', *Kajian Tadbiran Pembangunan* 1: 1 (January), 9–21.

ROBLESS, C. L. (1975), 'The Feasibility and Internal Consistency of the New Economic Policy', in Stephen Chee and Khoo Siew Mun (eds.), *Malaysian Economic Development and Policies* (Kuala Lumpur, Malaysian Economic Association), 37–56.

ROFF, MARGARET (1967), 'The Politics of Language in Malaya', *Asian Survey* 7: 5 (May), 316–28.

ROFF, WILLIAM R. (1967), *The Origins of Malay Nationalism* (Kuala Lumpur, University of Malaya Press).

ROGERS, MARVIN L. (1969), 'Politicization and Political Development in a Rural Malay Community', *Asian Survey* 9, no. 12 (December), 919–33.

ROSSI, PETER H. AND BLUM, ZAHARA D. (1968), 'Class, Status and Poverty', in Daniel P. Moynihan (ed.), *On Understanding Poverty. Perspectives from the Social Sciences* (New York, Basic Books), 36–63.

RUDNER, MARTIN (1970), 'The Malaysian General Election of 1969: A Political Analysis', *Modern Asian Studies* 4, 1–21.

______(1970a), 'The State and Peasant Innovation in Rural Development: The Case of Malaysian Rubber', *Asian and African Studies* 6, 75–96; reprinted in David Lim (ed.), (1975), 321–31.

RUEFF REPORT (1963), *Report on the Economic Aspects of Malaysia* (Kuala Lumpur, Government Press).

RYAN, N. J. (1967), *The Making of Modern Malaysia*, 3rd revised ed. (Kuala Lumpur, Oxford University Press).

SADKA, EMILY (1961), 'Singapore and the Federation: Problems of Merger', *Asian Survey* 1 (1961), 17–25.

______(1968), *The Protected Malay States 1874–1895* (Kuala Lumpur, University of Malaya Press).

SANDHU, KERNIAL SINGH (1961), 'Chinese Colonization of Malacca', *Journal of Tropical Geography* 15 (June), 1–26.

______(1962), 'Some Preliminary Observations on the Origins and Characteristics of Indian Migration to Malaya, 1786–1957', in K. G. Tregonning (ed.), *Papers on Malayan History* (Singapore, Journal of South-East Asian History), 193–213.

______(1969), *Indians in Malaya: Some Aspects of Their Immigration and Settlement, 1786–1957* (Cambridge, at the University Press).

SAW SWEE HOCK (1964), 'A Note on the Under-registration of Births in Malaya during the Intercensal Period 1947–1957', *Population Studies* 28: 1 (July), 35–52.

______(1965), 'State Differential Mortality in Malaya', *Ekonomi* 6, no. 1 (December), 103–6.

______(1966), 'Pattern of Fertility Decline in Malaya 1956–1965', *Kajian Ekonomi Malaysia* 3, no. 1 (June), 7–14.

______(1967), 'A Note on Fertility Levels in Malaya during 1947–1957', *Malayan Economic Review* 12, no. 1 (April), 117–24.

SCHMID, P. (1973), 'Report from Kuala Lumpur', *Encounter* 41 (August), 55–8.

SCOTT, JAMES C. (1968), *Political Ideology in Malaysia* (New Haven, Yale University Press).

Second Five-Year Plan 1961–1965 (1961) (Kuala Lumpur, Government Press).

Second Malaysia Plan 1971–1975 (1971) (Kuala Lumpur, Government Press).

SEERS, DUDLEY (1969), 'The Meaning of Development', *International Development Review* 11, no. 4 (December), 2–6.

______(1977), 'The New Meaning of Development', *International Development Review* 19, no. 3, 2–7.

SELVADURAI, S. (1968), *A Preliminary Report on the Survey of Coconut Smallholdings in West Malaysia* (Kuala Lumpur, Ministry of Agriculture and Co-operatives).

______(1972), *Padi Farming in West Malaysia* (Kuala Lumpur, Ministry of Agriculture and Fisheries).

SELVADURAI, S. AND ANI BIN AROPE (1969), *Socio-Economic Study of*

Padi Farms in Province Wellesley, 1968 (Kuala Lumpur, Ministry of Agriculture and Co-operatives).

SELVADURAI, S., ANI BIN AROPE AND NIK HASSANI BIN MOHAMMAD (1969), *Socio-Economic Study of Padi Farms in the Kemubu Area of Kelantan, 1968* (Kuala Lumpur, Ministry of Agriculture and Co-operatives).

SEN, AMARTYA (1973), *On Economic Inequality* (Oxford, Clarendon Press).

SHAMSUL BAHRIN, TUNKU (1969), 'A Preliminary Study of the Fringe Alienation Schemes in West Malaysia', *Journal of Tropical Geography* 28 (June), 75–83.

SHIBUTANI, TAMOTSU AND KWAN, KIAM M. (1965), *Ethnic Stratification: A Comparative Approach* (New York, Macmillan).

SHORT, D. C. AND JACKSON, JAMES C. (1971), 'The Origins of an Irrigation Policy in Malaya', *Journal of the Malaysian Branch of the Royal Asiatic Society* 44, Part 1.

SIEH-LEE MEI LING (1977), 'Size Distribution of Shareholdings in Manufacturing Companies of Malaysia, 1974–75', paper presented at the Fourth Malaysian Economic Convention, Kuala Lumpur, 19–21 May.

SILCOCK, T. H. (ed.), (1961), *Readings in Malayan Economics* (Singapore, Eastern Universities Press).

——— (1963), 'Approximate Racial Division of National Income', in T. H. Silcock and E. K. Fisk (eds.), 276–81.

——— (1964), 'The Role of Education in the Political and Economic Development of Southeast Asia', in Donald C. Piper and Taylor Cole (eds.), *Post-primary Education and Political and Economic Development* (Durham, N. C., Duke University Press).

——— (1965), 'The Effects of Industrialisation on Race Relations in Malaya', in Guy Hunter (ed.), *Industrialisation and Race Relations. A Symposium* (London, Oxford University Press for the Institute of Race Relations), 177–99.

SILCOCK, T. H. AND FISK, E. K. (eds.), (1963), *The Political Economy of Independent Malaya* (Berkeley, University of California Press).

SIMANDJUNTAK, B. (1969), *Malayan Federalism 1945–1963* (Kuala Lumpur, Oxford University Press).

SIMMONS, JOHN (1974), 'Education, Poverty and Development', Working Paper No. 188 (Washington, World Bank), (February).

——— (ed.), (1975), *Investment in Education; National Strategy Options for Developing Countries,* Working Paper No. 196 (Washington, World Bank), (February).

SINGH, S. (1965), 'Economic Aspects of Three New Land Development Schemes Organised by the Federal Land Development Authority in the Federation of Malaya', unpublished Ph.D. dissertation, Australian National University.

——— (1968), 'An Evaluation of Three Land Development Schemes in Malaysia', *Malayan Economic Review* 13, no. 1 (April), 89–100.

SLIMMING, JOHN (1969), *Malaysia: Death of a Democracy* (London, John Murray).

SMITH, ELDON D. AND GOETHALS, PETER R. (1965), *Tenancy among Padi Cultivators in Malaysia*, mimeographed (Kuala Lumpur, The Ford Foundation).

SMITH, T. E. (1962), *Population Growth in Malaya. An Analysis of Recent Trends* (London, Royal Institute of International Affairs).

——(1963), *The Background to Malaysia* (London, Oxford University Press).

SNIDER, NANCY L. (1970), 'Race, Leitmotiv of the Malayan Election Drama', *Asian Survey* 10 (December), 1070–80.

SNODGRASS, DONALD R. (1966), *Ceylon: The Export Economy in Transition* (Homewood, Ill., Richard D. Irwin).

——(1971), 'Some Development Implications of Political Integration and Disintegration in Malaysia', in Gustav Ranis (ed.), *Government and Economic Development* (New Haven, Yale University Press).

——(1972), 'The Growth and Utilization of Labor Supply in West Malaysia', mimeographed with appendices (Kuala Lumpur).

——(1974), 'The Fiscal System as an Income Redistributor in West Malaysia', *Public Finance* 29, no. 1, 56–76 [abridged version of Snodgrass (1975)].

——(1975), 'The Fiscal System as an Income Redistributor in West Malaysia', in David Lim (ed.), *Readings on Malaysian Economic Development* (Kuala Lumpur, Oxford University Press), 269–91 [complete version of Snodgrass (1974)].

——(1975a), 'Income Redistribution in West Malaysia and Recent Empirical Work on Budget Incidence: A Reply', *Public Finance* 30, no. 1, 136–7.

——(1975b), 'Trends and Patterns in Malaysian Income Distribution, 1957–70', in David Lim (ed.), 251–68.

——(1976), 'The Growth and Utilization of Labor Supply in West Malaysia', *Philippine Economic Journal* nos. 1 and 2, 273–313.

STALEY, EUGENE AND MORSE, RICHARD (1965), *Modern Small Industries for Developing Countries* (New York, McGraw-Hill).

SUMITRO DJOJOHADIKUSUMO (1969), *Trade and Aid in South-East Asia*, Vol. 1: *Malaysia and Singapore* (Kuala Lumpur, University of Malaya Co-operative Bookstore).

SUYAMA, TAKU (1962), 'Pang Societies and the Economy of Chinese Immigrants in Southeast Asia', in K. G. Tregonning (ed.), *Papers on Malayan History* (Singapore, Journal of South-East Asian History), 193–213.

SWIFT, M. G. (1957), 'The Accumulation of Capital in a Peasant Economy', *Economic Development and Cultural Change* 5, no. 4 (July), 325–37; reprinted in Silcock (1961).

——(1963), 'Malay Peasants', in Richard D. Lambert and Bert F. Hoselitz (eds.), *The Role of Savings and Wealth in Southern Asia and the West* (Paris, UNESCO), 219–44.

——(1964), 'Capital, Saving and Credit in the Malay Peasant Economy', in R. Firth and B. S. Yamey (eds.), *Capital, Saving and Credit in Peasant Societies* (London, Allen and Unwin), 33–56.

_____ (1967), 'Economic Concentration and Malay Peasant Society', in Maurice Freedman (ed.), *Social Organization: Essays Presented to Raymond Firth* (London, Frank Cass and Co.), 241–69.

TAIB BIN HAJI ANDAK (1964), 'The Work of the Federal Land Development Authority', mimeographed.

_____ (1968), 'Land Development in Malaysia under the Federal Land Development Authority—Description of Programme and Techniques of Development Administration', in Malaysian Centre for Development Studies, *Report on 1st Seminar on Development, 24th October–3rd November, 1966* (Kuala Lumpur, Government Printer), 7–23.

TAKEI, YOSHIMITSU (1971), 'Ethnic Sponsorship in Education: A Case Study of West Malaysia', Ph.D. dissertation, University of California, Berkeley.

TAKEI, YOSHIMITSU, BOCK, JOHN C. AND SAUNDERS, BRUCE (1973), *Educational Sponsorship by Ethnicity: A Preliminary Analysis of the West Malaysian Experience*, Papers in International Studies Southeast Asia Series No. 28 (Athens, Ohio, Ohio University Center for International Studies Southeast Asia Program).

TAN, AUGUSTINE H. H. (1964), 'Special Development Problems of a Plural Society: The Malayan Example—A Comment', *Economic Record* 40, no. 89 (March), 114–21.

TAN BOCK THIAM (1975), 'Returns to Investment in Land Development from Settler and Government Viewpoints', in Stephen Chee and Khoo Siew Mun (eds.), *Malaysian Economic Development and Policies* (Kuala Lumpur, Malaysian Economic Association), 205–18.

TAN SIEW SIN, TUN (1969), *The 1969 Budget* (Kuala Lumpur, Department of Information).

TAN SOO HAI, DING EING (1963), *The Rice Industry in Malaya 1920–1940* (Singapore, Malaya Publishing House).

TAN TAT-WAI (1977), 'Income Distribution and Determination in West Malaysia', Ph.D. dissertation, Harvard University.

TEITELBAUM, MICHAEL S. (1975), 'Relevance of Demographic Transition Theory for Developing Countries', *Science* 188 (2 May), 420–5.

TELLANDER, ROBERT W. (1970), Review of Kernial Singh Sandhu, *Indians in Malaya: Some Aspects of their Immigration and Settlement, 1886–1957*, *Journal of Asian Studies* 30 (November), 232–4.

THILLAINATHAN, R. (1970), 'The Second Malaysia Plan—Notes on the Objectives of Balanced Distribution of Wealth and Employment', *Kajian Ekonomi Malaysia* 7, no. 2 (December), 57–71.

_____ (1974), 'Balanced Distribution of Wealth and Income in Malaysia', *Kajian Ekonomi Malaysia* 11, no. 2 (December), 40–50.

_____ (1975), 'Public Enterprise as an Instrument for Restructuring Society: Prospects and Implications', in Stephen Chee and Khoo Siew Mun (eds.), *Malaysian Economic Development and Policies* (Kuala Lumpur, Malaysian Economic Association), 73–88.

_____ (1976), 'Inter-Racial Balance in Malaysian Employment and Wealth: An Evaluation of Distributional Targets', *Developing Economies* 14, no. 3 (September), 239–60.

_____ (1976a), 'Malaysia', in Nguyen Truong (ed.), *The Role of Public Enterprise in National Development in Southeast Asia: Problems and Prospects* (Singapore, Regional Institute for Higher Education and Development), 1–149.

_____ (1976b), 'Public Enterprises in Malaysia—Problems and Prospects', *UMBC Economic Review* 12: 2, 37–45.

THIO, EUNICE (1969), *British Policy in the Malay Peninsula 1880–1910*, Vol. 1: *The Southern and Central States* (Singapore, University of Malaya Press).

Third Malaysia Plan 1976–1980 (1976), (Kuala Lumpur, Government Press).

THOBURN, JOHN T. (1977), *Primary Commodity Exports and Economic Development: Theory, Evidence and a Study of Malaysia* (New York, Wiley).

THOMAS, P. O. AND FONG CHU CHAI, A. (1968), *Rubber Industry Statistics* (Kuala Lumpur, Rubber Research Institute of Malaya).

THOMPSON, VIRGINIA (1943), *Postmortem on Malaya* (New York, Macmillan).

THOMSON, A. M. (1954), *Report on the Marketing of Rice in the Federation of Malaya* (Rome, United Nations Food and Agriculture Organization).

THOMSON, FLORENCE A. (1960), *Child Nutrition. A Survey in the Parit District of Perak, Federation of Malaya*, Bulletin No. 10 (Kuala Lumpur, Institute for Medical Research).

THUROW, LESTER C. (1969), *Poverty and Discrimination* (Washington, The Brookings Institution).

TILMAN, ROBERT O. (1963), 'Malaysia: The Problems of Federation', *Western Political Quarterly* 16 (1963), 897–911.

_____ (1964), *Bureaucratic Transition in Malaya* (Durham, N. C., Duke University Press).

TREASURY (1974), *Economic Report 1974–75* (Kuala Lumpur, The Treasury).

_____ (1975), *Economic Report 1975–76* (Kuala Lumpur).

TREGONNING, K. G. (1963), *A History of Modern Malaya* (London, University of London Press).

_____ (1965), *The British in Malaya: The First Forty Years, 1786–1826* (Tucson, University of Arizona Press for the Association for Asian Studies).

TURNHAM, DAVID J. (1972), 'Income Distribution: Measurement and Problems', in Andrew E. Rice (ed.), *Development for the 70's: Jobs and Justice*, papers from the 12th World Conference of the Society for International Development (Dobbs Ferry, N.Y., Oceana Publications), 37–59.

UNITED NATIONS FOOD AND AGRICULTURAL ORGANIZATION (1970), *Provisional Indicative World Plan for Agricultural Development* (Rome).

UNITED NATIONS RESEARCH INSTITUTE FOR SOCIAL DEVELOPMENT (1969), *Research Notes* No. 2 (Geneva), (July).

UNITED STATES INTERDEPARTMENTAL COMMITTEE ON NUTRITION

FOR NATIONAL DEFENSE, Office of International Research (1964), *Report on a Nutrition Survey of the Federation of Malaya* (Washington, U.S. Government Printing Office).

VAN THEAN KEE (1949), 'Cultivation of Taiwan Padi in Perak during the Japanese Occupation', *Malayan Agricultural Journal* 31: 2 (April).

VASIL, R. K. (1965), 'The 1964 General Elections in Malaya', *International Studies* 7 (July 1965), 20–65.

_____ (1972), *The Malaysian General Elections of 1969* (Kuala Lumpur, Oxford University Press).

VLIELAND, C. A. (1932), *British Malaya. Report on the 1931 Census and on Certain Problems of Vital Statistics* (London: Crown Agents).

VON DER MEHDEN, FRED R. (1975), 'Communalism, Industrial Policy and Income Distribution in Malaysia', *Asian Survey* 15, no. 3 (March), 250–61.

VON VORYS, KARL (1975), *Democracy without Consensus. Communalism and Political Stability in Malaysia* (Princeton, N. J., Princeton University Press).

VOON PHIN KEONG (1976), *Western Rubber Planting Enterprise in South-east Asia 1876–1921* (Kuala Lumpur, Penerbit Universiti Malaya).

WALTERS, DOROTHY (1963), *Report on the National Accounts of the Federation of Malaya*, Report No. TAO/MAL/10 (New York, United Nations).

WANG, CHAN BEE-LAN (1977), 'Governmental Intervention in Ethnic Stratification: Effects on the Distribution of Students among Fields of Study', *Comparative Education Review* 21, no. 1 (February), 110–18.

WANG GUNGWU (ed.), (1964), *Malaysia: A Survey* (Singapore, Donald Moore Books).

WEBER, MAX (1930), *The Protestant Ethic and the Spirit of Capitalism* (New York, C. Scribner's Sons).

WEISSKOFF, RICHARD (1970), 'Income Distribution in Puerto Rico, Argentina and Mexico', *Review of Income and Wealth*, New Series 16, no. 4 (December), 308–32.

WHARTON, C. R. JR. (1962), 'Marketing, Merchandising and Moneylending: A Note on Middleman Monopsony in Malaya', *Malayan Economic Review* 7, no. 2 (October), 24–44.

WHEELWRIGHT, E. L. (1965), *Industrialization in Malaysia* (Melbourne, Melbourne University Press).

WIKKRAMATILEKE, R. (1964), 'Variable Ethnic Attitudes in Malayan Rural Land Development', *Pacific Viewpoint* 5, no. 1 (May), 35–50.

_____ (1965), 'State Aided Land Colonization in Malaya: An Appraisal of the F.L.D.A. Program', *Annals of the Association of American Geographers* 53, no. 3 (September), 377–403.

_____ (1972), 'Federal Land Development in West Malaysia 1957–1971', *Pacific Viewpoint* 13: 1 (May), 62–85; reprinted in David Lim (ed.), *Readings on Malaysian Economic Development* (Kuala Lumpur, Oxford University Press), (1975), 111–24.

WILCOX, CLAIR (1965), *The Planning and Execution of Economic Development in Southeast Asia*, Occasional Papers in International

Affairs No. 29 (Cambridge, Mass., Center for International Affairs, Harvard University).

WILDER, WILLIAM (1968), 'Islam, Other Factors and Malay Backwardness: Comments on an Argument', *Modern Asian Studies* 2, no. 2 (April): 155–64; reprinted in David Lim (ed.), *Readings on Malaysian Economic Development* (Kuala Lumpur, Oxford University Press) (1975).

WILSON, ALAN B. (1972), 'General Education and Unemployment in West Malaysia', *Journal Pendidekan* 3 (October).

______ (1972a), 'Educational Qualification and Participation in Labour Force: A Further Note on the Relationship between General Education and Unemployment in West Malaysia', *Journal Pendidekan* 3 (October).

WILSON, PETER J. (1967), *A Malay Village and Malaysia* (New Haven, HRAF Press).

WILSON, T. B. (1954), 'The Marketing of Durian Fruit from Parit District, Perak', *Malayan Agricultural Journal* 37, no. 4, 211–17.

______ (1958), *The Economics of Padi Production in North Malaya. Part I. Land Tenure, Rents, Land Use and Fragmentation* (Kuala Lumpur, Ministry of Agriculture).

WINSTEDT, RICHARD (1961), *The Malays. A Cultural History* (London, Routledge and Kegan Paul).

WITTFOGEL, KARL A. (1957), *Oriental Despotism* (New Haven, Yale University Press).

WONG LIN KEN (1965), *The Malayan Tin Industry to 1914* (Tucson, University of Arizona Press for the Association of Asian Studies).

WORLD BANK (1975), *Health Sector Policy Paper* (March).

______ (1978), *World Bank Atlas.*

YIP YAT HOONG (1968), 'Recent Changes in the Ownership and Control of Locally Incorporated Tin Dredging Companies in Malaya', *Malayan Economic Review* 13, no. 1 (April), 70–88.

______ (1969), *The Development of the Tin Mining Industry of Malaya* (Kuala Lumpur, University of Malaya Press).

ZAINAL AZNAM YUSOF AND KHAIRUDDIN YUSOF (1974), *Some Socio-Economic and Medical Aspects of Malay Mortality in Urban and Rural Areas*, Occasional Paper No. 1 (Kuala Lumpur, Malaysian Centre for Development Studies).

Index

Numbers in italics refer to Tables.